D1690493

Veröffentlichungen des Arbeitskreises
für historische Hexen- und Kriminalitätsforschung
in Norddeutschland

herausgegeben von

Katrin Moeller
und Burghart Schmidt

Band 5

Burghart Schmidt / Rolf Schulte (Hg.)

Hexenglauben im modernen Afrika

Hexen, Hexenverfolgung und magische Vorstellungswelten

Witchcraft in Modern Africa

Witches, Witch-Hunts and Magical Imaginaries

Wissenschaftlicher Verlag
Dokumentation & Buch

Titelbild: Ablution *(kuoga)*. Painting by Max Kamundi, Njenga/Tanzania, 2002.
Abbildung Rückseite: Ablution of witchcraft influence from a child, Nachingwea / Tanzania
Privatbesitz, Abdruck mit freundlicher Genehmigung.

Bibliografische Information der Deutschen Bibliothek:
Die Deutsche Bibliothek verzeichnet diese Publikation in der Deutschen
Nationalbibliografie; detaillierte bibliografische Daten sind im Internet
über http://dnb.ddb.de abrufbar.

Hexenglauben im modernen Afrika. Hexen, Hexenverfolgung
und magische Vorstellungswelten / Witchcraft in Modern Africa. Witches,
Witch-Hunts and Magical Imaginaries. Burghart Schmidt / Rolf Schulte (Hg.)
Hamburg: DOBU Verlag, 2007

1. Auflage 2007
© Copyright 2007 by DOBU Verlag, Hamburg
Tel.: ++49(0)40 64891 334 Fax: ++49(0)40 64891 359
www.dobu-verlag.de info@dobu-verlag.de

ISBN 3-934632-15-7
EAN 9783934632158

Inhaltsverzeichnis

Burghart Schmidt / Rolf Schulte
Vorwort 7

Burghart Schmidt
Einführende Bemerkungen zum Hexenglauben im modernen Afrika 9

Michael Schönhuth
Theorien zu Hexerei in Afrika: Eine Exkursion ins afrikanische
Hexendickicht 16

Dirk Kohnert
On the Renaissance of African Modes of Thought:
The Example of Occult Belief Systems 32

Dirk Kohnert
On the Articulation of Witchcraft and Modes of
Production among the Nupe, Northern Nigeria 55

Erhard Kamphausen
Hexenglauben, Magie und Besessenheitsphänomene in Afrika.
Religions- und missionswissenschaftliche Anmerkungen 88

Johannes Harnischfeger
Sozialer Niedergang und Kampf gegen das Böse:
Hexerei im postmodernen Afrika 96

Johannes Harnischfeger
Rückkehr der Dämonen:
Wandlungen des Christentums in Afrika und Europa 110

Walter Bruchhausen
Repelling and Cleansing 'Bad People' The Fight against Witchcraft
in Southeast Tanzania since Colonial Times 130

Katrin Pfeiffer
Buwaa: Cannibals of supernatural power and changing appearance.
A term from the Mandinka language (Gambia, Senegal, Guinea-Bissau) 153

Rolf Schulte
Okkulte Mächte, Hexenverfolgungen und Geschlecht in Afrika 167

Oliver Becker
„Muti Morde" in Afrika: Töten für okkulte Medizin 187

Joan Wardrop
Soweto witchcraft accusations in the transition
from apartheid through liberation to democracy 213

Jan-Lodewijk Grootaers
„Criminal Enemies of the People": Water Wizards
among the Zande, Central African Republic (1950-2000) 230

Rolf Schulte / Burghart Schmidt

Vorwort

Das Phänomen der Hexenverfolgungen findet seit längerer Zeit das Interesse einer breiten Öffentlichkeit und wird in unterschiedlichster Ausprägung sowohl in literarischer als auch in wissenschaftlicher Form thematisiert und diskutiert. Der inzwischen seit gut sechs Jahren bestehende Arbeitskreis für historische Hexen- und Kriminalitätsforschung in Norddeutschland hat es sich zum Ziel gesetzt, in diesem Kontext eine Plattform für den Austausch von Forschungsergebnissen zu schaffen, die Vernetzung von Forschungsprojekten zu erleichtern und persönliche Kontakte zu fördern. Obwohl ein Schwerpunkt seiner Tätigkeit auf der Kriminalitätsgeschichte und den Hexenverfolgungen der Frühen Neuzeit im nördlichen Deutschland liegt, beschäftigt er sich darüber hinaus auch aus interdisziplinärer und epochenübergreifender Perspektive mit den vielfältigen Aspekten des Magie- und Hexenglaubens in anderen Teilen Europas und der Welt. Neben regelmäßigen Arbeitstreffen, auf denen neuere Forschungsergebnisse präsentiert und diskutiert werden, veranstaltet er in loser Folge größere Konferenzen oder Workshops, die unter interdisziplinären Gesichtspunkten wichtige aktuelle Fragestellungen aufgreifen.

In diesem Kontext wurde im Jahre 2004 eine größere internationale Konferenz zum Hexenglauben im modernen Afrika veranstaltet, deren Ergebnisse jetzt im fünften Band der Veröffentlichungsreihe des Arbeitskreises herausgegeben werden. Tatsächlich werden große Teile Afrikas seit etwas mehr als zwei Jahrzehnten mit einem enormen Bedeutungsgewinn verschiedenster religiöser Bewegungen konfrontiert. Am sichtbarsten sind dabei diejenigen, die aus den großen Universalreligionen hervorgingen: die Pfingstkirchen, christliche Heils- und Freikirchen, charismatische Erneuerungs- und Erweckungsbewegungen, islamische und islamistische Glaubensbewegungen. Aber daneben besteht auch eine Vielzahl unterschiedlichster traditioneller und neotraditioneller sowie synkretischer religiöser Bewegungen, die zunehmend an Einfluss gewinnen, von den Heilkräften der Menschen überzeugt sind, an gute und böse Geister sowie an Magie und Zauberkraft glauben. Die Religion war und ist in Afrika ein wesentlicher Bestandteil des vielfältigen kulturellen und sozialen Lebens. Sie spielte und spielt für die Menschen eine wichtige Rolle. Im letzten, durch tiefgreifende wirtschaftliche und soziale Krisen gekennzeichneten Vierteljahrhundert erlangten dabei in der Öffentlichkeit auch der Hexenglauben und verschiedene Repräsentationsformen spiritueller okkulter Kräfte nachhaltig an Bedeutung.

Will man diese Entwicklung nachvollziehen und analysieren, genügt es nicht, auf die sozialen und wirtschaftlichen Krisenerscheinungen zu rekurrieren, so gravierend diese auch sind, die fatalen Folgen der Globalisation auf dem afrikanischen Kontinent zu hinterfragen oder sich mit den dramatischen innenpolitischen und administrativen Verhältnissen einzelner afrikanischer Staaten auseinander zu setzen. Das Beziehungsgeflecht zwischen dem „Materiellen" und „Spirituellen" ist sehr viel komplexer und erfordert einen interdisziplinären Zugang, der Religions-, Politik-, Wirtschafts- und Kulturwissenschaft, Anthropologie und Ethnologie miteinander verbindet und auch das erforderlichen

Wissen über historische Zusammenhänge und Entwicklungen umfasst. Glücklicherweise haben Anthropologie, Ethnologie und Geschichtswissenschaft in den letzten beiden Jahrzehnten wieder intensiver den Dialog gesucht, der unter der Dominanz eindimensionaler Modernisierungstheorien der 1960er und 70er Jahre fast verstummt war. Historikerinnen und Historiker, die sich mit der europäischen Hexenverfolgung auseinandersetzten, beschäftigten sich nur selten mit Material aus Afrika, Lateinamerika oder Asien. Der historische Diskurs endete oft an den Grenzen eines kulturhistorischen Relativismus, der davon ausging, dass kulturelle Eigenheiten verschiedener Völker komparative Sichtweisen nahezu unmöglich machen. Umgekehrt griffen anthropologische und ethnologische Forschungen, die sich mit außereuropäischen Magiebildern beschäftigten, auf Forschungsergebnisse zurück, die in der Geschichtswissenschaft längst als überholt galten.

Der hier vorgelegte Band hofft dazu beitragen zu können, die inzwischen wieder verschränkten Diskurse zwischen ethnologischer und historischer Hexenforschung weiter zu beleben. Er möchte einen ersten, wenn auch naturgemäß bescheidenen Beitrag zu einem interdisziplinär gestalteten Erkenntnisgewinn über Hexen, Hexenverfolgung und magische Vorstellungswelten im gegenwärtigen Afrika leisten. Er geht damit erstmals nicht nur geografisch, sondern auch chronologisch über das bisherige, auf die Frühe Neuzeit ausgerichtete Tätigkeitsfeld des Arbeitskreises hinaus. Um den erforderlichen internationalen Dialog zu erweitern, wurde bewusst auf eine zweisprachige Publikationsform zurückgegriffen.

Burghart Schmidt & Rolf Schulte

Burghart Schmidt

Einführende Bemerkungen zum Hexenglauben im modernen Afrika

„Der Mond verschwindet, wenn er groß gewesen ist, die Sterne leuchten weiter, obwohl sie klein sind".[1]

„Frau Muwulene war eine berüchtigte *feticheira* gewesen, damals, als die weißen Kolonialherren ungeschickt und mit wachsender Resignation versucht hatten, zu verbieten, was sie als unseren primitiven Aberglauben betrachteten. Die Weißen hatten nicht verstanden, welche Bedeutung die Geister für das Leben eines Menschen haben. Sie hatten nicht begriffen, dass es notwendig ist, sich mit den Seelen der Ahnen gut zu stellen, sie hatten nicht begriffen, dass das Leben eines Menschen ein ständiger Kampf ist, um die Geister bei Laune zu halten. Das ist vermutlich der Grund, weshalb die Weißen den Krieg am Ende verloren haben und unser Land zurückgeben mussten. Es waren die gekränkten Geister, die den Krieg gewonnen haben, nicht in erster Linie die jungen Revolutionäre. Doch zur Verwunderung von Frau Muwulene und uns anderen waren die jungen Revolutionäre noch entschiedener in ihrer Verurteilung unserer Gewohnheit, die Geister anzubeten und unser Leben ihren Wünschen entsprechend einzurichten." Doch auch sie sollten dabei, folgt man der weiteren Erzählung des schwedischen Schriftstellers Hennig Mankell, letztlich erfolglos bleiben.[2]

Was der 1948 in Härjedalen bei Stockholm als Sohn eines Richters geborene Autor, Theaterregisseur und Intendant, der seit 1985 einen erheblichen Teil seines Lebens in Maputo (Mosambik) verbrachte, hier romanhaft schildert, rekurriert in mancher Hinsicht auf reale Gegebenheiten. Magische Vorstellungswelten, Geister und Hexen waren und sind noch immer –vielleicht mehr denn je – keineswegs nur literarische Denkfiguren oder kulturelle Deutungsmuster wissenschaftlicher Theorien westlicher Prägung. Afrikanische Gespräche kreisen um satanische Banknoten, Kinderhexen und Wassergeister. Erzählungen über Dämonen, Neuigkeiten über rituelle Morde, Gerüchte über Politiker und Sportvereine, die magische Mittel einsetzen, um zum Erfolg zu gelangen, Berichte über familiäre und nachbarschaftliche Konflikte, die auf Hexereibeschuldigungen beruhen, spielen eine zentrale Rolle in einer häufig als bedrohlich empfundenen Alltagsrealität eines im Umbruch befindlichen Kontinents, werden dementsprechend von den örtlichen Medien aufgegriffen und von der internationalen Forschung rezipiert.[3]

---

1   Afrikanisches Sprichwort (Opixa murima orèra. Mweri wahòkhwa ori mutokwène, etheneri ehala yàraka), hier wiedergegeben nach Hennig MANKELL: Der Chronist der Winde, 6. Aufl., München 2003, S. 199.
2   Ebd., S. 44ff.
3   Auf wissenschaftliche Verweise zur Entwicklung der Forschung und zu ihren unterschiedlichen theoretischen Ansätzen wird in dieser kurzen Einführung verzichtet. Ausführliche Angaben finden sich diesbezüglich in den theoretischen Überlegungen von Michael Schönhuth und in den nachfolgenden Beiträgen dieses Tagungsbandes.

Anders als es zahlreiche sozial- und religionstheoretische Interpretationsansätze der 1930er bis 1980er Jahre nahelegten, die eine Abnahme derartiger Vorstellungswelten unter dem Druck der wirtschaftlichen Entwicklung und Urbanisierung, sich ausbreitender schriftlicher Kulturen und monotheistischer Religionen vorhersagten, sind Hexenglauben und Hexenverfolgungen aus dem gegenwärtigen Afrika genauso wenig wegzudenken wie magische Überzeugungen. Sie gehören zu den zentralen Kategorien des öffentlichen und privaten Lebens, sind integraler Bestandteil einer allgemeinen Krisensituation im Kontext eines Globalisierungs- und Modernisierungsprozesses, der auch in anderen Teilen Welt zu einem verstärkten Rückgriff auf religiöse und religionsähnliche Glaubensvorstellungen führte, denkt man nur an die Pfingstkirchen und andere Erweckungsbewegungen in Nordamerika, an den Aufschwung islamischer und islamistischer Glaubensbewegungen in vielen Teilen der Welt, an den Bedeutungsgewinn esoterischer Gruppierungen in Europa oder an die Vielzahl traditioneller und neo-traditioneller sowie synkretischer religiöser Bewegungen, die in den letzten Jahren nicht nur in Afrika an Einfluss gewannen.

Fragt man nach den Gründen und Kriterien für diese Entwicklung, so sind diese vielschichtig und kaum in einem einzigen Modell zu erfassen. Die Suche nach Problemlösungsstrategien und Erklärungsmustern in einer sich nicht nur wandelnden, sondern auch zunehmend unverständlich erscheinenden Welt mag eine Rolle spielen, die Suche nach Halt in einem solchen Kontext ebenfalls. Es geht um die stets aktuelle Frage nach den Ursachen der Leiden und Übel in einer Welt, in der Flüchtlingsströme, Kriege und Hungersnöte zum Alltag gehören, die Folgen des Klimawandels und der extensiven Ausbeutung natürlicher Ressourcen das Leben unsicher erscheinen lassen, die Globalisierung zunehmend einem globalen Verteilungskampf weicht und die sozialen Lebens- und Überlebensbedingungen vieler Millionen Menschen einer Katastrophe ähneln.

Obwohl es weder im frühneuzeitlichen Europa noch im heutigen Afrika einheitliche Hexereivorstellungen gab bzw. gibt, sich sowohl die diesbezüglich verwendeten Begrifflichkeiten als auch deren Inhalte in der Vergangenheit und Gegenwart regional unterschieden bzw. nach wie vor sehr stark voneinander unterscheiden und es sicherlich verfehlt wäre, die frühneuzeitliche Hexenverfolgung in Europa und den Hexenglauben im modernen Afrika als gleichartig zu betrachten, lässt sich der Hexenglauben allgemein als „anthropologisches Phänomen mit historischer Dimension" begreifen,[4] das über die Zeiten und Kontinente hinweg gewisse Ähnlichkeiten aufweist. So zählt es zu den Charakteristika dieses Phänomens, dass es sich monokausalen Erklärungsansätzen entzieht und in komplexe Beziehungsgefüge eingebunden ist. Ökonomische und soziale Krisen, Mentalitätsverschiebungen, übergreifende Veränderungen in den Kommunikationsstrukturen, Umstrukturierungsprozesse in der Agrargesellschaft, das langsame Erstarken politischer Zentralgewalten, kirchliche Versuche zur Ausgrenzung von „Aberglaube" und Volksmagie – um nur einige Beispiele zu nennen, deren relative Gleichzeitigkeit zu betonen ist – gehörten im frühneuzeitlichen Europa genauso zu den auslösenden Momenten der Hexenverfolgungen wie spezifische Interessen einzelner Personen und Institutionen,

---

4 Wolfgang BEHRINGER: Hexen. Glaube, Verfolgung, Vermarktung, München 1998, S. 10.

soziale Spannungen in kleinräumigen Lebensgemeinschaften, anhaltende Missernten, Seuchen oder Wetterunbilden.

Ähnliches könnte man für Teile des modernen Afrika behaupten, wobei dem territorialen und politischen Staatsbildungsprozess des frühneuzeitlichen Europa hier teilweise ein entsprechender Zerfallsprozess gegenübersteht. Hexereivorstellungen waren in Europa und sind auch heute in Afrika weder gleichförmig noch gleichmäßig verteilt. Afrikanische „Hexerei" als solche gibt es genauso wenig wie einheitliche magische Vorstellungswelten südlich der Sahara. Gerade deshalb erscheinen generalisierende theoretische Erklärungsmodelle und wissenschaftliche Diskurse nur bedingt weiterführend. Sie sind wie der Mond, leuchten einige Zeit hell und groß und verschwinden dann nach und nach in der Versenkung, um einem neuen Mond in Form einer veränderten theoretischen Zuschreibung Platz zu machen, die nach einer gewissen Zeit demselben Schicksal erliegt. Hell scheint der Mond darüber hinaus immer nur für einen kleinen Teil der Betrachter. Ersten funktionalistischen Forschungsansätzen folgten in der Nachkriegszeit konfliktsoziologische und mikropolitische Ansätze, denen sich später psychologisch geprägte und kulturhistorisch inspirierte Interpretationsmuster anschlossen, die seit den 1970er Jahren durch konstruktivistische Erklärungsansätze ergänzt wurden. Seit dem letzten Jahrzehnt des vergangenen Jahrhunderts dominieren Globalisierungs- und Modernisierungstheorien, die die Hexerei in Afrika als Antwort auf die Herausforderungen der Moderne verstehen, als wechselnde und sich verändernde Ausdrucksform in einem sich wandelnden wirtschaftlichen, sozialen und politischen Kräfteverhältnis – eine Ausdrucksform, die allen Gesellschaftsmitgliedern offensteht und keineswegs auf den engen Kreis der *witchdoctors, traditional healers, féticheurs* oder *ngangas* beschränkt ist.

Auch diese Theorie wird in absehbarer Zeit durch neue Erklärungsmuster ersetzt werden, was ihren Wert nicht schmälert, aber darauf verweist, dass es letztlich weniger das einzelne, zeit- und gesellschaftsgebundene wissenschaftliche Interpretationsmodell ist, das der Vielfältigkeit realer Vorstellungs- und Glaubenswelten gerecht werden kann, als vielmehr die jeweils unterschiedlich zu gewichtende Zusammensetzung einzelner Faktoren und Interpretationsmuster in Abhängigkeit der jeweils spezifischen politischen, wirtschaftlichen und kulturellen Rahmenbedingungen in den einzelnen Territorien und Regionen des afrikanischen Kontinents. Auch wenn die aufeinanderfolgenden Monde theoretischer Ausrichtung für das Gefüge der wissenschaftlichen Forschung unabdingbar erscheinen, diese strukturieren, leiten und jeweils ihren eigenen Wert behalten, so erscheint es zunächst einmal wichtig, ihnen durch vermehrte Einzelstudien eine ausreichende und empirisch abgesicherte Basis zu verleihen. Es sind, um noch einmal auf das Bild des eingangs zitierten afrikanischen Sprichwortes zurückzukommen, die vielen Sterne, die kontinuierlich leuchten, obwohl sie klein zu sein scheinen; es sind die fundierten wissenschaftlichen Einzelstudien, die am ehesten der Vielfältigkeit afrikanischer Lebenswelten gerecht werden können. Wie sonst sollte man erklären, dass Hexereivorstellungen in manchen afrikanischen Gesellschaften keine Rolle spielen, während in anderen unter ähnlichen sozialen und wirtschaftlichen Bedingungen die überwiegende Mehrheit der Bevölkerung an Hexen glaubt und dieser Glaube das soziale Leben in hohem Maße beeinflusst. Gemeinsam bilden Sterne und Monde, empirische Studien und

Theorien mittlerer Reichweite ein Firmament, das nur wenig mit „himmlischen" Zuständen zu tun hat, aber die konkreten irdischen Gegebenheiten des heutigen Afrika etwas besser zu verstehen gestattet.

Einen kleinen und bescheidenen Schritt in diese Richtung zu unternehmen, versucht der folgende Tagungsband. Er wird eingeführt durch eine „Reise in das afrikanische Hexendickicht", d. h. durch einen Überblick von *Michael Schönhuth* über die theoretischen Interpretationsansätze der wissenschaftlichen Forschung seit den Zwanziger Jahren des zurückliegenden Jahrhunderts. Ähnlich wie er, geht auch *Dirk Kohnert* in seiner Analyse okkulter afrikanischer Glaubenssysteme davon aus, dass aus westlicher Sicht „rückständig" scheinende Vorstellungswelten in Wirklichkeit sehr modern sein können und einen erheblichen Einfluss auf die Gesellschafts- und Wirtschaftsstrukturen der betroffenen Völker ausüben. In einem empirisch fundierten Beitrag über Hexereianschuldigungen bei den *Nupe* im nördlichen Nigeria belegt er darüber hinaus, dass es lohnend erscheint, derartige Anschuldigungen in Relation zu bestehenden wirtschaftlichen Produktionsweisen und politischen Machtansprüchen bzw. Herrschaftsinteressen zu setzen.

Aus religions- und missionswissenschaftlicher Perspektive hinterfragt *Erhard Kamphausen* ein afrikanisches Wirklichkeitsverständnis, das über den westlichen Dualismus von Diesseitigkeit und Jenseitigkeit, Leib und Seele, Geist und Materie, Transzendenz und Immanenz, sichtbarer und unsichtbarer Welt weit hinausreicht und dabei von der Voraussetzung ausgeht, dass das gesamte Universum von mystischen Kräften durchdrungen ist, die an sich weder gut noch böse sind, sich sowohl als Heil bringend und nützlich erweisen können, als auch als schädlich und bösartig. Diese Kräfte können sich in der religiösen Erfahrung der Gläubigen auch in verschiedenen Erscheinungsformen der Besessenheit manifestieren. Sie werden in den letzten Jahrzehnten von zahlreichen unabhängigen Gemeinschaften charismatisch-pentekostalen Ursprungs in ihren theologischen Referenzrahmen und ihre religiöse Praxis integriert und auf diese Weise instrumentalisiert.

Dass das Ende der Kolonialzeit für die Geschichte der Hexerei in Afrika von geringer Bedeutung war und es erst zwei bis drei Jahrzehnte später mit dem Verfall des postkolonialen Staates zu einem nachhaltigen Aufleben okkulter Gewalt kam, unterstreicht *Johannes Harnischfeger* in seinen Überlegungen über ein Zeitalter, das in mancher Hinsicht der alten vorstaatlichen Welt ähnelt und zugleich von Globalisierungstendenzen geprägt wird, ein Zeitalter des sozialen Niedergangs und wachsender Gewalt. Am konkreten Beispiel Nigerias betrachtet er verschiedene Aspekte der gegenwärtigen afrikanischen Krise näher, um der Frage nachzugehen, warum sich die Erfahrungen von moralischem und sozialem Verfall im Idiom von Hexerei, Zauberei und anderen unsichtbaren Bedrohungen ausdrücken. In seinen Überlegungen über Wandlungen des Christentums in Afrika und Europa geht er davon aus, dass das Projekt der Moderne, die Entzauberung der Welt, gescheitert ist. War die spirituelle Welt der traditionellen afrikanischen Gesellschaften insofern überschaubarer, als der Zugang zu ihr gesellschaftlich geregelt wurde, ist es heute weitgehend dem Einzelnen überlassen, seine Beziehung zu dieser Welt zu organisieren. Auch wenn es für europäische Beobachter befremdlich erscheinen mag, dass christliche Gebete und Rituale in erster Linie dazu dienen, sich vor dämonischen Kräften zu schützen, treibt dieser Wunsch den Kirchen Millionen von Gläubigen zu.

Staatsverfall und soziale Desintegration, verbunden mit dem eindeutigen Legitimationsverlust der politischen Eliten, der durch die Massenmedien und das Internet verstärkte spirituelle Pluralismus, das immer intensivere Werben um Kunden im Supermarkt der magischen Techniken und religiösen Vorstellungen führen dazu, dass die Verfolgung von Hexen auch in Zukunft von rivalisierenden Gruppen, von Kirchen, Kulten und Milizen betrieben werden wird. Während sich in Afrika eine Rückbesinnung auf die spirituellen Wurzeln des Christentums abzeichnet, eine Afrikanisierung christlicher Orientierungen, erscheinen Harnischfeger auch außerhalb Afrikas die Bemühungen weitgehend gescheitert, den Glauben mit aufklärerisch-säkularen Prinzipien in Einklang zu bringen. Traditionelle Formen des Glaubens dringen dabei nicht nur von außen nach Europa ein, sie kommen auch aus der eigenen Kultur.

Sich im Laufe der Zeit verändernde Reaktionsformen auf Hexerei untersucht *Walter Bruchhausen* am Fallbeispiel Südost-Tansanias. Er arbeitet heraus, auf welche Weise die Auflösung traditioneller politischer und religiöser Autoritäten durch den Islam und die Kolonialherrschaft sowie die koloniale und nachkoloniale Gesetzgebung die gesellschaftlichen Antworten auf dieses Phänomen veränderten. Von der Giftprobe und anderen Orakelformen durch die Führer lokaler Gemeinschaften über das öffentliche Hexenaufspüren und -reinigen durch auswärtige „Experten" bis hin zu privaten und religiösen Methoden durch sogenannte Geistmedien wandelte sich dabei in Abhängigkeit sich verändernder gesamtgesellschaftlicher Rahmenbedingungen auch der konkrete Umgang mit dem Phänomen der Hexereibeschuldigungen.

Zeigt dieses Beispiel erneut, dass Verallgemeinerungen über afrikanische Hexenvorstellungen mit einer gewissen Skepsis zu betrachten sind, unterstreicht diesen Tatbestand auch der Überblick von *Katrin Pfeiffer* über verschiedene Begriffe aus der westafrikanischen Sprache *Mandinka* aus dem Kontext des Übernatürlichen. Sind bereits Übersetzungen von einer europäischen Sprache zur anderen bei einzelnen Ausdrücken nur durch Umschreibungen möglich, so gilt dieses noch mehr für Begriffe aus einem gänzlich anderen Kulturkreis, die selbst in der eigenen Volksgruppe unterschiedlichen Interpretationen unterliegen. Wie das Beispiel des Wortes *Buwaa* zeigt, das in europäischer Tradition lexikalisch als „Hexe", „witch" oder „sorcier" übersetzt wird, handelt es sich dabei eher um „eine Person, von der man sagt, dass sie ein Kannibale mit übernatürlichen Kräften und wandelnder Erscheinung sei", eine Interpretation, die dennoch nichts anderes als einen Annäherungswert an eine Realität darstellt, der wir als Europäer in gewisser Weise immer als Fremde und Aussenstehende gegenübertreten werden. Wie sagte schon Michael Schönhuth: „Als ‚Ungläubige' können wir uns über die vergangenen und heutigen Hexereidiskurse durch Quellenstudium, konkrete Beobachtung oder Befragungen informieren und versuchen, sie zu erklären. In einem tieferen Sinne verstehen können wir Hexerei auf diese Weise nicht. Wir müssten bereit sein, Mitspieler zu werden in einem gefährlichen Spiel, das eigentlich keine teilnehmenden Beobachter kennt",[5] das zudem eine kulturelle und sprachliche Akkulturation voraussetzt, die nur in den seltensten Fällen auch tatsächlich gewährleistet ist. In diesem Sinne sagen viele europäische Forschungsbeiträge über den Hexenglauben und über magische Vorstellungswelten im modernen

---

5   Siehe das entsprechende Zitat im nachfolgenden Beitrag von Michael Schönhuth.

Afrika nicht nur etwas über diese Thematik aus. Sie zeugen auch von den eigenen Rationalisierungsbemühungen im Rahmen kultureller Übertragungsmechanismen.

Dass es interessant und weiterführend sein kann, okkulte Kräfte, Hexenverfolgungen und Geschlecht in Afrika mit frühneuzeitlichen europäischen Entwicklungen zu vergleichen, unterstreicht der Beitrag von *Rolf Schulte*, der seine empirischen Forschungen zu geschlechtsspezifischen Ausprägungen europäischer Hexenverfolgungen in Relation zur afrikanischen Moderne setzt. Während Erstere tatsächlich signifikant geschlechtsspezifisch waren, lässt sich Ähnliches für Afrika nicht belegen. Auf diesem Kontinent besteht innerhalb der vielfältigen ethnischen, regionalen, wirtschaftlichen und kulturellen Differenzen weder ein einheitliches Hexenbild, noch ein einheitliches geschlechtsspezifisches Hexenstereotyp. Dennoch sind massive Hexenverfolgungen auch in Afrika häufig geschlechtsbezogen. Neben sozialen, wirtschaftlichen, kulturellen und anderen Faktoren gehört der Gender-Aspekt zu den Variablen, die je nach Konstellation eine mehr oder minder bedeutende Rolle im Kontext afrikanischer Hexenverfolgungen spielen können und dementsprechend aus analytischer Sicht beachtenswert erscheinen.

Auf den Resultaten einer mehrjährigen Recherche zur Produktion eines Dokumentarfilms basieren die Überlegungen von *Oliver G. Becker* über die Hintergründe einer extremen Form okkulter Aggression in Afrikas Sub-Sahara-Zone. Bestimmte, oft besonders grausame Mordfälle, sogenannte „Muti-Morde", werden von der Forschung häufig zusammen mit der Ver- oder Austreibung und der anschließenden Tötung von Hexen unter der Bezeichnung *witchcraft violence* subsumiert. Sie stellen jedoch im Hinblick auf ihre psychologische Motivation und Ausführung eine eigene Kategorie dar, eine extreme Form okkulter Gewalt, die auf drastische Weise den Konflikt von Markt und Moderne in Afrika repräsentiert und dabei inzwischen auch den europäischen Kontinent erreicht hat. Der Bezug zwischen traditionellen afrikanischen Glaubensvorstellungen und medizinischen Anwendungen, verbunden mit dem ökonomischen Niedergang vieler Regionen, spielt bei der Suche nach den Tatmotiven eine ebenso bedeutende Rolle wie der Glaube an Magie und okkulte Mächte.

Auf erweiterten Feldforschungen in Soweto, dem größten schwarzen Township in Südafrika, beruhen die Ausführungen von *Joan Wardrop*, die sich Mitte der 1990er Jahre in Zusammenarbeit mit einer speziellen Polizeieinheit, der *Soweto Flying Squad*, mit einem signifikanten Anstieg von Hexereianschuldigungen befasste. Der Vorwurf, dass Hexerei im Spiel ist, wenn Unglück oder Tod einen Menschen befällt, war in dieser Zeit im südafrikanischen Township weit verbreitet. Mit der Zahl der Aids-Toten nahmen auch die Hexereiverdächtigungen drastisch zu. Die Menschen, die mit der ständigen Angst lebten, Opfer der Hexerei zu werden, suchten Schutz und forderten Gerechtigkeit. Für den Rechtsstaat wurde dieses auch insofern zum Problem, als die Jagd auf Hexer und Hexen in Form von Selbstjustiz erhebliche Ausmaße annahm. Allein in der *Northern Province* wurden zwischen 1990 und 1999 insgesamt 587 Menschen als angebliche Hexer oder Hexen erschlagen oder lebendig verbrannt.[6] Nicht nur der Fluch einer Krankheit, sondern auch die tiefe kulturelle Verunsicherung im Übergang vom Apart-

---

6   Adam ASHFORTH: Witchcraft, Violence and Democracy in South Africa, The University of Chicago Press, Chicago 2005.

heid-Regime zur Demokratie verbunden mit einem schnellen politischen und sozialen Wandel führten zu einer Krisensituation, die in den Schilderungen und Berichten der örtlichen Bevölkerung über unerklärliche Phänomene einen deutlichen Widerhall fanden und dabei auch geschlechts- und schichtenspezifische Charakteristika aufwiesen.

Gewissermaßen zu den Anfängen der wissenschaftlichen Hexenforschung zurückkehrend, beschließt *Jan-Lodewijk Grootaers* diesen Tagungsband, in dem er sich in eingehenden Feld- und Archivforschungen der zentralafrikanischen Gesellschaft der *Zande* widmet. Diese diente seit der Veröffentlichung von Evans-Pritchards *Witchcraft, Oracles and Magic among the Azande* im Jahre 1937[7] den meisten ethnologischen Studien als Bezugspunkt, ohne dass die Veränderungen ihrer Glaubensvorstellungen und Lebenserfahrungen in den zurückliegenden siebzig Jahren Berücksichtigung fanden. Grootaers zeigt sich nicht nur bestrebt, den wissenschaftlichen Diskurs über die *Zande* historisch zu verorten und den gegenwärtigen Realitäten anzupassen, er analysiert auch den Unterschied zwischen innewohnender Hexerei und erworbener Zauberei, beschäftigt sich mit der Problematik des Kannibalismus als Ausdrucksform schädlicher Zauberei und erörtert den veränderten Umgang mit Personen, die der Ausübung derartiger Praktiken verdächtigt werden. Er unterstreicht dabei, dass Diskurse über Hexerei und Zauberei soziale Beziehungen und gesellschaftliche Veränderungen nicht nur reflektieren, sondern diese auch konstitutiv prägen. In diesem Sinne sind okkulte Glaubensvorstellungen und Praktiken nicht nur eine Begleiterscheinung afrikanischer Modernität, sondern integraler Bestandteil derselben.

---

7   Eward EVANS-PRITCHARD: Witchcraft, oracles and magic among the Azande, Oxford 1937.

Michael Schönhuth

Theorien zu Hexerei in Afrika:
Eine Exkursion ins afrikanische Hexendickicht

Abstract

The article takes the reader along to an anthropological excursion into the brushwood of African witchcraft. First, the destinations are delimited and hints are given on the purpose of the journey and the fellow passengers. Then the article immerges into the forest of anthropological theories and typologies on witchcraft in Africa. With this structuring help, aisles are cut into the bushes of African witchcraft, which for outsiders are not easily seen through. Before returning to the safe base camp an outlook is offered, where the journey could be bound for.

Zusammenfassung

Der Beitrag geleitet die LeserInnen auf eine ethnologisch geführte Exkursion ins afrikanische Hexendickicht. Zuerst werden die Reiseziele abgesteckt und Hinweise über den Gegenstand der Reise und die Mitreisenden gegeben. Dann taucht der Beitrag ein in den Wald der ethnologischen Theorien und Typologien zur Hexerei in Afrika. Mit dieser Strukturierungshilfe im Gepäck werden Schneisen in das für den Außenstehenden nicht immer leicht zu durchschauende afrikanische Hexendickicht geschlagen. Die ExkursionsteilnehmerInnen werden eingeladen, einen Blick auf die modernen Hexenmuster und Alltagstheorien zur Hexerei in Afrika zu werfen. Vor der Rückkehr ins sichere Basislager wird noch ein Ausblick angeboten, wohin die Reise weitergehen könnte.

Reiseziele

Auf den folgenden Seiten wird der Stand der ethnologischen Hexereiforschung in Afrika für ein nicht ethnologisches, vor allem historisch geschultes Publikum skizziert. Mit den großen Theorierichtungen der letzten 80 Jahre und einem ursprünglich für eher geschlossene bäuerliche Gesellschaften entwickelten Modell im Gepäck werden die ExkursionsteilnehmerInnen eingeladen, die Entwicklung der modernen Hexenmuster und Alltagstheorien zur Hexerei in Afrika in ihren lokalen wie transnationalen Einbettungs- und Wiedereinbettungsprozessen zu verfolgen. Richtigen Hexen werden wir auf dieser Reise nicht begegnen. Da bräuchten wir Eintrittskarten, und die sind auf einer wissenschaftlichen Exkursion wie dieser nicht zu haben. Auch werden anschauliche Beispiele auf ein Minimum beschränkt. Die liefern im weiteren Verlauf dieses Bandes die Reiseführerkollegen Kohnert, Kamphausen, Harnischfeger, Bruchhausen und Becker, die sich mit je eigenem Fokus empirisch dem Thema ‚Hexerei in Afrika' genähert haben. Der vorliegende Beitrag liefert den Rahmen und Strukturierungshilfen zur Einordnung des Phänomens.

Hinweise über den Gegenstand der Reise

Zur besseren Einordnung unterschiedlicher Herangehensweisen und für ein gemeinsames Verständnis des Gegenstandes möchte die Reiseleitung die historisch in Europa forschenden Reiseteilnehmer auf Folgendes hinweisen: Hexerei in Europa und Hexerei in Afrika sind zwei Paar Stiefel. Wenn von Hexerei „witchcraft" (mangu, bayi, buwaa, ...) in Afrika die Rede ist, hat dies mit europäischen Hexenmustern unter Umständen genauso wenig zu tun, wie der christliche Teufel mit Sasabonsam. Sasabonsam ist ein boshafter, aber eher menschenscheuer Waldgeist bei den Akan-sprechenden Ethnien in Ghana, der auf Urwaldriesen hockt, mit seinen spinnenlangen, bis auf den Waldboden reichenden Beinen unachtsame Jäger aufgreift, und sie, wenn er schlecht gelaunt ist, auch schon mal verspeist. Würden wir uns auf die Beschreibung in lokalen Quellen beschränken, käme wohl auch ein europäischer Beobachter kaum auf eine Verwandtschaft mit dem christlichen Teufel.

Es ist dem Eifer früher Bibelübersetzer zu verdanken, dass Sasabonsam, in Ermangelung anderer lokaler Entsprechungen, zum Gegenspieler Gottes mutierte. Er wurde häufig genannt, wenn von den Missionaren nach bösen, gemeinschaftszerstörenden „übernatürlichen Wesen" gefragt wurde. Sasabonsam ist ein unangenehmer Bursche. Für eine semantische Vereinnahmung in das im Spätmittelalter von der katholischen Scholastik ausgebildete Konzept Satans als Inkarnation des Bösen und Führer der Hexen ist Sasabonsam allerdings denkbar schlecht geeignet, und mit ihm die meisten anderen ambivalenten Figuren afrikanischer Kosmologien, die in der christlichen Terminologie das Teufelsattribut verpasst bekamen.[1]

Übersetzungsprobleme treten auch in der historischen Hexenforschung in Europa auf. Während sie hier aber eher historisch-etymologischer Natur sind, also den diachronischen Wandlungen des Begriffs in einem kulturellen Austauschraum folgen, sind sie in der interkulturellen Begegnungssituation mit Afrika vor allem ein Problem historisch unabhängig voneinander entwickelter, unterschiedlich geknüpfter semantischer Systeme. Einen Eindruck von der für Außenstehende verwirrenden Vielfalt und den sich oft überlappenden Begriffsfeldern lokaler Hexereidiskurse gibt Kathrin Pfeiffer anhand des wandlungsfähigen und immer nur kontextspezifisch verständlichen Hexenbegriffs im westafrikanischen Mandinka in diesem Band. Wo nicht schon früh durch den Einfluss hegemonialer Macht- und Religionssysteme (die es natürlich auch in Afrika gab) eine Einbettung in größere Systeme stattgefunden hat, sind wir in jedem Fall gut beraten, den lokalen Hexereidiskursen auf den Grund zu gehen, sie in ihrem Kontext zu verorten, bevor wir vergleichen. Vor einer Aneignung afrikanischer Hexenbilder im europäischen Diskurs ist es deshalb nützlich, sich folgende einschränkenden Punkte zu vergegenwärtigen:

---

1 Eine den afrikanischen Tricksterfiguren vergleichbare, ambivalente Rolle nimmt der europäische Teufel allenfalls im weitab kirchlicher Dualisierung von Gut und Böse entwickelten Volksdiskurs des späten Mittelalters ein, der sich im Sagenkreis des geprellten Teufels gehalten hat. Vgl. August WÜNSCHE: Der Sagenkreis vom geprellten Teufel, Leipzig / Wien 1905. Peter DINZELBACHER: Die Realität des Teufels im Mittelalter, in: Peter SEGL (Hg.): Der Hexenhammer. Entstehung und Umfeld des Malleus malficarum von 1487, Köln / Wien 1988, S. 177-194.

- Das afrikanische Phänomen hat mit dem europäischen Muster der frühen Neuzeit eigentlich nur das Maleficium, die schlechte oder üble Tat gemein. Alle anderen typischen Kennzeichen der europäischen Hexerei sind nicht notwendigerweise vorhanden. Das hat unter anderem mit dem Fehlen bzw. der marginalen Rolle eines für die Normierung und Verbreitung des europäischen Musters ab dem 12. Jahrhundert entscheidenden Akteurs zu tun: der Katholischen Kirche.

- Hexerei und Besessenheit in Afrika müssen als zwei getrennte Objektbereiche verstanden und behandelt werden. Das Ergriffenwerden von Wesen, die von außerhalb des menschlichen Einflussbereiches kommen, bietet in der Regel für den Träger die Möglichkeit, ihre nützlichen (expressiven, diagnostischen oder kurativen) Eigenschaften über eine Lehrzeit zu kontrollieren und dann in den Dienst der Gemeinschaft zu stellen. Nur wenn das Geistwesen asozial ist, rein destruktiven Charakter hat, bzw. den Träger überfordert, besteht die Notwendigkeit, es wieder loszuwerden. Dies steht in deutlichem Widerspruch zur Dämonologie des Mittelalters und der frühen Neuzeit, die ausschließlich negativen Charakter hat[2] und in der über das Wirken Satans eine enge funktionale Verbindung zwischen (absichtsvoller) Hexerei und (meist unabsichtlicher) Besessenheit hergestellt wurde.

- Hexerei ist im Gegensatz zum postmodernen europäischen Diskurs in Afrika eine überwiegend den sozialen Zusammenhalt zerstörende Kategorie. Ihr asozialer, Leben verzehrender Zug steht im Vordergrund. Die Gegenspieler der Hexen, die Praktiker der „weißen Magie" („witchdoctors", „traditional healers", „féticheurs", „ngangas") führen dagegen kein Nischendasein wie bei uns. Sie sind nicht selten geschätzter, gefürchteter oder geachteter Teil der lokalen Machtelite. Der westliche Diskurs schätzt Hexereigeschichten vor allem wegen ihrer Fähigkeit, modernistische Gewissheiten zu unterminieren. Im afrikanischen Diskurs dienen Gerüchte über Hexerei weniger zur Belustigung, zur Befriedigung intellektueller Neugierde oder gar der individuellen Sinnsuche. Sie sind viel mehr Teil einer manchmal bedrohlichen Alltagsrealität, mit der die Leute in der einen oder anderen Weise fertig werden müssen.

- Hexerei in Afrika ist keine vom Establishment oder einer aufstrebenden Schicht moderner Mediziner unterdrückte archaische Religionsform. Auch die These, die von Bruchhausen[3] kürzlich – wenn auch vorsichtig – formuliert wurde, es könne sich bei der afrikanischen Hexerei um eine real existierende „okkultistische Subkultur" handeln, führt nicht weiter. Dort, wo wir traditionellerweise Formen okkultistischer Macht finden, sind sie in der überwiegenden Zahl mit Geheimgesellschaften verbunden. Diese halfen in der Regel, die gerontokratische Macht (also das Establishment) abzusichern, bzw. die Jüngeren ins System einzubinden. Oder aber sie boten ein probates Mittel, auf die ersten Modernisierungsschübe des europäisch-afrikanischen Handels (Sklaven, Handelswaren) im 18. und 19. Jahrhundert mit einem adäquaten Vertriebssystem z. T. Ethnien übergreifend zu re-

---

2 Zentral sind dabei die Begriffe der „Versuchung" und „Austreibung".
3 Walter BRUCHHAUSEN: Hexerei und Krankheit in Ostafrika. Betrachtungen zu einem missglückten interkulturellen Diskurs, in: DERS. (Hg.): Hexerei und Krankheit. Historische und ethnologische Perspektiven, Münster 2003, S. 93-124, hier S. 108f.

agieren.⁴ Die heutige okkultistische Subkultur in Afrika ist, wie ich noch skizzieren werde, ein Globalisierungs- und Modernisierungsphänomen.

- Afrikanische Hexerei als solche gibt es nicht. In Europa bestand mit dem Hexenhammer, dem Buchdruck, der Inquisition und den über päpstliche Verlautbarungen (Bullen) gelenkten Kanzeln ein ausgefeiltes System zur Verbreitung eines relativ einheitlichen Musters über mehrere Jahrhunderte. Für die nicht Schrift führenden, traditionell bäuerlichen Kulturen des südlichen Afrikas, deren kommunikatives Gedächtnis lediglich über wenige Generationen reichte, können wir historisch eigentlich immer nur von „Hexerei" bei den x am Ort y zum Zeitpunkt z sprechen. Dies macht Kulturvergleiche und generalisierte Aussagen einigermaßen schwierig. Die Bereitschaft, über „afrikanische Hexerei" zu sprechen, steht bei europäischen Wissenschaftlern in der Regel umgekehrt proportional zur Dauer eigener lokaler Feldforschungstätigkeit in Afrika.

Hinweise über die Mitreisenden ins Hexendickicht

Die westlichen Diskurse über das Hexereiphänomen in Afrika und die Art seiner Aneignung sind so verschieden, wie die Gruppen, die sich mit ihm beschäftigen oder beschäftigt haben. Es gibt dabei wissenschaftliche und nichtwissenschaftliche, theologisch, politisch und persönlich motivierte Herangehensweisen. Bevor die ethnologischen Erklärungsansätze eingeführt werden, sollen die anderen Akteure und Erklärungs- / Handlungsansätze zumindest aufgezählt werden:

- Weiße und später mit anderer Schwerpunktsetzung schwarze Missionare und Theologen (theologischer Erklärungsansatz: von skeptisch ablehnend bis moralphilosophisch annehmend);⁵
- Die Kolonialjustiz bis in die 50er Jahre des 20. Jahrhunderts (juristisch: basierend auf der europäischen Rechtsprechung, aber inkonsistent und teils widersprüchlich in der Praxis);⁶
- Medizin und Ethnomedizin (naturwissenschaftlicher Erklärungsansatz: zuerst aufklärerisch-bekämpfend, dann seit den 1970er Jahren dialogbereit, zumindest gegenüber der pharmakologisch-wirksamen und natürlich auch wirtschaftlich verwertbaren Seite der lokalen Kräuterheilkunde);⁷
- Die Ethnopsychiatrie (individual- oder sozialpsychologischer Erklärungsansatz: Hexenmuster entweder eine dem depressiven Formenkreis angehörende Geistes-

---

4 Erika DETTMAR: Markt – Macht – Moral. Interkulturelle Wirtschaftsbeziehungen zwischen Afrika und Europa, Frankfurt a. M. / New York 2000.
5 Während der Kampf gegen okkulte und magische Praktiken in der frühen Phase ein Hauptmotor und Rechtfertigungsinstrument für die weißen Missionsanstrengungen darstellte, ging mit der Afrikanisierung des Klerus eine zunehmend differenzierte Haltung einher, die in Hexenvorstellungen weniger heidnische Verirrung, als einen Ausdruck gestörter Sozialbeziehungen und die Verkörperung einer Kategorie des moralisch Schlechten erkannte, vgl. BRUCHHAUSEN: Hexerei und Krankheit in Ostafrika, S. 102.
6 Zusammenfassend BRUCHHAUSEN: Ebd., S. 102ff.
7 vgl. zur Spaltung zwischen naturwissenschaftlich akzeptabler Kräuterheilkunde und „magischem Heilwesen" die Position der WHO 1978, cit. in: BRUCHHAUSEN 2003b:99, Fn13.

gestörtheit, Angstneurosen oder ein Phänomen von Gruppensuggestion oder Gruppenpsychose);[8]
- Die Ethnopsychoanalyse (kulturtraumatologischer Erklärungsansatz: Hexenmuster als kollektive Antwort auf die Verschiebung und Projektion der fressenden phallischen Mutter aus der symbiotischen Phase des Kleinkindes);[9]
- Die Vertreter eines Neuheidentums und so genannter frei fliegender Hexen, die sich die afrikanische Hexe zum Vorbild eines mit den Naturkräften in Einklang befindlichen persönlichen Lebensentwurfes genommen haben.[10] Mit dem aus dem Mittelmeerraum entlehnten Bild der großen Göttin im Gepäck findet dabei meist eine Verwechslung der Rolle von Hexe und Hexendoktor / traditionellen Heilern statt.

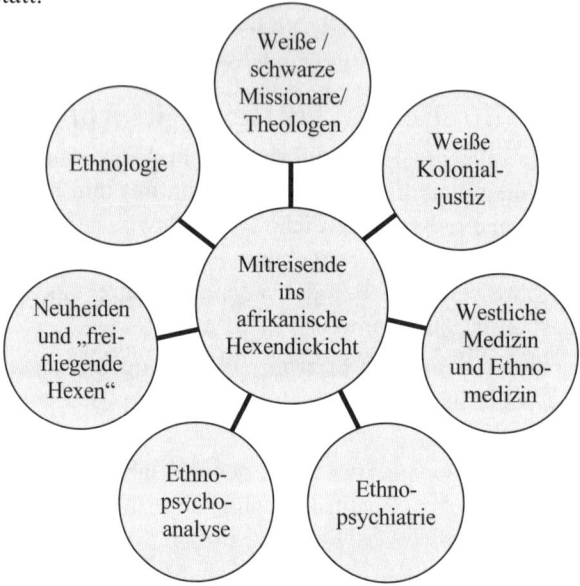

Abb. 1: *Wissenschaftliche und nichtwissenschaftliche Repräsentationen des afrikanischen Hexenmusters.*

---

8 Margaret J. FIELD: Search for Security. An ethno-psychiatric study of rural Ghana, Evanston 1960 Ill. E. O. HAAF: Hexenwahn in Afrika, in: Bild der Wissenschft. Naturvölker in unserer Zeit. Stuttgart 1971, S. 80-100. E. B. WITTKOVER / H. H. WEIDMAN: Magic, witchcraft and sorcery in Relation to Mental Health and Mental Disorder, in: N. PETRILOWITSCH / K. FLEGEL (Hg.): Social Psychiatry, Vol. 8, New York 1969, S. 169-185.

9 Paul PARIN / Fritz MORGENTHALER / Goldy PARIN-MATHEY: Fürchte Deinen Nächsten wie Dich selbst. Psychoanalyse und Gesellschaft am Modell der Agni in Westafrika, Frankfurt 1971. Zur Kritik: M. RUTSCHKY: Unser Agni. Ein ethnologisches Vexierbild, in: Merkur, Nr. 10 (1978), S. 977-992. Thomas HAUSCHILD: Ethno-Psychoanalyse. Symboltheorien an der Grenze zweier Wissenschaften, in: W. SCHMIED-KOWARZIK / J. STAGL (Hg.), Grundfragen der Ethnologie, Berlin 1980, S. 151-168.

10 Praktisch-naturphilosophischer Erklärungsansatz; vgl Donate PAHNCKE: Gibt es eine Hexenreligion? Das Phänomen Hexe und die deutsche Hexen- und Heidenszene, in: Wulf KÖPKE / Bernd SCHMELZ (Hg.): Hexen im Museum, Hexen heute, Hexen weltweit. Museum für Völkerkunde Hamburg 2003, S. 213-229. Christopher McINTOSH: Die Entstehung und Perspektive des Neuheidentums, in: Ebd., S. 230-238.

All diese Gruppen haben Anteil an der westlichen Form der Aneignung und Repräsentation des Phänomens `Hexerei in Afrika´. Sie erzählen viel über die unterschiedlichen Rationalisierungsstrategien ihrer Protagonisten – im Bemühen, das Phänomen zu bannen, bzw. es dem eigenen Diskurs zu unterwerfen und weniger über das Phänomen selbst. Davor ist natürlich auch die Ethnologie nicht gefeit. Allerdings verfügt sie – ähnlich der geschichtswissenschaftlichen Herangehensweise an Quellen – über den Vorteil eines hermeneutischen Vorgehens in der Feldforschung, das vor jeder Theoriebildung versucht, die lokalen Repräsentationen von innen her, aus den Kategorien der untersuchten Gruppen selbst, verstehend zu erschließen.

Ethnologische Theorien zu Hexerei in Afrika

Die Aussagen westlicher Sozialtheoretiker in den 1940er und 50er Jahren ließen darauf schließen, dass afrikanische Hexereivorstellungen mit dem Greifen westlicher moderner Institutionen aussterben würden. So sagte Godfrey Parrinder 1958 voraus, dass „... eine aufgeklärte Religion, Erziehung, Medizin und bessere soziale und rassische Bedingungen dazu führen werden, Hexereivorstellungen zu vertreiben". Margaret Field war als Ethnopsychiaterin auf der Basis ihrer Untersuchungen bei ghanaischen Antihexereischreinen sogar der Meinung, dass Hexerei nur in den Köpfen bestimmter gemütskranker Menschen existieren könne. Eine erfolgreiche Bekämpfung depressiver Krankheiten in Afrika hätte ihr Aussterben zur Folge.[11]

Heute haben Islam und Christentum die indigenen Religionen zahlenmäßig überrundet. Die Institutionen der Moderne mit ihrer funktionalen Ausdifferenzierung und konkurrierende Wertesysteme sind auch in Afrika überall anzutreffen. Massenmedien und Internet sind Teil der afrikanischen Moderne und zumindest in den städtischen Agglomerationen allgegenwärtige Pforten zum Marktplatz globalisierter Informationen, Muster und Sichtweisen. Afrika setzt sich mit den Folgen der Globalisierung genauso auseinander wie wir. Trotzdem haben die Propheten eines „hexenfreien Afrikas" nicht recht behalten. Hexerei ist ein Thema in Afrika und es ist in manchen Teilen des Kontinents aktueller als noch vor zwanzig oder dreißig Jahren. Die Fragen der Globalisierung werden überall gleich oder ähnlich gestellt – die Antworten sind so verschieden wie das jeweils für die Akteure verfügbare „kulturelle Gedächtnis", um eine Figur von Jan Assmann aufzugreifen.[12]

Gehen wir aber einen Schritt zurück in der Geschichte der wissenschaftlichen Auseinandersetzung mit afrikanischer Hexerei. Welche Theorieangebote hat uns die Afrika bezogene empirische Forschung für das Hexereiphänomen in den letzten 80 Jahren ge-

---

11 Margaret J. FIELD: Search for Security. An ethno-psychiatric study of rural Ghana, Evanston 1960.

12 Das kulturelle Gedächtnis verbindet nach Assmann soziale Gruppen in zweifacher Richtung: Auf sozialer Ebene durch das Zusammengehörigkeitsgefühl untereinander, in historischer Dimension durch das Verbundenheitsgefühl mit früheren Generationen. Dieses kommunikative Gedächtnis reicht in mündlichen Kulturen nur drei bis vier Generationen weit, ihr Erinnerungshorizont wandert mit den Generationen mit. Schrift stabilisiert die Tradierung des kulturellen Wissens. Es entwickelt sich nach Assmann dadurch ein echtes Geschichtsbewusstsein im heutigen Sinne, vgl. Jan ASSMANN: Das kulturelle Gedächtnis. Schrift, Erinnerung und politische Identität in frühen Hochkulturen, München 2002 (1992)

macht? Grob vereinfachend lassen sich folgende, gleichzeitig auch mit Paradigmenwechseln verbundene Ansätze unterscheiden:[13]

(1990er-heute)
Hexerei als Ausdruck
globalisierter okkulter Ökonomien

(1970er-1990er)
Hexerei als kulturelles Konstrukt
im Rahmen von Alltagstheorien

(1960er-1980er)
Hexerei als Exklusionskategorie
in Kulturwandelsituationen

(1950er-1960er)
Hexerei als Element
sozialer Ausgleichsprozesse

(1950er-1980er)
Hexerei als Projektion
kompensierter Schuldgefühle

(1920-1940er)
Hexerei als Ausdruck
unterschiedlicher Denkstile

Abb. 2: Chronologie der Paradigmenwechsel ethnologischer Theorien zur Hexerei in Afrika

Die mit den Forschungsansätzen von Lévy Bruhl[14] und Evans-Pritchard verbundenen Ansätze der 1920er bis 1940er Jahre sahen die Hexerei als Manifestation angenommener, grundsätzlich unterschiedlicher Denkstile im Vergleich zur abendländisch-cartesianischen Denktradition. Evans-Pritchard stellte im Rahmen seiner damals bahnbrechenden Feldforschung bei den Azande im Sudan fest: „The European is right, the Azande wrong. (...) A witch cannot do what he is supposed to do and has in fact no real existence".[15] Das magische Denken stört sich nach dieser Diktion nicht am logischen Widerspruch und erlaubt gerade deshalb die Beantwortung sozial relevanter Fragen nach den mystischen bzw. moralischen Ursachen für erfahrenes Unglück. Diese frühen funktionalistischen Ansätze dominierten die erste Phase der Forschung zwischen 1920 und 1940.[16]

---

13 Vgl. Michael SCHÖNHUTH: Das Einsetzen der Nacht in die Rechte des Tages. Hexerei im symbolischen Kontext afrikanischer und europäischer Weltbilder, Münster 1992, S. 52ff.. Wim VAN BINSBERGEN: Witchcraft in modern Africa as virtualised boundary conditions of the kinship order (2001). Elektronisches Dokument: http://www.shikanda.net/african_religion/witch.htm (Aufruf am 17.11. 2007).

14 „mentalité primitive / prälogisches Denken" M. LÉVY-BRUHL: La mentalité primitive. The Herbert Spencer Lecture, Oxford 1931.

15 Edward E. EVANS-PRITCHARD: Witchcaft, in: Africa 8, 4 (1935), S. 417-22, hier S. 417.

16 Die Diskussion um „different modes of thought" wurde in den 1960er und 1970er Jahren in der sozialwissenschaftlichen Kontroverse um das Verstehen fremden Denkens wieder aufgenommen. Sie hat auch in Deutschland in Sammelbänden wie „Der Wissenschaftler und das Irrationale" ihren

In einer zweiten Phase in den 1950er bis 1960er Jahren kamen Erklärungsansätze auf, die Hexerei als Element sozialer Ausgleichsprozesse verstanden. Diese an die funktionalistische Tradition anknüpfenden konfliktsoziologischen bzw. mikropolitischen Ansätze sahen in Hexenanklagen vor allem ein Mittel zur Aufdeckung von Rollenkonflikten und zur Auflösung von spannungsgeladenen („redundanten") Sozialbeziehungen in einem auf Stabilität ausgelegten Sozialsystem. Sie versuchten, auch eine Rechtfertigung afrikanischer Rationalität über die Betonung der Logik sozialer Beziehungen hinter den Hexereivorwürfen.[17]

Neben den mikropolitisch argumentierenden Ansätzen etablierte sich in dieser Zeit auch eine Richtung, die die normativen Aspekte der Hexereianklagen hinsichtlich des Erhalts der sozialen Organisation einer Gesellschaft betonte. In der Hexereianklage haben die Gesellschaftsmitglieder nicht nur die Möglichkeit, redundante Beziehungen zu lösen, sondern auch, sich gegenseitig ihrer moralischen Werte zu versichern. Als negative Rollenmodelle[18] fungieren Hexen für die moralische Mehrheit gleichzeitig als Bestärkung bestehender Normen und Grenzmarker für gesellschaftlich gebilligtes Verhalten.

In der dritten Phase zwischen den 1950er und 1980er Jahren etablierten sich sozialpsychologisch inspirierte Ansätze, die unterdrückte Aggression, Frustration und deren Abfuhr und Verschiebung durch kollektive Sündenbockfantasien als Motor für die gesellschaftliche Entwicklung des Hexenmusters ausfindig machten. Immer und überall, wo Menschen um die gleichen Gratifikationen wetteifern – so die Argumentation – entstehen feindliche Impulse gegenüber anderen Menschen. Gleichzeitig begrenzt und kanalisiert jede Gesellschaft das Ausleben feindlicher Impulse. Als Reaktionsformen bleiben Rückzug in Scheinwelten (z. B. durch Narkotika), Sublimierung, Flucht, vor allem aber Aggression. In Sozialbereichen, wo offene Aggression nicht legitimiert ist, wo das Ideal des Familialismus und der guten Nachbarschaft herrscht, benötigt die Gesellschaft legitime Sündenböcke, auf die die Aggression projiziert wird: die Hexen.[19]

In einer vierten Phase zwischen den 1960ern und Ende der 1980er Jahre kamen auch Ansätze auf, die die symbolische, die normativ-moralische und die Kulturwandeldimension der Hexerei aufeinander bezogen. Sie begriffen Hexerei als moralische Kategorie der Ausgrenzung („Exklusion"), in der sich die Verwerfungen sozialen und politischen Wandels zeigen. Im prekär gewordenen moralischen Kosmos steht die Hexe symbolisch für die Umkehr des traditionell gesellschaftlich gebilligten Verhaltens: „Die Hexen verkörpern, was ein Mensch qua Kulturdefinition nicht ist. Sie werden mit Eigenschaften

---

Niederschlag gefunden. Vgl. Hans-Peter DUERR (Hg.): Der Wissenschaftler und das Irrationale. 2 Bde. Berlin 1981.

17 Manchester-Schule um Max Gluckman; Sammelbände von Marwick: Max MARWICK (Hg.): Witchcraft and Sorcey. Selected Readings, Harmondsworth 1970; und Douglas als Kulminationspunkt: Mary DOUGLAS (Hg): Witchcraft, confessions and accusations, London u. a. 1970.

18 „the antimodel of approved behaviour": Lucy MAIR: Magie im schwarzen Erdteil, München 1969.

19 Klassisch s. Kluckhohn für die Navajo: Clyde KLUCKHOHN: Navaho Witchcraft, Boston 1944. Für verschiedene afrikanische Ethnien vgl. S. F. NADEL: Witchcraft in Four African Societies. An Essay in Comparison, in: American Anthropologist 54 (1952), S. 18-29. Godfrey PARRINDER: Witchcraft. European and African, London 1958. J. G. KENNEDY: Psychological and social explanations of Witchcraft, in: Man 2 (1967), S.216-225; verknüpft mit Freudscher Theorie ethnopsychoanalytisch: PARIN / MORGENTHALER / PARIN-MATHEY: Psychoanalyse und Gesellschaft.

belegt, die einem Menschen nicht zur Verfügung stehen und leben aus, was Menschen tunlichst unterlassen sollten. Sie sind ontologisch gesprochen eine negative Seinskategorie, sie sind moralisch gesprochen die Perversion der gesellschaftlichen Ethik und sie sind symbolisch gesprochen die Verkörperung der verkehrten Welt".[20]

Der Unterschied zu früheren normativ-moralischen Ansätzen ist, dass dieser Akt der Ausgrenzung die tradierten Gesellschaftsstrukturen nicht mehr stabilisiert, sondern selbst zum Kennzeichen des Verfalls der alten Ordnung wird. Hexereivorwürfe werden so zum Versuch, die Verhältnisse in einer Übergangsphase zur Moderne noch aus der Perspektive der alten Ordnung zu betrachten und zu bewerten.[21]

Eine fünfte Phase in den 1970er bis 1990er Jahren brachte konstruktivistische Erklärungsansätze ins Spiel. Konstruktivisten begreifen Hexerei als von den Kulturmitgliedern „kulturell hergestellt". Das Hexenmuster ist Teil der Alltagstheorien, auf die sich Menschen in ihrer sozialen Praxis einigen, und nach denen sich das Handeln in der Regel richtet. Dabei spielt Diskursmacht zur Herstellung von Realität eine zentrale Rolle.[22]

Globalisierungsansätze der 1990er Jahre schließlich verstehen die Hexerei als eine afrikanische Antwort auf die Herausforderungen der Moderne im Kontext der Globalisierung.[23] In einer Welt, die sich zunehmend ihrer Kontrolle entzieht, ist der Zugang zu okkulten Kräften gerade für Globalisierungsverlierer ein probates Mittel, sich noch als Handelnde zu erfahren.

Alle diese Theorieansätze haben auch heute noch einen gewissen Erklärungswert für das Fortbestehen des Phänomens und keiner erklärt uns das Phänomen ganz. Bemerkenswert ist die Tatsache, dass von den frühen zu den späteren Theorieansätzen die Frage der „objektiven" Basis für Hexerei immer weniger bedeutsam wird. War für Evans-Pritchard noch klar, dass Hexen nicht real sind, so machen die neueren Untersuchungen keinen Unterschied mehr zwischen in unserem Sinne möglichen (weil beobachtbaren) magischen Handlungen und unmöglicher (weil nur in den Köpfen der Beteiligten existierender) Hexerei.

Typen von Hexereianklagen in Afrika

Ergebnisse der empirischen Hexereiforschungen der 1930er bis 1970er Jahre in Afrika legen einen engen Zusammenhang zwischen der Gesellschaftsformation und dem vorherrschenden Typ von Hexenanklagen nahe. So schlug Mary Douglas in dem erwähnten Sammelband 1970 eine Typologie vor, die nach der sozialen Position fragt, von der aus Hexereianklagen gemacht werden.

---

20 SCHÖNHUTH: Hexerei, S. 166.
21 Wim VAN BINSBERGEN: Witchcraft in modern Africa as virtualised boundary conditions of the kinship order (2001). http://www.shikanda.net/african_religion/witch.htm (Aufruf am 5.11. 2003).
22 „Wer die Macht hat, definiert den Diskurs"; vgl. dazu die neueren Beiträge in: Max MARWICK (Hg.), Witchcraft and Sorcey. Selected Readings. Second Edtion, Harmondsworth 1986.
23 Jean COMAROFF / John L. COMAROFF (Hg.): Modernity and Its Malcontents: Ritual and Power in Postcolonial Africa Chicago 1993. Peter GESCHIERE: The Modernity of Witchcraft. Politics and the Occult in Postcolonial Africa, Charlottesville VA/London 1997. D. CIEKAWY / P. GESCHIERE: Containing Witchcraft: Conflicting Scenarios in Postcolonial Africa, in: African Studies Review 41, 3 (1998), S. 1-14.

Theorien zur Hexerei in Afrika 25

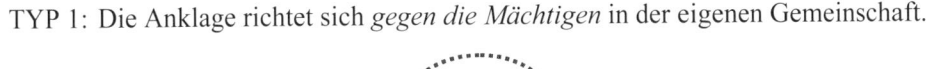

TYP 1: Die Anklage richtet sich *gegen die Mächtigen* in der eigenen Gemeinschaft.

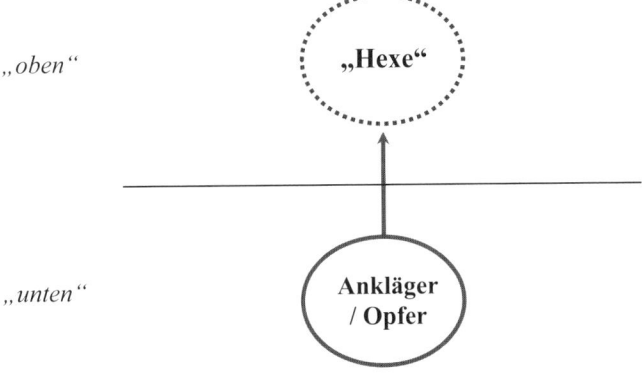

TYP 2: Die Anklage richtet sich *gegen die Unterprivilegierten* in der eigenen Gemeinschaft.

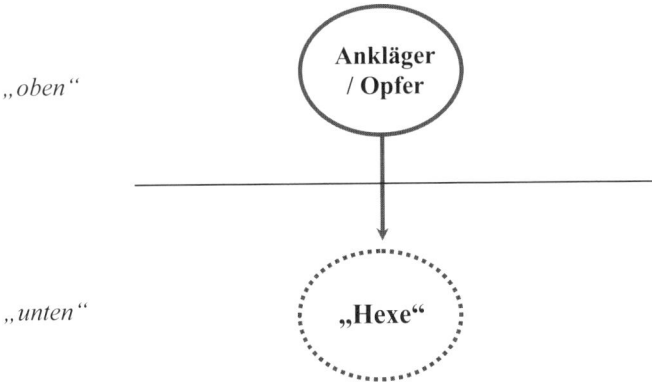

TYP 3: Die Anklage richtet sich *gegen Fremde* bzw. außerhalb des Binnenraums stehende Personen.

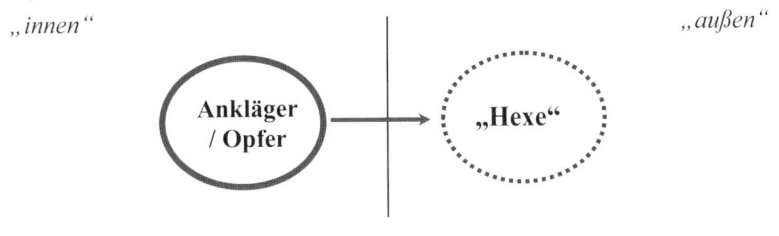

Abb.3: Drei Typen von Hexereivorwürfen in Afrika (verändert nach Douglas 1970).

Der erste Typ ist z. B. für die Azande im Sudan oder die Cewa in Zimbabwe beschrieben. Er betont den nivellierenden Einfluss von Hexereivorwürfen als Korrosiv gegen materielle Anhäufung in Gemeinschaften mit nur gering ausgeprägter sozialer Schichtung. Er ist typisch für segmentäre Verhältnisse, in denen Formen der materiellen und symbolischen Umverteilung die Basis für das sozioökonomische und politische Gleichgewicht bilden.

In der zweiten Variante richten sich Hexereianklagen gegen die Unterprivilegierten innerhalb der eigenen Gemeinschaft (wie z. B. bei den Tiv in Nigeria oder in verschiedenen kamerunischen Gesellschaften). Diese Form ist typisch für eine Situation, in der sich eine städtische, Kapital akkumulierende Schicht aus den Verpflichtungen einer reziproken Verwandtschafts- oder ständischen Ordnung zu lösen beginnt. Es ist deshalb nicht verwunderlich, dass dieser Typ auch die Geburtswehen der europäischen Moderne begleitete.

Der dritte Typ, bei dem sich der Vorwurf gegen Außenstehende oder Fremde richtet, die die eigene Ordnung bedrohen, war für afrikanische Gesellschaften mit Hexereimuster eher untypisch. Er ist zum Beispiel für den mittelamerikanischen „brujo" beschrieben, aber auch in pazifischen Gesellschaften anzutreffen. Im europäischen Hexereidiskurs entspricht ihm am ehesten das Stereotyp des „Brunnen vergiftenden" oder „weltverschwörenden" Juden – der aber interessanterweise weitgehend außerhalb des eigentlichen Hexenparadigmas verhandelt wurde.[24]

Moderne Hexenmuster

Drei Monate vor den allgemeinen Wahlen in der tansanischen Provinz Sansibar im Jahr 2000 wurden kleine mit Blättern und einem Talisman gefüllte Schachteln an Orten gefunden, an denen vorwiegend für die Regierungspartei Stimmen abgegeben wurden. Einige Wochen später fand man unter dem Festplatz einer Veranstaltung der Opposition eine vergrabene Ziege. Solche Ereignisse, über die regelmäßig in afrikanischen Gazetten berichtet wird, sind Ausdruck für die verstärkten Bemühungen von Politikern, über die Konsultation von traditionellen spirituellen Experten ihre Karrieren zu fördern und Wahlen in ihrem Sinne zu beeinflussen. Das seit 14 Jahren in Tansania eingeführte Mehrparteiensystem und der damit verknüpfte größere Wettbewerb um Posten und politischen Einfluss haben diese Tendenz noch verstärkt. Mindestens ein Viertel der fast 8.000 Kandidaten von 13 politischen Parteien konsultieren traditionelle Spezialisten vor den Wahlen, schätzt eine politologische Untersuchung der Universität Dar es Salaam. Auch der plötzliche Tod bekannter Politiker wird von den Bürgern häufig auf den von politischen Gegnern initiierten Einfluss schwarzmagischer Experten zurückgeführt. Welche bizarren Formen solche Aktivitäten annehmen können, wurde an der Warnung von König Mswati von Swaziland an die Politiker seines Landes im Jahr 2003 deutlich, im bevorstehenden Wahlkampf keine rituellen Morde mehr in Auftrag zu geben, um aus Körperteilen der Getöteten Erfolg versprechende Medizin zu machen.

Warum wird Moderne in Afrika so leicht mit Hexerei verbunden? Hexerei-Diskurse sind explizit mit „Home" und Familie verknüpft; sie stellen die dunkle Seite der Verwandtschaft dar, die in Afrika die klassische Form der „Schließung" darstellt.[25]

---

24 Norman COHN: Die Protokolle der Weisen von Zion. Der Mythos von der jüdischen Weltverschwörung, Baden-Baden 1998.
25 CIEKAWY / GESCHIERE: Containing Witchcraft, S. 5.

In diesen dörflichen Kosmos hinein weist das Hexereiphänomen zurück. In weiten Teilen Afrikas stellten die verwandtschaftlichen Bindungen ein soziales Universum dar, dessen Funktionieren von einem heiklen Fließgleichgewicht zwischen Gegenpolen abhing: Himmel und Erde, die Lebenden und die Ahnen, Männer und Frauen, Endosphäre und Exosphäre.[26] Die Familie ist der Hort einer nicht gewalttätigen, sozialen, reziproken Ordnung, und damit eine permanente Herausforderung für alle individuellen Bestrebungen und Sehnsüchte. Solange die Dorfgemeinschaft noch den Kontext von Produktion und Reproduktion darstellte, repräsentierte die Hexe die Grenzbedingung dieser Existenz. Sie war, was auch der altdeutsche Wortstamm des Wortes Hexe ausdrückt: „Hagazussa", Zaunreiterin: illegitimer Grenzgänger zwischen Wildnis und Zivilisation, innen und außen, Tag und Nacht, Kultur und Natur. Ihr Wirken richtete sich gegen die dörflichen Existenzbedingungen schlechthin: die Produktion und Reproduktion auf materieller Ebene, die Gemeinschaftsnormen auf sozialer Ebene und die kosmologische Ordnung auf moralischer Ebene. Sie verkörperte die fleischgewordene Antithese des gebilligten Verhaltens.

Zwar werden die modernen Produktionsverhältnisse in Afrika nicht mehr durch die Verwandtschaftsordnung bestimmt, aber sie werden vielfach noch aus der Perspektive dieser Ordnung betrachtet und bewertet. Hexerei hat sich, um mit Wim van Binsbergen zu sprechen, in der Moderne eingerichtet, aber im Rahmen der alten kosmologischen Ordnung. Im Hexereiparadigma und anderen okkulten Praktiken finden die Bemühungen der Menschen Ausdruck, sich selbst Macht zuzuschreiben. Damit versuchen sie, ein gewisses Maß an Kontrolle über eine Welt zurückzugewinnen, die sich zunehmend ihrem Einfluss entzieht.[27] Weil die Welt von der Stadt aus gesehen ganz anders aussieht, als von der Warte des Dorfes, figuriert die Hexe aus der Perspektive ihrer Opfer im je anderen Kosmos. Für diejenigen, die den Dorfkontext hinter sich gelassen haben, und versuchen, sich in der städtischen Moderne einzurichten, wird Hexerei zum Inbegriff neidischer Verwandtschaft, die das Vermögen der Abwesenden auffrisst, und so für das eigene Fortkommen in der Stadt zur existenziellen Gefahr wird.

Für die im Dorf Gebliebenen stellen die Hexen die personifizierte Selbstsüchtigkeit der Städter dar. Diese saugen die Menschen, Güter und Geld auf, ohne Gegengabe. Sie werden als illegitime Räuber wahrgenommen, die sich aus ihren Verpflichtungen gestohlen haben und die Früchte der Moderne für sich selber konsumieren. Das Problem für die zu kurz Gekommenen ist nicht die Ankunft der Moderne an sich. An ihr möchten die meisten nur zu gerne partizipieren. Die Frage, die sie umtreibt, ist, wie eine gerechte Umverteilung aussehen müsste. Hexerei gehört zur Verwandtschaftsordnung, aber sie ist gleichzeitig der Verrat an ihren Grenzen.[28] Die prinzipielle Grenzenlosigkeit der Hexerei verbindet sie mit dem globalen Kapitalismus. Angesichts der Zirkulation von Menschen, Gütern und vor allem Bildern über den Globus[29] drücken Hexereigerüchte

---

26 VAN BINSBERGEN: Witchcraft, S. 238.
27 COMAROFF / COMAROFF: Modernity, S. XIV.
28 CIEKAWY / GESCHIERE: Containing Witchcraft, S. 5.
29 Arjun APPADURAI: Globale ethnische Räume, in: Ulrich BECK (Hg.): Perspektiven der Weltgesellschaft, Frankfurt/M. 1998, S. 11-40.

die Angst wie auch die Besessenheit aus, mit neuen Möglichkeiten Reichtum und Macht anzuhäufen.

So finden sich in den postkolonialen Staaten alle Typen von Hexereianklagen. Der Pfeil der Anklage zeigt einmal nach oben gegen die Modernisierungsgewinner. Er verbindet sich dann mit dem Ideal der ökonomischen Umverteilung, der sich die Modernisierungsgewinner zusehends entziehen. Der Pfeil kann ebenso gut nach unten gerichtet sein bei denen, die sich vor der Rache Zurückgelassenen fürchten, vor allem, wenn sie vom Kuchen der Moderne trotz ständigen Bemühens nichts abbekommen, beim Spiel um Geld und Machtzuwachs ins Straucheln geraten, oder gar unter die Räder kommen. Auch nach außen kann sich der Pfeil richten, z. B. wenn ganzen Volksgruppen hexerische Umtriebe unterstellt werden oder politische Gegner (oft anderer ethnischer Zugehörigkeit) mit Hilfe von Hexerei ausgeschaltet werden sollen.

Hexerei und andere okkulte Kräfte können je nach Region und Kontext im Dienste der Mächtigen wie der Ohnmächtigen, der Emporkömmlinge wie der Zurückgelassenen, der Gewinner wie der Verlierer stehen. Auch die Grenzen zwischen nach unserem Verständnis imaginären und realen Angriffen werden fließend. Gerüchte über angebliche hexerische Aktivitäten von Geschäftsleuten und Politikern und tatsächliche rituelle Mordaufträge, Selbstbekenntnisse von überführten „Hexen", und auf ihr Wirken zurückgeführte, tatsächliche mysteriöse Todesfälle, verstärken und bestätigen sich gegenseitig.

Was in früheren Untersuchungen als Unterscheidungskriterium für verschiedene Gesellschaftsformationen diente, taucht nun als Versatzstück in komplexen Gesellschaften mit okkulten Ökonomien wieder auf. In ihnen basteln unterschiedliche Akteure ganz im Sinne von Levi Strauss' „homme le bricoleur" an ihrer je eigenen Version des Hexereidiskurses im modernen Kontext. Sie tun dies unter der selektiven Mobilisierung traditioneller kultureller Ressourcen.

Hexenmuster auf der Reise

Durch Wanderarbeiter werden Hexenbilder und okkulte Praktiken auch über Landesgrenzen hinweg in neue Kontexte getragen und dort transformiert. Durch das Vorherrschen einer einheitlichen Landes- oder Verkehrssprache werden ethnische Hexenkonzepte in einen nationalen oder transnationalen Sprachdiskurs eingebunden (z. B. im Kiswahili); dort wo Englisch oder Französisch Nationalsprache ist, sogar in einen internationalen. Wie folgenreich das sein kann, zeigen schon die frühen Bemühungen europäischer Bibelübersetzer, für die Dreifaltigkeit oder den christlichen Teufel Entsprechungen in der Lokalsprache zu finden. Und die Katholische Kirche in Afrika tut sich heute noch schwer, bei der Frage, ob es sich bei afrikanischen Hexen um vom Teufel Besessene handelt, bei denen das „Rituale Romanum", der große Exorzismus anzuwenden sei. Die Pfingstkirchen wiederum machen sich genau dieses Muster zunutze und versprechen diesseitige Erlösung.

Der Markt des Okkulten ist dereguliert. Es herrscht ein Überangebot an globalen und lokalen Interpretationsexperten, von denen sich die wenigsten über die Natur der okkulten

Kräfte einig sind.³⁰ So beugen sich die Marktkräfte des Okkulten dem jeweils Definitionsmächtigeren. Das kann in einem Fall der Politiker sein, der seine durch anstehende Wahlen gefährdete Machtposition mithilfe okkulter Spezialisten sichern will, auch wenn dies Menschenopfer kostet.³¹ Das kann im anderen Fall eine Gruppe von Modernisierungsverlierern sein, die in der Mobilisierung traditioneller Muster eine Chance sieht, ihre real schwache Position im ins Schwimmen geratenen Sozialgefüge zu verbessern.

Man könnte sagen, Hexerei ist eine der „travelling theories", die heute weltweit als Interpretations- und Handlungsrahmen verfügbar sind. Sie muss aber, um wirksam zu werden, auf fruchtbaren Boden fallen. Sie muss an schon vorhandene Deutungsmuster in den Köpfen anschließen können. Sie ist auf die Macht des primordialen Arguments angewiesen und dies kann nur von den Akteuren selbst kommen. Förderlich für das Wiedererstarken des Musters ist eine Situation, die von unklaren Sozialbeziehungen, Rollenzuweisungen und Machtkonstellationen gekennzeichnet ist, eine kritische Masse von Personen, die das Muster mitträgt sowie ein Staat, der moderne Rechtsstandards nicht durchzusetzen in der Lage bzw. gewillt ist. Diese Faktoren erklären auch die regional so unterschiedliche Verbreitung des Phänomens im heutigen Afrika.

Wohin die Reise weitergehen könnte

Wohin entwickelt sich der Hexereidiskurs in Afrika? Was wird gegen seine Entgrenzung getan? Der moderne Vertreter des Gewaltmonopols, der postkoloniale afrikanische Staat, befindet sich in einer Zwickmühle. Lehnt er die Realität der Hexerei ab und ächtet die traditionellen Formen der Verfolgung, so schreibt er den Diskurs der Kolonialmächte fort. In einer Zeit schwindenden Vertrauens seitens der Zivilgesellschaft in die Legitimität staatlicher Macht und der Suche nach einer afrikanischen Identität erodiert dies seine Position zusätzlich. Trägt er der Realität von Hexerei Rechnung, und lässt Hexen den Prozess machen, so verabschiedet er sich aus dem Diskurs der modernen Weltgemeinschaft. Er macht sich unglaubwürdig in internationalen Institutionen und wird zur Zielscheibe von Menschenrechtskampagnen.

Die betroffenen Staaten gehen ganz unterschiedliche Wege. Während in etlichen Ländern die Kolonialgesetzgebung mit ihrer Unterscheidung zwischen möglicher Magie und unmöglicher Hexerei noch offiziell besteht, sind zum Beispiel in Südafrika Bestrebungen im Gange, Hexerei als Tatbestand wieder in die Strafgesetzgebung aufzunehmen.³² Kamerun schließlich zählt zu den Ländern, in denen der Hexerei angeklagten Menschen aufgrund der Expertise von Hexendoktoren bis zu zehn Jahre Gefängnis dro-

---

30 Adam ASHFORTH: AIDS, Witchcraft, and the Problem of Power in Post-Apartheid South Africa. May 2001 (Occassional Paper of the School of Social Sciences, 10). Elektronisches Dokument. http://www.sss.ias.edu/publications/papers/paperten.pdf (Aufruf am 17.11. 2007).
31 Eine Form sind die so genannten „Muti"-morde in Südafrika, aber auch in westafrikanischen Ländern, von denen BECKER in diesem Band berichtet.
32 N. V. RALUSHAI et al.: Report of the Commission of Inquiry into Witchcraft violence and ritual murders in the Northern Province of the Republic of South Africa, 1996 (unveröffentlicht). Dirk KOHNERT: Witchcraft and transnational Social Spaces: Witchcraft Violence, Reconciliation and Development in South Africa's Transition Process, in: Journal of Modern African Studies 41, 2 (2003), S. 1-29.

hen.³³ Die schwächste Institution zur Eingrenzung des Hexereiproblems ist anscheinend der Staat. Er produziert mehr Hexereidiskurse und -gewalt, als er bannt. Erfolgreicher bei der Behandlung – das zeigen Beispiele aus Südafrika und Kamerun – sind traditionelle *Chiefs*. Sie begrenzen zumindest den Wahn.

Am effektivsten allerdings sind die Pfingstkirchen, weil sie einerseits Hexerei als Realität akzeptieren, sie aber dennoch von außerhalb des Deutungssystems zu bekämpfen suchen. Zunehmend weltweit vernetzt und meistens in afrikanischen Ballungsräumen konzentriert, deuten sie Hexerei als Werk des Teufels um. Sie versprechen gleichzeitig göttlichen Schutz vor Hexerei und göttliche Erlösung für ehemalige Hexen innerhalb ihrer Gemeinden. Gegen die Einhaltung eines strikten ethischen Codes bieten sie eine neue Form der Schließung in dem freiwilligen Zusammenschluss ihrer egalitären Glaubensgemeinschaft.³⁴ Sie legitimieren persönliche Akkumulation von Geld und erlauben es gleichzeitig, die Forderungen armer Verwandter abzuweisen.

Es wäre interessant zu wissen, was Max Weber zu dieser Vermählung von Hexenglauben und protestantischer Ethik in US-amerikanischem Gewand sagen würde. Ihr hybrider Charakter zwischen dem Geist des Kapitalismus und der Macht des Okkulten macht die Pfingstkirchen jedenfalls zu einem der effektivsten, für eine demokratische Weltordnung aber auch problematischsten Akteure der kulturellen Globalisierung.³⁵

Zurück am heimischen Schreibtisch

Als „Händler des Fremdartigen" (Geertz) laufen wir Ethnologen leicht Gefahr, den gleichen voyeuristischen Exotismus von archaischer Primitivität und Rückständigkeit zu bedienen, den wir an der Darstellung in den Massenmedien kritisieren.³⁶ Hexerei und okkulte Praktiken sind weder eine Rückkehr zu traditionellen Strukturen noch ein Zeichen von Rückständigkeit.³⁷ Sie sind vielmehr Ausdruck moderner sozialer Praxis in der Auseinandersetzung mit überregionalen und globalen Einflüssen. Sie äußern sich in der Revitalisierung und der Erfindung von Traditionen. Sie äußern sich in der lokalen Aneignung des Fremden, der Domestikation der großen Erzählungen. Und sie äußern sich in der Expansion des Lokalen in die Außenwelt (der Diasporabildung und Transnationalisierung des Phänomens).

Generalisierte Aussagen über das Hexereiphänomen in einer Weltregion, die weder katholische Inquisition, noch Kanzel, Hexenhammer oder Gutenbergschen Buchdruck

---

33 CIEKAWY / GESCHIERE: Containing Witchcraft.
34 Johannes HARNISCHFEGER: „Unverdienter Reichtum. Über Hexerei und Ritualmorde in Nigeria", in: Sociologus 47/2 (1997), S. 129-156, hier S. 152. Dirk KOHNERT: Occult Beliefs, Globalization and the Quest for Development in African Societies: The example of South Africa. Religion and the Political Imagination in Changing South Africa, in: Gordon MITCHELL / Eve MULLEN (eds.): Religion and the political imagination in a changing South Africa, Münster 2002, S. 169-188.
35 Peter BERGER: Die vier Gesichter der globalen Kultur, in: Europäische Rundschau (Wien) 26, (1998), S. 105-113. Zur problematischen Rolle der Pfingstkirchen in Afrika siehe z. B. Philip JENKINS: Das Christentum der Zukunft wird vom Süden bestimmt, in: Der Überblick 03/2003.
36 Bruce KAPFERER: Beyond Rationalism: Rethinking Magic, Witchcraft, and Sorcery. New York 2003.
37 H. L. MOORE / T. SANDERS (Hg.): Magical Interpretations. Material Realities. Modernity, Witchcraft and the Occult in Postcolonial Africa, Routledge 2001.

zur Vereinheitlichung der Nomenklatur hatte, sind für die Modellbildung vielleicht hilfreich, halten der Empirie aber nur selten stand. Ich werde mich deshalb nach meinem Ordnungsversuch – wie jede vernünftige Hexe – bemühen, diese Ordnung gleich wieder durcheinanderzubringen. Ich möchte empfehlen, keiner großen Theorie zu Wesen oder Unwesen, zur Funktion oder Dysfunktion, zur Moral oder Unmoral, zum modernistischen oder antimodernistischen Potenzial des Hexereidiskurses in Afrika Glauben zu schenken.[38] Auch Hexenmuster vertragen nur Theorien mittlerer Reichweite. Die spannendsten Arbeiten der letzten Jahre, die ich kenne, nähern sich dem Thema lokal und fundiert empirisch.[39] Als „Ungläubige" können wir uns über die vergangenen und heutigen Hexereidiskurse durch Quellenstudium, konkrete Beobachtung oder Befragung informieren und versuchen, sie zu erklären. In einem tieferen Sinne verstehen können wir Hexerei auf diese Weise nicht. Wir müssten bereit sein, Mitspieler zu werden in einem gefährlichen Spiel, das eigentlich keine teilnehmenden Beobachter kennt. Die afrikanische Hexe ist eben nicht nur eine Denkfigur, Teil einer großen Erzählung oder ein kulturelles Deutungsmuster, zu der wir sie in der wissenschaftlichen Beschreibung gerne deklarieren.

Hexerei ist ein Feld, auf dem reale Männer und Frauen um okkultes Wissen, realen Einfluss und Macht kämpfen. Wer ernsthaft Forschung auf diesem Feld betreibt, weiß, dass er oder sie sich auf einem Minenfeld bewegt, bei dem Neid, Missgunst, Selbstsüchtigkeit, Eifersucht, Ausgrenzung, Verdächtigung, üble Nachrede, Machthunger und enttäuschte Hoffnungen die Ingredienzien sind; eine explosive Mischung, die jederzeit hochgehen kann und dabei ganz gewöhnliche Opfer findet. Wohl dem, der da seinen akademischen Kopf einziehen und unversehrt an den heimischen Schreibtisch zurückkehren kann, um über Hexerei als „afrikanischen Weg zur Moderne" zu räsonieren.

---

38 Als jüngster Versuch einer m. E. insgesamt missglückten aber in der Öffentlichkeit viel beachteten monokausalen Erklärung des Zusammenhanges zwischen wirtschaftlicher Stagnation und Hexerei in Afrika: D. SIGNER: Die Ökonomie der Hexerei oder Warum es in Afrika keine Wolkenkratzer gibt, Wuppertal 2004.

39 M. LAMBEK: Knowledge and Practice in Mayotte. Local Discourses of Islam, Sorcery, and Spirit Possession, Toronto, Buffalo, London 1993. GESCHIERE: Modernity. I. NIEHAUS: Witchcraft, power and politics. Exploring the occult in the South African lowveld, Cape Town 2001.

Dirk Kohnert

On the Renaissance of African Modes of Thought: The Example of Occult Belief Systems

Zusammenfassung

Die Analyse okkulter Glaubenssysteme in Afrika stellt eine einzigartige Möglichkeit dar, zu zeigen, dass angeblich rückständige afrikanische Denkweisen wie der Magie- und Hexenglaube höchst modern sind und erheblichen Einfluss auf die Gesellschafts- und Wirtschaftsstrukturen der betroffenen Völker haben. Offizielle Ansätze zur Bewältigung der durch Hexenanklagen bedingten gewaltsamen Konflikte bauen seit der Kolonialzeit auf eine durch eurozentrische Sichtweisen geprägte Kolonialgesetzgebung auf, die, legitimiert durch eine vorurteilsgeladene westlich geprägte Sozialwissenschaft, zum Bestandteil des Problems selbst wurde. Afrikanische Religionen bieten Ansätze für die Fortentwicklung tragfähigerer eigenständiger Lösungsansätze. Darüber hinaus können sie unter bestimmten Bedingungen auch westlichen Kulturbereichen neue, innovative Dimensionen philosophischen Denkens und emanzipativen Handelns bieten, zum Beispiel im Bereich der gesellschaftlichen Konfliktlösung und Versöhnung. Afrikanische Lösungsansätze für die Gewaltanwendung im Rahmen von Hexenanklagen greifen allerdings nur, insoweit sie gegen negative Einflüsse einer globalisierten liberal-kapitalistischen Wirtschaftsordnung geschützt werden können.

Abstract

The analysis of African occult belief systems provides a unique example for demonstrating that seemingly outdated and exotic African modes of thought, such as the belief in magic and witchcraft, are modern and have significant impact on social, economic and political structures. Official approaches, designed to cope with the problems of witchcraft violence in Africa, have since the advent of colonial rule been based on eurocentric views and colonial jurisdiction, legitimised by Western social science. These answers are inadequate; in fact, they constitute part of the problem itself. African religions could provide a framework for valuable indigenous solutions to actual problems of contemporary life, including the problem of witchcraft violence. Besides, they might, under certain conditions, provide the outside world with an inspiring new dimension of philosophic thought and emancipative action, for example, within the realm of conflict resolution and reconciliation. However, even in the case of the 'domestication' of witchcraft violence, this holds only in so far as appropriate African answers can be shielded against the negative impact of globalised liberal capitalism.

Modernity and African Renaissance: divided between rationalism and superstition

The history of African philosophies and development visions, from Nkrumah's Panafricanism *via* Senghor's Négritude to the current concepts of the New Partnership for Africa's Development (NEPAD)[1] and the related vision of an African Renaissance, is said to be a history of failures.[2] Certainly, the proponents of African Renaissance suggest that Africans are successfully continuing to rise out of slavery, colonialism, and neo-colonialism into liberation. Their vision is based on the rich intellectual and cultural heritage of Africa and the common dream of its renaissance.[3] Unfortunately, implementation of these concepts has so far been primarily restricted to myth-making, used by the new African elite as a mobilisation tool to unite their people in the fight against neo-colonialism, or even as an ideological political tool in the pursuit of particular class interests.[4]

„*21st century Africa will be rational, or it will not be at all*"[5] wrote the Cameroonian sociologist Axelle Kabou (1991) in her provocative bestseller more than a decade ago. This was by no means a reflection limited to the eurocentric modernisation ideology of the former colonial masters; it has been the prevailing view of both the European educated African power elite and the donor community who have been involved in Africa up to the present day. The globalisation of universal standards of governance and of neo-liberal economic concepts corresponding to Western standards was promoted, last but not least, by the political conditions imposed by the international donor community. Nevertheless, this was readily accepted by African rulers, as reflected in the NEPAD

---

1 New Partnership for Africa's Development (NEPAD); cf. www.nepad.org; 10.03.05. For an evaluation of NEPAD cf. Henning MELBER: The G8 and NEPAD – More than an elite pact? Institut für Afrikanistik, ULPA - University of Leipzig Papers on Africa. Politics and Economics 2004, p. 74. Sally MATTHEWS: Investigating NEPAD's development assumptions, in: Review of African Political Economy Vol. 31, Nr. 101 (September 2004), pp. 497-511.
2 Cord JAKOBEIT: Afrikanische Diskussionen zur Entwicklung des Kontinents – das Beispiel ‚African Renaissance', in: Journal für Entwicklungspolitik, Vol. 2 (2000), pp. 149-160. Axelle KABOU: „Et si l'Afrique refusait le développement"?, Paris 1991. MELBER: The G8, p. 74.
3 Mbulelo Vizikhungo MZAMANE: Where there is no vision the people parish: Reflections on the African Renaissance. Hawke Institute Working Paper Series, No 16; Hawke Institute, University of South Australia, Magill, South Australia 2001, (available online: http://www.unisa.edu.au/hawke/institute/resources/working%20paper%2016%20(Mbulelo).pdf; 26.01.05. Ulrich LÖLKE: Zwischen Altem und Neuem – Afrikanische Renaissance und die Geschichte afrikanischer Einheit. Epd-Entwicklungspolitik, Vol. 10 (2003), pp. 32-34. For an annotated detailed bibliography on the definition and concept of African Renaissance cf. Anne JANSEN / Claudia ROESKE: African Renaissance – Annotated online bibliography (in German), DÜI, Hamburg, 2001, <www.duei.de/dok/archiv/onlinebibl_afdok_01_3.pdf>; 20.01.2005; as well as online bibliographies, like <www.africavenir.com/elibrary/african-renaissance/index.php>; 26.01.05. African Renaissance Bibliography: <www.fu-berlin.de/afrosi/documents_pdf/AfricanRenaissanceBibliography.pdf>; 26.01.2005.
4 Ian LIEBENBERG: The African Renaissance: Myth, Vital Lie, or Mobilising Tool? African Security Review, Vol 7, No. 3 (1998): available online: http://www.iss.co.za/Pubs/ASR/7No3/Liebenberg.html; 26.01.05.
5 «L'Afrique du XXIe siècle sera rationnelle ou ne sera pas», cf KABOU: „Et si l'Afrique refusait le développement".

programme.[6] The (post) modernisation ideology contributed to the questioning of African local custom and of indigenous knowledge as outdated barriers to development. It was commonly assumed that modernisation would inevitably rationalise both social processes and human beliefs. This also holds for „traditional" African religions, and particularly for the occult belief, i.e. the belief in magic and witchcraft[7], characterised by modernists as superstition.

The proponents of modernisation in Africa and elsewhere would like to uproot this belief as soon as possible in the name of progress, preferably by legal means and educational campaigns (cf. below). To date, the cultural heritage of African societies is still unjustly seen by the majority of experts merely in terms of development constraints, dominated by characteristics such as rent seeking, informal sector trap, irrational economic actors or the prebend economy[8], without due regard to its historical roots and its dependency on the global economic system, as explained by Bilgin / Morton[9], Comaroff / Comaroff[10], Mazrui[11] and others.[12] However, apparently there coexist multiple moderni-

---

6   cf. MELBER: G8. MATTHEWS: Investigating NEPAD's development, pp. 497-511.

7   African scholars, religious leaders and healers, as well as politicians, maintain that they, with other Africans, share a common ground of 'basics' of occult belief, i.e. that witchcraft is a reality and principally evil; it is to be considered as an integral part of African culture. Therefore, analytical concepts of witchcraft should take this emic view on the subject into account: cf. Dirk KOHNERT: Witchcraft and transnational social spaces: witchcraft violence, reconciliation and development in South Africa's transition process. Journal of Modern African Studies, Vol. 41, Nr. 2 (2003), pp. 217-245. For a detailed discussion of definitions and concepts of witchcraft, sorcery and magic in different local contexts, as well as of the limitations and fallacies of the general delimitations of witchcraft, particularly in the African context, and finally on the ambiguities of the transfer of eurocentric concepts of magic and witchcraft to African societies, cf. Peter GESCHIERE: „The modernity of witchcraft. Politics and the occult in postcolonial Africa", London 1997, pp. 12-15, 215-224. Dirk KOHNERT: Magic and witchkraft: implications for democratization and poverty alleviating aid in Afrika. World Development, Vol. 24 (1996), pp. 1347-1355.

8   Patrick CHABAL / Jean Pascal DALOZ: Africa works. Disorder as political instrument, Oxford 1999. Ulrich MEZEL: Afrika oder – das neue Mittelalter – Eigenlogik und Konsequenzen der Gewaltökonomie, in: Blätter für deutsche und internationale Politik 9 (2003), S. 1060-1069. For examples of dubious oversimplifications of the role of African culture as an impediment to modern economic development cf. Lawrence HARRISON / Samuel P. HUNTINGTON (eds.): Culture matters: how values shape human progress, New York 2000, p. xiii; on Ghana and its harsh critique by Amartya SEN: How does culture matter? Paper, Conference on Culture and Public Action, World Bank, Washington D. C., April 2002, pp. 10-11. CHABAL / DELOZ: Africa, pp. 128-30.

9   Pinar BILGIN / Adam DAVID: Historicising representations of 'failed states': beyond the cold-war annexation of the social sciences?, in: Third World Quarterly, Vol. 23, Nr. 1 (2002), pp. 55-80, pp. 73-75.

10 Jean COMAROFF / John COMAROFF: Transparent Fictions, or the Conspiracies of a Liberal Imagination – An Afterword, in: H. G. WEST / T. SANDERS (eds.), Transparency and conspiracy: ethnographies of suspicion in the New World Order, Durham, NC 2003, pp. 287-300.

11 Ali A. MAZRUI: The African Renaissance – A Triple Legacy of Skills, Values and Gender. First presented as the Keynote Address at the 5th General Conference of The African Academy of Sciences, held in Hammamet, Tunisia, April 22-27, 1999; <www.africacentre.org.uk/renaissance.htm#Ali%20A.%20Mazrui>; 20.01.2005.

12 For a critique of the lack of regard for the pluralism of African cultures, of ethnocentrism and of the ideological facets of ethno-philosophy, cf. Paulin J. HOUNTONDJI: „African Cultures and Globalisation. A Call to Resistance. D+C Development and Cooperation, No. 6 (November/December 1997),

ties – including the modernity of occult belief systems – in Africa, each of which follows its own cultural traits.[13] Therefore, what would be required is both the emancipation of awkward aspects of witchcraft violence and the liberation from the Procrustes' bed of an individualistic and uncritical scientific Western tradition of Cartesian reason. As Jürgen Habermas[14] explained some twenty years ago, the European tradition of enlightenment is an „unfinished business". This is particularly the case when it is articulated in the form of technological reason, which often acts to support the concerns of dominant vested interests, shielded behind the supposed objectivity of rational actors. In fact, this specific culturally bound logic in itself constitutes a new form of superstition.

This has serious repercussions on both research and development politics. The realities of local politics and economics, notably the linkage between religious thought and political practice in Africa,[15] remained until recently neglected by the mainstream of academic research. This is particularly the case for economics and political science, but also for policy advisors and development experts, who base their analyses on eurocentric assumptions. The modernity and relevance of occult belief had crucial, hitherto unnoticed implications on shifting legitimacy and power relations at the local level of African societies. Representatives of the state, party leaders, political entrepreneurs, warlords, and civil society organisations contested the established power brokers, such as traditional rulers, healers or religious leaders, who were now competing strategic players in the local political arena.[16]

---

pp. 24-26. IDEM: Tempting traditions – Internal debate needed in traditional cultures, in Compas Magazine (March 2001), pp. 12-13. Jean-Marc ELA: Les voies de l'afro-renaissance – Refus du développement ou échec de l'occidentalisation? Le Monde diplomatique, (Octobre 1998), p. 3 analysed the wealth and dynamics of indigenous social innovations in sub-Saharan Africa at the grassroot level; he engaged in a passionate call for a new approach, in considering rural life in Africa with its enormous potential of creativity as a laboratory of social change with often surprising and highly competitive results, promising an African renaissance. – The growing awareness of the importance of cultural change for African development is also reflected in development policy: On 20 June 2003, the ministers of culture of the African, Caribbean and Pacific (ACP) countries, on their first meeting in Dakar (Senegal), adopted the Dakar Plan of Action to start an innovative approach with culture as a driving force for development; cf. The Courier ACP-EU, No. 199, July 2003, pp. 8-9 and <www.acpse.org>; 10.03.05.

13 cf. the ongoing debate on „African modernities", Jan-Georg DEUTSCH / Peter PROBST / Heike SCHMIDT (Hg.): African modernities – entangled meanings in a current debate, Portsmouth 2002, and on „multiple modernities" cf. Ibrahim KAYA: Modernity, openness, interpretation – A perspective on multiple modernities. Social Science Information, Vol. 43, Nr. 1 (2004), pp. 35-57. Arif DIRLIK: Global modernity? Modernity in an age of global capitalism, in: European Journal of Social Theory, Vol 6, Nr. 3 (2003), pp. 275-292.

14 Jürgen HABERMAS: The Philosophical Discourse of Modernity, MIT Press, Cambridge, Mass. 1987.

15 cf. Stephen ELLIS / Gerrie TER HAAR (eds.): Worlds of power – Religious thought and political practice in Africa, London 2004. Gordon MITCHELL / Eve MULLEN (eds.): Religion and the political imagination in a changing South Africa, Münster 2002. John COMAROFF: Governmentality, materiality, legality, modernity – On the colonial state in Africa, in: DEUTSCH / PROBST / SCHMIDT (Hg.), African modernities, pp. 107-134. V. FAURE (ed.): Dynamiques religieuses en Afrique australe, Paris 2000. Jean-François BAYART (ed.): Religion et modernité politique en Afrique noire. Dieu pour tous et chacun pour soi. Paris 1993.

16 cf. ELLIS / TER HAAR (eds.): Worlds of power. GESCHIERE: The Modernity of Witchcraft. Politics and the Occult in Postcolonial Africa, Charlottesville/London 1997. Thomas BIERSCHENK: Powers

In contrast to the post-modernist approach, contemporary African philosophers and sociologists maintained that far from rejecting development and rationalism in itself, „Africa is forging new trails towards the affirmation of its dignity".[17] But it would seem that the African quest for its own distinguished way of development has a long way to go. In the short run, the rapid rise of globalised neo-liberal capitalism, accompanied by the hyper-rationalisation of economic and social relationships on the one hand, and its aftermath of increasing social differentiation on a global scale on the other, simultaneously led to an unprecedented growth of occult belief systems and economies in Africa and elsewhere, as described in detail by the Comaroffs and others.[18] This had a negative impact on development, including gross violation on an unprecedented scale of human rights by witchcraft violence and instrumentalised ritual (muti) murder in various African countries.[19]

Surprisingly, in the emic world view, the major fault lines, created under the impact of globalisation, did not lead to a reinforcement of accusations against external enemies, as under the rule of colonialism or racism in South Africa. Rather, they materialised in growing confrontation with the alleged enemy within one's own society, village or peer group. In South Africa for example, the major lines of conflict of the apartheid regime between race and class, were replaced during the transition period by cleavages between different age-groups or generations, mediated by gender.[20] Black male underclass youth and ANC activists tried to translate their understanding of Western ideas of democratisation and socialism in specific actions to eradicate the evil, equated with black magic, by witchcraft accusations against certain elders, preferably deviant elderly women, whom they saw as a menace to their communities.[21] In the following paper I should like

---

in the Village. Rural Benin between Democratisation and Decentralisation. In: Africa, Vol. 73, Nr. 2 (2003), pp 145-173. IDEM.: The local appropriation of democracy. An analysis of the municipal elections in Parakou, Rep. Benin 2002/03. Working Papers of the Department of Anthropology and African Studies, Johannes Gutenberg University Mainz, 2004, Nr. 39.

17 Célestin MONGA: Anthropologie de la colère: Société civile et démocratie en Afrique Noire., Paris 1994. HOUNTONDJI: African Culture. DERS: African Philosophy: Myth and Reality (First published 1977, Sur la Philosophie Africaine), Indiana University Press 1996.

18 cf. Jean COMAROFF / John COMAROFF: Occult economies and the violence of abstraction: Notes from the South African postcolony, in: American Ethnologist, Vol. 26, Nr. 2 (1999), pp. 279-303. IDEM.: Alien-Nation: Zombies, immigrants, and millennial capitalism. CODESRIA Bulletin, Nr. 3-4 (1999), pp. 17-27. IDEM.: Privatizing the Millennium: New Protestant Ethics and the Spirits of Capitalism in Africa, and Elsewhere. In: Afrika spectrum, Vol. 35 (2001) Nr. 3, pp. 293-312. ELLIS / TER HAAR: Worlds of power. Isac NIEHAUS: Witchcraft, power and politics – Exploring the occult in the South African, London 2001.

19 cf. ELLIS / TER HAAR: Worlds of power. J. EVANS: On brûle bien les sorcières – Les meutres muti et leur repression. In: Politique Africaine, Vol. 48 (1992), pp. 47-57. KOHNERT: Witchcraft. K. PELTZER / P. MAKGOSHING: Attitudes and beliefs of police officers towards witchcraft (boloi) and their intervention role in the Northern Province, South Africa. In: Acta Criminologica, Vol. 14 (2001), Nr. 2, pp. 100-107.

20 COMAROFF / COMAROFF: Occult economies.

21 cf. I. KESSEL: From Confusion to Lusaka: the Youth revolt in Sekhukhuneland. In: Journal of Southern African Studies, Vol. 19, Nr 4 (1993), pp. 593-614. A. ASHFORT: Witchcraft, violence, and democracy in the new South Africa. In: Cahiers d'Etudes Africaines, Vol. 38 (1998), pp. 505-532. EVANS: On brûle bien les sorcières. FAURE (ed.): Dynamiques religieuses. Anthony MINNAAR: Witch purging in the Northern Province of South Africa: A victim profile and assessment of initia-

to substantiate two hypotheses: Firstly, the analysis of African occult belief systems provides a unique example for demonstrating that seemingly outdated and exotic African modes of thought, such as the belief in magic and witchcraft, are „modern", i.e. not only current and widespread, affecting relevant aspects of everyday life in Sub-Saharan Africa, but they also have significant impact on actual social, economic and political structures. Although often ill-adapted to the actual human environment of the stakeholders, occult belief systems in African societies reflect a cultural process which is not at all limited to remote places in the hinterland, but is based on African traditional religions and shaped by current linkages between transnational social spaces in a globalised world, as Geschiere[22] and others have demonstrated.[23] Secondly, African religious systems provided a framework for valuable indigenous solutions to current problems of contemporary life, for example within the realm of increasing violence of non-state actors, including the problem of witchcraft violence. Besides, under certain conditions, they might provide the outside world with an inspiring new dimension of philosophic thought and emancipative action, for example, within the realm of conflict resolution and reconciliation. However, even as regards the 'domestication' of witchcraft violence, this holds only if appropriate African answers can be shielded against negative impacts of globalised capitalism.

On the relevance of the political economy of African belief in magic and witchcraft

1. The political economy of occult belief systems is neither outdated nor exotic

The belief in magic and witchcraft is deeply ingrained in African society. It exerts a decisive structuring influence on everyday life, even in the informal sector of politics and economics. Occult belief systems in Africa have since pre-colonial times been continually adapted to the current needs of their stakeholders. Last, but not least, they are indicators of a growing alienation caused by individualisation processes and triggered by globalisation and subsequent social, economic and political transformations.

Contrary to a widely held view in economics and political science, the political economy of the belief in magic and witchcraft in Africa is neither outdated nor restricted to exotic fields of study of somewhat limited societal interest and which are occupied by traditionally minded anthropologists. In the past decade, the modernity of the belief in magic and witchcraft and its relevance for the everyday life of Africans has been proven by a vast body of cultural studies and scholarly analyses, based on innumerable case studies, summarised and conceptualised by internationally renowned scholars, such as

---

tive to deal with witchcraft. Unpublished paper, delivered to witchcraft summit, 28 September 1999, Giyani, mpd. J. MIHALIK / Y. CASSIM: Ritual murder and witchcraft: A political weapon. In: South Africa Law Journal, (1992), pp. 127-140. I.A. NIEHAUS: The ANC's dilemma: the symbolic politics of three witch-hunts in the South African lowveld, 1990-1995, in: African Studies Review 41, 3 (1998), pp. 93-118. NIEHAUS: Witchcraft, power and politics.

22 GESCHIERE: The modernity of witchcraft.
23 KOHNERT: Witchcraft.

Geschiere[24], Ellis[25], the Comaroffs[26] and others. It is not by chance that the connection between globalised capitalism and occult economics within the framework of economic and political transformation processes in Sub-Saharan Africa, which took place in the wake of the second wind of change in the 1990s, reminds one of an amazing resurgence and manifestation of Marxist concepts of alienation (*Entfremdung, Entäußerung*), objectification (*Vergegenständlichung*), and commodity fetishism in the spiritual African world.[27] During the transition period in South Africa, for example, the growing alienation of producers from the logic of the globalised economy led to people imagining the existence of migrant labourers, bewitched as zombies and employed by powerful entrepreneurs and witches in pursuit of their sinister and selfish interests.[28] Strikingly similar notions of zombies employed by witches were reported, according to Geschiere[29], from Cameroon, southern Ghana, eastern Nigeria, former Zaire and Sierra Leone.

In Ghana, Nigeria, and other African countries, faithful new-born Christians looked for comfort and spiritual protection from the diabolic powers of the world market. Quite worldly problems, such as diminishing terms of trade, falling farmgate prices of local export crops, increasing unemployment, and indebtedness were explained within the context of their religion. New charismatic churches offered ready assistance to cope with these problems. Pentecostals in Ghana for example, revealed the dangers inherent in foreign commodities and offered to remove the spell from the fruits of globalisation. As they understood it, any foreign goods imported from the world market and sold in the local markets of Accra or Kumasi could be infected with evil. However, unlike historical materialism, they did not relate the assumed evil powers of these commodities to alienated relations of production. Instead, they identified this evil as a direct materialisation of demonic forces, as a true and real fetish which requires a ritual of „de-fetishisation", before being suited and safe for local consumption.[30]

Another vivid example of the alienation of the ethics of African traditional religions and of the systems of checks and balances within the realm of informal politics which are connected with it, is the transformation of secret cults, and the politics of vigilance and ritual murder in Nigeria.[31] The police raid in August 2004 on the Okija-shrine, in

---

24 GESCHIERE: The modernity of witchcraft.
25 ELLIS / TER HAAR: Worlds of power.
26 COMAROFF / COMAROFF: Occult economies. IDEM.: Alien-Nation.
27 For a succinct description of the theory of alienation and related concepts cf. „Alienation in Hegel and Marx", in: The Dictionary of History of Ideas, Studies of Selected Pivotal Ideas, edited by Philip P. WIENER, published by Charles Scribner's Sons, New York, in 1973-74. <cf. http://etext.lib.virginia.edu/cgi-local/DHI/dhi.cgi?id=dv1-06>, 25.02.05.
28 COMAROFF / COMAROFF: Occult economies.
29 GESCHIERE: The modernity of witchcraft, pp. 147-51, 165, 254.
30 cf. E. KAMPHAUSEN: Pentecostalism and De-Fetishism. A Ghanaian Case Study, in: Journal of Constructive Theology, Vol. 6, Nr. 1 (2000), pp. 79-96. Birgit MEYER: The power of money. Politics, occult forces and Pentecostalism in Ghana, in: The African Studies Review, Vol. 41, Nr. 3 (1998), pp. 15-37.
31 cf. Johannes HARNISCHFEGER: Witchcraft and the state in South Africa, in: Anthropos, Vol. 95 (2001), pp. 99-112. www.africana.ru/biblio/afrocentrism/12_Harnischfeger.htm; 09.03.05. Daniel OFFIONG: Secret cults in Nigerian tertiary institutions, Enugu 2003. Amadu SESAY / Charles UKEJE

Ihiala Local Government Area, Anambra State, well-known also outside the boundaries of Igboland, was revealing. Traditional shrines and their nefast practices were by no means the last vestiges of bad governance in Nigeria, as the speaker of the Anambra state government wanted to make the Nigerian public believe.[32] On the contrary, the power which secret cults in Nigeria wield in contemporary life and in regional politics is still considerable, and this power has been continuously adapted, from pre-colonial times up to present-day political structures of formal multi-party democracy; the Okija-shrine was only the tip of the iceberg. Many Western educated Nigerians considered the continued existence and strength of the country's traditional and informal social control systems as a repulsive contradiction to the country's quest to become a „modern" state with good governance. The words 'shrine' or 'secret cult' assume quasi-automatically a diabolical meaning in the ears of those who advocated good governance and the rule of law. But there is strong evidence that Okija and similar secret cults remain very popular among Nigerians, honoured and feared at the same time.[33] Shrines and cults are not bad in themselves, but are symbols of faith for African or Christian religions alike, as Wole Soyinka rightly observed in deploring 'a lazy mental attitude', 'simplistic to the point of puerility', among many of those who commented the police raid on the Okija shrine.[34] The question is rather why many Nigerians have no confidence in the contemporary formal justice system, inherited from the British colonial masters, and why they would rather submit their fate to the crude and cruel approaches of informal justice offered by Okija or similar cults, as well as by vigilant groups, such as the Bakassi boys, scattered across the country.[35] Soyinka offered another perspective in asking what would happen if Nigerians, guided by the Okija deity, were to develop the power to take to task their selfish and corrupt political leaders? In fact, a similar vision had already been explored by the Nobel Laureate in one of his early novels „Season of Anomy" (1973), and in principle there is no reason why such a bold vision would be more utopic than the influence of the Christian Liberation Theology in Latin America.

However, the example of the Okija-shrine, the representation of the dreaded Ogwugwu cult, showed at the same time the harmful alliance between scrupulous entrepreneurs with political ambitions, politicians at all levels of regional administration, and cult leaders in a society which had for a long time been deprived of traditional checks and balances by a ruthless and greedy group of military rulers condoned, if not backed, by global players. In spring 2003, during the election campaign for the legislative and gubernatorial elections of 2003, leading politicians, such as the Governor of Anambra state, Dr. Chris Ngige, as well as Senators of the House of Representatives, had apparently been pressed by an influential political god-father, the rich entrepreneur Chief Chris Uba, to swear

---

/ Olabisi AINA / Adetanwa ODEBIYI (eds.): „Ethnic Militias And The Future Of Democracy In Nigeria", Obafemi Awolowo University Press, Ile-Ife, Nigeria 2003.

32 cf. Guardian (Nigeria daily) August 8th, 2004.
33 Nonso OKEREAFOEZEKE: Foundations of Okija justice. (2004), http://nigeriaworld.com/articles/2005/mar/033.html; 08.03.05.
34 cf. Wole SOYINKA, Sunday Sun, 19 September 2004, p. 17.
35 cf. Chichere EKWURIBE: „...In defence of Soyinka." Sun News, Sunday, 26 September 2004. George DANIEL: Soyinka & the Okija shrine. Sun News, 26 September 2004.

political allegiance to him before the Okija shrine. Ngige won the elections with the help of Uba, but apparently he refused to honour his oath as he was forced to resign and was abducted on 10 July 2003. Uba openly boasted with impunity that his former protégé won the election only because he had bribed the election authorities (INEC).[36] Ngige was reinstalled, but in the ensuing battle between supporters of the two adversaries and the ongoing quest to dispose the Governor, the latter was subject to assassination attempts and arsons by roving armed bands, allegedly masterminded by Uba and the Okija shrine.

In August 2004, a police raid of the shrine revealed some 80 corpses disposed of in the sacred forest of the shrine, several of them mutilated apparently for ritual purposes, and ostensibly displayed as a sign of the spiritual and worldly powers of the cult in order to frighten and subdue potential clients. The majority leader of the Anambra State House of Assembly, Hon. Humphrey Nsofor, confessed that he and 21 other parliamentarians had also been forced to swear allegiance to Uba under the threat that the cult would otherwise perform a spiritual killing. In addition, Nsofor confirmed that these spiritual practices had a generation-long tradition within the parallel structures of informal customary justice and the structures of law enforcement used by the godfathers of political leaders to ensure their political power in the state, otherwise „You can't have access to the grassroots, no matter how politically strong you are."[37] The 13 registers of clients of the Okija-shrine, confiscated by the Federal Police, comprised some 8,000 names of Nigerians from virtually all walks of life, including a respectable bishop of Rivers State, several members of parliament for Anambra and Rivers states, businessmen, traditional rulers and well-known politicians from all over Nigeria, including Lagos.[38] Ngige and others demanded the publication of the names of the patrons of the shrine who belonged to the political and economic elite of the country and who regularly consulted the cult, but the police refused to comply.[39] Allegedly, some important patrons of the cult, interested in the pursuit of the Ngige case, paid up to five Mio. Naira monthly to the Okija shrine to punish the „culprit", according to the cult's motto: 'Eziokwu bu ndu, asi bu onwu', i.e. 'truth is life, falsehood (lying) is death'.[40] Apparently, some of the shrines connected with the Ogwugwu cult, were hijacked by unscrupulous young indigenous businessmen in the 1990s to turn it into a money-making machine of fraudulent practices, similar to the illicit Advance Fee Fraud or '419 scam'.[41] Similarly,

---

36 cf. US-State Department, Country Reports on Human Rights Practices, Nigeria, 2004; February 28, 2005; http://www.state.gov/g/drl/rls/hrrpt/2004/41620.htm; 08.03.05.

37 cf. Collins EDOMARUSE: Anambra Lawmakers – We swore at Okija Shrine. This Day Sunday, 16.08.2004.

38 cf. The Sun, 31.08.04; „Living in Bondage", cover story, Tell-Magazine, 23 August 2004:12-20; „Manhunt for patrons", cover story of Tell, 6 September, 2004:18-25.

39 cf. The Sun, 13.08.04; 30.08.04.

40 cf. Anayo OKOLI / Tony EDIKE: Police uncover 10 fresh shrines, Ohanaeze scribe slams raid. Vanguard, Lagos, 6 August 2004.

41 cf. James EZE: „Okija – those who fed fat on the shrine", Saturday Sun, 14 August 2004. – Igbo economic and political history provides other famous examples of similar connections between economic, political and ritual interests of unscrupulous leaders, as shown by the revival of the Aro Long juju in the early 1920s, later destroyed by the British. This was a mighty and extensive trading

vigilante groups, like the infamous Bakassi Boys, cooperated closely with the Okija shrine and similar secret cults.[42] Preliminary findings of police investigations showed that in the past almost all Igbo shrines were involved in ritual killings within the system of parallel justice. However, some communities tried to moderate these practices while others abused the traditional principles of local deities as „custodians of truth and protectors of the oppressed" and misused the shrines for their own selfish purposes.[43] The secretary-General of the pan-Igbo group Ohanaeze, umbrella cultural organisation for all Igbos worldwide, the former Biafran military commander, Chief Joe Achuzia, as well as independent observers were unanimous in stating that similar shrines exist all over Nigeria and they demanded that they all receive the same treatment from the police.[44]

2. Conflict resolution within the realm of the political economy of occult belief systems in Africa becomes increasingly violent

The processes of modernisation, globalisation and the accompanying transition of African societies result in increasingly violent forms of conflict resolution by anti-witchcraft movements, for example in the Democratic Republic of Congo, Tanzania or South Africa. Apparently, the link between political power and witchcraft is becoming tighter,[45] which is explained by the crucial importance of occult power in the social control of violence in Africa. Modern and traditional rulers alike have to understand and speak the language of ritual violence if they want to guarantee anything approaching a state-monopoly of violence.[46] Although statistical data on the long-term trends of witchcraft related violence in Africa are not available, 'witchcraft violence', notably the extra-legal killing of alleged witches,[47] is on the increase compared with pre- and early colonial

---

network of Aro long distance traders collaborating with local secret cults in contracting humans for service to their oracle, but who, in fact, immediately channeled these people into the slave trade as cargo; cf. Omoniyi ADEWOYE: The Judicial System in Southern Nigeria, 1854-1954. London 1977. Yet another example is the Odozi Obodo Society, a secret society and law-enforcing structure, which terrorized Abakaliki in the 1950s and allegedly killed over 400 people in the guise of exacting punishment for their evil deeds cf. Mobolaji E. ALUKO: The barbarous acts of Okija (2004). http://www.dawodu.com/aluko93.htlm; 08.03.05.

42 cf. HARNISCHFEGER: Witchcraft, pp. 29-35. SESAY / UKEJE / AINA / ODEBIYI (eds.): „Ethnic Militias, pp. 37.

43 cf. Richard ELESHO / Uba AHAM: „Gory rituals", The News, Lagos, 23 August, 2004. Victor E. DIKE: „Our Belief System And The Deity-Based Shrines", Lagosforum.com; 07.09.04; at <www.lagosforum.com/comment.php?NR=1237>; 08.03.05.

44 Another example of the political and law-enforcing power of secret cults in Nigeria's informal sector is the traditional Ogboni-fraternity of the Yoruba, in South-Western Nigeria (not to be confused with the toothless Reformed Ogboni Fraternity; cf. Komolafe KOLAWOLE: African traditional Religion – Understanding Ogboni Fraternity. Ifa-Orunmila Organisation. Ife 1995. Nathaniel FADIPE: The sociology of the Yoruba, Ibadan University Press 1970. Peter MORTON-WILLIAMS: The Yoruba Ogboni cult in Oyo, in: Africa (1960), p. 30. Richard Edward DENNETT: The Ogboni and other secret societies in Nigeria. Africa Society, London 1916 (reprinted from the Journal of the Africa Society).

45 GESCHIERE: Modernity, p. 7.

46 ELLIS / TER HAAR: Worlds of power.

47 Here and in the following, 'witchcraft violence', considers both the emic view of serious harm and violence, inflicted by (imaginary or real) witches on innocent citizens, and all forms of violence ap-

times when less violent forms of punishment for witches (e.g. ransom, enforced migration etc.) were applied, according to the available ethnographic evidence. The politics of anti-witchcraft movements in the impoverished regions of the (former) Northern- and Eastern Cape Provinces in South Africa, for example, resulted in the murder of thousands of witches in the 1990s. The death-toll reached hitherto unknown dimensions, for example in the former homelands of Lebowa, Gazankulu and Venda, or in the districts of Tsolo and Qumbu (Transkei). The impact could be felt not just within the microcosmos of village communities, but also at the meso and macro level of society. Apart from the immeasurable harm that „witchcraft violence" inflicted on the individuals and families concerned, it also destabilised the social, economic and political set-up of a whole region, seriously endangered the state monopoly of force, and undermined the legitimacy of the new post-apartheid government. Public as well as civic institutions were at pains to stop the violence, but apparently with limited success. The strange collusion between occult belief systems and different trans-local and trans-national social networks, embedded in specific transformations of local and global modes of production, resulted in unique but reinforcing modifications of witchcraft belief, its underlying structures and its impact on the process of democratisation.[48]

3. The modern belief in magic and witchcraft in Africa is characterised by an increasing ambivalence of causes, intentions and effects

The underlying causes of witch-belief, its historical roots, as well as the effects it has may differ significantly according to the social strata and modes of production in which it is embedded.[49] Quite often it has been instrumentalised by conservative and radical African leaders alike (e.g. Eyadéma, Moboutu, Kérékou, or liberation movements in Guinea-Bissau, Mozambique, Zimbabwe etc.) to achieve their goals, for example by mystifying exploitation or by eliminating opponents, usually without any regard to the disintegrating long-term effects on society. But grass-root liberation movements throughout Africa have also been seen to use witchcraft accusations as „cults of counter-violence"[50] against political enemies. This often happened under the pretext of combating „the relics of feudalism", as in the politically motivated witch-hunt, either guided by

---

plied against people accused of witchcraft. The former can be at least as fatal as the latter in the view of the stakeholders. In any case, most Africans consider witchcraft as an evil, sometimes satanic force, cf. GESCHIERE: Modernity, pp. 12-5, 215-24. MEYER: Power of money.

48 KOHNERT: Witchcraft.

49 cf. Ralph AUSTEN: „The moral economy of witchcraft. An essay in comparative history", in: Jean COMAROFF / John COMAROFF (eds.): Modernity and its Malcontents. Modernity, Ritual and Power in Postcolonial Africa, Chicago 1993, pp. 89-110. Edwin ARDENER: „Witchcraft, economics and the continuity of belief", in: Mary DOUGLAS (ed.), „Witchcraft confessions and accusations", Tavistock, London 1970, pp. 141-60. GESCHIERE: Modernity, pp. 146-151. Monica HUNTER-WILSON: „Witch-beliefs and social structure", in: American J. of Sociology, Vol. 56 (1951), pp. 307-313; reprinted in: M. MARWICK (ed.): „Witchcraft and sorcery", Penguin, 1970, pp. 252-263. Dirk KOHNERT: On the articulation of witchcraft and modes of production among the Nupe, Northern Nigeria. In this volume.

50 K. B. WILSON: „Cults of violence and counter-violence in Mozambique", in: Journal of Southern African Studies, Vol. 18, No. 3 (1992), pp. 527-582.

„Marxist-Leninist" doctrines, as in Benin under the reign of its President Matthieu Kérékou (1973-89), or in the fight against apartheid and racism by the „comrades" in Gogoza, in the border region of Transkei/Natal in the late 1980s and early 1990s.[51] The concerned population might even see in these witch-hunters heroes who cleanse their areas of evil, rather than view them as evil itself. Thus, under certain historical conditions, witch-hunts constitute what Peter Geschiere[52], quoting D. C. Martin, called a „popular mode of political action", directed towards promoting the dawn of a new democratic order, towards equalizing the distribution of income and wealth, or towards defending the ideal of solidarity within acephalous village communities.

As shown above, scholarly analyses abound on the modernity of witchcraft in African societies, stressing its influence on current power relations, politics and development. However, one of the puzzling questions still to be solved concerns the ambiguous nature of witchcraft, which makes it difficult to predict the impact of occult belief systems in general, and the impact of witchcraft violence in particular, on politics in Africa.[53] This holds particularly true for the intriguing contradiction between the emancipative versus repressive impetus of different anti-witchcraft movements in the stakeholders' view, and the significance of this impetus for lasting reconciliation. Much of the ambiguity of occult belief systems may be explained by reference to the concept of Transnational Social Spaces (TSS[54]) complemented by an analysis of the articulation between witchcraft accusations and the modes of production in which they are embedded. More often than not, the change over time of content and meaning of witchcraft accusations appears to go unnoticed, by the population and researchers alike, because its outward guise is one of continuity.

Due to the process of globalisation, the conventional comparative analysis of different states, or geographical and social entities, no longer suffices to explain the 'interlacing coherence networks'[55], constituting new social facts that emerged outside the unit of analysis of national societies or their local representations. Rather than simple comparative studies, simultaneous multi-site research with due regard to trans-local social spaces

---

51 cf. EVANS: On brûle bien les sorcières, p. 56. David CHILDESTER: „Shots in the streets: violence and religion in South Africa", OUP, Cape Town 1992, pp. 43-66.

52 GESCHIERE: Modernity. IDEM. Sorcellerie et politique: les pièges du rapport élite-village. In: Politique Africaine, Vol. 63 (1996), pp. 82-96.

53 See Peter GESCHIERE: Sorcellerie et modernité: retour sur une étrange complicité. In: Politique Africaine, Vol 79 (2000), pp. 17-32, 28: 'Presque partout en Afrique, ces forces occultes sont considérées comme un mal primordial. Mais un autre principe général veut que ces forces puissent être canalisées et utilisées à fins constructives.' See also GESCHIERE: The modernity of witchcraft, pp. 9-12, 23, 233. NIEHAUS: Witchcraft, p. 192.

54 Ludger PRIES: Transnational social spaces: Do we need a new approach in response to new phenomena!?, in: L. PRIES (ed.), New Transnational Social Spaces. London 2001. Quoted according to online version of 09 March 2001, pp. 1-14. (http.//www.gwdg.de/~zens/transnational/pries.html). Saskia SASSEN: Cracked casings: Notes towards an analytics for studying transnational processes, in: L. PRIES (ed.): New Transnational Social Spaces, London 2001. Quoted according to online version of 09 March 2005 (www1.kas.de/international/konferenz02-06-17/Referententexte/ sassen_links.html).

55 Norbert ELIAS, quoted in PRIES: Transnational social spaces, p. 3.

is required. In fact, this constitutes a basic insight of the TSS concept and the general methodological working hypothesis of this paper which should be tested in subsequent case studies.[56] The profound links between witchcraft and modernity, promoted by globalisation, such as the 'odd complicity' between occult belief systems in Sub-Saharan Africa (SSA) and recent transformations of the world market, have already been aptly analysed by Geschiere[57], the Comaroffs[58] and others[59]. These authors stress the dialectical interplay between the local and the global as heuristic dimensions of analysis. Nevertheless, either the state or the nation, even in its magic representation as an 'alien-nation' of zombies[60], remained a crucial but defective methodological point of reference for analysis.[61] Certainly, the trans-local dimension of occult belief systems has also been noted by various other authors, but they perceived it as a heuristic concept, illuminating the linkage of local and global phenomena in its historical setting, rather than one which reflects empirical facts.[62] Yet, many stakeholders are caught up directly in trans-local social networks, which apparently exert an ever-increasing impact on modern structures of witchcraft accusations. These different roots of witchcraft violence have had serious repercussions on conflict resolution, as has been demonstrated elsewhere.[63]

African Renaissance: divided between rationalism and emotion?

1. Eurocentric approaches constitute a considerable problem

Since the advent of colonial rule, official approaches, designed to cope with the problems of witchcraft violence in Africa, have been based on eurocentric views and colonial jurisdiction, legitimised by Western social science. These solutions are inadequate; in fact, they constitute part of the problem itself.

Scholarly interpretation of African belief systems was dominated during colonial rule and its aftermath by eurocentric prejudices, oscillating between paternalistic homage of the natives' „primitive" mode of thought and its ethical devaluation by the colonial po-

---

56 KOHNERT: On the articulation of witchcraft. PRIES: Transnational social spaces.
57 GESCHIERE: Modernity.
58 COMAROFF / COMAROFF: Occult economies.
59 It goes without saying that 'modern' witchcraft accusations are often rooted in the colonial or even pre-colonial past, whereas 'tradition' has been invented time and again, by old and new authorities alike, e.g. to legitimise a change of power relations cf. COMAROFF / COMAROFF: Occult economies. GESCHIERE: Modernity, pp. 6-9.
60 cf. COMAROFF / COMAROFF: Alien-Nation, p. 21.
61 See GESCHIERE: Modernity, pp. 6-8: '… nearly everywhere on the continent the state and politics seem to be a true breeding ground for modern transformations of witchcraft and sorcery'. Nevertheless, COMAROFF / COMAROFF: Occult economies, Geschiere and others underline the surprising capacity of the customary discourse on witchcraft to link the 'global' and the 'local', or micro and macro levels of popular interpretations of transition in modern Africa: 'Le marché mondial représente, comme la sorcellerie, une brèche dangereuse dans la clôture de la communauté locale.' (GESCHIERE: Sorcellerie et modernité, p. 26).
62 cf. COMAROFF / COMAROFF: Occult economies, p. 294.
63 KOHNERT: Witchcraft.

licy under the pretext of the *moral education* of the natives.[64] Guided by an ideology of modernisation, formal institutions (such as the Christian churches and missionaries) and the (post) colonial state treated African belief in witchcraft as superstition which would be most probably eradicated by the process of modernisation by itself in the long run. In the mean time the judiciary enacted anti-witchcraft laws which stipulated that both witchcraft and the accusation of witchcraft were punishable according to the law, thereby effectively preventing colonial courts from taking an active part in resolving the witchcraft fears of their subjects.[65] The present jurisdiction in most African countries is still based on these biased colonial anti-witchcraft laws.

Under these conditions, in view of the apparent illegitimacy of state intervention along the lines of Western reasoning, the stakeholders sought help in the informal sector. That is, they were left on their own, and subsequently often engaged in self-justice. This contributed to a rapid erosion of the state's monopoly on force, which seriously affected the legitimacy of public institutions. Even traditional authorities, formerly considered to be the guardians of customary law, are now at pains to cope with the situation because of considerable changes in the incidence, content, and form of witchcraft accusations over time, and the compromising attitude of traditional authorities during the apartheid regime. African independent and Pentecostal churches, mushrooming all over Africa, as well as „modern" witch-finders, such as leaders of politically motivated ANC-youth organisations, have emphatically offered to cater more effectively for the felt needs of the people than have either the state or traditional leaders. But it is open to question whether institutions or personalities belonging to the informal sector are always likely to act in the best interests of society.

In post-apartheid South Africa, for example, government, political parties, and trade unions alike, were under increasing pressure to take account of witchcraft beliefs, not only in order to prevent further loss of lives and property, but in order to combat the loss of their legitimacy as well. However, in actual practice, the stakeholders differed widely on how to deal with witchcraft. In September 1998 the National Conference on Witchcraft Violence, organised by the Commission of Gender Equality (CGE) in the Northern Province, pushed government further to change its attitude towards witchcraft. Representatives of the CGE conceded an urgent need to develop new strategies which should not simply deny the existence of witchcraft, especially since this approach has utterly failed to work in the past. Besides educational and legal tasks, namely educational programmes and the revision of the anti-witchcraft act, the experts favoured among other things, spiritual alternatives, substitution of witchcraft violence by spiritual healing, and „activities to treat the communities' psychosocial needs".[66] According to a problem analysis by representatives of the South African Human Rights Commission (HRC), the

---

64 cf. Lucien LÉVY-BRUHL „La mentalité primitive", Paris 1922, who contrasted the supposed rational reasoning of European civilisation, based on exact observation and logical conclusions, with the way of thinking of the „primitives", based on emotion, intuition and magic-religious interpretation of the world around them.

65 KOHNERT: On the articulation on witchcraft.

66 CGE: „The National Conference on Witchcraft Violence", Conference Report, Commission of Gender Equality (CGE), Braamfontain 1999, p. 49.

„belief in witchcraft has the capacity to paralyse people", consequently witchcraft violence was seen as „a sign of a pathology in a community". Representatives of the Department of Constitutional Development declared witchcraft violence as „the number-one enemy of our society", and the Department of Justice deplored among other things its „negative effects on the economy of the country".[67]

However, in the past, neither the state nor liberation movements, political parties, or trade unions seemed to have cared very much about witchcraft. Only if social and political conflict boiled over to a veritable witch craze, was it deemed necessary to take notice officially. There is a growing awareness that current legislation such as the anti witchcraft legislation in Nigeria, Cameroon or South Africa, which still reflects colonial reasoning, is unable to cope with the problem.[68] By its salomonic phrasing it punishes both the alleged witch and the allegedly bewitched, i.e. those who express their fear by witchcraft accusations.[69] It thus protects the real culprits, at least from the perspective of people believing in the existence of witchcraft. Therefore, the South African state, for example, has been challenged by both independent bodies and political parties such as the ANC, to „review the legal system from being euro-centric to reflecting the reality of a multicultural nation".[70] The Commission of Gender Equality (CGE), the Department of Justice, and the Law Commission of South Africa set up a committee to draw up proposals for a new law. In February 2000 it presented parliament with a first draft of the „Regulation of Baloyi Practices Act"[71]; however, apparently there has so far been no follow-up to these initiatives.[72] The call of grassroot organisations, politicians and academics for an indigenisation of national laws and regulations, i.e. their adaptation to the African socio-cultural setting in general, and the official recognition of the existence of witchcraft in particular, are certainly justified, but only in as far as basic human rights are respected. Any attempt at a „domestication" of witchcraft violence by an opportunist indigenisation of legislation, based on the official recognition of witchcraft and of the accusers, e.g. traditional healers (sangomas, in South Africa) as plaintiffs, without due regard to universal concepts of human rights, is hardly to be considered as sustainable.

---

67 Ibid., p. 55.
68 cf. GESCHIERE: Modernity, pp. 169-72, 185-197. HARNISCHFEGER: Witchcraft. J. HUND: African witchcraft and western law – psychological and cultural issues, in: J. of Contemporary Religion, Vol. 19, Nr. 1 (2004), pp. 67-84. Anthony MINNAAR: Witchpurging and muti murder in South Africa – the legislative and legal challenges to combating these practices with specific reference to the Witchcraft Suppression Act (No 3 of 1957, amended by Act No. 50 of 1970). African Legal Studies, «Witchcraft violence and the law» Vol. 2 (2001), pp. 1-21, in: KOHNERT, On the articulation of witchcraft.
69 cf. the South African Witchcraft Suppression Act, passed in 1957, which sets a 20-year jail sentence for anyone who, professing a knowledge of witchcraft, names one person as having caused death, injury, grief, or disappearance of another. It also provides for up to five years in jail for anyone who „professes a knowledge of witchcraft, or the use of charms (and) supplies any person with any pretended means of witchcraft", cf. „Witchcraft law up for review, Parliament", February 11, 2000, Sapa.
70 CGE, p. 55.
71 Baloyi being the more precise Venda terminus for socio-cultural practices which could be loosely translated by the English word „witchcraft" cf. ANC-news 14.02.2000.
72 HUND: African witchcraft.

It could perhaps help the state to regain credibility and legitimacy in the short run, but it may even promote the witch craze, accentuate social cleavages or lead to despotism of charismatic rulers in the long run.

2. On the doubtful impact of African ethno-philosophy

African ethno-philosophers opposed both colonialism and basic concepts of Western social science by propagating the return to the roots of an authentic African culture. This provoked among other things a re-evaluation of African religions, including occult belief systems, which were seen as real and effective, but essentially defensive and utilitaristic.

Representatives of African ethno-philosophy, such as Placide Tempels, Alexis Kagame, and the Senegalese President Léopold Sédar Senghor (1906-2001), successfully opposed colonial rule and strengthened African identity. This holds particularly true for the concept of Négritude, as developed by Aimé Césaire of Martinique and Senghor, particularly in francophone Africa. Négritude was defined as comprising the totality of cultural values of the Black world, but the concept was nevertheless based on European cultural tradition, particularly of French intellectual origin.[73] It embraced nostalgic glorifications of the African philosophical tradition and the alleged harmony of African life. According to its advocates, there was a fundamental difference in philosophical thinking between Africans, who underlined their collective identity, „I feel (the other), … therefore I am"[74], and the identity of Europeans, based on the Descartian imperative of the separation of body and mind: „Cogito ergo sum; I think, therefore I am."[75]

Nevertheless, the proponents of Négritude maintained that Africans were not less rational than Europeans. However, according to Senghor, the African's reason is not discursive but synthetic, not antagonistic, but sympathetic. In short, it is another mode of knowledge. Reason does not impoverish the things, it does not grind them up in rigid schemes. The African is less interested in the appearance of an object than in its profound reality, i.e. in its sense. „The European reason is analytic through utilisation, the reason of Negroes is intuitive through participation."[76]

---

73 In fact, Senghor was the first African elected to the distinguished Académie Française in Paris in 1983. Jean-Paul Sartre, in his introduction to Senghor (1948) characterised Négritude as „a weak stage of a dialectical progression: the theoretical and practical affirmation of white supremacy is the thesis" cf. http://www.kirjasto.sci.fi/senghor.htm; 15.03.05; cf. J.-P. SARTRE: «Orphée Noir», in: L. S. SENGHOR, Anthologie de la nouvelle poésie nègre et malagache de langue française, Paris 1948, pp. ix-xliv.

74 «Voilà donc le Négro-africain qui sympathise et s'identifie, qui meurt à soi pour renaître dans l'autre. Il n'assimile pas; *il s'assimile*. Il vit avec l'autre en symbiose, *il con-naît à l'autre*, pour parler comme Paul Claudel. Sujet et objet sont, ici, dialectiquement confronté dans l'acte même de la connaissance, qui est acte d'amour. 'Je pense, donc je suis', écrivait Descartes. La remarque en a déjà été faite, on pense toujours *quelque chose*. Le Négro-africain pourrait dire: „Je sens l'Autre, je danse l'Autre, donc je suis.' Or, danser c'est créer, surtout lorsque la danse est danse d'amour. C'est, en tout cas, le meilleur mode de connaissance». Leopold Sédar SENGHOR: Liberté I, négritude et humanisme, Ed. du Seuil, 1964, p. 259. Italics by Senghor.

75 SENGHOR, ibid. In short: «*L'émotion est nègre, la raison est hellène.*» (emotion is Negro, reason is Hellenistic); cf. http://www.kirjasto.sci.fi/senghor.htm; 15.03.05.

76 SENGHOR: Liberté I, p. 203.

The ethno-philosophy of Négritude has had important repercussions on the interpretation of African religion and occult belief systems. Magic was seen by Senghor at the crossroads of the rational and the mystical, but nevertheless belonging to the realm of science: white magic, as an important means of defence against all sorts of misfortune; black magic, notably witchcraft, as an offensive weapon, which, however, was not peculiar to Africa. In both forms, magic was seen as strictly utilitaristic and individual.[77]

However, for the Africans concerned this victory had ambiguous effects. In implementing their vision of Négritude the new African rulers may have reinforced the self-consciousness and the collective identity of their people. But at the same time, the collusion of African ethno-philosophers and elites served the continued suppression of their subjects under the pretext of an African renaissance. Therefore, other African philosophers and sociologists highly critical of ethno-philosophy, such as Paulin J. Hountondji, sharply criticised both ethno-philosophy and the malevolent facets of globalised capitalism in Africa (cf. above). For them, ethno-philosophy only interpreted African realities differently, without contributing to its necessary transformations, treating it as an invariable ontological bond instead of a historical process. For Hountondji, African philosophy is an activity, a process that expresses and transcends itself, rather than a fixed system of truth, although it is inseparable from African science, the strength of which lies in its hypothetical nature and in the strive for knowledge and wisdom, since as with any science, there is no absolute truth in scientific research.[78] As far as the belief in witchcraft is concerned, indigenous African knowledge, used effectively by traditional healers to answer problems caused by witchcraft, showed the limits of Cartesian rationalism. The latter was qualified as a „reductionist approach, reducing and impoverishing the recognition of reality."[79] Hountondji called for the resistance of African cultures against globalisation as the only way to guarantee self-determination and sustainable development with a human and African face: „For Africans, there are two forms of losing one's way: by immurement in particularism, or dispersion in the universal".[80]

---

[77] «La magie ... n'est pas propre au Négro-africain. Elle n'est, en somme, qu'un recours contre l'anormal et, à ce titre, elle se trouve partout, même en Europe, chez le peuple. Pourtant il est intéressant de l'étudier, car l'accident est fréquent en Afrique noire, que *la magie se situe au croisement du rationnel et du mystique*. ... Il est question d'une *technique*, d'une *science*. ...Voilà la religion des Négro-africains dont Delafosse disait: 'Ces peuples, dont on a parfois nié qu'ils eussent une religion, sont, en réalité, parmi les plus religieux de la terre. Les préoccupations d'ordre divin l'emportent chez eux, le plus souvent, sur les préoccupations d'ordre purement humain'. ... La magie entre dans le cadre de la religion négro-africaine en tant qu'elle est *défensive*, c'est à dire s'il s'agit de se protéger contre des actes de magie comme de tout malheur. ... Et, en effet, sous sa forme offensive, la plus caractéristique (la sorcellerie, D. K.), la magie n'est pas proprement négro-africaine. ... C'est que la magie, même sous sa forme défensive, a un *but strictement utilitaire et individuel*». SENGHOR: Liberté I, pp. 72-74; italics by Senghor.

[78] cf. HOUNTONDJI: African Philosophy. IDEM. (ed.): Les savoirs endogènes – pistes pour une recherché, Paris 1994. D. A. MASOLO: African philosophy in search of identity, Indiana University Press, Bloomington 1994, p. 199-203.

[79] cf. HOUNTONDJI: Les savoirs endogène, p. 23-27. Comlan Th ADJIDO: La médecine psychosomatique dans se rapports avec la sorcellerie, in: HOUNTONDJI: Les savoirs endogène, p. 247-256. HOUNTONDJI: African Cultures and Globalisation.

[80] Quoted by HOUNTONDJI: „African Cultures and Globalisation, p. 24, with reference to one of the founding fathers of the Négritude, Aimé CÉSAIRE: Aimé Césaire in a letter to Maurice Thorez, 1956.

In the same vein, Ali A. Mazrui called for a qualified modernisation, i.e. for a development that is based on modernisation without dependency. Indigenisation of material and social resources, above all the use of African languages, of domestication, diversification, regional integration and counter-penetration, was seen as a strategy for promoting sustainable self-reliance.[81]

3. Evans-Pritchard's fallacy

The Cartesian credo of the separation of body and mind, of emotion and reason, is to date the base for scholarly discussions of African belief in witchcraft. Generations of anthropologists since Evans-Pritchard (1937) have been at pains to prove that the Western logic of cause and effect is perfectly compatible with African magic reasoning. However, this credo reflects only half of the truth, as body and mind are intimately linked together, which makes rational action without strong emotions impossible. The combined effects of Descarte's error[82] and Evans-Pritchard's fallacy lead to unfeasible rationalistic propositions for solutions concerning the eradication of witchcraft violence.

In general, Western educated experts, European and African alike, consider witchcraft basically as an „illogic and mistaken belief" which should be eradicated as soon as possible through education and critical assessment.[83] As stated by Wyatt MacGaffey in the preface to Geschiere's (1997) reader, African systems of occult belief are anything but „irrational", as was demonstrated in 1937 by Evans-Pritchard's classical study of the Azande. Although its inherent logic can hardly be grasped in patterns of thought of natural science, its methodological structure is no less rational than the impulse-giving ethics of the Protestant spirit of capitalism in 19th century Europe, and Geschiere (1997) points out astonishing parallels between powerful African „marabouts" and the role attributed to public relations experts in current American politics. The relevant distinction in this respect is that each adheres to a different rationality with different degrees of concern for values such as equality, solidarity, achievement and development orientation. In short, methodologically, the difference between the rationality of African witchcraft beliefs and Western forms of reasoning lies more in the degree of its „reduction of complexity", to borrow an expression from Niklas Luhman, than in the degree of rationality.[84]

---

81 „... development is modernization minus dependency. But what is modernization? One possible answer is that modernization is change which is compatible with the present stage of human knowledge, which seeks to comprehend the legacy of the past, which is sensitive to the needs of the future, and which is increasingly aware of its global context. This is the positive interpretation of modernization. Skills and values are at the core. ... Where does culture enter into this? If development equals modernization minus dependency, there is not doubt about the relevance of the African Renaissance in at least that part of the equation which concerns 'minus dependence'. African culture is central to this process of reducing dependency in the dialectic of modernization. One strategy of transcending dependency is indigenization, which includes greater utilization of indigenous techniques, personnel, and approaches to purposeful change": cf. MAZRUI: The African Renaissance, pp. 3-11.

82 Antonio DAMASIO: „Descartes' Error. Emotion, reason and the human brain", New York 1994 (Dt. „Descartes Irrtum. Fühlen, Denken und das menschliche Gehirn", Stuttgart, 1997. Quotiation according to German edition).

83 CGE, pp. 49, 53.

84 „Zande belief in witchcraft in no way contradicts empirical knowledge of cause and effect. The world known to the senses is just as real to them as it is to us ... They are foreshortening the chain

Although Evans-Pritchard[85] was right in confronting common Western prejudices of the 1920s on primitive African thinking with the intrinsic logic of the belief in magic and witchcraft, this was just half of the truth. Evans-Pritchard's fallacy consisted in his focus on the rationality of occult belief systems, which deflected attention from its decisive role as an emotional base for survival. This fallacy may be illustrated in analogy to the results of research in neuro-physiology as developed by Antonio Damasio[86] some ten years ago. Evans-Pritchard, and with him much of conventional economic anthropology, was probably wrong in underestimating the profound structural links between emotion and rational reasoning in human beings in general. Rational behaviour is at least as much influenced by deep seated emotions as by empirical knowledge. In fact, man can not act rationally without moving emotions. In contrast to the Cartesian postulate on the fundamental separation of body and soul (*cogito, ergo sum*), human decision making, by its very biological structure, is never determined by rational reasoning alone, but guided by emotions grown on, and deeply embedded in, the respective culture of the actor.[87] One may even go one step further in discussing the relevance of Gerald Edelman's[88] hypothesis that the biological self, or at least vital parts of the human brain, have been conditioned and structured in the course of human genesis by basic values needed for survival. Thus, the evolution of mankind provided for the acceptance of basic human value-systems which guide its actions; Edelman's thesis possibly even sheds new light on the controversy concerning the existence of universal human rights. According to neuro-physiological theories on cognition, the perception of the world in the human brain has been directed through the filter of positive and negative sentiments from the very moment of birth onwards. There exists a close neuro-biological link between feeling and thinking, which makes the existence of emotions (based on the respective socio-cultural setting) a precondition for any rational action of both Africans and Europeans. But even more important in this context, the linkage of ratio and emotions, born out of and developed within specific socio-cultural settings,[89] is of immediate relevance for the resolution of the pressing social and political problems mentioned above, such as education or the propensity to violent mob actions against witches.

Rational action without deep emotions is impossible, because the lack of these emotions deprives the mind of a vital driving force and measure gauge which enables the actor to choose an adequate action from a universe of different options. This argument can by no means be reduced to the age-old debate on value judgements in social science. The underlying vision of Cartesian rationality as a remedy for major ills of development was in itself a fallacy. Some three centuries ago, Francisco Goya chastised a similar form

---

of events, and in a particular social situation are selecting the cause that is socially relevant and neglecting the rest" Edward EVANS-PRITCHARD: Witchcraft, oracles and magic among the Azande, 1937, p. 73. Reprinted: Oxford, 1963. (Thus) „witchcraft explains why events are harmful to man and not how they happen. A Zande perceives how they happen just as we do" (ibid., p. 72).

85 EVANS-PRITCHARD: Witchcraft, pp. 21-39, 63-83, 99-106.
86 DAMASIO: „Descartes' Error.
87 DAMASIO: Descartes' Error, pp. 325-328.
88 Gerald M. EDELMAN: „Bright air, brilliant fire - On the matter of the mind", New York 1992, pp. 232-236.
89 DAMASIO: Descartes' Error, p. 327.

of hubris in his famous Capricho „*The dream [sleep] of reason produces monsters*".[90]

These fundamental emotional guidelines of every human being are not only rooted in the general biological history of mankind but to at least as great an extent in the specific socio-cultural setting responsible for the education and upkeep of any rational actor from birth. Because they are embedded in the respective cultures, these emotions are not easily exchangeable, and one would deprive Africans believing in witchcraft of the necessary means of survival if one were to try to eradicate this belief without providing similar strong and sustainable emotional alternatives.

Now, occult belief systems, like religions in general, induce not just a certain vision of the world and of human relations, but they also provide, as shown above, for strong emotions. This relates not just to individual hate, fear, or other emotions directly linked to witchcraft, but to the whole fabric of the human emotional system, as indicated above.

Fig. 1: „The dream [sleep] of reason produces monsters". Francisco Goya, 1797.

The state, NGOs or other progressive institutions of civil society would literally deprive the concerned of their ability to survive if they were to categorically deny them their belief in magic and witchcraft without providing, jointly within the framework of educational programmes and a gradual scientific dismantling of witchcraft belief (as advocated by the CGE and other institutions), a convincing source of equally strong alternative „development-enhancing" emotions. No wonder that most education programmes which concentrated on rational reasoning, whether implemented by missionaries, schools or the state, have utterly failed since the beginning of colonial rule.

If it are specific culturally determined manners of reducing complexity, and not different rationalities which constitute the major distinction between African magic and Western rational reasoning, then generations of social anthropologists since Evans-Pritchard have been right in stressing (apparently without much effect) that Western educated scientists, experts, and politicians should be especially careful not to cultivate the hubris of rationality in their dialogue with African stakeholders. „Irrational behaviour" due to methodologically unsound reduction of complexity is common in Western so-

---

90 Francisco GOYA: „El sueño de la razón produce monstrous" (1797), in English, „The dream [sleep] of reason produces monsters", which derives its ambiguity from two antagonistic interpretations, arising from the fact that the Spanish word *sueño* means „sleep" as well as „dream". For a description of the image cf. website: www.museum.cornell.edu/HFJ/handbook/hb128.html, 10.03.05.

cieties, too.[91] Thus, I revert to the central theme of my argument: the open society and its enemies, to borrow a phrase from Karl R. Popper, the Nestor of neo-positivist philosophy. The given socio-cultural setting and social structure have become the cornerstones of the Western delimitation of objectivity and rationality, just as the denunciation of persons as witches by their fellow citizens depends finally, at least according to the classical interpretation of African witchcraft by Evans-Pritchard (as quoted above), on the social recognition of certain worldviews on cause and effect.

4. African religion provides crucial answers to current problems

African religious systems provided a framework for valuable indigenous solutions to current problems of contemporary life, including the problem of witchcraft violence. Besides this, they might, under certain conditions, provide the outside world with an inspiring new dimension of philosophic thought and emancipative action, for example, within the realm of conflict resolution and reconciliation. However, even in the case of the 'domestication' of witchcraft violence, this holds only in so far as appropriate African answers can be shielded against the negative impact of globalised capitalism.

The concept, methods and lessons learned for example from the South African Truth and Reconciliation Commission (TRC)[92], later on copied by other African states like Rwanda, Sierra Leone or Ghana, might be highly relevant, not just for fellow Africans, but also for conflict solving cultures of industrialised countries.[93] Deliberative processes of truth and reconciliation in politics, as organised by the TRC, could, in transforming a plurality of people into a community, make our hopes and opinions at the same time ethical and rational. Public and attentive discussion of individual truth with respect to violent conflicts opens up the chance to create ethical knowledge and shared ethical

---

91 In order to avoid ethnocentric misconceptions I want to stress again that many aspects of occult belief systems and their rationality are not restricted to African countries. Even in the USA, the belief in witchcraft was officially recognised as a religion in 1982 by the High Court, under the term *Wicca*. The latter, as contemporary anti-witchcraft cults in Africa, is far from being a traditionally-minded belief system. It propagates its objectives with the help of modern concepts and technology, and even has its own website. The revival of occult belief systems around the world has different, hitherto unexplored sources which call for comparative in-depth investigations by ongoing research. The obsession with isolating and fixing the „true" ideas and emotions of human beings by technical investigation must, however, inevitably fail, as it is based on a methodological fallacy. Our conception of both human nature and scientific objectivity in general can not be isolated and fixed by science once and for all, as both depend on the unremitting evolution of knowledge, the possibility of mutual exchange and critique, and last but not least, on actual social conventions and social structures encouraging or averting critical reflection of our present knowledge. The latter is decisive in setting the limits between legitimate critical discourse on the one hand, and dogmatic pursuit of „enemies to society" or witch-hunts on the other.

92 T. MALULEKE: 'Can lions and rabbits reconcile? The South African TRC as an instrument for peace-building', in: The Ecumenical Review, Vol. 53, Nr. 2 (2001), pp. 190-201. P. J. CAMPBELL: 'The Truth and Reconciliation Commission (TRC): human rights and state transitions: the South African model', in: African Studies Quarterly, Vol. 4, Nr. 3 (2000), pp. 1-30.

93 cf. Philippe-Joseph SALAZAR / Sanya OSHA / Wim VAN BINSBERGEN (eds.): Truth in politics – rethorical approaches to democratic deliberation in Africa and beyond. Leiden, African Studies Centre (from: Quest – An African Journal of Philosophy, 16.2002,1/2; special issue; published in March 2004); cf. intergral text: <www.quest-journal.net/2002.htm>; 02.03.05.

truth.[94] Unfortunately, it is beyond the scope of this paper to deal with the general implications of this thesis in more detail. In the following, I would like to focus on the societal problems caused by occult belief systems, and especially on witchcraft violence.

In May 2000 the South African Truth and Reconciliation Commission (TRC) began its hearings on politically motivated witchcraft violence in Northern Province. ANC supporters, convicted in 1990 and serving long-term sentences for their attacks, applied for amnesty with respect to the murder of 26 villagers in the former Bantustan of Venda between 1989 and 1993. The applicants claimed they perceived their victims as persons who were practising witchcraft and who, in doing so were collaborating with traditional chiefs and politicians of the hated „homeland" government of Venda in order to strengthen their position. The TRC finally granted amnesty to 33 applicants in June 2000, ten others were refused amnesty. In summary, reconciliation in Northern Province proved to be difficult, but not impossible.

The official post-apartheid vision of the reality of witchcraft represented an important shift in the public discourse on witchcraft.[95] The massive and hitherto unimaginable involvement of the state, trans-local and even trans-national social, political and academic networks in a local discourse on witchcraft, driven by an understanding attitude vis-à-vis the stakeholders concerned (unlike early colonial administration and missionaries), and the weakness of counteracting vested interests of other implicated groups, opened new chances for conflict resolution. Beside the impact of trans-local forces on conflict resolution, such as the Commission of Gender Equality (CGE), it was probably facilitated by the relatively strong inward orientation of the population: characterised firstly by the remarkable absence of strong migrant, civic or underground informal political organisations, and secondly, by the low key profile, if not absence, of trans-local social networks who wanted to profit from the violence, the strong backing of witch-hunts by the co-villagers, and the corresponding legitimacy the persecutors had in the emic view.

In contrast, the different nature of trans-local networks and modes of production fuelling the hotbed of violence in the Transkei[96], put local reconciliation efforts at risk right from the beginning. Witchcraft related violence, although not open visible, was considerable here, as in the Northern Province, but it did not draw the same sympathetic attention of external actors like the CGE, as in Northern Province. Therefore, the „case" of Tsolo and Qumbu was handled by the post-apartheid authorities with the conventional means which most democratic governments used to handle outbreaks of domestic violence in disfavoured regions: i.e. policing, awareness campaigns and development programmes, as usual hampered by the constraints of inadequate resources and ineffective projects. Yet, it would be misleading to excuse the lack of interest in the violence, par-

---

94 Eugene GARVER: Truth in politics – Ethical argument, ethical knowledge, and ethical truth, in: SALAZAR / OSHA / VAN BINSBERGEN (eds.), Truth in politics, pp. 220-237.
95 Isac A. NIEHAUS: 'Witchcraft in the new South Africa: from colonial superstition to postcolonial reality?', in H. L. MOORE / T. SANDERS (eds.), Magical Interpretations, Material Realities: modernity, witchcraft and the occult in postcolonial Africa, London 2002, pp. 184-205, here pp. 184f., 199.
96 KOHNERT: Witchcraft.

ticularly in its occult dimension, merely by ignorance. Last but not least because of its sensitive political nature, the conflict was obscured by a longstanding „culture of silence and untruth"[97], comparable only with what was apparently a politically motivated disguise of the aftermath of the conflicts in KwaZulu Natal in the 1990s by the post-apartheid regime. Neglected by the outside world, the villagers decided in May 1999 to take matters in their own hands in order to achieve peace and reconciliation. Trusting in their own local culture, in which public confession of the truth behind the aggression was considered to be the ultimate condition of any conflict resolution, they, in fact, applied similar principles to the TRC on the national level, but unfortunately with different results. The outside interference of conflicting political forces (e.g. ANC, South African Communist party and the ultra right Afrikaner Weerstandsbeweging (AWB), rival trade unions in the mines, and other trans-local networks with vested interests (e.g. a „Third World Mafia" trading in drugs and weapons), by no means congruent with the legitimate interests of the local community, and of a quite different nature from those involved in Northern Province, proved to be too strong to be handled by the villagers alone. They had to tackle unknown forces, the involvement of 'modern' elements of globalised markets of violence, brought to their villages by way of integration into new trans-national social spaces propelled by the forces of globalisation in general, and the transition process of the apartheid regime in particular. Once this Pandora's box had been opened, there was apparently no way out that the villagers themselves could have made use of.

---

[97] J. B. PEIRES: Secrecy and violence in rural Tsolo. Unpublished paper, read at the South African Historical Association Conference, Univ. of Western Cape, July 1999, p. 1f.

Dirk Kohnert

On the Articulation of Witchcraft and Modes of Production among the Nupe, Northern Nigeria[1]

Zusammenfassung

Die politische Ökonomie okkulter Glaubenssysteme in Afrika kann versteckte soziale und politische Konflikte in Transitionsphasen erhellen, die anderenfalls unentdeckt bleiben. Dies wird gezeigt am Indikator der Entwicklung von Hexereianschuldigungen im Zeitablauf, wobei eine Fallstudie der Nupe in Nordnigeria als empirische Grundlage dient. Eine Langzeitstudie der Entwicklung des Nupe-States seit vorkolonialer Zeit weist auf einen engen Zusammenhang zwischen dem Inhalt und der Form von Hexereianschuldigungen und der Produktionsweisen hin. Im Zeitablauf dienten Hexereianschuldigungen unter den Nupe unterschiedlichen, sogar konkurrierenden Zielen, und zwar in Abhängigkeit von der Produktionsweise, mit denen die Betroffenen lebten und arbeiten. Viel Verwirrung in der Literatur über die scheinbaren Widersprüche zwischen den ‚emanzipativen' und ‚unterdrückenden' Funktionen des Hexenglaubens könnten vermieden werden, wenn man den Zusammenhang zwischen Produktionsweisen, Hexenanschuldigungen und zugrunde liegenden Interessen der Herrschenden stärker berücksichtigen würde.

Abstract

The political economy of occult belief in Africa can highlight hidden social and political conflict in times of transition which remain otherwise undetected. This has been demonstrated in taking the development of witchcraft accusations over time as indicator, and the Nupe of Northern Nigeria as an example. A tentative long-term study on the growth of the Nupe state since pre-colonial times points towards a close relationship between the content and form of witchcraft accusations and the mode of production under which the stakeholders used to life and work. Over time, witchcraft accusations among the Nupe apparently served different, even antagonistic ends, depending on the mode of production in which they were embedded. Much confusion in literature on the apparent contradiction between 'emancipating' and 'oppressive' functions of witchcraft beliefs could be avoided by considering this articulation between modes of production, witchcraft accusations, and the underlying vested interests of the ruling powers.

---

1 This paper is based on the author's hitherto unpublished empirical material, which, although collected some twenty to thirty years ago, is not simply of historical value, but remains crucial in backing the major theses of the article.

Introduction[2]

Since pre-colonial times the Nupe are renowned throughout Northern Nigeria for their knowledge of witchcraft. This is so widely accepted in general public that even newspapers are reporting on it occasionally. The virulence of occult belief among the Nupe had serious repercussions even in regional party politics. One outstanding example was the notable shift in political power in Bida Emirate (Niger state), which became apparent during the gubernatorial elections in 1983 and its aftermath of violent conflicts that were related to witchcraft by the concerned population.[3]

Nupe witchcraft belief has already been subject to a rigorous analysis in pioneering studies on comparative witchcraft in Africa by S.F. Nadel.[4] Though Nadel did his fieldwork among the Nupe about seventy years ago, his subject is by no means outdated. Witchcraft accusations still flourish in Nupeland, and they are an important sign of social stress and strain in Sub-Saharan Africa in general.[5] The Nupe are no exception in this respect. Most Nupe informants interviewed in 1976, 1982 and 1990 insisted that the

---

2   Thanks for valuable suggestions go to Lars Clausen, Georg and Karola Elwert, Max Marwick, Mike Mason, and two anonymous referees. The responsibility for any fallacies or inaccuracies in the paper remains of course with the author. The article is a thoroughly revised and updated version of my working paper, distributed in 1983 by the Sociology of Development Research Centre, Univ. of Bielefeld, titled: „ Indicators of Social and Political Conflict in African Societies: On the Articulation of Witchcraft among the Nupe, Northern Nigeria".

3   The surprising switch in the allegiance of the Nupe from the conservative National Party of Nigeria (NPN) to the Nigerian People's Party (NPP) in 1983 resulted in terrible incidences of disorder, especially in Bida, were houses and vehicles were destroyed and a number of officials of the Federal Electoral Commission (FEDECO) were burnt to death. Law and order had virtually broken down, with thugs hired by both sides and a mounting casualty list. No wonder that in this tense political climate, witchcraft accusations flourished and were used by both parties to meet their ends. Before the 1983 elections, the fortunes of the NPN in Niger state had already declined, as indicated by the election results, where the proportion of votes they received fell from 74.12% in 1979 to 64.72% in the gubernatorial elections, although these were probably rigged in favour of the NPN. In Bida most NPP supporters had hoped to win, but they polled only 30.95% for the gubernatorial election in Niger state. Disappointed Nupe as well as some minority groups in the state, for example, the Gwan people, protested against the Hausa-Fulani hegemony. In addition, Sulaiman Takuma, Nupe candidate for the post of the national Secretary of the NPN was defeated by his rival Uba Ahmed from Bauchi state, last but not least, because of his unguarded remarks on the sensitive issue of zoning; although this was intended to conserve the power base of the northern Emirs, it was opposed by Takuma, who was campaigning in Niger State for the rotation of governorship between the Hausa-Fulani group of the incumbent governor and his own Nupe group. Cf. Lai OLURODE: A political economy of Nigeria's 1983 elections, John West Publications, Ikeja / Lagos 1990, pp. 54, 64, 80. Lindsay BARRET: Nigeria's Elections – The method and the implications, in: West Africa, No. 3461 (12.12.1983) pp. 2865-2868.

4   S.F. NADEL: Witchcraft in four African Societies, in: The American Anthropologist, Vol. 54 (1952), pp. 18-29, reprinted in: Max MARWICK (ed.): Witchcraft an Sorcery. Selected Readings, Harmondsworth 1975, pp. 264-279. IDIM: Nupe Religion, London 1954, reprinted 1970.

5   Dirk KOHNERT: Magic and witchcraft: implications for demoncratization and poverty-alleviating aid in Africa, in: World development, Vol. 24 (1996), pp. 1347-1355. IDEM: Witchcraft and transantional social spaces, in: Journal of Modern African Studies, Vol. 41 (2003), pp. 1-29. Peter GESCHIERE: The Modernity of Witchcraft. Politics and the Occult in Postcolonial Africa, Charlottesville / London 1997. Stepfen ELLIS / Gerrie TER HAAR (eds.): Worlds of power – Religious thought and political practice in Africa, London 2004.

incidence of witchcraft increased since the early days of colonial rule.[6] In the peasants' view, this growth of witchcraft is mainly related to the growing ineffectiveness of traditional means of witchcraft control, an assertion which will be analysed in detail later. But increasing social and political cleavages, caused by growing social and economic differentiation as consequence of globalisation seem to lay at the roots of this problem.[7]

Up to now there has been a common understanding in the Western World that witchcraft accusations in Africa are based on superstition and strange occult belief which cause harm to a society and should be eradicated as soon as possible in the name of progress. Since the beginning of colonial rule, missionaries and colonial officers tried to destroy „*juju* medicine" and anti-witchcraft cults, first often by mere force, later also by legal means,[8] but apparently without great success. Despite the existing laws against „ordeal, witchcraft, and juju",[9] there is, according to a Nigerian scholar in religious studies

> „no belief more profoundly ingrained than that of the existence of witches ... To the Yorùbá as well as other ethnic groups in Africa, witchcraft is a reality. It is a belief very prevalent among literates and illiterates, among the high and the low in the society."[10]

Although it is undisputed that in most individual cases witchcraft accusations were directed against innocent people, there is a growing awareness among social scientists that occult belief systems may have a social justification, and that they are not necessarily a sign of backwardness, but quite to the contrary, symptoms of modern development.[11]

---

6   Own field studies on Nupe witchcraft belief were conducted mainly within the framework of investigations in the economic history and socio-economic differentiation of the Nupe peasantry in 1975/76, cf. Dirk KOHNERT: Klassenbildung im ländlichen Nigeria. Das Beispiel der Savannenbauern im Nupeland. Institute of African Affairs (IAK), Hamburg, 1982. Semi-structured and narrative interviews were the major methods employed, complemented by research at the National Archives, Kaduna. Further enquiries were conducted during an additional field visits in 1982 and 1990.

7   Jean COMAROFF / John COMAROFF: Alien-Nation: Zombies, immigrants, and millennial capitalism, in: Codesria Bulletin 3-4 (1999), pp. 17-27.

8   Soon after the invasion of Bida by the British colonial forces (1897), the Church Missionary Society (CMS) opened stations all over Nupeland, e.g. in Bida (1902), Kutigi (1904), Mokwa (1906), and Wodata near Baro. Later on, other missionary societies, like the Sudan Interior Mission and the United Mission Church (of Africa) (UMCA), followed. However, Samuel Crowther, Rev. of the CMS and one of the first missionaries who entered Nupeland, opened a station near Rabba (in the present Mokwa District) already in 1857 (cf. CMS, Northern Nigeria Mission, files, G3, A9/0", 1908, Nos. 1-113; G/3,A9/3, 1913; and Crowther/Taylor 1859: 157/58). – At least from the missionaries at Mokwa it is known that they burnt the masks of the *ndakógbòyá*, i.e. the Nupe anti-witchcraft cult, and forbade the performance of the cult (cf. Leo FROBENIUS: „ Und Afrika sprach", Vita, Berlin, 1912, vol. 2, „ An der Schwelle des verehrungswürdigen Byzanz", S. 39). The rationale behind these actions of the missionaries seems to be quite clear. As Mr. Derwar, A.D.O. in the Colonial Service of Northern Nigeria, put it in a memo on witchcraft to the Resident, Niger Province: „ In practice, if not always in theory, ' black' and ' white' magic are inextricably mingled in primitive philosophy and ... religion and magic (including ' black magic' or witchcraft) are similarly associated. Any attempt, therefore, to interfere with or destroy witchcraft ... must certainly interfere with and might altogether destroy the religion into the fabric of which they are so closely woven" (cf. DERWAR: Notes on Witchcraft in its Relations to Administrative Problems, National Archives, Kaduna (NAK), MINPROF, M 1228, 1934).

9   cf. for example the Nigerian Penal Code Law, 4th ed., 1976, Sec., pp. 214-19.

10 J. Omosade AWOLALU: Yoruba beliefs and sacrificial rites, London 1979, p. 81.

11 E. BEVER: Witchcraft fears and psychological factors in disease. Journal of Interdisciplinary History, Vol. 30/4 (2000), pp. 573-590. Peter GESCHIERE: The modernity of witchcraft. Politics and the

Witchcraft beliefs satisfy a deeply rooted desire to be sure that the world is concerned with us, our fate and happiness, and that nothing happens simply by chance. The acceptance of a domain of life where malevolent forces, like the witch, can be defined and attacked makes it possible to bear a universe devoid of such design. This is the case in the Nupe religious system too, as Nadel rightly observed.[12]

The occult reduction of complex social and political conflicts, as expressed by its personalisation in witchcraft accusations, was considered to be a legitimate option by the indigenous population *vis à vis* external enemies, like the colonial oppressors, thereby opening new doors for political action. At least this was an option pursued by (anti-) witchcraft movements directed against colonial domination, like the *Ijov-*, *Haakaa-*, and *Inyambuan* movements of the Tiv in Northern Nigeria or by the Mpondo of the Transkei, South Africa, in the 1880s.[13] More recent examples are the messianic grass-root movements which used magic and witchcraft accusations to fight their enemies by „cults of counter-violence", like the *Naprama* of Mozambique;[14] similar traits of occult thought and political action were to be found in Sierra Leone and Liberia in the 1990s.[15] Other witchcraft accusations with a strong „liberating", „emancipative" or „egalitarian" impetus are directed against enemies within the own community. Examples are witchcraft accusations directed against rich peasants and traders in East- and West-Africa, who accumulate large sums of grain or money individually, without due regard to their obligation – under the traditional solidarity-system of the village community – to assist the poor in case of hardship. In the latter case the rich are suspected – quite correctly in the logic of a communitarian redistribute social system – of obtaining their wealth through evil powers.[16] We shall return later in more detail to this question.

---

occult in postcolonial Africa", London 1997. Dirk KOHNERT: Local Manifestations of Transnational Troubles: Different Strategies of Curbing Witchcraft. Violence in Times of Transition in South Africa, in: Jürgen OSSENBRÜGGE / Mechthild REH (eds.), Social Spaces of African Societies. Applications an Critique of Concepts of "Transnational Social Spaces", Münster 2004, pp. 175-198.

12 NADEL: Nupe Religion 1954, p. 205.

13 cf. J.I. TSEAYO: Conflict an incorporation in Nigeria, Zaria, ABU 1975, pp. 57-74. For further examples of witchcraft-control movements caused by stress and strain resulting from colonial conditions cf. Audrey RICHARDS: A Modern Movement of Witch-Finders, in: Africa, Vol. 8 (1935), pp. 448-461. Marwick (ed.): (1950), Goody (1957), and Lee (1976). – Early local resistance against colonial oppression in South Africa followed similar avenues, as shown by the Transkei rebellion of 1880 against the introduction of a hut tax register. This, it was believed locally, provided intimate knowledge of the tax payers, which could be used by colonial administrators, who were believed to collude with witches and sorcerers, to inflict serious harm; cf. Redding (1996: 257): „People's survival, as they saw it, may have depended upon the removal of a state that was prohibiting them from discovering and punishing all the 'evilly disposed' people." Apparently, it was not the individual European, who was suspected of sorcery or witchcraft, but the colonial administration as such, reinforced by collaborating local chiefs with renowned occult power.

14 K.B. WILSON: Cults of violence and counter-violence in Mozambique, in: Journal of Southern African Studies 18 (1992), 3, pp. 527-582.

15 ELLIS / TER HAAR: Worlds of power.

16 For similar examples cf. Frank A. SALAMONE: Gbagyi Witchcraft. A Reconsideration of S.F. Nadel' s Theory of African Witchcraft, in: Afrika und Übersee 63 (1980), S. 1-20, on '*abujanke*' witchcraft among the Gbayi (Gwari), Northern Nigeria; cf. Kyari TIJANI: Research priorities for agricultural development. A critique of the irrigation project south of lake Chad (Nigeria), in: Research and Public Policy in Nigeria, Report of a Conference, unpublished, ABU, Zaria (1977), pp.

Thus witchcraft accusations, notable those, which are organised in anti-witchcraft cults or secret societies by social groups with vested political interests, are often related to stress and anxieties resulting from the economic and social cleavages caused by the articulation of different or even antagonistic modes of production and the violation of the social laws which they represent. As will be demonstrated in the subsequent chapters, the communal mode of production in the village communities of peasant societies in Nupeland for example, conflicted with the rules of the semi-feudal mode of production of the 19th century Nupe state, the colonial mode of production installed in the early 1900s, as well as with modern rural capitalist development, induced by the Nigerian Oil-boom in the 1970s.[17] It is against this background that the forms and changes in the meaning of Nupe witchcraft over time will be investigated and tentative hypotheses on the articulation of witchcraft accusations and modes of production in the course of Nupe history developed.

The aim of this study is threefold: firstly, to test whether the analysis of occult belief is a meaningful methodology with which to uncover the origins of past and current social conflicts. Secondly, to obtain better insight into covert social conflicts during a crucial stage of the development of rural capitalism in Nigeria, taking the Nupe society as an example. And thirdly, to give a re-evaluation of Nadel's witchcraft theory, including a reconsideration of the history of the *ndakógbòyá*, a secret society intended to control witchcraft, and at the same time a major pillar of occult belief among the Nupe.[18] Finally, I should like to test the preliminary hypothesis of an interdependency between the form and content of witchcraft belief and the modes of production in which the different actors involved were embedded. As with most social and economic concepts intended to explain long-term historical developments, this hypothesis can be of heuristic value

---

117-143; on witchcraft accusations connected with enrichment through development projects in Bornu Emirate, Northern Nigeria; and Chyntia BRANTLEY: An historical perspective of the Girama and witchcraft control. Africa, Vol. 49, 1979, Nr. 2, pp. 112-33. D.J. PARKIN: Medicine and Men of Influence, in: Man 3 (1968), pp. 424-39; IDEM.: Politics of ritual syneretism – Isam among the Non-Muslim Giriama of Kenya. Africa, Vol. 40, 1979, Nr. 3, pp. 217-33, on the „equalizing" effects of witchcraft accusations among the Giriama trading communities of Kenya. COMAROFF / COMAROFF: Alien-Nation, analyse the accusation of migrant farm labourers in South Africa as zombies, employed by capitalist farmer, blamed to be witches.

17 For a detailed discussion of the concept of „modes of production" and its relevance for the analysis of Nupe economic history cf. KOHNERT: Klassenbildung, S. 62-242. On the links between globalisation, the rise of neo-liberal capitalism and the political economy of occult belief systems in Africa and elsewhere cf. COMAROFF / COMAROFF: Allien-Nations. ELLIS / TER HAAR: Worlds of power. KOHNERT: Witchcraft.

18 If we talk of „the Nupe" here, it should not obscure the fact that the Nupe are an extremely pluralistic society [cf. S.F. NADEL: A Black Byzantium. The Kingdom of Nupe in Nigeria, London, OUP, 1942, reprinted 1973. 1942, pp. 12-26]. Of course this holds even more when we speak of „the African". For obvious reasons it is difficult to say whether the research results are representative for all Nupe or not [cf. NADEL: Byzantium, pp. ix-x]. This is all the more valid as we are dealing with an extremely sensitive cultural and social aspect of African life. It must therefore be understood that where I limit my description to single events or attitudes, these can only claim to be 'typical' for the groups or villages which I investigated - unless stated otherwise. Although witchcraft belief in Africa is expressed in many different forms (according to region, religion, and ethnic affiliation) I have explained elsewhere (cf. KOHNERT: Magic and Witchcraft) that, nevertheless, there are some essential common grounds which allow general insights.

only, as a sound data base for more rigid methodological testing is still lacking. This is all the more so as the scanty data and analyses available on the origins of the Nupe state and society are clouded by myth and ignorance.

The Origins of Witchcraft Accusations among the Nupe: Nadel's witchcraft theory reconsidered

As stated above, witchcraft and magic beliefs may indicate the precise nature of the social conflicts of which they are symptoms.[19] This holds especially for conflicts which dominant forces in a given society are obliged to camouflage, because the open discussion of these conflicts may put into question the whole social fabric on which their well-being depends.

In such a case witchcraft accusations tend to act as a kind of safety valve which canalises existing hostilities towards a few scapegoats, rather than towards those, who would be regarded by the stakeholders as the real enemies of society. There can be no doubt that a society which needs such a safety valve has been badly constructed (cf. Nadel 1954: 206/206). But for research purposes, the study of magic beliefs provides us with a unique instrument to uncover and analyse social conflicts which otherwise might pass through undetected. In fact the latter has been stressed already by S.F. Nadel in a well-known article on comparative African witchcraft, in applying the Durkheimian method of concomitant variances in an analysis of the differences between Nupe and Gwari witchcraft beliefs.[20] However, Nadel's study underwent severe criticism by Salamone (1980), because of the alleged use of poor ethnographical data on the Gbagyi (Gwari).[21] This criticism certainly does not apply to Nadel's well founded Nupe studies which contain a wealth of valid information. But a secondary analysis of Nadel's data – complemented by results of my own field work among the Nupe – support a different interpretation of these data and subsequently a revision of Nadel's witchcraft theory. It is not Nadel's empirical base, but his witchcraft theory itself which will be challenged in the following.

In light of general theories of functional anthropology and social psychology, fashionable in the 1940's,[22] Nadel considered witchcraft accusations as a kind of „social illness", analogous to psycho-pathological symptoms of mentally disturbed persons.[23] This „illness" is based, according to Nadel, on sex-antagonism, resulting from the specific marriage system and the sexual and economic independence of women from their husbands in Nupe society.[24] Nadel holds that the symptoms are „easy to read; for in

---

19 cf. NADEL: Witchcraft, p. 264. Max MARWICK: Witchcraft as a social strain-gauge, Australian Journal of Science Nr. 26 (1964), pp. 263-268; reprint in: MARWICK (ed.): Witchcraft and Sorcery, pp. 280-295.
20 cf. NADEL: Witchcraft, p. 264.
21 According to Salamone, Nadel's inaccurate ethnographical data was not sufficient to test his theory adequately and forced him to modify it, thus „impeding the advancement of sound theory" (SALAMONE: Gbagyi Witchcraft, p. 16).
22 cf. NADEL: Byzantium, pp. vi-vii; IDEM.: Nupe Religion, pp. 163-206.
23 NADEL: Witchcraft, p. 264.
24 cf. NADEL: Witchcraft, pp. 266-269. IDEM.: Nupe Religion, pp. 172-180, for a detailed account.

Nupe witchcraft expresses the social threats and tensions from which they spring with little disguise".[25] As a proof he lists three points of reference:
  (a) The existing legends on the development of witchcraft
  (b) The concrete accusations against witches
  (c) The explicit reference to the market organisation of Nupe women, with respect to witchcraft-control.

But quite contrary to Nadel, the interpretation of these symptoms might be not easy at all, but highly controversial. This will be shown in analysing his arguments one by one.

The first reason given by Nadel, i.e. the analysis of existing legends on the origin of witchcraft, is of course highly speculative, but it may be accepted for the sake of argument against the background of the methodological concepts of social psychology, current at his time. As far as Nupe concepts of the historic origins of witchcraft, as well as counter measures to defeat it are concerned, Nadel[26] refers to two founding legends of the anti-witchcraft cult of the Nupe, the *ndakógbòyá*[27], taking them as decisive indicators of the social psychology of Nupe society. One of these legends centres around people living under the reign of *Etsu* Shago (the founding father of the Nupe state), leading a lawless life and refusing to listen to their elders.

„Men would steal each other's wives and commit adultery without shame. The older women, especially, caused much trouble; they quarrelled among themselves and 'gave no peace'. The more law-abiding among the men grew angry and spoke harshly to the women; but these 'replied with insolence'."[28]

In trying to solve this problem, a young man of great strength invented a mask (later called *ndakógbòyá*) to frighten away the insolent women. But one woman refused to run away; she was caught and killed with an iron rod (*sányŋ*, a slave chain, cf. below). This legend was still widely known among the heads of the *ndakógbòyá* lodges to the north and south of the Niger whom I interviewed in 1982. However, the legend, used by Nadel to back his thesis of „sex-antagonism" as the principal source of witchcraft accusations among the Nupe, lends itself for other interpretations of the origins of the *ndakógbòyá*. It hints at the police functions of the cult, meant to maintain the moral values of the village community which were disregarded by both men and women, although especially the older women are blamed. As Nadel rightly observed, the „evilness" of the elderly women implied undermined the authority of the „Great Men". The reference to the „insolence" of women in the legend may hint at an event in a very early period of Nupe history, i.e. the transformation of a matrilineal to a patrilineal society. This

---

25 IDEM.: Nupe Religion, p. 172.
26 ibid., p. 172f.
27 Literally, „Grandfather Gboya", in Nupe, i.e. a traditional „secret society", specialised in the control of witchcraft in Nupe (cf. NADEL: Nupe Religion, pp. 188-201), but used for centuries, also for many other purposes of political oppression and extortion. According to Laing, Acting Resident at Bida in 1920, who investigated in the extortion cases of the *ndakógbòyá*, the latter means „big father of echo", a meaning derived from the fact „that the gongola, supporting the long body of the mask, is pierced at the bottom, and the man bearing it speaks into this cavity, his voice then appears to come out of the top of this 15' pole"; cf. NAK, SNP 10/8, 340p/1920. The Hausa name for the *ndakógbòyá* was *masugirro* or *magiro*, pl. *magirai*, according to Laing (ibid.).
28 NADEL: Nupe Religion, p. 173.

transformation streched over a long period and started, according to Frobenius[29], during the reign of the Bini dynasty, probably during the 14th and 15th century, i.e. at about the same time as in the Hausa kingdoms further to the North.[30] The transformation probably coincided with the transformation from communal rule in acephalous village societies to the semi-feudal mode of production under the despotic rule of the kings of the emerging Nupe state. Remains of matrilineal rule, especially at the village level and in the Nupe rank and land tenure system, were still evident in colonial times.[31]

This reinterpretation of Nadel's hypothesis seems to be backed by the second founding legend, rendered by Nadel, which tells of a Nupe king whose mother was an interfering woman, constantly meddling in his affairs.[32] The king in question might have been the last of the Nupe Kings before the Fulani invasion (the Nupe/Fulani *jihad*), *Etsu* (Ali) Kolo (Ta-)Nagari, who lived at the end of the 18th century. *Etsu* Kolo had been installed by his predecessor *Etsu* Maazu, although the former was the heir to the throne according to the then already outdated rules of matrilineal descent. Therefore he was rejected by the Nupe elders, who had got accustomed to the advantages of patrilineal organisation in the meantime.[33] One of the early European travellers who visited the court of *Etsu* Masaba, wrote of *Etsu* Kolo: „He took his mother's advice so constantly that the Nupe people said they wanted not to be governed by a woman, and, rising against him, drove him to Yauri".[34] The legend, however, tells a different story, i.e. the king himself succeeded in overwhelming his mother (i.e. matrilineal rule, D. K.) with the help of the *ndakógbòyá* mask[35]; details from different historical events have probably been merged, a familiar feature of myth-making.

However, these founding-legends are not the only ones, and in addition they do not necessarily back Nadel's theory of sex-antagonism as a source of witchcraft accusations, neither in the colonial, nor in the present social and economic order of the Nupe. For reasons subject to speculation, Nadel and others completely ignored the valuable and detailed account on Nupe witchcraft by Leo Frobenius, published about twenty years before the publication of the relevant articles by Nadel.[36] Interesting enough, the two

---

29 FROBENIUS: Schwelle, S. 274.
30 cf. M.G. SMITH : TheAffairs of Daura. Berkeley/London 1978, on the transformation of matrilineal rule in Dauwa Emirate, the oldest of the Hausa kingdoms, which counted the Nupe to one of its seven *banza bakwài*, i.e. „ bastard" or vassal states.
31 cf. FROBENIUS: Schwelle, S. 274. IDEM.: Volkserzählungen und Volksdichtungen aus dem Zentral-Sudan – Der Geist des Quorra, Jena 1924, pp. 9, 87-89. O. TEMPLE (ed.): Notes on the Tribes, Provinces, Emirates and States of the Northern Provinces of Nigeria, Cass, 2nd ed. 1922; new impr., 1965; 1922, p. 329. NADEL: Byzantium, pp. x, 31-32, 51, 54, 147-49, 278. Michael MASON: The Nupe Kingdom in the Nineteenth Century - A Political History, Ph.D. thesis, Birmingham, Centre of West African Studies, 1970, pp. 194-196.
32 cf. NADEL: Nupe Religion, p. 172.
33 cf. FROBENIUS: Schwelle, p. 41.
34 W.B. BAIKIE: Notes on a Journey from Bida in Nupe to Kano in Hausa, in: Journal of the Royal Geographic Society 37 (1867), pp. 92-109,105.
35 cf. NADEL: Nupe Religion, pp. 184, 164.
36 cf. FROBENIUS: Schwelle. IDEM.: Volkserzählungen, 9, p. 9. Even Murdock and the co-authors of the „*Human Relations Area Files*" did not consult the works of Frobenius as a source on Nupe

legends given by Frobenius did not fit into Nadel's sex-antagonism theory. According to one of them, the *ndakógbòyá* represents the spirit of *Etsu* Guschi, one ancient local Nupe king in Epa (in the Northwest of Nupeland) who refused to come out of his *katamba* to „greet", i.e. to bow to Edegi (also called „Tsoèdè" in Hausa, the mystical founder of the Nupe kingdom), who had presumably invaded his country during the 14th and 15th century. Thereupon, the Guschi died (was killed?), and his son became the follower of the new emperor. The spirit which rose out of the grave of the late Guschi was – according to this legend – the incorporation of the spirit of resistance which created the *ndakógbòyá*.[37] According to the second legend reported by Frobenius, the *ndakógbòyá*, in olden times named *Lata*, came from the East via Atagara[38] into Nupeland. It was directed against „social enemies" of the people, and at this time the mask had greater power than most of the Nupe kings.[39]

Apparently there is no reference to any kind of „sex-antagonism" in these legends. According to them the *ndakógbòyá* originally represented the resistance of Nupe peasant communities against enemies of their society, especially against the usurpation of despotic power by outside forces. Concerning the latter aspect of these legends there are interesting parallels with the *gunnu* ritual of the Nupe – the most important of all traditional Nupe cults according to Nadel – where the *ndakógbòyá* used to play a dominant role as *dògiri nyá gunnu*, lit. „policeman of the *gunnu*". According to Nadel the *gunnu* priest, assisted by the *ndakógbòyá* mask, which is also called *gunnukó*, lit. „great *gunnu*", holds all power in his hand during the week-long ceremonies: „Neither parents nor chiefs, not even the *Etsu* of Nupe, retain any authority ... The legal system (introduced and enforced by the 'feudal' overlords of the Nupe, D. K.) is upset rather than confirmed by the *gunnu* organisation."[40] The *gunnu* guards the community against intruders and ties the whole village periodically to its common values.[41]

---

   witchcraft. Although Frobenius' work on the Nupe has a heavy ideological bias which may even sometimes distort the facts, it is nevertheless interesting to read because it avoids another equally serious source of confusion, i.e. the „Fulani bias" in the „official" Nupe history, on which Nadel's accounts are mainly based (cf. NADEL: Byzantium, p. 76. KOHNERT: Klassenbildung, p. 90, 380, fn. 212). Frobenius got his information mainly from peasants in the Mokwa area who have a long tradition of resistance against „Fulani domination".

37 cf. FROBENIUS: Schwelle, pp. 377-378. IDEM.: Volkserzählungen, 9, pp. 78, 81; unfortunately the memory of this legend was lost to all of my present informants in the Zugurma/Mokwa area, including the *Etzu* Zugurma, one of the descendants of a branch of the pre-Fulani Nupe Kings, living in a small palace at Eba.

38 I.e. Idah, the capital of the *Atta* of Gara (Igara or Igala), who became the master of Edigi, when the latter was brought to Igalaland as a slave.

39 cf. FROBENIUS: Volkserzählungen, 9, pp. 78-81. This account by Frobenius fits well into another legend, which was related to me in 1976 by the elders of Mokwa, namely that the *ndakógbòyá* had already been created before there was a king in Nupeland. It originated in Tata - near Onitsha. The man who invented the cult was not a Nupe, but he was the first to protect the Nupe by means of his *kuti* (magic) against warriors from that area.

40 S. F. NADEL: Gunnu – a fertility cult of the Nupe in Northern Nigeria. Journal of the Royal Anthropological Institute of Great Britain and Ireland, Vol. 67, pp. 91-130, here 100, 113

41 IDEM, p. 120.

The evidence for the new interpretation of the historical origins of witchcraft and of the *ndakógbòyá* (as reconstructed from the legends) given above may not be very strong. But one has to keep in mind that Nadel himself admitted that the legends, althought talking of gender-cleavages, failed to corroborate his concept of „sex-antagonism" in its narrow sense, since the empirical base of Nadel's view on the weakening effects of sexual intercourse on the strength of men as a principal cause of witchcraft accusations among the Nupe was not confirmed by the legends. On the contrary, the first of his legends tells about the sexual dominance of the male (through adultery), and frustrations of the (male) elders which concentrate on the old women, not the young and attractive ones.

The same is valid for the second point of reference for Nadel's „sex-antagonism" theory, the actual accusations against witches. First, they fasten rather on the woman's character as a whole, which rejects the submissiveness expected of women,[42] especially on the dominating character of older women, than on their sexual dominance in particular. Why then did Nadel insist on his „sex-antagonism" theses, although he himself mentioned several times the important political role played by the *ndakógbòyá*? Might it not be possible that - at least at the beginning - the *ndakógbòyá* ritual was not a „social illness", but a legitimate political instrument, developed by the peasantry, to fight injustice and exploitation by their overlords? An instrument, which only later on was taken out of the hands of the peasants and occupied by the despotic central powers during the emergence of the state in Nupe society whose representatives turned it against the peasantry?[43]

Second, if the witch in Nupe religion is correctly identified as a person openly and successfully setting aside fundamental values of society, as Nadel presumes, does this not suggest that the most ostensible neglect of these values by the despotic rulers would be somehow connected with such witch accusations? Especially, as the *ndakógbòyá* was most virulent in Trans-Kaduna, a region where the peasants were notorious rebellious. Such a suggestion would also be backed by far reaching analogies, within the realm of the social psychology of Nupe peasants, between the characteristics of a witch (*gici*, pl. *gicizi* in Nupe for witches of both sexes) and those of despotic rulers, namely:

(a) Both have power over life and death reaching everywhere.
(b) This (evil) power is conscious, and ordinary persons are powerless against it.[44]
(c) Both the *Etsu* and the witch have power over the profane and in the spiritual world;[45] this view is widespread even nowadays according to own investigations cf. below).

---

42 cf. NADEL: Nupe Religion, p. 187.
43 For a description of the ruthless exploitation of the peasantry by the institutionalised and closed lodges of the *ndakógbòyá* under the leadership of the *Maji Dodo* (lit. the „Master of the Terrible") and the *Etsu* see S.F. NADEL: Nupe State and Community, in: Afrika 8 (1935), p. 442. IDEM.: Nupe Religion, p. 197. Apparently, it reached its peak in the second decade of colonial rule, when the British Resident became afraid that no tax-money would be left for the British, and therefore forbade the cult in 1921. For the exploitative aspect of the cult see also: FROBENIUS: Schwelle, p. 268. IDEM.: Volkserzählungen 9, pp. 78-80). S. CROWTHER / J. TAYLOR: The Gospel on the Banks of the Niger, Journals and Notices of the Native Missionaries Accompanying the Niger Expedition of 1857-59, 1859, reprinted London 1968, 1859, p. 215 and TEMPLE: Notes, pp. 331-332.
44 cf. NADEL: Nupe Religion, p. 166. FROBENIUS: Schwelle, p. 262.

(d) The most powerful witches are rich, they accumulate their wealth for their own selfish purposes. And if they wanted money (in pre-colonial times) they would have sold their victims to another country as slaves.[46]
(e) Witches attack in the dark of the night – like the Nupe slave-raiders in pre-colonial times did. They suck the blood out of their victims,[47] which, in a metaphorical sense, may be said of the ruling class, too.

Third, if witchcraft accusations are mainly based on „sex-antagonism", how then can the important role of male witches (*eshe*, pl. *eshezi*, in Nupe) be explained, be it as „partners in crime",[48] or even as male evil witches, said to exist in Nupeland – contrary to the assertion of Nadel – already by Frobenius?[49]

In addition, the connection between magic and worldly power is not restricted to analogies which may appear more or less accidental or superficial, but is very real in the person of the *Lelu*. The latter is said to be the head of all witches in a village, and, at the same time, as S*agŋ* or *Nakó*, respected as the most powerful and rich woman in the village, held to be a „good" witch, who is expected to keep witchcraft within reasonable bounds.[50] But we have to admit that with the emergence of the Nupe state, even the *Lelu* had to bow before the superior authority of the male village chief and district head.

Since the establishment of Fulani dominance over the Nupe peasantry, the *Etsu* Nupe is supposed to be even more powerful. He is said to control witchcraft himself within a wide range around his residence.[51] The alleged magic power of the *Etsu* served, at least until the end of the 19th century, as a well defined political means to maintain the despotic feudal order and the „king's law". This had been done notably by invocation of the *kútí* (i.e. magic) of the *èḡba Tsoèdè*, i.e. the slave-chains of Tsoede (or Edegi), used for strangling political opponents and for uncovering crimes in the manner of an ordeal.[52]

The fear among the peasants that the Emir might employ black magic to achieve his goals did not vanish after this period: Whitaker[53], for example, reported that even during the electoral campaigns of 1959 local opposition to the Emir of Bida proved to be extremely difficult, among other reasons, because of the prevailing belief among the villagers, that the Emir would pronounce a curse, should they not vote for him or his candidate. Some twenty years later, in 1976, similar fears were still virulent among the peasantry with respect to Local Government elections, as I was able to observe myself. As the „open ballot

---

45 cf. FROBENIUS: Schwelle, pp. 261-267.
46 cf. NADEL: Nupe Religion, pp. 165, 167.
47 cf. FROBENIUS: Schwelle, pp. 41, 261-271. IDEM.: Volkserzählungen 9, p. 68.
48 I.e. as medicine man, cf. NADEL: Nupe Religion, p. 169.
49 FROBENIUS: Volkserzählungen 9, pp. 65, 67.
50 cf. NADEL: Nupe Religion, p. 168.
51 cf. NADEL: Nupe State and Community. Africa, Vol. 8, 1935, pp. 257-303. IDEM: Byzantium, p. 87.
52 cf. NADEL: The King's Hangman; a Judical Organisation in Central Africa in: Man 35 (1935) 143, pp. 129-132. Parts of this iron chain, which is similar to the old Portuguese slave chains (cf. NADEL: Nupe Religion, pp. 32, 194), were still a cult object of the *ndakógbòyá* in 1982, at least in its lodges south of the Niger.
53 C.S. WHITAKER: The Politics of Tradition Continuity and Change in Northern Nigeria 1946-1966, Princeton Univ. Press, 1970, p. 296.

Fig. 1: The The Lelu of Dabba (Trans-Kaduna) with her entourage in 1982.

system" was still in practice at that time, the above mentioned threat proved to be very effective indeed, because the voters had to queue behind their candidate.

Altogether, major factors which constitute a witch in the eyes of Nupe peasants, i.e. illegitimate spiritual and worldly power over life and death, and the disregard of fundamental human rights concerning health and property of their victims, seem to be very similar to the qualities of a traditional ruler in the view of the peasantry, at least in pre-colonial and colonial times. All this leads to my working hypothesis that the belief in witchcraft in Nupeland, namely the origin of the institutionalised anti-witchcraft cult (*ndakógbòyá*), was causally related to the resistance of the peasants within a communal mode of production against illegitimate power accumulation of despotic rulers of the emerging Nupe state. At least, this thesis corresponds neatly to the second legend on the origin of the *ndakógbòyá* as rendered by Frobenius.[54] At the beginning, the actual witchcraft accusations may have been directed either directly against the usurper, or they may have been the result of repressed frustrations, derived from the peasants' impotence *vis à*

---

54 FROBENIUS (cf. above) Volkserzählungen 9, pp. 65, 67.

vis illegitimate force, which was then directed against a few scapegoats. Of course, this hypothesis would have to be confirmed by sound empirical evidence. Although this hypothesis runs contrary to Nadel's witchcraft theory, Nadel was certainly right in his general description of the effect of witchcraft accusations when he said: „Attacks against witches are thus attacks upon the successful enemies of the ideal society ... witchcraft fears and accusations only accentuate concrete hostilities and in fact give them free reign."[55]

Even though the *ndakógbòyá* was forbidden by the British Resident in Bida in 1921 for the reasons stated above, it continued to be practiced, though on a smaller scale. In any case, the proscription applied only to Bida Emirate, and not to the Nupe districts south of the Niger. There the *ndakógbòyá* remained active, though it seems to have changed its character, and the cult is now even referred to as a „festival" by a tourist guide.[56] Whether it is really completely void of any exploitative aspect nowadays, and whether new forms of witchcraft control have been developed, will be explored in the following chapter.

Witchcraft accusation in present-day Nupeland

As said in the beginning, even today the Nupe are renown (and sometimes feared) among other ethnic groups of Nigeria, like the Hausa or the Yorùbá, for their knowledge of powerful magic and the prevalence of witchcraft in their society.[57] Nupe informants whom I interviewed during visits in several Nupe villages and towns in 1976, 1982 and 1990 insisted that witchcraft was by no means a minor aspect of Nupe cultural life, but, on the contrary, had increased very much during the past decades. However, this is very difficult to confirm by sound empirical investigation, due to the sensitivity of the subject.[58]

---

55 NADEL: Witchcraft, p. 279.
56 cf. S.A. EMIELU: Guide to Kwara, Ilorin, 1981, p. 27.
57 Some authors maintain that every ethnic group believes its neighbours to have more dark and potent magic than its own (cf. G. PARRINDER: Witchcraft, Harmondsworth 1958, p. 196). But this certainly does not hold for the Nupe, as their „authorities" in anti-witchcraft matters are proud that they harbour the most powerful anti-witchcraft magic, a secret which is anxiously protected against disclosure to members of other tribes. In fact, the cult has even been 'exported' to other Nigerian provinces, e.g. to Yorùbáland. Named „*igunnu*" by the Yorùbá, the *ndakógbòyá* mask came to Abeokuta, Lagos and other Yorùbá towns through Nupe who migrated from the Gbado area during World War I, according to the present *Lile* (i.e. Village Head) of Gbado. (cf. also G. PARRINDER: Religion in an African City, London, OUP, 1953, pp. 58, 69, on *ndakógbòyá* masks in Ibadan).
58 Some of the reluctance to discuss the whole issue of witchcraft with outsiders was apparently due to the fear that other tribes could come into possession of the secrets of the *ndakógbòyá* as a result of the carelessness of talkative members of the cult. There is, however, also a more general suspicion among the Nupe concerning the discussion of witchcraft, as already observed by Nadel (cf. NADEL: Nupe Religion, p.164): Since only witches can really know about their evil deeds, nobody would like to betray too much knowledge lest he or she be accused of being a witch him/herself. This is especially true of women - those most likely to be accused. It is difficult for males to interview these women, especially in an Islam dominated society like the Nupe. Thus, I hardly received any information from them, even though women such as the *Nakó* (lit. „grandmother") of Dabba, a well known herbalist and head of the women of this village in Trans-Kaduna were said to know *ex officio* about this craft. Needless to say, this imposes serious limitations on the value of the following analysis, which can only scratch the surface of a strong belief which is still deeply rooted in Nupe society.

Fig. 2: The ndakógbòyá *mask, welcoming the Oba of Benin and the Etsu Nupe on their arrival in Bida 1982; the mask resembles exactly the* ndakógbòyá *masks already documented and photographed by L. Frobenius in Mokwa in 1909 and S.F. Nadel in 1936.*

Although belief in black magic is still ingrained in both members of the ruling class in Bida, the capital of Nupeland, and the peasants in the countryside, this does not mean that there have been no changes since Nadel made his investigations among the Nupe. Probably the most noticeable transformation did take place in the realm of control of the supposed witchcraft activities. The *ndakógbòyá*, in the 1920s one of the most powerful means in the hands of the *Etsu* of detecting witches and thereby of exploiting the peasantry, is now also used for entertainment purposes, as a masquerade, a „cultural performance", which features on occasions of social enjoyment, devoid of its original social and religious meaning. Nowadays, the great masks of Kusogi[59], for example, are invited to perform their dance at Sallah, at agricultural shows of the Bida Agricultural Development Project (established in the early 1980s), or to „greet" important state guests who visit the Emir in Bida. Such events, like the performance on the occasion of the recent visit of the *Oba* (king) of Benin, who toured the northern Emirates in October 1982 to weld all traditional rulers of Nigeria together in a united front against attacks on their „historic privileges" in the course of the upcoming 1983 elections (cf. above), must have been experienced as degrading, especially for the mask bearers.[60] After they had been waiting in vain for about two hours for the arrival of the *Oba* and the *Etsu*, who were supposed to ride through the main streets of Bida on horseback as in olden times, the latter rushed through the cheering crowd within seconds in their extravagant Mercedes and Volvo cars, concealed by the darkened car windscreens, and accompanied by

---

59 The second Kusogi, was founded near Doko under *Etsu* Masaba (1859-73), and since that time has been headquarters of the *ndakógbòyá* lodges in Bida Emirate. The original Kusogi is situated east of Pategi. It finally lost its significance when its last *Majin Dodo* died in about 1970. The new title holder is a teacher of Arabic who is said not to be very interested in keeping up the tradition of the *ndakógbòyá*.

60 The performance in question took place on October 8, 1982, just in front of and in the courtyard of the guest house, or more precisely the palace, of one of the biggest and most important businessmen in Bida, thus demonstrating the emerging alliance between the old traditional rulers and the aspiring new class of the national bourgeoisie; on the latter on the latter cf. Dirk KOHNERT: Unternehmer und Grundherren Nord-Nigerias im Kampf um die politische Macht, in: Afrika-Spectrum 13 (1978), 3, pp. 269-286.

their entourage (including the private TV-team of the *Oba*), hardly taking any notice of the frustrated dancing masks and drummers who tried in vain to follow them. But it may be that those concerned held their mere presence as sufficient to chase away any evil minded spirits or witches.

Minor masks, such as the *ndakógbòyá* of Lade to the south of the Niger, now even dance for entertainment on the occasion of important local football matches. But again, there could also be more serious, less overt reasons for the presence of the masks, such as the protection of the players against the witchcraft of their opponents. There are several examples in African football history where violent clashes resulted from witchcraft accusations in connection with football matches allegedly „rigged" by means of black magic.[61]

Nevertheless, the *Májin Dòdo* of Kusogi admitted during my interview that the cult and its members had lost much of their former authority. Many villages and lodges had ceased altogether to perform the ritual. They had to invite the *ndakógbòyá* from other villages, mainly from the Nupe areas south of the Niger, e.g. from Gbado, Tankpufu, Tsambafu, Patizuru, Etsuvun or Lade, if they had serious cases of witchcraft with which they could not cope themselves. One of the cases in the Mokwa area, remembered very well by a Reverend of the UMCA, happened at Kpaki (about 18 miles from Mokwa on the road to Bida) in 1963: A culmination of strange events, such as the outbreak of smallpox, a significant increase in snake bites, and the beating of young men by invisible hands which allegedly resulted in an outbreak of yellow fever, set the village in turmoil. The village authorities called the *ndakógbòyá* from Tsambufu to discipline the witches who were supposed to be the instigators of this sudden outbreak of evil.

The reason most readily given by educated Nupe for the decreasing importance of the *ndakógbòyá* was the ever growing influence of Islam in the already Muslim dominated Northern Emirates and the impact of modern education. Nowadays, fewer and fewer youngsters are prepared to undergo the harsh initiation rituals which involve flogging, staying in the bush at night, or the participation in strange customs such as exhuming of human bones in the graveyard at full moon. Another obvious reason for the decreasing incidence of witch cleansing rituals by the *ndakógbòyá* is directly related to the considerable costs involved in such performances. Most villages, such as Kusogi, Mwuo, and Gbado that could still afford these expenses, exercised the ritual only once a year, most often at the beginning of the dry season, in November or December; some villages, such as Gada, had their annual performance already in September. Of course, the costs were heavy only in relation to the average annual peasants income. As the organised extortion tours of the past had apparently ceased since they were forbidden by law in 1921, and as there has also been a decreasing demand for such cleansing rituals over the past decades

---

[61] cf. Paul RICHARDS: Soccer and Violence in War-Torn Africa: Soccer and Social Rehabilitation in Sierra Leone, in: Gary Armstrong / Richard Giulianotti (eds.), Entering the Field: New Perspectives on World Football, Oxford 1997, pp. 141-157. In 2002 the Ivorian Government settled a 10-year dispute with disgruntled witch doctors who claimed to have had a hand in the country's African Nations Cup triumph (cf. BBC News, 08.04.2002;http://news.bbc.co.uk/sport1/hi/sports_talk/1917251.stm; 04.02.05). In Tanzania there were allegations that the national team used money earmarked for players to pay a witch doctor (cf. BBC News, 20.10.04; http://news.bbc.co.uk/2/hi/africa/3756910.stm.; 04.02.05). Witchcraft was also part and parcel of Ugandan football.

Fig. 3: A performance of the cleansing ritual of the ndakógbòyá-*mask at Kusogi in 1982.*

(due to reasons to which we shall return later), a considerable number of the lodges of the *ndakógbòyá* still existing to be at pains to cover the expenses for the ceremonies, dances, and the maintenance of the masks.

It is doubtful that under such circumstances they still contribute any considerable amount to the shadow household of the Bida emirate, like the *ndakógbòyá* did during the reign of *Etsu* Bello (1916-26), when the lodges, beside gifts in kind, got ransoms of £ 20 on the average (up to £ 100) per village, a profit which they shared with the *Etsu* in Bida.[62] An investigation by Laing, the Acting Resident of Bida in 1920, revealed that the *ndakógbòyá* extortion concentrated on the districts to the West of the Kaduna river, notorious for their quest for independence.[63] The range of gross family-income from

---

62 cf. NADEL: Nupe State. IDEM.: Nupe Religion, p. 196.
63 According to inquiries of the colonial administration into the extortion tours of the *ndakógbòyá* in the early 1920s, the acting resident in Bida, Mr. Laing, came to the following conclusion: „the parties of the *masugirro* (*ndakógbòyá*, D. K.) who were found to have visited the Districts of Labozhi, Egbako, Sakpe and to a small extend Jima-Doko, the details are as follows: (37) Egbako Dist. Livestock and goats extorted £ 471.0.0. It was obvious that these depredations could not have been carried out without the knowledge of the DH and Alkalin Egbaki. (38) 11 *maigirro* arrested; (39) Labozhi Dist. Goods, livestock, money taken: £ 367.2.10.; (40) Skape Dist., Goods, livestock, money taken: £ 165. 1.2; (42) 13 *magirro* arrested at Kutegi; (43) From the forgoing it was obvious that extortions on such a large scale could not have been carried out without the knowledge of the Hakima (the DH, D.K.). After further investigation ... I arrived at the conclusion that the Emir alone was the instigator and prime mover of the sending out of these *masugirro* parties; (45) ... after a half hearted denial the Emir acknowledged his guilt. (47) This catastrophe has been a severe blow to the N.A. and has done an incalculable amount of harm. The District Heads were witness of the daily extortion, carried on with the sanction of their paramount chief, and the District Alkalai were not permitted to exert their authority. The Alkalin Bida, whose court is a Court of Appeal, was ren-

farming at that time was estimated at between £ 2 and £ 12 per year, corresponding to the different resource positions of peasant families.[64]

According to the *Lílé* of Gbado, every villager – „even the child in the womb"– had to give the „traditional one shilling" for a performance still in 1982 according to my interviews, whereas the elders in Mokwa said that they themselves gave a total of about Naira 200 (2 Naira ~ 1 £ in 1982) in cash. Apart from money, the villagers had to contribute in kind: a he-goat, food and drinks, - even Indian hemp in one village to the south of the Niger. So the total value of the contributions for one performance of the *ndakógbòyá* was estimated at about Naira 400 to 600 in 1982 by the elders of Mwuo, a village in southern Mokwa District.

Thus, according to the author's own rough estimates, the income of the cult per performance has decreased in real terms within the past six decades by about 20 to 50 per cent.[65] Of course the performance may have yielded additional income, in case the *ndakógbòyá* discovered a witch. The accused, or her/his relatives, would have to give a ransom, like a black goat, cloth, and money, according to the seriousness of the supposed offence and the willingness to undo their spell or misdeed. But, as said above, such incidences were few in the 1980s, compared with the past, and the deflated total annual net income from witchcraft eradication by the *ndakógbòyá* decreased certainly much more than by mere 50 per cent.

The potential of systematic exploitation, based on the social structure of a semi-feudal kingdom, which did not exist any more, decreased even further. On the other hand, the cult might have guarded, consolidated or even extended its political influence into the realm of party politics, as indicated by the witchcraft accusations linked with the switch of party allegiance of the Nupe in 1983, mentioned at the beginning. In this respect, the *ndakógbòyá* might resemble nowadays more to the *Ogboni* secret society of the Yoruba, or the *Okija* cult, i.e. the *Ogwugwu*-shrines in Okija, Anambra State. The gruesome spiritual and worldly powers of the latter, and its strong influence on high ranking politicians in Anambra government and parliament, including the governor himself, became known to the Nigerian public in August 2004.[66] However, again we enter the sphere of mere speculation, and further investigation would be required.

---

dered powerless to act in this matter; on referring the complainant, the Alkalin Sakpe to the Emir, he was practically told to mind his own business and turn a deaf ear to the allegations which were daily taking place." (cf. NAK, SNP, 10/8, 340p/1920. „Nupe Province – Report, no 37, for half year ending 30th June 1920") „ ... (6) 'smelling out' witchcraft was a lucrative branch of these charlatans, who levied their tolls, at times on individuals or on the whole community. Men and women have been tied up and beaten on the slightest pretext and only obtained their freedom on payment. It will be easily understood what scope this afforded to individuals having grudges against their fellow villagers; a word spoken to the '*magirro*' accompanied by a douceur, would speedily occasion 'a certain weakness' in the household of the unfortunate accused." (ibid.; I am grateful to Mike Mason who allowed me to quote from his copy of the relevant files).

64 cf. KOHNERT: Klassenbildung, pp. 226-227.
65 The nominal growth rate of the income for one performance between 1920 and 1980 was about 4 to 4.6% per annum, whereas the price per unit of staple food, like sorghum or rice, increased about 5 to 5.6% p.a. during the same period (cf. KOHNERT: Klassenbildung, p. 487).
66 cf. Peter MORTON-WILLIAMS: The Yoruba Ogboni cult in Oyo, in: Africa 30 (1960) and Nathaniel FADIPE: The sociology of the Yoruba. Ibadan University Press 1970 on the traditional Ogboni soci-

Although the *ndakógbòyá* is still a „secret society" in the sense in which Nadel used this expression,[67] as the members of the lodges still guard certain important secrets on the rules and the magic of the cult, the very source of their power, and as they threaten any adept with serious punishment (even death penalty) should he dare to betray their secrets, the cult can not any longer be described as a „closed society", apart from the still existing strong gender bias. According to the Heads of the lodges in Gbado and Tankpufu, i.e. the two major centres of the cult to the south of the Niger, any self-confident and reliable man who feels strong enough to stand the initiation rites and to keep the secret of the *kútí* (i.e. ritual or magic), may apply for membership. The high initiation fees of former times which rose up to £ 20 (or twice the customary bride price)[68] have been reduced to a token payment of one cock and some 60 Kobos (1 Naira = 100 Kobos) intended for the initiation sacrifice.

The attitude of the villagers towards the *ndakógbòyá* seems to have changed considerably, too. The terrifying influence which the dancing had in former times especially on women has almost gone, as far as I can judge from my limited experience with two performances at Tsambafu and Bida, which may be taken as another sign of the vanishing influence of the cult in general.

And although one of my informants, a high ranking Nupe officer from Koro (east of Patigi), but resident in Ilorin, would not exclude that the *ndakógbòyá* still served the aim of upholding the authority of men over women and to extract resources from them, he also agreed that most villages which still harbour one of the lodges of the society perform their dances mainly to honour a cherished tradition.

It remains to be added that now, as in the past, the purpose of the masquerade is not restricted to social entertainment or to fighting actual cases of witchcraft, but is still used to ensure the well-being of the village at large, e.g. the cult pleads for rain at times of drought, helps women to become pregnant, or protects the villagers against illness.[69] When there was a change in the District Headship at Doko in 1976, even the compound of the D. H. (District Head or *hakŋmi*, pl. *hàkŋmai*) had to be cleansed by the *ndakógbòyá* to protect the new D. H. against any evil magic which might have been placed in his official residence during the interregnum. Although the new District Head – as usual belonging to the Majigi royal family in Bida – ridiculed this performance a bit in the presence of a European like me, he was nevertheless eager to point out that he is the major authority over all movements of the *ndakógbòyá* in his district. He claimed that even the *Etsu* Nupe had to consult him before he could send the mask to any village in his district. But, according to him, the villages preferred to handle all witchcraft cases which they couldn´t settle themselves through mediation by the D. H.

Therefore, it is no wonder that during the three years of tenure (1973-76) of the D. H. at Doko, the *ndakógbòyá* of Kusogi (which was under his jurisdiction) was not called at

---

ety, and The Sun, of 05. & 19.08.2004, as well as other Nigerian newspaper reports in the following month on the Okija-affaire. Cf. my first article in this volume.

67 cf. NADEL: Nupe Religion, p. 196.
68 cf. NADEL: Nupe Religion, p. 194.
69 cf. NADEL: Nupe Religion, p. 195.

Fig. 4: The local ruler of the ndakógbòyá, *the District Head of Jima/Doko, at his home, surrounded by his councillors (in 1976).*

all for the purpose of detecting and punishing witches, although the D. H. himself had to deal with three witchcraft cases during this time, according to his own statement. The first happened in Ebagi, a hamlet south of Doko, where he was called at night because the inhabitants had accused a witch of poisoning the village well. The second and third cases occurred in Doko itself; the issues centred around marriage disputes (i.e. jealousy and adultery). The D. H. asserted that he was capable of telling at once – if necessary with the help of the *Sagi* – whether the accused was a witch or not. And, in the D. H.'s own words, „because the peasants still fear and respect my authority, I normally succeed in convincing the evil-doers to loosen their spell on their victims, - otherwise they are threatened with jail". As, however, only Upper Area Courts, like that of Bida, are allowed to deal with witchcraft cases, simple Area Courts, such as that of Doko, Kutigi, or Mokwa, can make just preliminary investigations. One of such cases in Doko happened in 1975 and involved one local policeman who had an argument with a prostitute whom he „forgot" to pay. According to the D. H., she tried to impress the policeman with the following incident: Some days after the dispute, the policeman took a kettle as he wanted to clean his mouth and hands for prayer and suddenly heard a voice, coming from nowhere saying, „Don't touch me, I am poisoned". Though he was surprised and startled he tried again, but the warning was repeated. The case was reported to the local Judge and investigated with the help of the *Sagŋ*. The detected „witch" confessed of being responsible for this incident and of wanting to teach her customer a lesson. This example may serve as an illustration that witches are supposed not just to kill randomly, but that as a rule there is a kind of „Dantesque appropriateness" between the offence of the victim and the punishment by the witch, as Salamone observed already concerning the neighbouring Gbagyi.[70]

The range of such „punishments" is said to stretch from impotence to pauperisation and murder. This became evident in a case related to me by a Hausa assistant to the Irrigation Officer in Patigi: In 1976 the Irrigation Officer laid off some of his workers for unknown reasons. Two weeks later he had a road accident under strange circumstances, escaping narrowly with his life. Some days later, my informant overheard a conversation between two of the sacked Nupe workers in which one of them boasted of having bewitched the officer in causing the accident expressively to serve as a first warning, but that this „idiot" would not escape so easily the second time. It seems to be noteworthy that this time the self-confessed „witch" was a male, who in addition belonged to the *ndakógbòyá* society, according to his own words. This indicates the general ambivalence of many Nupe towards medicine-men or witch finders that they often equate – unconsciously or not – with witches themselves, as we shall see later in detail on Gbagyi medicine-men.[71]

How many of such or similar cases are brought to the courts annually, or whether the number is increasing or decreasing over the years is difficult to tell.[72] But since most Nupe peasants are still bewildered by the ambivalent attitude of Western educated judges towards the handling of witchcraft cases, and as they do not feel sure about the intentions of the existing law[73], it is doubtful that there is asignificantly larger amount of witchcraft cases handled by the courts today compared with the 1930s. As in the past, the courts are most likely to be involved only if witchcraft cases assume strong political overtones, or if serious offences, like murder, were committed. The following two case histories may serve as an illustration:

The first case, which got nationwide attention, happened in spring 1973 in Mwuo, a remote village at the western border of Nupeland.[74] As usual, there are different versions of the story. According to one version the victim was a 28 year old patent medicine seller, born in a Christian family and a staunch member of the UMCA (United Missionary Church of Africa) in a village, whose population was almost equally made up of Moslems and Christians. The medicine seller, G., had a quarrel with his mother and other co-villagers, possibly because of his recent marriage with an 18 year old girl, and was warned by his brother, a pastor at the Salaka Bible School, to leave his village over New Year. However, G. disregarded this warning and subsequently fell seriously ill. Two days later he died. The villagers suspected that he died as a result of some „evil prac-

---

70 cf. SALAMONE: Gbagyi Witchcraft, p. 9.
71 cf. similar SALAMONE: Gbagyi Witchcraft, p. 15.
72 Both the former Chief Àlkali of Bida, who was among the members who drafted the Nigerian Penal Code (including section 214 to 219 on ordeal, juju, and witchcraft) and who was one of the chief members of the Emir's Council at the time of the interview, and the Àlkali at the Bida Upper Area Court in 1976 were very reluctant to provide any useful information on this issue.
73 cf. NADEL: Nupe Religion, pp. 163-164.
74 The incident received nationwide publicity, as one Nigerian magazine carried a photo-story on this witchcraft case; cf. „Mystery man of Mwuo", in: „Spear - Nigeria's National Magazine", July 1973, pp. 15-18.

tices", they buried him in the village cemetery after a funeral service conducted at the local church. Four months later, the dead and buried man was found alive again – though distressed and confused – in the bush near Ndafu, a hamlet some 18 miles from Mwuo. The story of this apparent rise from the dead spread rapidly, and the Local Administration – fearful of the religious and political disorder that might entail this story - instructed all religious leaders in Mwuo to tell their congregation that no human being could ever arise from the dead. The case of the „resurrected" man was later investigated by the police of Mokwa, a medical officer from Bida General Hospital, and even the *Etsu* Nupe himself. A skeleton of doubtful origin from G.'s grave was dug up, which some villagers had found unusually depressed shortly after the burial. It was suspected that the Christian community of Mwuo, or at least its representatives, took part in a religiously motivated campaign to destabilise the traditional (Islamic) authorities. The former Village Head and others were tried in the courts for inciting religious unrest, first at Mokwa, then at Bida and Minna (the division and state capital, respectively). The accused Village Head goz deposed, whereas the victim could apparently coin the newly acquired fame into money. At least, G. owned a Toyota van and ran a prosperous medicine selling business in 1982.[75]

The second case happened long ago, in 1953, but is still of interest because it throws light on the close relationship between Nupe and Gwari witchcraft beliefs, which exist, quite contrary to Nadel's theory[76], at least in the peasants view.[77] The incident took place at Yidna, a Gwari village of Paiko District (neighbouring Badeggi District of the former Bida Division). It centred around accusations of unlawful trials by ordeal administered by three Nupe medicine-men.[78] At that time mass ordeals were also endemic in Nupeland, probably because, with the official prohibition of the witch hunts of the *ndakógbòyá,* the people thought they had no alternative for detecting witches than taking recourse to individual witch finders. The people of Yidna feared that their village was troubled by an evil spirit, which among other things had caused illness and an attempted murder of the *Nákorjí,* the Nupe title of the Village Head of Yidna, when the latter was riding through the bush. In November 1952, the *Nakorjí* sent for three travelling Nupe „witch doctors" (*bocizi*[79]) who had been seen practising in some neighbouring villages (Gawu and Buku). As the *bocizi* had never before been in that area, they first asked the *Sarkin* Paiko, the District Head, for permission to come to Yidna, which was granted after they had sent a tribute of £ 5, as well as a calabash of cola nuts to the D. H.. When the Nupe *bocizi,* two brothers and one of their friends from Bida, who earned their living by such extortion tours, arrived at the village, they told the population that the *Sarkin* Paiko had given them authority to dispense a liquid potion for eve-

---

75 However, according to another local source of information, G. was later accused of being a witch himself because two children died shortly after he treated them with an injection.
76 cf. NADEL: Witchcraft, p. 267.
77 cf. similar SALAMONE: Gbagyi Witchcraft, p. 4.
78 cf. here and in the following: NAK, MINPROF. 2478, „Preliminary inquiry: Regina vs. Moh. Kusogi Bida and 5 others", trial at the court of Minna, Jan. 16, 1953.
79 Medicine men or „witch doctors" are called *boci* (pl. *bocizi*) or *cigbeci* (pl. *cigbecizi*) in Nupe; the suffix *ci* indicating the actor or owner of the medicine (*cigbe,* in Nupe). The Gwari equivalent is *beki.*

rybody to drink in all the hamlets of his District, which would reveal any witch among the population. Anyone who should refuse to drink their „medicine" would be arrested. The next morning, the whole village assembled in front of the door of the *Nákorji's* compound, and everybody, including babies, had to drink from the potion, mixed from water and different powders by Moh. Kusogi, the leading *boci*. Some of the villagers fell down immediately after drinking the potion, while three of them - all women - died on the spot and were buried the same day. This caused some concern among the *bocizi* because, according to their own statement, all their victims had recovered from similar ordeals in the past, if treated with an antidote (in this case lemon juice). But since the villagers were convinced that the women who died were indeed witches, the travellers could nevertheless collect ransom money or fines from the victims and their relatives, respectively. One unlucky man, whose mother and wife died, had to give £ 3, two lengths of cloth, and a chicken. Others gave a big gown, three lengths of cloth, and five chicken or 35 sh. and a chicken, etc.

It is interesting to note that there was little opposition to the dealings of the *bocizi*, even among the relatives of the deceased victims. When one of them dared to protest, the elders replied: „Why has your mother died, others drank and are still alive?" The husband of another woman who died during the ordeal even agreed that „she died as a consequence of her evil ways" as revealed by the ordeal. And again another villager confessed to one of the *bocizi* that he was an evil person and had attempted to kill the *Nakorji* by witchcraft. Eventually, in spite of the attempt by the villagers to cover-up the incident, the colonial administrators heard about it, albeit by chance.

At about the same time, another famous *boci* called Ndasogba, from Badeggi, used to tour the southern and eastern Districts of Nupeland on invitation of villages senting for him to cleanse their villages from witchcraft. He was known as the leading herbalist in the Cis-Kaduna area in the last two decades of colonial rule and was in the habit of organising public trials to prove the innocence of persons who were suspected of being witches. Reasons for such suspicion were described by the Nupe as follows: If a person is bewitched and falls ill, there is a chance that he (or she) will signify the name of the person who has bewitched him in his dreams. The dream figure will be only dimly recognizable through a column of smoke.[80] However, the victim himself will not be able to remember either his dream or the name he uttered. Therefore, the cooperation of the *boci* or the watcher at the sick-bed is required to note the name of the accused that usually belongs to a person with whom the victim is in close contact. The relatives of the bewitched or the *boci* himself will then visit the accused person and demand the release of his or her spell. Should the accused refuse or deny the accusation, he or she will be

---

[80] cf. „Note on witchcraft in Badeggi District", A.H.M. Kirk Greene, Badeggi, September 24, 1954; included in: NAK, Bida Div., Non-Current Papers, B118, 1933, „Witchcraft cases and anti-witchcraft in Nupe society"; cf. similar, FROBENIUS: Volkserzählungen 9, p. 65. - The reference to smoke in this report probably indicates the use of a certain anti-witchcraft medicine, called *toràri*, which is put beside the sick person on a fire and is supposed to cause the bewitched person to utter the name of the evil spirit. According to the *Etsu* Zugurma, the *toràri* was one of the most powerful anti-witchcraft medicines in the 1980s, and had replaced the *ndakógbòyá*, at least in the Eban/Zugurma area of Nupeland.

forced (normally moral coercion will suffice, as the whole story will be spread round the village) to prove innocence by ordeal. There are two well known Nupe potions applied: *ukpa* and *kpakangici*, made from the powdered bark of a poisonous tree.[81] Similar kinds of witch finding in other parts of the country were already used in the twenties as a means to extort money, as a report from H.M. Irwin indicated. The report was included in the above mentioned memo on witchcraft prepared for the Resident of the Niger Province.[82] Whether this report, together with the sad experience of the extortion tours of the *ndakógbòyá* described above, caused the British Resident to exert some moral pressure on the *Etsu* Nupe is not known. But it is likely that the Colonial Officers persuaded the *Etsu* and his council to take a closer look at such mass ordeals. At least in the above mentioned case of Ndasogba the *Etsu* told his District Heads that such public trials would spread only worries and fears among their people and would cause disunity among them. He ordered the *hakimai* (D. H.) to announce that any community inviting witch doctors, as well as those who would apply the ordeal, would be seriously punished. Apparently, this order was implemented immediately. After Ndasogba was caught a third time, the *Àlkalin Àlkaki* of Bida fined him, as well as the inhabitants of Tswakoko, the village which had invited him, £ 5.[83]

However, this reflects just the official handling of the subject. Similar to the prohibition of tribute payments (under the pretext of *zakkat*) – which the British tried to enforce in vain because it ran contrary to the interest of the ruling class[84] – the traditional authorities apparently were not very eager to stop the business of „witch finders". Even after the death of the Ndasogba, other travelling *bocizi* continued to perform „witch trials" in Nupeland unmolested.

One well-known *boci* in western Trans-Kaduna, who continued to earn his living in 1982 by touring villages on invitation, was the Ndagena of Ebi. His junior brother, a *boci* himself at Mokwa, told me that both of them, assisted by other villagers, conducted a witch hunt in Mokwa just four weeks before my arrival. Altogether four witches were detected and punished. They were all females, one old and three younger women, married, but from different families. None of them could be called rich, though each of them had her sideline occupation, e.g. petty trading in foodstuffs. All cases centred around conflicts within the extended family. In two of the cases the mother of the family head

---

81 In the court case against Moh. Kusogi, mentioned above, the potion, analysed by a Government chemist, revealed a lethal dose of *aworoso*, which is sometimes used as a purgative in a smaller dose.

82 „Sometimes, however, this belief in witchcraft was only used as an excuse for raising money by the chiefs. When someone died, the relatives when bearing away the corpse would approach as if voluntary the door of a certain man, who would at once be accused of causing the death of the deceased. The victim would always be a man of means which would be appropriated by the Chief. The latter would previously give his instructions to the deceased's relatives and probably a present also for their pains... The natural effect of such a custom was to militate against the acquisition of wealth, as its possession was a source of temptation to the accuser. Even today no pagan will make a display of wealth..." H.M. Irwin, D.O., „Extract from Kumbashi Assessment Report, 1920", NAK, MINPROF, M. 1228, 1934.

83 cf. the correspondence of *Etsu* Nupe, Muh. Ndayako, on „Ndasogba Mai-Maganin Maita" and related subjects, Nov. 1952 to Feb. 1954; included in: NAK, Bida Div., Non-Current Papers, B 118.

84 cf. KOHNERT: Klassenbildung, pp. 99-119.

Fig. 5: A convicted 'witch' - One of the three framed photographs of detected 'witches' displayed, together with a diploma, certifying that the owner was a recognised witch-doctor, on the wall of the compound of a boci in Mokwa in 1982.

was accused of having bewitched her son and husband „to give his mother money", i.e. to guarantee the social security of his mother. In another case a small schoolboy fell seriously ill. He was allegedly bewitched by a barren older woman living in the same compound, said to be jealous of the fertility of her female co-residents. In both cases, the accused women „confessed" their evil deeds and loosened their spell, i.e. their „victims" recovered from their illness.[85] Whether these confessions were made without coercion is doubtful, last but not least, because my informants in Mokwa agreed that if an accused person tried to argue, he or she would be forced to prove his or her innocence by an ordeal, applied either by the *ndakógbòyá* or a *boci*. In the Mokwa region the accused was given a certain potion, called *fien* or *tagan*, which is meant to cause him to confess im-

---

85 According to the elders of Mokwa there are seven different kinds of illness caused by witchcraft in Nupeland: (1) *shamu*, i.e. stomach trouble which causes severe pain to the victim right from birth; (2) *zana-zana* which can be seen in the eyes; (3) *lan-jwan-jwa* which is witnessed through continuous headache; (4) *esu*, i.e. severe pains under the ribs; (5) *wuregi*, an illness which paralyses the whole body; (6) *kparagi*, i.e. convulsions which are lethal for children; (7) *bogun*, which will cause the body of the victim to swell up so that he loses his power.

mediately if he or she is a witch. Innocent people, they say, do not feel anything if they drink the medicine.[86]

Beside payments in cash and/or kind to the *boci* or the *ndakógbòyá*, witches were also punished by flogging, and in more serious cases by exposing them naked in the streets of the village in broad daylight still in 1982. First of all, however, they were ordered to repair the harm they were accused of having done. The failure or success to obey this order was a decisive element in determination of the degree of the punishment. Though at least Nadel's informants maintained that a witch was never killed, since that would entail only revenge by other witches,[87] this information was apparently falsified by the evidence of violent clashes connected with the „witchcraft riots" in Bida in 1931, when even troops had to be called out to quell the riots.[88] Also one of my informants, a Nupe from Kataeregi, confessed that as a young boy he had taken part in the stoning of a witch in his village. The witch in question was an old woman who confessed to having bewitched her co-wife out of jealousy. This case, however, happened in the late thirties and it seems unlikely that such an incidence of stoning would occur today, although one should not rule out the possibility, last but not least in view of the heated international controversy around the stoning verdicts of Sharia courts, related to cases of adultery, in other Northern Emirates in 2003 and 2004. Generally speaking, according to the elders of Mokwa the most serious cases will nowadays be handed over to the police and the courts.

The *bocizi* are often assisted in their search for evil magic by the Village Head and the *Lelu* of affected villages. The use of the word *Lelu* is ambiguous in Nupe. In pre-*jihad* times (i.e. before 1806) it denoted the office of the Head Woman of a village, and it still refers to the supposed spiritual qualities of this woman.[89] But as many Nupe villagers used to call any woman who is suspected of being experienced in witchcraft *Lelu*, rather in an abusive sense,[90] the existence of a *Lelu* in a village will often be denied by the inhabitants. Therefore it is doubtful whether the assertion of the *Majin Dodo* of Kusogi that today the *Lelu* is found only in Patigi Emirate is valid. At least other informants, natives of Doko, insisted that they still have a *Lelu* in this village, which is only a few kilometres from Kusogi. In Dabba, a medium-sized village in Trans-Kaduna, they even have four *Lelu*, one for each of the four village wards. These women were so much re-

---

86 Yet another ordeal, known as *wasa*, was applied in the Doko area. This is a snake bite medicine, the belief being that a true witch would be killed or at least frightened and subdued by a snake after drinking the medicine (cf. also NADEL: Nupe Religion, p. 188). As the former D. H. of Doko told me, the *wasa* medicine was still applied in Jima/Doko District in 1982, also to detect thieves. The same is valid for the *sòrògi* dance, mentioned already by Nadel (Nupe Religion, p. 188), which was still applied as recently as 1982 in villages south of the Niger, to detect and to punish witches, who are supposed to get a swollen throat from watching the dance, according to the *Lile* of Gbado. The ordeal where the suspect had to scratch the ground with his finger-nails until blood appeared from under his nails (cf. FROBENIUS: Volkserzählungen 9, p. 66. NADEL: Nupe Religion, p. 188), however, disappeared some generations ago, at least in the Mokwa region.
87 cf. NADEL: Nupe Religion, p. 188.
88 cf. NADEL: Byzantium, p. 127. IDEM.: Nupe Religion, p. 163.
89 cf. NADEL: Nupe Religion, pp. 167-168.
90 cf. memo of M. Aliyu on witchcraft and related subjects" NAK, Bida Div., Non-Current Papers, B118, 1938.

Fig 6: The author during his interviews with Nupe peasants in Dabba, 1976.

spected by the *Nkó*, the Head Woman of Dabba and a great herbalist herself, that she had to consult them first before granting me an interview, out of fear that otherwise these women would take her to task because of single handed decisions on such important matter providing information to strangers. It is therefore evident that many Nupe villages still have their *Lelu*, but as witchcraft remains such a sensitive issue, people would rather avoid calling her by that title.

Anyway, everybody agreed that a *Lelu* is not sufficient to check evil magic at the village level. Despite the relatively dense network of „witch finders" described above, most Nupe authorities ehich I interviewed insisted that the number of witches in Nupeland must have increased over time. Three reasons were given to explain this development. The first two of these explanations seem to be quite obvious with regard to the inner logic of occult belief systems: Firstly, population growth caused a growing effective demand for witchcraft medicine. The growth of population meant that, other figures being equal, the absolute number of witches would double every 25 years.[91] In addition, it was said that the incidence of witchcraft per village increased also in relative terms. This was explained by the growing impact of the market economy and the aftermath of the Nigerian Oil Boom (both in terms of economic growth and the spread of corruption and social differentiation), which had its side effects in Nupeland, too; more money became available in the villages, leading to more opportunities and a greater effective demand for witchcraft medicine.[92] The Nupe as a rule believe that witchcraft is not necessarily hereditary since there are various methods of acquiring it.[93] The most common method, they say, is to buy the *cigbè*, either from other witches or from a *cigbèci* or *boci*, the crucial implication being that the evil deed of the witch is intended. In view of the legal situation no *boci* would ever admit openly selling such witchcraft medicine, but nevertheless some offer „guestimates" on the costs involved, namely some £ 5 in the

---

91 Population increase in Nigeria was estimated at about 2 to 2.5% per annum in 1982 in the countryside and 3% in the urban areas. This would imply that the population - and *ceteris paribus* with it, the absolute number of witches - doubled within one generation (or every 23 to 35 years).

92 The Nupe have various names for such medicines (*cigbe*): They call them *ega(n)*, like witchcraft in general, *eshe*, like the name for male witches, or *bàdufù*, literally, „dark place" (cf. NADEL: Nupe Religion, pp. 158-159).

93 cf. NADEL: Nupe Religion, pp. 165-166, 170.

olden days, probably Naira 400 - 600 in 1982.[94] Therefore, my informants reasoned, someone who is really poor could hardly be a witch. But you never know, since a young girl could have been initiated into this sinister occupation free of charge by her mother, who was already a witch.

The growth of the market economy also played a crucial part in the closely related reasoning of some of my informants, that with the Oil Boom and its socio-economic effects spreading well into the country-side, it became easier to accumulate capital, the impact could be easily seen in the growing farms of rich peasants and capitalist absentee farmers and the flourishing business of big traders all over Nupeland. But the growing social differentiation, even within the village,[95] raised the envy of the poorer villagers, and some of them accused their wealthy neighbours of having enriched themselves by evil means. However, as we have already seen, this widely reported „natural effect" of witchcraft accusations to militate against unequal acquisition of wealth, is nothing new. It was already noted by British colonial officers in the 1920's (cf. the touring notes of H. M. Irwin, D. O., quoted above), and it is common in other African societies, too.[96] However, there is no empirical evidence available to back the working hypothesis that witchcraft accusation as a means of defending traditional egalitarian community structures against the intrusion of rural capitalism in Nupeland increased in importance over time, relative to other factors, like jealousy, greed.

The most worrying local explanation for the growing incidence of witchcraft accusations in Nupeland was given by „Papa Angulu", a former Reverend of the Church Missionary Society (CMS) at Doko. His account was confirmed later by similar reasoning of other informants and runs as follows: In view of the official ban of the *ndakógbòyá* and of witchcraft ordeals, many Nupe were afraid to be left unprotected against the evil intentions of the witches, now supposed to spread all over the country without any effective control. In addition, the power and influence of the *ndakógbòyá* and the *Lelu* deteriorated due to other reasons listed above. Under these adverse circumstances, it might happen that a desperate family head or a mother would feel pressed to resort him- or herself to witchcraft to protect the family against evil magic from outsiders. The argument behind this reasoning being that it is possible to drive out the devil with Beelzebub – similar to the concept of the *Lelu* and the *ndakógbòyá*.[97] However, this could lead to the tragic situation that a mother, in her despair about an actual incidence of witchcraft, might see no alternative than to commit a ritual murder, either to appease the witches, or

---

94 FROBENIUS: Volkserzählungen 9, p. 68, mentioned that a „Boschi" would ask a price of 30,000 cowries in 1909, i.e. roughly the equivalent of the price of a slave in pre-colonial times.

95 cf. Dirk KOHNERT: Rural Class Differentiation in Nigeria - Theory and Practice, in: Afrika-Spectrum 14 (1979), 3, pp. 295-315. IDEM.: Klassenbildung.

96 cf. SALAMONE: Gbagyi Witchcraft on the Gbagyi (Gwari). PARRINDER: Religion, p. 54 on the Yoruba. Brantley (1979:131/32) and D.J. PARKIN: Politics of Ritual Syncretism: Islam among the Non-Muslim Giriama of Kenya, in: Africa 40 (1979), 3, pp. 217-233, 223 on the Giriama of Kenya. COMAROFF / COMAROFF: Alien-Nation on South Africa.

97 cf. NADEL: Nupe Religion, p. 191.

as a precondition for acceptance into the witch order as the Nupe see it.[98] Since the easiest available victims to get at for a mother are likely to be young children (notably young girls) of the own extended family, especially the kin of her husband or co-wives, she was said to be placed before the tragic choice, either to kill one of her own relatives in order to be able to protect the rest of the family against the evil intentions of co-witches, or of leaving the family unprotected.[99] This indicates that there existed also altruistic reasons for practising witchcraft, beside the usual selfish reasons given, like greed or jealousy. Regarding the logic fabric of Nupe religion, this certainly had serious repercussions concerning the evaluation of the commited witchcraft by the relatives and neighbours of the witch as well as by the *bocici,* and may be, even the Alkali courts. Besides it is an additional explanation, why in the view of the Nupe, the evilness of the witch is so often directed against his or her husband's or co-wives' kin. And as the woman is considered to be the traditional keeper of the family by the Nupe, this was finally given by my informants as an explanation why more women than men are accused of witchcraft.[100]

Towards a new conception of Nupe witchcraft

In summary, a consistent local concept of Nupe witchcraft, if existent, would have to distinguish between at least two different kinds of witchcraft: First, the employment of black magic – e.g. the sacrifice of own family members – for good ends, i.e. to protect the rest of the family.[101] And second, the use of black magic to harm anyone in order to

---

98 cf. NADEL: Nupe Religion, p. 165; a more prosaic, but no less tragic, situation would arise if a family head or a mother, in desperate need of protection against witchcraft, were requested by the consulted witch-doctor to commit ritual murder in order to get parts of the human body considered to be necessary for the preparation of an anti-witchcraft medicine. Cases of ritual murder are reported periodically in the newspapers, not only from Nupeland, but from all parts of Nigeria, one of the outstanding cases being the Okija-cult incident in Anambra state, mentioned before. The spread and commercialisation of so called *muti*-murder, i.e. ritual murder for the purpose of enhancing the business success of greedy businessmen, has been widely commented in Southern Africa in recent years (e.g. in South Africa, Tanzania, Zimbabwe); it has already been subject to scholarly analyses (cf. COMAROFF / COMAROFF: Alien-Nation).

99 Exactly this protection of the family against witchcraft might be the strange „special" and „unintelligible pleasure" which FROBENIUS (Volkserzählungen 9, p. 67) narrated 80 years ago from the Nupe in Mokwa in the following, somewhat confused statement on the reasons and methods by which the male (!) would-be Nupe witch acquired his evil craft from the *boci*: „If a man has many children, he may very well fear for them, or else entertain the hope, by means of their help, namely in sacrificing some of them, to gain a special pleasure, which is of course unintelligible to us ... The man (asks the boci, D.K.): 'Give me a good medicine which I can take home ... and which I can use for me and for my children ... Give me a good Tschibe (i.e. cigbe, D.K.) so that I can prove my power to everybody.',, The medicine which the family head eventually gets from the 'Bassa-tschi' or 'Boschi' has to be eaten by the witch himself 'and all his children'. (Translation from German, D.K.). Probably, Frobenius confused and mixed the protective and the greedy reasons for acquiring witchcraft medicine, which, however, had significantly different repercussions in the logic of Nupe religion.

100 At Mokwa, my informants estimated the proportion of male to female witches to be one male (*eshe*) to 20 female (*ega(n)* or *gaci*, as witch is called in general in Nupe) in a gang of witches in 1976. But as the female cannot kill without the help of the male (cf. NADEL: Nupe Religion, pp. 169-170), the latter were considered to be more dangerous. However, as nowadays the males are said normally not to kill themselves, they are hardly ever detected and punished.

101 It goes without saying that even in this case the end does not justify the means, killing of family members or co-villagers, for whatever reason, is regarded by any Nupe as a capital crime.

satisfy unsocial, selfish desires, such as greed, envy, jealousy, private redress, or other sinister reasons (killing for fun is also held to be possible, according to my informants). Apparently there are – contrary to Nadel's comparative witchcraft theory[102] – close similarities between these two types of Nupe witchcraft and the *nwando* and *abujanke* witchcraft of the neighbouring Gwari (Gbagyi). My Nupe informants agreed to this, though they do not distinguish the two types by separate names. However, among the Gwari the *nwando* witchcraft is restricted to personal gains resulting from witchcraft of males within the family, and *abujanke* is restricted to female witchcraft against outsiders or social enemies for reasons of revenge.[103] But it seems necessary to point out some differences between these two indigenous witchcraft theories. First, among the Nupe there is not such a strong correlation between the type of witchcraft and the sex of a witch, the victim, and the client, respectively, as among the Gwari.[104] Second, the Nupe do not differentiate between the „real evil-doer" (i.e. the client of the witch) and the witch, who performs the evil for him, like the Gwari. Again, this separation between the witch and his or her client in Salamone's witchcraft account seems to be more of a theoretical nature, as the Gwari hold that in practice the real evil-doer is the person who intends to harm other people by the help of either a witch or a witch-doctor.[105] This is similar to the Nupe belief, where the would-be-witch has to consult the *boci* or another witch before her/his evil intentions can become effective. The most sinister effect of witchcraft, the murder of one's enemies or rivals, depends anew in each of the case on the co-operation of the *boci*.[106] At other occasions the Nupe witch may act directly, without the help of others, provided that he/she has been initiated into the witch order, again depending on the *boci*.[107] Third, whereas in Gwari society, according to Salamone, witchcraft itself acts as a means of social control, it seems that among the Nupe, witchcraft accusation, i.e. the anti-witchcraft activities, are meant to fulfil this function. This thesis may need some explanation: According to Salamone, the Gwari witches are „tragic" figures. They get their evil power already with their mothers' milk, and their victims have been selected for them by their clients. These clients again seek revenge for a harm previously caused by the victim. So the witch's victims are not innocent, on the contrary, certain social norms of Gwari society have been violated by every victim.[108]

---

102 cf. NADEL: Witchcraft.

103 cf. SALAMONE: Gbagyi Witchcraft, pp. 6-8, 12.

104 In Gwari witchcraft theory the client is the „real evil-doer" who consults the witch (or the witch-doctor) and selects the victim for him/her. However, it may be that Salamone overstated this point, as his case histories underline that this correlation between sex and type of witchcraft is a vague „general tendency" (cf. SALAMONE, ibid.).

105 cf. SALAMONE: Gbagyi Witchcraft, p. 10.

106 cf. NADEL: Nupe Religion, pp. 169-170.

107 However, it remains an open question, why – contrary to the Nupe – the Gwari should punish not the „ real evil-doer" but their partners in crime (i.e. the consulted witch) as Salamone (Gbagyi Witchcraft, pp. 10-11) maintains. This is even more puzzling, as the Gwari say – contrary to the Nupe – that one becomes a witch not by intention but by birth, unconsciously and involuntary (cf. SALAMONE, Gbagyi Witchcraft, p. 9).

108 cf. SALAMONE: Gbagyi Witchcraft, p. 5, 13). Those violations are „jealousy, hatred, refusing to share good fortune, withholding love, injustice, and resorting to magic to advance your fortune to

As shown above, under certain conditions also the Nupe are said to employ black magic against victims who openly set aside the customary social norms of Nupe society, thus punishing the social deviant, or at least accused of having done so. This happens especially in cases of rich people, who refuse to share their resources in times of hardship. Even in such cases, where witchcraft against outsiders is employed to serve good ends, the witches would be considered as evil persons because they seek to settle their grievances individually and by illegitimate force. This egoistical impudent use of individual power, however, is contrary to the social norms of Nupe religion. As in most African societies, the prerogative of punishing enemies of the society is restricted to the community, the state, or its representatives. In this respect there is no difference between the Nupe and the Gwari.[109] For the Nupe, however, the important point is that the use of power is not considered as such to be evil – as maintained by Salamone for the Gwari.

On a theoretical level, the evil embodied in the illegitimate use of individual power for selfish purposes, is a necessary, but not sufficient condition of witchcraft within the realm of the occult belief system of the Nupe. Other things being equal, anti-witchcraft cults are a means for a society to effect sanctions against egoistic private redress, which represents the illegitimate use of individual force; illegitimate, of course, only from the stand-point of the dominant ideology, which reflects more often than not the ideology of the rulers. However, in different socio-economic formations this could have a completely different meaning which may be camouflaged by seemingly insignificant changes in the appearance of witch purge.

Under the conditions of the communal mode of production, e.g. among the stateless village communities of the Nupe *zányi* (i.e. the „pure" Nupe) in pre-Edegi times up to the 15th century,[110] such socially organised witch accusations might have been used as a direct defence against the usurpation of private power by despotic invaders (like Edegi, cf. the first legend quoted above), similar to witchcraft accusations in other parts of Nigeria, as among the Tiv of the „Middle Belt".[111] Under the slave (or semi-feudal) mode of production of the 18th and 19th century they were used by the Nupe state, first as a method of securing and consolidating the appropriation of power from the gentile organisation.[112] Afterwards, during a period, stretching from the Nupe *jihad* (i.e. during the 19th century) well into the colonial mode of production (i.e. the first half of the 20th

---

the detriment of another. All can be reduced to the formulation that violators have not acted like true Gbagyi" (ibid., p. 13). – This statement raises some doubts again: According to the case histories that Salamone provides as examples to clarify his point (ibid., p. 9), at least jealousy and hatred were motives of the witches and their clients, respectively, not of their victims. In fact, the latter interpretation would appear more reasonable and is common not only among the Nupe, but also in many other African societies. However, this interpretation would fail to back Salamone's thesis that among the Gwari the witches act as agents of social control.

109 cf. SALAMONE: Gbagyi Witchcraft, p. 15.
110 cf. NADEL: Byzantium, pp. 19-20, 25, 73.
111 cf. TSEAYO: Conflict, pp. 57-65.
112 According to narratives of the Nupe, as recorded by Frobenius in 1912, the Head of the *ndakógbòyá* and the *Etsu* Nupe already shared the extortion money, which is said to have been paid in cash (200,000 cowries, i.e. the price of 4 - 7 slaves) and in kind (e.g. cola, goats, chicken) per village, at the time of Edegi (cf. FROBENIUS: Volkserzählungen 9, S. 79-81. Cf. also KOHNERT: Klassenbildung, S. 62-90, on the articulation of the slave mode of production in Nupeland).

century), the witch hunts were used as extortion tours of the *ndakógbòyá*.[113] This might have been welcomed by the ruling class in Bida as a substitute for the expropriation of the peasantry through tribute and slave hunts, which were first restricted and finally forbidden by the British colonial power.[114] Thus the anti-witchcraft cult in this period reconfirmed the power of the ruling class in threefold respect: Apart from acting as a substitute for the punitive expeditions against disloyal or resistant tributary villages, especially in Trans-Kaduna, it was an open sign of the power of local rulers in the profane as well as in the spiritual world and signified their judicial authority even over the occult enemies of the society, as they themselves defined them. And third, it served to disguise their true goals of aggression, of exploiting the peasantry by promoting the witch craze in Nupeland. In this respect, it is revealing that not just individual women were accused, but whole villages, and the Village Head had to pay heavy ransom to the members of the lodges. Quite often, the villagers appealed to the *Etsu* Nupe, to order the *Maji(n) Dodo* to recall his servants.[115] But in fact, the *Etsu* himself was considered to be the prime instigator of the extortion tours of the *ndakógbòyá*, as mentioned above. This lends further support to the thesis that anti-witchcraft cults among the Nupe were principally based on class antagonism and only to a lesser extent on gender-specific cleavages, although the latter should by no means be excluded from consideration as another determinant.

However, I do not think that it is necessary to take sides, either for or against cognitive, political, feminist, or any other „pure" witchcraft theory. All of then are likely to be too restrictive, although each of them may contain valid arguments. The point is, that anti-witchcraft movements may change their content and meaning over time, although their outer appearance remains the same; a change which is closely related to and interdependent with the different modes of production in which they are embedded.

It seems equally important to note that witchcraft accusations themselves may not only have served opposite ends under different modes of production, but might also have done so in quite different manners, i.e. the societies concerned, in adhering to the *ndakógbòyá*, used quite different social or socio-psychological mechanisms to make their ends meet.

As Nadel[116] rightly observed, Nupe peasants, similar to peasants all over Africa, do not face the choice between faith and knowledge concerning the explanation of the realities of their life. They generally believe that hard work and good weather will provide a good harvest, but may hold that under certain conditions good or evil spirits would bring the same results. Notwithstanding the fact that in African as well as in Western societies, religious or magic and scientific knowledge are complementary to rather than exclusive. This absence of conflict between the supernatural and natural science be-

---

113 Already CROWTHER / TAYLOR: Gospel, 1859, p. 215, who were among the first missionaries to arrive in Nupeland, wrote about the big mask (*gunnukó*) of the *ndakógbòyá* in the Rabba-Mokwa-Region of Trans-Kaduna: „These (Gunoko) dance about from village to village and receive cowries. They exercise some tyrannical influence over the people during the time of their appearance."
114 cf. KOHNERT: Klassenbildung. MASON: Foundation.
115 cf. NADEL: Nupe State, p. 441. IDEM.: Nupe Religion, p. 196.
116 NADEL: Nupe Religion, pp. 4-5.

comes relevant on different levels of explanation. It is against this background that I would like to forward three working hypotheses which would challenge Nadel's witchcraft theory if they should prove to be valid.

First, the anti-witchcraft cult among the Nupe was created in the beginning as a direct means of defence against an aggressor, i.e. the Nupe openly pointed at the true enemy of the community whom they tried to eliminate; therefore, at this stage of development of Nupe society, anti-witchcraft accusations would be misinterpreted as symptoms of mental stress in the society. Second, even if one were to agree that witchcraft accusations of the Nupe were developed to cover social frustrations and anxieties, it does not necessarily follow that they are to be interpreted as pathological symptoms of the society, i.e. as an (social) illness which had to be cured. If, as I maintained at the beginning, under certain circumstances (e.g. anti-colonial witchcraft movements, accusations against selfish accumulation of resources), witchcraft accusations act to attack directly or indirectly (through scapegoats) true enemies of the society, they might prove to be a powerful antidote – serving to prevent the destruction of the valid social structure. The fact that from the Western point of view of rational science there exists better medicines (i.e. social strategies) may not be of great help to the stakeholders, as long as the actual relations of production in which they are embedded, do not favour the development of such a superior social medicine. Third, socially organised witchcraft accusations (e.g. organised by anti-witchcraft cults) are to be interpreted as pathological symptoms of social conflicts only if they are mainly used (consciously or unconsciously) by dominant forces in a society to repress or exploit other social groups, i.e. if they serve the same purpose as ideologies.[117] In this respect, the degree of ritualisation of the witch hunt may serve as an indicator of the strength of the ideological component of such a purge:[118] a high degree, like that of the *ndakógbòyá* performances described by Frobenius[119] and Nadel,[120] indicating a strong exploitative character, and a comparatively low degree, like that of the current performances of the *ndakógbòyá* lodges (see above), pointing to a diminishing exploitative content. Only in this context do witch hunts tend to canalise social antagonism by diverting the interest from the real source of the conflicts. But to stress it again, „canalise" does not mean that they solve the conflict. In the long run they rather tend to build up social tensions even further. Finally, it goes without saying that the Durkheimian methodology of „concomitant variations", i.e. to detect relevant social divergences by further, concomitant divergences – a method which, according to Nadel[121] „any enquiry concerned with social facts must employ", will be meaningful in the latter two cases only.

---

117 Here, 'ideology' is not meant in the totalitarian Mannheimian sense, but in the stricter sociological meaning of wrong or dependent consciousness.
118 A.J. BERGENSEN: Political witch hunts: The sacred end the subversive in cross-national perspective. American Sociology Review, 42 (2), 1977, pp. 220-233.
119 FROBENIUS: Volkserzählungen 9, pp. 65-68, 78-82.
120 NADEL: Nupe Religion, pp. 188-201.
121 NADEL: Witchcraft, p. 264.

However, let us be clear about it. Much further and deeper empirical investigation is necessary, before we can arrive at any conclusive theory on the social function and meaning of Nupe witchcraft, especially in its present function and its relation to changes in the past. Currently available information bears more resemblance to some pieces of an incomplete puzzle than to a meaningful picture. The shift from a subsistence to a market economy provoked not only the dissolution of the production unit of the extended family (*efakó*, in Nupe) in favour of smaller consumption units, which could hardly afford to support the sick and „unproductive" elder members. It also led to the deterioration of the economic and social independence of the female members of the farming household.[122] Could it be that the remarkable increase of witchcraft accusations in Nupeland is related to an individualisation of the socialisation-process caused by the growth of the market economy, rural-urban migration, and class differentiation within the peasantry that promotes the personification of evil powers and the apostasy from traditional beliefs in collective actions of gods or one's ancestors?[123] Could it be that the increasing prominence of females as targets of witch accusations in Nupeland over the past two or three generations was caused by the combined effect of the above mentioned socio-economic development patterns, just as during the witch craze in medieval Europe?[124] Was the source of witchcraft accusations against females thus not the jealousy of the male regarding the independent economic and sexual position of the Nupe women in the 1940s[125] but, on the contrary, the growing dependence of the women on their men, whereby the latter were tempted to consolidate their newly acquired power by witchcraft accusations, which may have compensated them for the dim prospects of their own economic future? Could the predominance of accusations against old women as murderers of young children result from a fear of the guilt-ridden young, male and female alike, concerning imaginary (or real) threats of their elders, feeling neglected by their kin? Had the projection of this hatred into witch fantasies been promoted by the fact that still the only legitimate method to question the authority of senior relatives in cases of social conflict within the family was to press them into the role of an outsider? All these, and many more questions await an answer, which could be provided only by painstaking further grass-root research.

---

122 cf. KOHNERT: Klassenbildung, pp. 232-242.

123 A similar argument has been put forward by G. ELWERT (Bauern und Staat in Afrika, Frankfurt 1983) concerning witchcraft movements in rural Benin, and by COMAROFF / COMAROFF (Alien-Nation) concerning Southern Africa.

124 cf. Nachman BEN-YEHUDA: The European witch craze of the 14th to 17th centuries: A sociologist's perspective, in: American Journal of Sociology 86 (1980), 1, pp. 1-31, 17-18.

125 NADEL: Nupe Religion, pp. 172-181.

Erhard Kamphausen

Hexenglauben, Magie und Besessenheitsphänomene in Afrika. Religions- und missionswissenschaftliche Anmerkungen

Abstract

The following text tries to interprete various phenomena of occult experiences like sorcery, magic and spirit possession in the context of African traditional religion (ATR) and philosophy. It is necessary to analyse the supernatural phenomena not from a narrow western perspective but to give cognition to the indigenous frame of reference. African theologians adopt the concepts of traditional religiousness and spirituality – as for example the idea of a divine mystical power – to understand and communicate the experience of the invisible world of spirits and supernatural forces. Today new religious movements of pentecostal and charismatic origin are mushrooming all over the African continent. The members of these movements reject the enlightened expression of Western Christianity and take up ideas of the ATR (African Traditional Religions). Glossolalia, the expulsion of evil spirits, the eradication of witchcraft and sorcery and various rites of healing are integral parts of their religious practice.

Zusammenfassung

Der folgende Beitrag versucht, die verschiedenen Phänomene okkulter Erfahrungen wie Schadenszauber, Magie und Geistbesessenheit im Kontext der afrikanischen traditionellen Religion und Weltanschauung zu interpretieren. Dabei ist es notwendig, die übernatürlichen Erscheinungen nicht einseitig aus westlicher Perspektive zu analysieren, sondern den indigenen Referenzrahmen zu berücksichtigen. Afrikanische Theologen übernehmen die Konzepte traditioneller Religiosität und Spiritualität – wie etwa die Vorstellung von der göttlichen mystischen Kraft –, um die Erfahrungen der unsichtbaren Welt der Geister und anderen übernatürlichen Mächten versteh- und vermittelbar zu machen. Heute breiten sich in Afrika neue religiöse Bewegungen meist pentekostaler und charismatischer Ursprungs explosionsartig aus. Diese Bewegungen lehnen das westliche aufgeklärte Form des Christentums ab und knüpfen die Vorstellungswelt der ATR (African Traditional Religions) an. Glossolalie, die Vertreibung böser Geister, der Kampf gegen Hexerei und Zauberei sowie diverse Heilungsriten sind integrale Bestandteile ihrer religiösen Praxis.

Vorbemerkung

Der kenianische Theologe und einer der Väter der Afrikanischen Theologie,[1] John S. Mbiti beklagt in seinem bahnbrechenden Buch: Afrikanische Religion und Weltanschauung[2] die verzerrenden Darstellungen durch europäische Wissenschaftler gerade im Blick auf das Verständnis religiöser Phänomene wie Hexerei, Zauberei oder Magie: „Man ist unangenehm berührt, wenn man sieht, wie viel Unwissenheit, Vorurteile und Fälschungen in den Büchern, Zeitungen und Unterhaltungen unserer Zeitgenossen zum Ausdruck kommen. Die Diskussion findet zwischen zwei gegnerischen Lagern statt. Im größeren Lager befinden sich jene, die gröbste Unkenntnis, irrige Ideen, übertriebene Vorurteile und eine abschätzige Gesamthaltung an den Tag legen, um den Begriff der mystischen Kraft herabzusetzen und zu schmähen. Das andere, kleinere Lager ist durch ein paar Gelehrte vertreten, die die Ansichten der Afrikaner über diese mystische Kraft, die Ängste, die sie auslöst, sowie ihre Anwendung und Handhabung durch einheimische Spezialisten durchaus ernst nehmen. Die meisten Zerrbilder sind durch europäische und amerikanische Missionare und Kolonialbeamte entstanden."[3]

In der Tat besteht kein Zweifel, dass im wissenschaftlichen Diskurs des 19. und bis weit ins 20. Jahrhundert abwertende Theorien über afrikanische Kultur und Religion kolportiert wurden, die oft von christlichen Missionaren vorgeprägt waren und unkritisch von Vertretern anderer Disziplinen übernommen wurden. Ein unverdächtiger Zeuge ist Georg Friedrich Hegel, der sich zu dem „eigentümlich afrikanischen Charakter" in seinen Vorlesungen über die Philosophie der Geschichte folgendermaßen äußert: „Der Neger stellt, wie schon gesagt worden ist, den natürlichen Menschen in seiner ganzen Wildheit und Unbändigkeit dar; von aller Ehrfurcht und Sittlichkeit, von dem was Gefühl heißt, muss man abstrahieren, wenn man ihn richtig auffassen will: Es ist nichts an das Menschliche anklingende in diesem Charakter zu finden. Die weitläufigen Berichte der Missionare bestätigen dieses vollkommen."[4] Demgemäß charakterisiert Hegel die afrikanischen religiösen Äußerungen im Wesentlichen als „Zauberei", denn „in der Zauberei liegt nun nicht die Vorstellung von einem Gott, von einem sittlichen Glauben, sondern sie stellt dar, dass der Mensch die höchste Macht ist, dass er sich allein befehlend gegen die Naturmacht verhält." Der große, die europäische Geistesgeschichte zutiefst prägende Aufklärer Hegel vermag also „nichts an das Menschliche anklingende" im afrikanischen Wesen zu entdecken; die afrikanische Religion wird von

---

1 Zur Entstehungsgeschichte der Afrikanischen Theologie s. Erhard KAMPHAUSEN: „An den Flüssen Babylons saßen wir und weinten". Die afrikanische Klage über anthropologische Armut, in: Parabel 10/11 (1989), S. 106-117. DERS.: Afrikanische Theologie im Spannungsfeld von Abhängigkeit und Befreiung, in: Ökumenische Rundschau 33 (1984), S. 556-567. DERS: 'African Cry'. Anmerkungen zur Entstehungsgeschichte einer kontextuellen Befreiungstheologie in Afrika / 'African Cry'. Remarks on the genesis of a contextual theology of liberation in Africa, in: Klaus KOSCHORKE / Jens H. SCHJORRING (Hg.): African Identities and World Christianity in the Twentieth Century, Wiesbaden 2006.
2 John S. MBITI: Afrikanische Religion und Weltanschauung, Berlin 1974.
3 MBITI: Afrikanische Religion, 246f.
4 Georg Wilhelm F. HEGEL: Werke in zwanzig Bänden. Bd 12: Vorlesungen über die Philosophie der Geschichte, Frankfurt/M. 1973, S.120ff.

ihm bestimmt als „Zauberei", „Fetischismus" und gar als „Kannibalismus", Begriffe, die in der weiteren Forschungsgeschichte in verschiedenen Varianten immer wieder auftauchen, wenn es um das Verstehen der sog. „Naturreligionen", „primitiven Religionen" etc. geht. Wie Hegel sind auch viele andere Geisteswissenschaftler, die sich zu dem Thema äußerten, nie aus eigener Anschauung zu ihren Beurteilungen gekommen. Keiner von ihnen war jemals in Afrika, sondern sie zogen ausschließlich Berichte von Reisenden und besonders Missionaren zurate.

Die destruktive Rolle der christlichen Mission und der Paradigmenwechsel in der afrikanischen Theologie

Ohne an dieser Stelle ausführlich auf die missionsgeschichtlichen Zusammenhänge eingehen zu können, lässt sich vereinfacht sagen, dass die Haltung der in Afrika tätigen Missionare bestimmt war durch eine scharfe Ablehnung der einheimischen kulturellen und religiösen Traditionen. Man zielte darauf ab, die „heidnischen" Religionen, die meist pauschal als Götzendienst, Dämonenglaube, Zauberei, Magie und Ahnenkult diffamiert wurden, auszumerzen und damit das gesamte kulturelle und soziale Gefüge der afrikanischen Gesellschaften zu zerstören. Es ging ihnen darum, neue, nach dem Vorbild der westlichen Zivilisation ausgerichtete Lebensformen zu schaffen. Afrikanische Glaubensvorstellungen und -praktiken galten als heidnischer Aberglauben, der durch das aufgeklärte Denken Europas überwunden werden sollte. „Man hat unsere Religionen verächtlich gemacht, verspottet und als primitiv und unterentwickelt abgetan", klagt Mbiti. „Im Dunstkreis der Heidenmission wurden sie als Aberglaube, Satanswerk und Höllengeburt verdammt. ... Wer mit einer solchen Einstellung an die Erforschung afrikanischer Religionen herantritt, kommt bestimmt nicht weit. Seine Methode dürfte auch wissenschaftlich und theologisch äußerst dürftig sein."[5]

In Bezug auf die Erforschung afrikanischer Religiosität und Spiritualität erfolgte in der Missionstheologie ein wirklicher Paradigmenwechsel erst in den Studien afrikanischer Wissenschaftler, die sich nach der Unabhängigkeit der meisten Kolonien in den 1960er-Jahren auf den Weg machten, um eigene kontextuelle afrikanische Theologien zu entwickeln. Man suchte nach theologisch verantwortbaren Möglichkeiten, das Christentum europäischer Prägung so in den afrikanischen Boden zu verwurzeln, dass es nicht mehr als Fremdkörper empfunden werden konnte.[6] Diesen Bemühungen vorangegangen waren zwei wegweisende Arbeiten europäischer Forscher, an die die afrikanischen Theologen anknüpften. Es handelt sich dabei um den flämischen Franziskanermissionar Placide Tempels und den französischen Ethnologen Marcel Griaule. In seinem 1945 erschienen Buch „La Philosophie Bantu"[7] versucht Tempels, mithilfe scholastischer Kategorien eine einheitliche afrikanische Ontologie zu rekonstruieren. In dieser Ontologie wird nicht nur die menschliche Lebenswelt, sondern auch das ganze Universum als geordnete, innig zusammenhängende Vielfalt von Kräften verstanden. Das Sein wird bestimmt als „Dynamis", als mystische Kraft, als „force vitale" – wie Tem-

---

5 MBITI: Afrikanische Religion, S. 10f.
6 Vgl. dazu die Publikationen von E. KAMPHAUSEN (wie Anmerkung 1).
7 Placide TEMPELS: Bantu-Philosophie: Ontologie und Ethik, Heidelberg 1956.

pels formuliert. Das Buch von Marcel Griaule mit dem Titel „Dieu d' Eau" erschien 1948 in Paris.[8] In ihm bringt der Verfasser am Beispiel der Mythologie der Dogon überzeugend den Nachweis, dass der afrikanische Mensch nach komplexen, aber wohlgeordneten Vorstellungen und gemäß einem System von Einrichtungen und Riten lebt, in dem nichts dem Zufall oder der Fantasie überlassen ist. Der anfangs zitierte Wissenschaftler John S. Mbiti folgte als erster protestantischer Theologe dem neuen Paradigma und wandte es auch auf die Themenbereiche Geistbesessenheit, Zauberei, Magie und Hexenglauben an.

Die mystische Kraft

Mit John S. Mbiti stimmen heute fast alle afrikanischen Theologen darin überein, dass Geistbesessenheit und Hexerei als genuin religiöse Phänomene zu verstehen sind, die die afrikanische Spiritualität in starkem Maße charakterisieren und das Leben sowohl in den traditionsbestimmten Dorfgemeinschaften, als auch in den modernen Großstädten noch weitgehend beeinflussen. Die religiösen Überzeugungen und Praktiken der meisten Afrikaner gründen in einer bestimmten theologischen Weltsicht oder einer „Philosophie", die in den meisten europäischen sozial- oder kulturwissenschaftlichen Forschungen über Zauberei, Magie und Hexerei nicht adäquat berücksichtigt und ernst genommen wird.[9] Diese Weltsicht geht von der Voraussetzung aus, dass das gesamte Universum von einer mystischen Kraft durchdrungen ist. Das All und damit auch alle Dimensionen der menschlichen Lebenswelt sind in dieser Auffassung als dynamisches „lebendiges" und mit Kraft erfülltes All zu verstehen. Die gesamte psychische Atmosphäre des Lebens ist von der konkreten Erfahrung und dem Glauben an die allgegenwärtige und alles durchdringende mystische Kraft erfüllt. Jeder afrikanische Dorfbewohner und jede afrikanische Dorfbewohnerin ist sich den vielfältigen Äußerungen der im Universum waltenden unbekannten Mächte und schwer bestimmbaren Kräfte durchaus bewusst. Ein Zweifel an deren Realität ist undenkbar. Auch kann die konkrete Erfahrung der mystischen Kraft nicht als Ergebnis des psychischen Zustands der sie erlebenden Menschen

---

8 Marcel GRIAULE: Schwarze Genesis. Ein afrikanischer Schöpfungsbericht. Aus dem Französischen von Janheinz Jahn, Freiburg 1970.

9 Zur einschlägigen Literatur über Afrikanische traditionelle Religionen (ATR) s. E. Idowu BOLAJI: African Traditional Religion. A Definition, London [4]1976. E. IKENGA-METUH: Comparative Studies of African Traditional Religions, Onitsha 1987. N. Q. KING: African Cosmos. An Introduction to Religion in Africa, Belmont, CAL 1986. DERS.: Religions of Africa, New York u. a. 1970. John S. MBITI: Afrikanische Religion und Weltanschauung, Berlin 1974. N. MNDENDE: The Pride of Izizikazi. Some Aspects of African Indigenous Religion, Cape Town 2000. J. K. OLUPONA (Hg.): African Traditional Religions in Contemporary Society, New York 1991. E. G. PARRINDER: African Traditional Religion, London 1962. B. C. RAY: African Religions, Symbol, Ritual, and Community, Englewood Cliffs, NJ 1976. Th. SUNDERMEIER: Nur gemeinsam können wir leben. Das Menschenbild schwarzafrikanischer Religionen, Gütersloh 1988. L.-V. THOMAS / R. LUNEAU: La terre africaine et ses religions, Paris 1975. S. A. THORPE: African Traditional Religions, Pretoria [5]1996. E. M. UKA (Hg.): Readings in African Traditional Religion. Structure, Meaning, Relevance, Future, Bern u. a. 1991. D. WESTERLUND: African Religion in African Scholarship. A Preliminary Study of the Religious and Political Background, Stockholm 1985. D. ZAHAN: The Religion, Spirituality and Thought of Traditional Africa, Chicago u. a. 1979.

erklärt werden. „Die mystische Kraft ist keine Erfindung. Was sie auch sein mag, sie ist Wirklichkeit, eine Wirklichkeit, mit der jederzeit gerechnet werden muss" (Mbiti).

Es handelt sich dabei nicht um ein theoretisches oder abstraktes Konzept, sondern die mystische Kraft wird im Vollzug des Lebens physisch und psychisch als Wirklichkeit erfahren. Damit überschreitet das afrikanische Verständnis von Wirklichkeit den westlichen Dualismus von Diesseitigkeit und Jenseitigkeit, Leib und Seele, Geist und Materie, Transzendenz und Immanenz, sichtbarer und unsichtbarer Welt. Es ist radikal „holistisch".

Die Hierarchisierung der Mächte

Das sichtbare und das unsichtbare Universum oder die mit mystischen Kräften erfüllte Wirklichkeit lässt sich grafisch in fünf konzentrischen Kreisen veranschaulichen. Im Mittelpunkt des Kreises steht der Mensch, genauer der dependente Mensch in Gemeinschaft mit anderen Menschen und verbunden mit der ihn umgebenen sichtbaren Natur. Die ihm nächste Welt, die der Tiere, gehört noch in den sichtbaren Bereich. Doch in mancher Hinsicht sind die Tiere schon Brücke zur unsichtbaren Welt: Als Opfertiere ermöglichen sie die Kommunikation mit den Ahnen. Sie können aber auch als Medien von Schadgeistern und bösen Mächten benutzt werden.

Die unsichtbare Welt der Geister bildet den nächsten Kreis. Auch die Geister gehören noch weitgehend zum Bereich der Menschen, sind sie ihnen aber in vieler Hinsicht überlegen und wirken von außen auf sie ein. Die Geister haben in der Regel leichteren Zugang zum mystischen Kraftfeld als die Menschen. Die Ahnen oder „Totenseelen" stehen den Menschen näher als die Geister, da sie ihnen als Familienmitglieder vertrauter sind. Andererseits haben die Ahnen oft eine größere Nähe zu den Gottheiten als die nichtmenschlichen Geister: Sie bilden quasi eine Brücke zu Gott.

Gott – das höchste Wesen – wird durch den fünften Kreis symbolisiert. Er ist allumfassend und stellt damit die äußere Grenze aller menschlichen Erfahrung dar.

Die Metapher von den konzentrischen Kreisen muss noch weiter differenziert werden. Die fünf Kreise liegen nicht eindimensional auf einer Ebene, sondern sie haben eine vertikale Stufung, die eine pyramidale Hierarchie der Kräfte andeutet. Auch der Zugang zur mystischen Kraft ist hierarchisch geregelt. Gott ist Schöpfer und Ursprung der mystischen Kraft und nur er hat die absolute Verfügungsgewalt über sie. Er lässt es zu, dass sich Geister und Ahnen Teile dieser Kraft aneignen und dass sich auch die lebenden Menschen in beschränktem Maße ihrer bedienen. In der Praxis kann sie also sowohl materiellen bzw. physischen Gegenständen, als auch spirituellen Mächten oder Geistwesen innewohnen und von diesen ausgehend auf die Außenwelt wirken.

Die Ambivalenz der mystischen Kraft

Die mystische Kraft an sich ist weder gut noch böse. Sie hat zwar ihren Ursprung in Gott, aber in der Praxis erfahren die Gläubigen die Auswirkungen dieser Kraft oder Macht durchaus ambivalent.

Denn sie kann sich als gut, Heil bringend und nützlich erweisen, sie kann aber auch Schaden bringen und wird dann als bedrohlich und böse erfahren. Im ersteren Fall dient die mystische Kraft dem Heil und Schutz der Gemeinschaft und wird zur Vorbeugung von Krankheiten und Unglücksfällen und zu produktiven Zwecken verwandt. Die religiösen Funktionsträger wie Priester, Heiler und Wahrsager sind diejenigen, die sich am besten in der Herstellung, Verteilung und Verwendung dieser als Kraftträger wirkenden Gegenstände auskennen und die ihre Kenntnisse zum Wohle der Gemeinschaft einsetzen. Als Eingeweihte verfügen sie über verborgene Informationen, durchdringen die Geheimnisse von Gegenwart und Zukunft und haben die Fähigkeit, Übeltäter, die der Gemeinschaft schaden, zu entlarven. Die Heiler werden konsultiert, wenn die Gemeinschaft oder ein Individuum unter Krankheiten leidet. Man bittet sie auch um Hilfe, wenn Gegenmaßnahmen gegen Unheil erforderlich sind. Die religiösen Funktionsträger verfügen über Mittel bei der Abwehr, Schwächung oder Zerstörung böser Kräfte – einschließlich der Hexerei. Die Heiler verschaffen den Menschen mystische Kraft in Form von Amuletten, Pulvern, Federn, besonderen Beschwörungsformeln oder Einschnitten am Körper. Man muss geschulte Augen haben, um die Bedeutung der Zeichen und der Symbole, die man in afrikanischen Häusern, auf den Feldern, an ihren Besitzgegenständen und auch am Körper findet, zu entdecken, zu lesen und zu entschlüsseln. Es handelt sich dabei in der Regel um Praktiken der weißen oder guten Magie. Die religiösen Spezialisten sagen, dass die von ihnen erschlossene Kraft, die der Gemeinschaft zugutekommt, letzten Endes von Gott stammt. Es gehört zu ihrem Beruf, unmittelbar oder mithilfe der Ahnen und Geister mit Gott in Verbindung zu treten und seine Hilfe zu erflehen.

Der antisoziale Missbrauch der Macht

Die mystische Kraft kann aber auch von gewissen antisozialen Elementen in bösartiger Weise manipuliert und in böswilliger Absicht verwendet werden; sie tritt dann als Schwarze Magie, Zauberei oder Hexerei[10] in Erscheinung. Im afrikanischen Kontext bedeuten Hexerei und Zauberei in erster Linie den antisozialen Gebrauch mystischer Kraft. Von den Zauberern, bösen Magiern und Hexen glaubt man, dass sie Fliegen, Fledermäuse, Vögel und andere Tiere sowie Geister und magische Gegenstände – wie die magische Schlange, die nicht blutet – aussenden, um ihre Zwecke zu erreichen. Sie richten mit dem „bösen Blick" Schaden an, sie vergraben Medizin an einer Stelle, an der das Opfer vorbeigehen muss, sie verstecken in seinem Haus oder seinem Feld magische Gegenstände oder senden ihm aus der Entfernung den Tod. Vielleicht verwandeln sie sich auch selbst in Tiere, um ihre Opfer anzugreifen. Zauberer und Hexen verfügen über okkulte Kräfte, die sie befähigen, Fluch oder Leid, ja den Tod aus der Ferne zu senden, sich in Tiere zu verwandeln (Lykanthropie) und unbelebte Dinge in biologische Lebewesen zu verwandeln. Sie schicken Insekten, Schlangen oder wilde Tiere aus, um ihre Gegner anzugreifen oder sie mit Krankheiten zu behaften. Sie wühlen Gräber auf, um Menschenfleisch oder Menschenknochen für ihre üblen Zwecke zu fleddern, sie beschwören böse Geister, um andere Menschen anzufallen oder Besitz von ihnen zu ergreifen.

---

10 Besonders gut erforscht ist das Hexenwesen bei den Zande. Vgl. Edward E. EVANS-PRITCHARD: Hexerei, Orakel und Magie bei den Zande, Frankfurt/M. 1978.

Die meisten Afrikanerinnen und Afrikaner sind zutiefst davon überzeugt, dass all die vielen Übel, Unglücke, Krankheiten, Tragödien, Unfälle, die sie erfahren und die Kümmernisse und unseligen Geheimnisse, mit denen sie sich konfrontiert sehen, durch den Missbrauch der mystischen Macht, durch einen Zauberer oder einer Hexe verursacht werden. Nichts geschieht durch Zufall, alles wird von irgendjemand entweder direkt oder mithilfe der mystischen Kraft verursacht. Im Falle der Hexerei gilt das Böse als unabhängiges und äußeres Objekt, das allerdings nicht aus sich selbst heraus handeln kann, sondern immer von Kraftträgern – Menschen oder Geistern – zur Entfaltung gebracht werden muss. Hexen sind sich oft ihrer Untaten nicht bewusst, da sie ihr Unwesen nachts außerhalb des schlafenden Körpers treiben, Zauberer dagegen verfolgen zielgerichtet ihre bösen Pläne.

Geistbesessenheit

Die mystischen Kräfte können sich in der religiösen Erfahrung der Gläubigen auch in vielfachen Erscheinungsformen der Besessenheit manifestieren. Die Geistbesessenheit ist eine besonders machtgeladene Äußerung, die in fast allen afrikanischen Gesellschaften und besonders in der afrikanischen Diaspora (z. B. in Brasilien: Candomblé – Macumba-Umbanda; in Haiti: Voodoo-Kult; in Kuba: Santeria; in Trinidad: spiritual baptists) zu beobachten ist. Besessenheit bedeutet, dass ein Geist aus einer anderen unsichtbaren Dimension der Wirklichkeit die Kontrolle über den menschlichen Körper übernimmt. Der Geist dringt in die von ihm ausgewählte Person ein und benutzt diese, um sich zu Wort melden, zu den Gläubigen zu sprechen, zu tanzen, zu singen, wahrzusagen, aber auch zu heilen. Meist werden besondere Rituale entwickelt, um Menschen zum Empfang des entsprechenden Geistes vorzubereiten. Das Hauptziel dieser Rituale ist es, etwa durch rhythmische Stimulation neurophysiologische Veränderungen im Körper des geistbesessenen Mediums herbeizuführen. Diese Veränderungen werden in der Religionswissenschaft als ekstatische Trance bezeichnet. Nachdem der Geist den Körper des Mediums wieder verlassen hat, kann sich die besessene Person gewöhnlich nicht an die Aktivität des fremden Geistes erinnern. Die neuere Forschung[11] hat darauf aufmerksam gemacht, dass Geistbesessenheit sozusagen als „kulturelle Sprache" verstanden werden kann, die dazu dient, bestimmte als psychosomatisch erfahrene und spirituell wahrgenommene Phänomene zu erklären.

Die mächtigen Geister, die Besessenheit hervorrufen, sind meistens dem Menschen freundlich gesonnen. Allerdings können auch gelegentlich böse Geister heraufbeschworen werden. Dies geschieht, wenn Schadgeister oder Dämonen aufgrund einer bösen Tat des Besessenen oder des Fluchs eines Feindes in das Medium eindringen. Dämonische Besessenheit kommt allerdings relativ selten vor; sie ist aber sehr gefährlich, da die unerwünschte Gegenwart eines bösen Geistes die besessene Person krank macht und sogar deren Tod bewirken kann. In einem solchen Fall ist es unbedingt notwendig, dass der Schadgeist so schnell wie möglich mithilfe der Durchführung eines exorzistischen Ri-

---

11 Z. B. E. BOURGIGNON: Possession (1976). Vincent CRAPANAZO / V. GARRISON: Case Studies in Spirit Possession, Sydney u. a. 1977. I. M. LEWIS: Exstatic Religion, London ²1989. Felicitas D. GOODMAN / J.H. HENNEY / E. PRESSEL: Trance, Healing and Hallucination, New York u. a. 1974.

tuals ausgetrieben wird. Die Fähigkeit der Austreibung von Dämonen ist eine spezielle Gabe der religiösen Funktionsträger Heiler und Heilerinnen.

Im Urteil der christlichen Afrikamission wurde das Phänomen der Geistbesessenheit als primitive abergläubische Einbildung abgetan, und als Ausdruck nicht überwundenen Heidentums verdammt. Wie auch andere Elemente afrikanischer Religion wurde die Geistbesessenheit fast ausschließlich unter ihren negativen Aspekten gesehen.

Kontextualität von unten: Die Aneignung der mystischen Kraft durch charismatisch/pentekostale Bewegungen

Das Programm der afrikanischen Theologie wurde nur selten in den Gemeinden der aus der westlichen Missionstätigkeit hervorgegangenen Kirchen, den sog. mainline churches verwirklicht. Die Forderung nach einer Afrikanisierung des Christentums blieb ein Desiderat in akademischen Zirkeln. Allerdings bildete sich in den letzten Jahrzehnten eine Unzahl unabhängiger Gemeinschaften charismatisch/pentekostalen Ursprungs heraus, die Hexerei und Geistbesessenheit in ihren theologischen Referenzrahmen und ihre religiöse Praxis integrieren. Aber anders als in der Tradition löst der Pentekostalismus die Ambivalenz des Numinosen auf und führt den klassischen christlichen Dualismus wieder ein. Die sich in Hexerei und Geistbesessenheit manifestierenden mystischen Kräfte werden grundsätzlich als böse dämonische Mächte verstanden, gegen die man einen gnadenlosen geistlichen Krieg – „spiritual warfare" – führen muss. Auf der einen Seite steht der Teufel mit seinen satanischen Heerscharen, auf der anderen Seite treten die christlichen Gotteskrieger an, die unter dem Schutz des Heiligen Geistes stehen. Die guten göttlichen Geister nehmen Besitz von den Gläubigen, die über die Gaben des Zungenredens (Glossolalie), der Austreibung dämonischer Mächte (Exorzismus) und der Heilung von Krankheiten verfügen. Wie die Funktionsträger der afrikanischen traditionellen Religion sind die Führer der neuen religiösen Bewegungen von Gott mit charismatischen Kräften ausgestattet, die es ihnen möglich macht, die Ursachen von Zauberei und Hexerei zu erkennen und zu beseitigen.

Johannes Harnischfeger

Sozialer Niedergang und Kampf gegen das Böse: Hexerei im postmodernen Afrika

Abstract

Witchcraft and State Decline in Postmodern Africa. For the history of witchcraft in Africa, the end of colonialism and the beginning of independence, around 1960, did not have much impact. Massive fear of occult forces began to spread two or three decades later, with the decline of state institutions. Since power is hardly regulated anymore, it has become unpredictable and seems to be connected to invisible forces that can be manipulated by secret techniques. A world which is ruled by dark forces cannot be renewed by transforming its political and economic structures. Evil which is personified in witches and sorcerers has to be fought by spiritual means.

Zusammenfassung

Mit dem Verfall staatlicher Institutionen wird es schwierig, die politischen Eliten öffentlicher Kontrolle zu unterwerfen. Zugang zu Macht und Reichtum ist kaum noch institutionell geregelt, sondern scheint von der Manipulation verborgener Kräfte abhängig zu sein. Angesichts der Bedrohung durch unkontrollierte okkulte Mächte ändern sich die Strategien kollektiven Handelns. Der Kampf gegen den sozialen Verfall wird mit spirituellen Mitteln geführt, nicht durch die Transformation politischer und ökonomischer Strukturen, sondern durch die Eliminierung des Bösen.

Einleitung

Für die Geschichte der Hexerei in Afrika sind das Ende der Kolonialzeit und der Übergang zur Unabhängigkeit, um 1960, kaum von Belang. Zum Aufleben okkulter Gewalt kam es erst zwei, drei Jahrzehnte später, mit dem Verfall des postkolonialen Staates. Da der Versuch, sich mithilfe staatlich geplanter Sozialtechnologie zu modernisieren, gescheitert ist, beginnt ein neues Zeitalter, das in mancher Hinsicht der alten, vorstaatlichen Welt ähnelt und zugleich von Globalisierung geprägt ist.[1] Mit dem Begriff ‚Postmoderne' verbindet sich meist die Vorstellung einer Welt, die traditionelle Bindungen hinter

---

1 Da nicht abzusehen ist, wie sich das nachmoderne Afrika gestalten wird, gibt es für die neue Zeit noch keinen Namen. Das Wort ‚Postmoderne' ist nur ein Platzhalter; man könnte auch von einer ‚afrikanischen Moderne' sprechen. Der Begriff ‚postkolonial' dagegen erscheint mir zur Charakterisierung der gegenwärtigen Krise irreführend: Vgl. Crawford YOUNG: The End of the Post-Colonial State in Africa? Reflections on Changing African Political Dynamics, in: African Affairs 103 (2004), S. 23-49. Es ist gerade der Niedergang postkolonialer Staatlichkeit, der zur Rückkehr des Okkulten entscheidend beigetragen hat.

sich gelassen hat, sodass die Menschen frei sind, wie in einem Spiel, die verschiedensten Identitäten anzunehmen und wieder abzulegen. Dagegen zeigt die Erfahrung vieler afrikanischer Gesellschaften, dass Gruppenidentitäten mit relativ starren ethnischen und religiösen Grenzen wieder Macht über die Individuen gewinnen. Wenn der Staat seine Bürger kaum noch schützt, müssen sie sich Milizen, Geheimgesellschaften oder Patronagenetzwerken anschließen.[2] An die Stelle von Rechtsverhältnissen treten persönliche Abhängigkeitsverhältnisse, die keiner öffentlichen Kontrolle unterliegen.[3] Politische Macht, die sich nicht hegen und einfrieden lässt, nimmt einen dämonischen Charakter an. Es scheint, als sei der Zugang zu Macht und Reichtum von unsichtbaren Kräften bestimmt, die man nur durch okkulte Techniken zu seinen Gunsten manipulieren kann. Neben dem Bestreben, magische und spirituelle Kräfte für sich zu nutzen, unternehmen viele Menschen auch den Versuch, aus der Welt gegenseitiger Verdächtigungen auszubrechen und sich durch kollektives Handeln von der Last des Okkulten zu befreien. Als Wege aus der Krise suchen sie freilich nach religiösen Lösungen. Christliche Priester oder islamische Geistliche veranstalten Exorzismen, zerstören Schreine und identifizieren Hexen, aber all diese Anstrengungen bestärken nur den Glauben an okkulte Bedrohungen.

Hexerei und Zauberei werden im Folgenden begrifflich getrennt, auch wenn es in vielen afrikanischen Kulturen keine klaren Grenzen zwischen ihnen gibt. Peter Geschiere, in seinem Buch über *Sorcellerie et politique en Afrique*, verzichtet auf die Unterscheidung und subsumiert beides unter den Begriff *sorcellerie*, aber er erwähnt eine Form von *sorcellerie*, die zwischen Nachbarn und Verwandten wütet und die jener Vorstellung von Hexerei entspricht, die in den klassischen Studien der *Social Anthropolgy* beschrieben wurde. Die Hexe ist demnach der Feind im Innern und entspricht darin dem Typ des Verräters. Zauberer dagegen betreiben ein mehr oder weniger legales Gewerbe. Sie bieten okkulte Dienstleistungen an, die von jedem Kunden zu kaufen sind und die sich, in der Form von Schadenszauber, auch gegen gänzlich fremde Personen einsetzen lassen.

Hexerei in Afrika und Europa

Die meisten Ethnologen, die Hexerei während der Kolonialzeit untersuchten, hielten das Phänomen für ein Relikt traditioneller Gesellschaften. Zu Hexerei-Anschuldigungen kam es in der Regel zwischen Angehörigen der eigenen Familie oder Dorfgemeinschaft, d. h. zwischen Menschen, die sich nicht ausweichen konnten, weil sie in fest gefügte Lebensverhältnisse eingebunden waren. Was sich unter ihnen an Neid, Missgunst und Hass ansammelte, durfte sich häufig nicht offen artikulieren, verwandelte sich also in Ressentiments und führte zu gegenseitigen Verdächtigungen: „People accuse one another of witchcraft when they are prohibited from expressing their aggression in other ways".[4] Die Neigung, den eigenen Nachbarn und Verwandten verborgene Aggressionen zu unterstellen, war auch unter der dörflichen Bevölkerung Europas weit verbreitet. Die

---

2 Martin VAN CREVELD: Die Zukunft des Krieges, München 1998.
3 Patrick CHABAL / Jean-Pascal DALOZ: Africa Works. Disorder as Political Instrument, Oxford 1999, S. 16, 30.
4 Philip MAYER: Witches. Inaugural Lecture Delivered at Rhodes University, Grahamstown 1954, S. 13.

großen Hexenverfolgungen zu Beginn der Neuzeit lassen sich aber daraus nicht erklären. Sie waren nicht Ausdruck von Rückständigkeit und sozialer Isolation, sondern „Begleiterscheinung der Öffnung".[5] Mit dem Übergang zur Moderne wurde die europäische Zivilisation von kollektiver Angst überwältigt. Der Schrecken der Pestepidemien, das Vordringen des Islam sowie das Schisma der Kirche erzeugten eine apokalyptische Stimmung, in der sich auch die gebildeten Schichten vom Hexenglauben der einfachen Bevölkerung anstecken ließen.[6] Es schien, als habe Gott der Christenheit seinen Schutz entzogen, als sei die Heilsordnung massiv gestört. Insbesondere für die plötzliche Klimaverschlechterung, für die Kälteeinbrüche und Hungersnöte, gab es, soweit die Erinnerung der Menschen reichte, keine Erklärung, außer dem Hinweis auf dämonische Verschwörungen.

Historiker können nur schwer rekonstruieren, was den Hexenglauben in den Augen der gebildeten Elite diskreditiert hat. Der Übergang zu einem mechanistischen Naturverständnis, bei Newton und anderen Wissenschaftlern, führte zunächst nicht dazu, die Existenz dämonischer Kräfte zu verwerfen.[7] Wichtiger als solche wissenschaftlichen Paradigmenwechsel waren vermutlich politische und soziale Umwälzungen, etwa der Übergang zu neuen Formen der Sozialisation, die zunächst im Bürgertum, später auch in anderen sozialen Schichten Gewissensbildung und Internalisierung förderten. Das Böse wurde nicht mehr nach außen projiziert, sondern im eigenen Innern gesucht.[8] Der Einfluss, den die allmähliche Ausbildung neuer Persönlichkeitsstrukturen auf den Hexenglauben hatte, lässt sich jedoch kaum abschätzen. Deutlicher beobachtbar ist dagegen ein anderer Zusammenhang: Wo staatliche Institutionen gefestigt waren, kam es nur selten zu Hexenverfolgungen.[9] Vielleicht hat die Angst vor okkulter Gewalt aufgehört, als die Menschen lernten, einander weniger zu fürchten, also mit der Befriedung der Gesellschaft durch den Staat und sein Gewaltmonopol. Der Vergleich mit dem zeitgenössischen Afrika ist hier interessant, denn er lässt erkennen, was passiert, wenn der umgekehrte Prozess einsetzt und staatliche Autorität sich zurückbildet. Da staatliche Behörden nicht mehr in der Lage sind, Rechtsverhältnisse zu garantieren, verfallen viele moderne Institutionen, die den Menschen Sicherheit gaben, und es breitet sich auch in den großen Städten panische Angst vor unsichtbaren Kräften aus. Die Bürgermeisterin von Soweto, in Südafrika erklärte, das größte Problem in ihrer Stadt sei die Hexerei.[10]

---

5 Arno BORST: Anfänge des Hexenwahns in den Alpen, in: Andreas Blauert (Hg.), Ketzer, Zauberer, Hexen. Die Anfänge der europäischen Hexenverfolgungen, Frankfurt/M. 1990, S. 43-67, hier S. 55.
6 Wolfgang BEHRINGER: Witches and Witch-Hunts. A Global History, Cambridge 2004, S. 60-61.
7 Stuart CLARK: Thinking with Demons. The Idea of Witchcraft in Early Modern Europe, Oxford 1997, S. 294-311.
8 Heinz D. KITTSTEINER: Die Entstehung des modernen Gewissens, Frankfurt/M. 1995.
9 Johannes DILLINGER: Hexenverfolgungen in Städten, in: Gunther Franz / Franz Irsigler (Hg.), Methoden und Konzepte der historischen Hexenforschung, Trier 1998, S. 129-165, hier S. 161-163. BEHRINGER: Wiches, S. 26, 116, 119, 126, 138, 159, 194, 215.
10 Adam ASHFORTH: Witchcraft, Violence, and Democracy in the New South Africa, in: Cahiers d'Études africaines 38 (1998), S. 505-532, hier S. 525.

Gescheiterte Modernisierung

Blickt man zurück in die Kolonialzeit, dann fällt auf, dass die Angst vor Hexerei damals keine so zerstörerische Gewalt entfaltete. Ethnologen hatten sogar den Eindruck, als führe die allmähliche Modernisierung unweigerlich dazu, dass der Glaube an okkulte Kräfte abnimmt: „Beliefs in witchcraft and sorcery began to decline (…) when small-scale, intimate communities began to be displaced by large, impersonal, urban complexes." „In the towns, a preponderance of strangers not linked intimately or emotionally makes it possible for hostility and opposition to be expressed openly rather than supernaturally".[11] Die Modernisierung schien ein unilinearer Prozess zu sein: von Stämmen zu Nationen, von der Subsistenzwirtschaft zu Marktbeziehungen, von askriptiven Identitäten, die kollektiv festgelegt wurden, zu individuell erworbenem Status. Doch die europäische Form von Staatlichkeit war nur eine flüchtige Episode in der langen Geschichte Afrikas. Und damit dürfte zusammenhängen, dass die Entwicklung der Hexerei einen unerwarteten Verlauf genommen hat.

Im Nachhinein betrachtet ist es erstaunlich, dass die Erschütterungen der Kolonialzeit so wenig Ängste vor dämonischen Kräften ausgelöst haben. Denn die forcierte Modernisierung, die über die Afrikaner hereinbrach, wurde von einer fremden, undurchschaubaren Macht betrieben. An der westafrikanischen Küste, wo die Erinnerung an den transatlantischen Sklavenhandel noch gegenwärtig war, kursierten Gerüchte, dass die europäischen Eroberer Kannibalen seien. Das dunkle Leder ihrer Schuhe, so hatte man sich zur Zeit der Sklavenjagden erzählt, sei aus der Haut von Afrikanern gemacht.[12] In einigen Städten Ostafrikas trauten sich, in den 1930er Jahren, viele Bewohner nachts nicht aus den Häusern, weil die Angst umging, dass die anämischen Weißen Afrikaner entführten und ihnen das Blut aussaugten. Besonderen Verdacht erregte die Feuerwehr, nicht nur wegen des leuchtenden Rots ihrer Fahrzeuge, sondern auch, weil sie Zugang hatte zu einem Labyrinth unterirdischer Wasserleitungen.[13] Doch solche Ängste waren für das Verhältnis zur Kolonialmacht nicht bestimmend. Die fremden Herrscher nahmen kaum dämonische Züge an, und auch im Innern der afrikanischen Gesellschaften war das Gefühl okkulter Bedrohungen, verglichen mit der heutigen Situation, wenig verbreitet. Im Südosten Nigerias, bei den Igbo, unter denen ich einige Jahre lebte, gab es zwar indigene Konzepte von Hexerei, doch soll es kaum zu gegenseitigen Anschuldigungen gekommen sein.[14] Dass die Kolonialverwaltung die Verfolgung von Hexen und Zauberern durch Strafandrohung einzudämmen suchte, erklärt vermutlich nur zum Teil, wa-

---

11 M. G. MARWICK: Sorcery in its Social Setting. A Study of the Northern Rhodesian Cewa, Manchester 1965, S. 295. Max MARWICK: Postscript. The Decline of Witch-Beliefs in Differentiated Societis, in: Max MARWICK (Hg.), Witchcraft and Sorcery. Selected Readings, Harmondsworth, Middlesex, England 1975, S. 379-382, hier S. 380.

12 Rosalind SHAW: The Production of Witchcraft/Witchcraft as Production. Memory, Modernity, and the Slave Trade in Sierra Leone, in: American Ethnologist 24 (1997), S. 856-876, hier S. 868. John ILIFFE: Africans. The History of a Continent, Cambridge 1995, S. 136.

13 Luise WHITE: Bodily Fluids and Usufruct. Controlling Property in Nairobi, 1917-1939, in: Canadian Journal of African Studies 24 (1990), S. 418-438.

14 G. I. JONES: A Boundary to Accusations, in: Mary Douglas (Hg.), Witchcraft Confessions & Accusations, London 1970, S. 321-332, hier S. 322. Natürlich gab es, wie in vorkolonialer Zeit, Geheimgesellschaften, Orakelpriester und Zauberer, die sich berufsmäßig mit Okkultem beschäftigten.

rum damals, trotz der politischen und sozialen Verwerfungen, keine spirituelle Panik um sich griff. Mir scheint, die Kolonialherrschaft wurde in vielen Regionen Afrikas nicht als sehr traumatisch erfahren. Im heutigen Nigeria z. B. hatte die Einführung der *Pax Britannica* eher den Effekt, das Leben sehr viel sicherer zu machen. Alte Männer im Igboland, die nach ihren Erinnerungen an die vorkoloniale Welt gefragt wurden, trennten deutlich zwischen der relativ friedlichen Kolonialzeit und der alten vorstaatlichen Zeit, als die Angst vor Gewalt allgegenwärtig war: „It was a time when might was right", when life „was nasty and brutish".[15] Die Angst vor bewaffneten Banden, die ihren Opfern außerhalb der Dörfer auflauerten, war so groß, dass Frauen oft nur in größeren Gruppen oder in Begleitung bewaffneter Krieger die Gehöfte verließen, um Wasser zu schöpfen oder Feuerholz zu sammeln. Im Norden des heutigen Nigeria, wo islamische Dschihadisten mit ihren Sklavenjagden ganze Landstriche entvölkerten, war die Erfahrung von Gewalt vermutlich noch traumatischer.

Mit der Auflösung des staatlichen Gewaltmonopols lebt religiöse und ethnische Gewalt heute wieder auf, sodass viele Nigerianer den Eindruck haben, in eine Art Hobbes'schen Naturzustand zurückzusinken.[16] Professor Wole Soyinka, der Nobelpreisträger für Literatur, sprach von einer „unglaublichen Brutalität", die „den humanen Umgang miteinander (…) völlig verdrängt" habe.[17] So gefährlich wie in vorkolonialer Zeit ist das Leben zwar (noch) nicht, dennoch sehen sich die Menschen mit einem unfassbaren Niedergang konfrontiert. Zu Beginn der Unabhängigkeit 1960 hatten viele erwartet, dass der schwarze Kontinent, von den Fesseln des Kolonialismus befreit, mit großen Schritten die soziale und technologische Entwicklung Europas nachholen werde. Die demokratische Verfassung Nigerias mochte freilich von Anfang an nicht funktionieren; es kam zu Militärputsch und Bürgerkrieg. Nach dem Ende des Krieges 1970 brachte der Ölboom immerhin beträchtlichen Wohlstand ins Land. Das Bruttosozialprodukt pro Einwohner lag höher als in Malaysia oder Indonesien, und Nigerias Präsident verkündete 1979, dass sein Land bis zum Ende des Jahrhunderts zu den zehn führenden Industrienationen der Welt gehören werde.[18] Doch seitdem hat eine beispiellose Welle von Disinvestment die Produktionsstätten veröden lassen. Fast alles, was die 140 Millionen Nigerianer an Industriegütern konsumieren, wird im Ausland hergestellt. Selbst die Landwirtschaft, die früher Überschüsse exportierte, ist weitgehend in die Subsistenzwirtschaft zurückgefallen, sodass sich Nigeria in einen Netto-Importeur von Lebensmitteln verwandelt hat.

Wie will man diesen Niedergang erklären? Ein Großteil der Menschen macht für ihr persönliches Elend die Machenschaften von Hexen und Zauberern verantwortlich, ja viele vermuten, dass auch im Zentrum der politischen Macht okkulte Kräfte am Werk sind. Für europäische Beobachter eine irrationale Reaktion. Statt die Ursachen der Krise

---

15 Zit. nach Elizabeth ISICHEI: Igbo Worlds. An Anthology of Oral Histories and Historical Descriptions, London / Basingstoke 1977, S. 61, 125.
16 Jibrin IBRAHIM: Ethno-Religious Mobilisation and the Sapping of Democracy in Nigeria, in: Jonathan HYSLOP (Hg.), African Democracy in the Era of Globalisation, Johannesburg 1999, S. 93-111, hier S. 93.
17 Der Spiegel, 35 (1995), S. 148.
18 Chinua ACHEBE: The Trouble with Nigeria, Enugu 1985, S. 9.

zu analysieren, richten die Menschen ihre Aufmerksamkeit auf den Kampf gegen imaginäre Kräfte. Sie legen sich Amulette zu, schützen sich mit Heiligem Wasser oder lassen sich mit Rasierklingen Abwehrzauber in die Haut ritzen. Aber damit lösen sie nicht ihre Probleme. Der Kreislauf von Zauber und Gegenzauber treibt sie nur noch weiter in eine paranoide Verfeindung mit der Umwelt.

Ich möchte, am Beispiel Nigerias, einige Aspekte der afrikanischen Krise näher betrachten, um der Frage nachzugehen, warum sich die Erfahrungen von moralischem und sozialem Verfall im Idiom von Hexerei, Zauberei und anderen unsichtbaren Bedrohungen ausdrücken.

Reichtum, Macht und okkulte Gewalt

Ein Teil der Krise besteht darin, dass die Kluft zwischen Arm und Reich größer ist als je zuvor. Eine angemessene Reaktion darauf wäre, aus europäischer Sicht, wenn die Unterprivilegierten sich zusammenschließen würden, um für ihre Rechte zu kämpfen. Doch auf welche Rechte sollen sie sich gegenüber den Reichen und Mächtigen berufen? Ihre Armut gründet ja nicht darauf, dass sie von Großgrundbesitzern oder kapitalistischen Unternehmern ausgebeutet würden.[19] Ganz im Gegenteil. Ob es um das Millionenheer von Arbeitslosen geht, die sich in Lagos oder Kano mit Gelegenheitsjobs durchschlagen, oder um Subsistenzbauern, die auf den ausgelaugten, erodierten Böden Hackbau betreiben: Sie können oft nur überleben, weil Angehörige, die etwas besser gestellt sind, ihnen ab und zu etwas Geld zustecken. In Nigerias Rentenökonomie geht es nicht um die Produktion von Reichtum, sondern um seine Distribution.[20] Was die Oberschicht an Luxus zur Schau stellt, verdankt sich im Wesentlichen den Öleinnahmen des Staates: Milliardentransfers von Shell, BP und Texaco, die dem Land 98% seiner Exporterlöse einbringen. Manches stammt auch aus Schmuggel, aus Drogen-, Waffen- und Kinderhandel, oder es wurde seinen Besitzern durch Angehörige aus Europa oder den USA zugeschickt. In jedem Fall steht der rasch wachsenden Bevölkerung nur eine begrenzte Menge an Reichtum zur Verfügung, und so ist der Kampf darum ein Nullsummenspiel, ähnlich wie in jenen Dorfgemeinschaften, in denen die Ethnologen der Kolonialzeit ihre Hexerei-Studien betrieben. Damals wie heute gilt die Regel: Was ich mir an Reichtum aneigne, ist stets anderen genommen, löst also Neid und Missgunst aus, zuweilen auch Hexerei-Vorwürfe. Individueller Eigennutz ist notwendig böse, weil er andere in ihren Überlebenschancen bedroht.

Wie kommt es, dass Europäer sich von dieser Vorstellung des Bösen gelöst haben? Selbstsucht und Geiz, die Kardinalsünden des christlichen Mittelalters, werden heute nicht mehr so sehr als Bedrohung erfahren, sondern als notwendige Bedingung für das Wohlergehen aller: „It is not from the benevolence of the butcher, the brewer, or the baker that we expect our dinner, but from their regard to their own self-interest".[21]

---

19 Goran HYDEN: The Anomaly of the African Peasantry, in: Development and Change 17 (1986), S. 677-705.

20 Claude AKE: Time for a Democratic Agenda, in: Tell [eine Zeitschrift aus Lagos], 22.8.1994, S. 33-34, hier S. 34.

21 Adam SMITH, zit. nach Maurice BLOCH / Jonathan PARRY: Introduction, in: DIES., Money and the Morality of Exchange, Cambridge 1989, S. 1-32, hier S. 17.

Durch die ökonomische und soziale Arbeitsteilung wurden die Menschen in ein Geflecht von horizontalen Beziehungen eingebunden, in denen sie sich gegenseitig als Rechtspersonen anerkennen. In Afrika dagegen setzen sich Klientelbeziehungen durch, sodass Rechtsverhältnisse mehr und mehr durch persönliche Abhängigkeitsverhältnisse ersetzt werden. Ansprüche auf die Protektion lokaler *strongmen* kann man nicht vor Gericht einklagen. Man muss um die Gunst der Reichen und Mächtigen buhlen, und dabei sind all die anderen Mittellosen nicht Verbündete, sondern Rivalen.

Der Reichtum, der Geschäftsleuten und Politikern wie aus dem Nichts zufließt, hat etwas Mysteriöses.[22] Da er von niemandem erzeugt wurde, unterliegt er keinen klaren, verbindlich geregelten Besitzverhältnissen. Jeder versucht, sich einen Teil dieses Reichtums anzueignen, und dabei kommen gelegentlich auch junge, unbekannte Männer wie über Nacht zu fantastischem Wohlstand. Wer sich in dem Wettbewerb um Macht und Reichtum durchsetzen wird, lässt sich nur schwer voraussagen, denn Auf- und Abstieg der Akteure hängen von stets wechselnden, undurchschaubaren Allianzen ab: „The most amazing changes of fortune are possible." „Laurent-Désiré Kabila, a small-time bandit chief and smuggler (…) dropped almost entirely from international view, before emerging from nowhere, as it were, to become president of Congo."[23] Politische Macht befindet sich nicht dort, wo sie laut Verfassung sein sollte.[24] Sie lässt sich nicht hegen und einfrieden. Sie geht nicht von Institutionen aus, sondern liegt in der Hand von Personen, die die Fähigkeit besitzen, anderen ihren Willen aufzuzwingen. Wie sie diese Macht über andere erworben haben, ist für Außenstehende nicht einsehbar und damit nicht kontrollierbar. Die Arkana der Macht werden daher, ähnlich wie in vorkolonialer Zeit, mit okkulten Praktiken in Verbindung gebracht: nicht so sehr mit Hexerei, sondern mit Ritualmorden, Zauberei und Geheimgesellschaften. Die Verdächtigen geben sich auch keine Mühe, den Gerüchten entgegenzutreten: „As rational social structures collapsed, (…) politicians would hire traditional rainmakers to scatter opponents' political rallies with heavy rains."[25] Selbst Minister und Präsidenten umgeben sich ganz offen mit Zauberern und Wahrsagern, um ihre Widersacher einzuschüchtern. Solche spirituellen Experten können tatsächlich großen Einfluss auf den Gang der Dinge nehmen, was damit zusammenhängt, dass sie, als Vertraute der Herrschenden, detaillierte Informationen über die geheimsten Bestrebungen ihrer Klienten erhalten.[26]

Die Welt der Politiker, mit ihren düsteren Intrigen, spielt jedoch eine geringe Rolle, wo es um Hexerei-Anklagen im engeren Sinne geht. Für die meisten Nigerianer findet der Kampf zwischen Arm und Reich innerhalb der Verwandtschaft statt. Der wirtschaftliche und politische Niedergang präsentiert sich ihnen als eine Krise der persönlichen Bezie-

---

22 Jean COMAROFF / John L. COMAROFF: Occult Economies and the Violence of Abstraction: Notes from the South African Postcolony, in: American Ethnologist 26 (1999) 2, S. 279-303, hier S. 281, 292-295.
23 Stephen ELLIS / Gerrie TER HAAR: Worlds of Power. Religious Thought and Political Practice in Africa, London 2004, S. 45.
24 Ebd., S. 190.
25 Ogbu U. KALU: The Religious Dimension of the Legitimacy Crisis, 1993-1998, in: Toyin FALOLA (Hg.), Nigeria in the Twentieth Century, Durham, North Carolina 2002, S. 667-685, hier S. 675.
26 ELLIS / TER HAAR: Worlds of Power, S. 87.

hungen. In einer extrem unberechenbaren Welt, in der auch auf Patronagebeziehungen und politische Allianzen wenig Verlass ist, stellen Verwandtschaftsbeziehungen die einzig unhintergehbare soziale Realität dar: ein Geflecht von Beziehungen, die sich, weil man in sie hineingeboren wurde, nicht einfach aufkündigen lassen. Wer arm und rechtlos ist, kann finanzielle Zuwendungen und Protektion im Prinzip nur von den eigenen Angehörigen einklagen. Sie sind die einzig natürlichen Verbündeten. Doch Familienangehörige, die es in der Stadt zu Reichtum gebracht haben, sind oft nicht geneigt, mit den Daheimgebliebenen zu teilen. Für sie ist es wenig sinnvoll, in die Aufrechterhaltung von Familienbeziehungen zu investieren, denn die armen Verwandten mit ihren unersättlichen Ansprüchen geben nicht Rückhalt und Schutz, sondern werden zu einer Belastung, und deshalb suchen sich die Reichgewordenen ihren traditionellen Verpflichtungen wenigstens teilweise zu entziehen. Der Vorwurf, sie würden Hexerei betreiben, ist eines der Mittel, sie unter Druck zu setzen, damit sie ihr anti-soziales Verhalten aufgeben.[27]

Mit dem Vorwurf, Hexe zu sein, ist zugleich ein moralisches Urteil gesetzt. Die Hexe ist der Feind im Innern, der Verräter, der die Mitglieder seiner Gruppe unterstützen müsste, aber insgeheim auf ihr Verderben sinnt. Zwischen den Vertretern verfeindeter Gruppen, etwa zwischen Igbo- und Hausa-Politikern, würde es wenig Sinn machen, sich gegenseitig okkulter Praktiken zu bezichtigen. In der Presse war gelegentlich zu lesen, dass Präsident Abacha bizarre Rituale veranstalten ließ, um Macht über seine Feinde zu gewinnen.[28] Aber mit welchem Recht hätte man ihm daraus einen Vorwurf machen können? Warum sollte er sich gegenüber Politikern aus anderen Ethnien, die ihn zu Fall bringen wollten, fair verhalten? Trotz der Verbitterung über den Militärherrscher, der für sich und seine Anhänger vier Milliarden Dollar veruntreut hat, konnte man ihm im Grunde nicht einmal vorwerfen, dass er sich auf Kosten anderer bereicherte. Denn er hat nur im großen Stil vorgeführt, was fast jeder von den eigenen Führern erwartet: „We, the ordinary people, will expect the man at the top to be corrupt and if the man is not corrupt, we say that the man has no senses."[29] Mit dieser Haltung ist an eine demokratische Kontrolle der Regierenden nicht zu denken. Gleichgültig, ob unter militärischer oder ziviler Herrschaft, die Nigerianer sind kaum in der Lage, auf die Bedingungen, unter denen sie leben, Einfluss zu nehmen. Ihre Lebenswelt wird von fremden Kräften beherrscht, die sie nicht zurückdrängen oder vertreiben, sondern bestenfalls zu ihren eigenen Gunsten manipulieren können.

---

27 Misty L. BASTIAN: 'Bloodhounds Who Have No Friends': Witchcraft and Locality in the Nigerian Popular Press, in: Jean COMAROFF / John COMAROFF (Hg.), Modernity and Its Malcontents. Ritual Power in Postcolonial Africa, Chicago / London 1993, S. 129-166, hier S. 134, 140-143. Peter GESCHIERE: The Modernity of Witchcraft. Politics and the Occult in Postcolonial Africa, Charlottesville / London 1997, S. 11, 42-46, 168, 211-214.

28 KALU: Religious Dimension, S. 679.

29 Achike UDENWA, Gouverneur von Imo State, in: Tell, 25.3.2002, S. 35. „If a fraudulent public official were prosecuted, his village elders would go on a delegation of protest": KALU: Religious Dimension, S. 674. Ähnlich wie in vorkolonialer Zeit sind Angehörige fremder Ethnien oder Dorfgemeinschaften nicht Teil des eigenen moralischen Universums, so dass es nicht verwerflich erscheint, sie zu schädigen: „,:The fact that one succeeds in gaining money among strangers is generally considered as a new equivalent to heroic acts in the outside world – kill a beast of prey, come back with an enemy's skull – by which, in the olden days, a young man could establish his reputation in his village": GESCHIERE: Modernity of Witchcraft, S. 162.

Die Ursachen der Krise

Die Gewalt, die im Innern der Gesellschaft, zwischen Nachbarn und Verwandten ausbricht, verwischt die Grenzen zwischen Gut und Böse, Innen und Außen, Eigen und Fremd. Dass sich diese traumatische Erfahrung als eine Überwältigung durch dämonische Kräfte darstellt, hängt auch damit zusammen, dass die Ursachen der Krise unklar sind. Nehmen wir als Beispiel den Westen Ugandas, wo sich seit den 1990er Jahren die Angst vor Hexen und Kannibalen wie eine Epidemie verbreitet hat. Die Angst der Menschen voreinander ist Ausdruck einer „existenziellen Krise", die durch den Verfall öffentlicher Institutionen und den Terror von Rebellenbewegungen, durch die krassen Gegensätze von Arm und Reich sowie die AIDS-Epidemie verursacht wurde.[30] Doch die „moralische Panik"[31] lässt sich nicht allein aus solchen leidvollen Erfahrungen erklären, denn Korruption, Massenarbeitslosigkeit und Gewalt waren in den Jahrzehnten davor weitaus gravierender. Durch den Terror des Idi-Amin-Regimes und den Bürgerkrieg nach seinem Sturz starben mehr als eine halbe Million Menschen. Warum hat sich die Angst vor okkulter Gewalt erst danach epidemisch verbreitet? Mir scheint, die Wirren des Bürgerkriegs haben den Bürgern zwar mehr Elend und Zerstörung gebracht, aber was ihnen widerfuhr, war verständlicher, weil die Feindseligkeiten sich aus der Logik des Bürgerkriegs erklärten. Was dagegen heute, in vielen Teilen Afrikas, als interner Terror erfahren wird, ist mysteriös. Warum hat sich die Welt in einen Krieg aller gegen alle verkehrt? Die Menschen spüren, dass sich ihr Leben langsam in einen Albtraum verwandelt, aber sie sind unfähig, diese Entwicklung zu stoppen: „When you look at yourself as an African, it is easy to think that God has cursed you".[32] Bei einer Dichterlesung von Wole Soyinka in Heidelberg wurde ich auf eindringliche Weise daran erinnert, wie verstört und fassungslos Afrikaner diesem unaufhaltsamen Niedergang gegenüberstehen: Ein Student aus Nigeria meldete sich zu Wort und erzählte, dass er immer wieder an das Elend in seiner Heimat denken müsse. Schon in den 1980er Jahren war alles im Verfall begriffen. Seitdem haben sich zivile und militärische Herrscher abgewechselt, aber alles wurde immer nur schlimmer. Darauf fragte er beinahe hilflos: „Professor Soyinka, tell me, what is our problem? Why is there no hope? What is the problem in Nigeria?" Wole Soyinka wurde verlegen und stammelte: „Bad leadership of our politicians, Kongo Conference in Berlin 1885" etc. Aber es war mit Händen zu greifen, dass diese Erklärungsmuster nicht weit führen. Natürlich weiß jeder, dass Nigerias Politiker korrupt sind, so wie Polizisten, Lehrer und Verwaltungsangestellte. Aber warum funktionieren die Staatsorgane in Europa und Nordamerika? Auch die Intellektuellen sind weitgehend ratlos. Manchmal erzählten mir Studenten oder Professoren, dass die Überlegenheit der Europäer darin gründe, dass sie stärkere Hexen oder Zauberer haben. Wie sonst sollte es ihnen gelungen sein, Computer zu bauen oder Raketen zum Mond zu schicken? Vielleicht lag das Geheimnis ihrer Stärke auch darin, dass sie Wege gefunden hatten, mit dem Okkulten weniger destruktiv umzugehen. Statt die verborge-

---

30 Heike BEHREND: Man ist, was man isst. Zur Eucharistie und ihren Variationen: Kannibalen und Katholiken in Westuganda, in: Kursbuch 143 (2001), S. 167-183, hier S. 170.
31 Ebd., S. 168.
32 Zit. nach Paul GIFFORD: African Christianity. Its Public Role, London 1998, S. 324.

nen Kräfte gegeneinander zu richten, wie Afrikaner es tun, zogen sie aus dieser Ressource gemeinsame Stärke.

Die Spekulationen der Afrikaner, dass dämonische Wesen ihrem Glück und Erfolg im Weg stehen, lassen erkennen, dass sie keinen Ausweg aus der Krise wissen. Für sie sieht es so aus, als seien sie in einer untergehenden Welt gefangen. Alle Anstrengungen, die erfolgreiche Entwicklung der Weißen nachzuahmen, indem man ihr technisches und administratives Wissen übernimmt, haben in eine Sackgasse geführt. Nigerias Universitäten haben mehr als eine Million Akademiker produziert, alles Experten in westlichem Know-how, doch ihr Wissen ist offenbar nicht geeignet, den Kern des Problems zu fassen. Für Menschen, die über den „moralischen Kollaps der Nation"[33] nachsinnen, sind es tatsächlich dunkle, unverstandene Kräfte, die sie dazu treiben, sich miteinander zu verfeinden. Der Hinweis auf Hexen und Zauberer führt in der Tat ins Zentrum des Problems. Den Europäern gelang es, effektive Verwaltungen und Nationalökonomien aufzubauen, als sie lernten, die Dämonen im Innern zu bändigen (eine Selbstdomestikation, die sich, wie die Nazi-Zeit zeigt, nur mit Mühe aufrechterhalten lässt).

Statt die Ursache der Probleme in sozialen oder ökonomischen Strukturen zu suchen, vermutet man sie in den finsteren Machenschaften bösartiger Wesen. Damit ändern sich die Lösungsstrategien. Soziale Strukturen können durch bewusstes, gesamtgesellschaftliches Handeln transformiert werden, am effektivsten mithilfe staatlicher Sozialtechnologie. Dämonische Kräfte dagegen lassen sich nicht reformieren. Man kann nur versuchen, sie zu vertreiben, und da sie hartnäckig wiederkehren, muss man Wege finden, sich mit ihrer überlegenen Macht zu arrangieren. Niemand kann sich dem Einfluss unsichtbarer Kräfte auf Dauer entziehen, und so bleibt nur die Möglichkeit, diese Kräfte zu seinen eigenen Gunsten zu manipulieren. Die Menschen verstricken sich dadurch in einen spirituellen Kampf, der sie anderen gegenüber misstrauisch macht und die Angst vor versteckter Aggression weiter steigert. Aus dem Gefühl der Unsicherheit und Vereinzelung heraus entsteht immer wieder das Bedürfnis, aus dieser Welt gegenseitiger Verdächtigungen auszubrechen und sich durch kollektives Handeln von der Last des Bösen zu befreien. Menschen, die gegen Hexen in ihrer Mitte vorgehen, konstituieren sich damit als eine moralische Gemeinschaft, die ihre inneren Spannungen zu lösen sucht. Das Bemühen, unheilvolle Einflüsse zu vertreiben, kann Tausende von Menschen zusammenführen. Im Südosten Nigerias, im Bundesstaat Anambra, stürmten aufgebrachte Demonstranten den Regierungssitz des Gouverneurs, um zu erzwingen, dass ein notorischer Zauberer öffentlich hingerichtet wird.[34] Doch solche sozialen Bewegungen fallen schnell wieder in sich zusammen, und damit zerfällt auch der Konsens über Gut und Böse.

Wege aus der Krise

Politische Führer, wie Thabo Mbeki in Südafrika, rufen die Bevölkerung dazu auf, sich wieder auf die eigene afrikanische Kultur zu besinnen. Offizielle Darstellungen der Vergangenheit beschwören ein goldenes Zeitalter, das erst durch das Eindringen der

---

33 KALU: Religious Dimension, S. 674.
34 Johannes HARNISCHFEGER: The Bakassi Boys. Fighting Crime in Nigeria, in: Journal of Modern African Studies 41 (2003), S. 23-49, hier S. 32-35.

Europäer ein Ende nahm. Ein Mitglied der staatlichen Afrikanische-Renaissance-Kommission informierte uns 1998 an der Universität Natal, wie wir die Vergangenheit zu sehen haben: Europäer hätten die Sklaverei nach Afrika gebracht. Ihre gotischen Kathedralen seien mit dem Blut der Schwarzen erbaut worden, usw. - lauter Geschichten, die sich dem alten Muster fügen, wonach der Reichtum und Erfolg des Einen stets auf Kosten Anderer erworben ist. Während die Weißen prosperieren, werden die Schwarzen immer ärmer. Um diese Ordnung der Dinge aufrechtzuerhalten, müssen die Europäer - wie es scheint - ihre afrikanischen Rivalen schwächen und abhängig halten. Ihnen werden daher monströse Verschwörungen unterstellt. Die angebliche AIDS-Epidemie sei von westlichen Medien erfunden, um Afrikaner zu veranlassen, Kondome zu benutzen und sich nicht mehr zu vermehren. Oder aber: Das AIDS-Virus sei vom CIA entwickelt worden, um die Schwarzen auszurotten. Wer sich mit Hilfe von Kondomen schützen wolle, habe keine Chance, denn auch die Kondome seien mit dem tödlichen Virus infiziert.[35] Die Beschäftigung mit der Boshaftigkeit anderer wird den Menschen nicht helfen, ihre Probleme zu lösen. Trotzdem sind Verschwörungstheorien auch unter Intellektuellen populär, helfen sie doch, sich von der Schuld für den „katastrophalen Niedergang"[36] zu entlasten. Die meisten Afrikaner wollen freilich nicht die vorkoloniale Vergangenheit auferstehen lassen, und sie reagieren eher misstrauisch, wenn Parteifunktionäre und Minister ihnen von *ubuntu* erzählen, dem angeblichen Gemeinsinn der Ahnen. Zumindest unter älteren Afrikanern ist noch die Erinnerung daran lebendig, dass die alte, dörfliche Lebenswelt nicht von Solidarität und Menschenrechten geprägt war, sondern von einem rabiaten Individualismus.[37]

Afrikanische Politiker und Intellektuelle, die der bedrückenden Gegenwart die Harmonie der traditionellen Gesellschaften entgegenstellen, stoßen damit in Europa und Nordamerika, besonders unter der schwarzen Diaspora, auf viel Verständnis. In ihrer Heimat dagegen betrachtet die Bevölkerung die vorkoloniale Vergangenheit in einem anderen Licht. Die erfolgreichsten sozialen Organisationen im heutigen Afrika, die Pfingstkirchen, zeichnen sich gerade dadurch aus, dass sie die ‚heidnischen' Traditionen dämonisieren.[38] Mit der Konversion zu einem strikten, buchstabengläubigen Christentum sollen die Gläubigen einen radikalen Bruch mit der Vergangenheit vollziehen. Dieser Bruch meint vor allem, sich individuell, im alltäglichen Leben, von der Verstrickung in Magie und heidnische Kulte zu lösen.[39] Satanische Kräfte werden durch fromme Riten vertrieben, doch das Abgespaltene behält Macht über das Ich und drängt sich ihm immer wieder auf, in bedrohlichen Träumen und Krankheiten, diabolischen Verführungen und Geisterattacken. Da sich der Einfluss der Dämonen nicht abschütteln lässt,

---

35 New African [London], December 1998, S. 34-42. ELLIS / TER HAAR: Worlds of Power, S. 45f.
36 GIFFORD: African Christianity, S. 348.
37 Jean-Francois BAYART: The ‚Social Capital' of the Felonious State, in: Jean-Francois BAYART / Stephen ELLIS / Béatrice HIBOU (Hg.), The Criminalization of the State in Africa, Oxford 1999, S. 32-48, hier S. 34.
38 GIFFORD: African Christianity, S. 324, 333.
39 Birgit MEYER: 'Make a Complete Break with the Past.' Memory and Post-Colonial Modernity in Ghanaian Pentecostalist Discourse, in: Journal of Religion in Africa 28 (1998), S. 316-349, hier S. 329.

unternehmen religiöse Gruppen auch kollektive Anstrengungen, um das Böse zu vertreiben. Als in der Nähe eines traditionellen Schreins einige Dutzend Leichen entdeckt wurden, brannten Gegner der Schreinpriester den heiligen Hain mitsamt der alten Kultstätte nieder. Ein Bischof der „Overcomer Christian Mission" übernahm dafür die spirituelle Verantwortung: „God gave me victory. I called on God to kill them and burn their shrine to ashes."[40] Der Kampf im Namen Gottes richtet sich jedoch nicht nur gegen die Geister der Vergangenheit, denn das Böse lässt sich in vielen Gestalten imaginieren. Der Antichrist, so vermuten manche christliche Prediger, ist in der dekadenten Welt des Westens wieder erstanden. Europa sei ein gottloser Kontinent, ein neues „Babylon"[41], in dem Homosexuelle zu Bischöfen gewählt werden und Satanisten ungehindert ihre Rituale abhalten.

Ähnlich wie die übergroße Mehrheit der Christen wollen auch Muslime keine Renaissance traditioneller Werte oder Lebensformen. Sie kämpfen eher für die „Ent-Afrikanisierung" ihrer Kultur.[42] Im Norden Nigerias, wo einige Bundesstaaten, die Scharia eingeführt haben, soll ‚Götzenanbetung' nun ebenso hart bestraft werden wie Hexerei und Zauberei: „Whoever (...) takes part in the worship or invocation of any juju (...) shall be punished with death."[43] In einigen Regionen sind selbst Singen und Trommeln, öffentlicher Tanz und Flötenspiel unter Strafe gestellt.[44] Durch die religiöse Wiedergeburt soll in Nigeria, wie in anderen Ländern, eine Gesellschaft entstehen, die nach dem zeitlosen Modell göttlicher Gerechtigkeit konzipiert ist: „Islam (…) is universal. It is the same all over the world. And it has never changed from the beginning and will not change till the end."[45] Für die Gläubigen verbindet sich damit der Traum von einer modernen Welt, die wohlhabend ist wie der Westen, aber seine Laster nicht teilt. Strikte Gesetze, die jeden Bereich des privaten und öffentlichen Lebens normieren, sollen dafür sorgen, dass jedes gottlose Verhalten sogleich sichtbar wird. Auf diese Weise kann die Gemeinschaft der Gläubigen anti-soziales Verhalten ächten und ihre innere Harmonie (zurück)gewinnen. Einheit entsteht nicht aus dem freien Spiel konkurrierender Interessen, sondern aus der Eliminierung des Bösen.

Globale Verschwörungen

Menschen, die zusammenkommen, um Hexen in ihrer Mitte zu verfolgen, konstituieren sich nur episodisch zu einer moralischen Gemeinschaft, und so können sie Angst und Misstrauen voreinander bestenfalls vorübergehend überwinden. Durch die Mobilmachung gegen äußere Feinde lässt sich dagegen mehr Geschlossenheit gewinnen, und

---

40 Alexander EKEWUBA, in: Newswatch [Lagos], 6.9.2004, S. 48.
41 Emmanuel MILINGO: The Demarcations, Lusaka 1984, S. 25.
42 William F. S. MILES: Shari'a as De-Africanization: Evidence from Hausaland, in: Africa Today [London] 50 (2003), S. 51-75, hier S. 65.
43 ZAMFARA STATE OF NIGERIA: Gazette No. 1. 15th June, 2000. Vol. 3. Law No. 10. Shariah Penal Code Law. Gusau, Zamfara State: Ministry of Justice, § 406. – Der Begriff 'Juju' wird in § 405 definiert: „'Juju' includes the worship or invocation of any object or being other than Allah".
44 MILES: Shari'a, S. 63.
45 Dr. Lateef ADEGBITE, Generalsekretär des Supreme Council for Islamic Affairs, in: Vanguard [eine Tageszeitung aus Lagos], 24.3.2002, S. 21.

diese Möglichkeit nutzen besonders Nigerias Muslime, indem sie die Grenze zwischen Gut und Böse, Eigen und Fremd durch eine Fülle religiöser Regeln hervorheben. Was sie an bösen, destruktiven Kräften bekämpfen, wird mit fremden, vor allem westlichen Einflüssen gleichgesetzt. Korruption, Prostitution und Straßenraub sollen erst mit der europäischen Kultur in die eigene Gesellschaft eingedrungen sein.[46] Ja es scheint, als sei der Niedergang der islamischen Welt, von dem nur die Europäer profitierten, mit Bedacht herbeigeführt worden: „Fundamentalists have little time for the idea of unintended consequences. If things happen, they must have a meaning, and meaning is found in the intentions of the agent (...). Bad things occur because bad people desire them."[47] Den Ungläubigen ist nicht zu trauen, selbst wenn sie angeblich uneigennützig handeln. Der Rat der Islamgelehrten in Kano, der Metropole Nordnigerias, forderte daher, sämtliche westliche Hilfsorganisationen des Landes zu verweisen.[48] Besonderen Verdacht erregten die vom Kinderhilfswerk der Vereinten Nationen organisierten Impfungen gegen Kinderlähmung. Es hieß, das Impfprogramm sei Teil einer amerikanischen Verschwörung, um das Land zu entvölkern. Der Impfstoff enthalte Substanzen, die AIDS übertragen oder die Menschen unfruchtbar machen. Laboruntersuchungen in Kano bestätigten diesen Verdacht, sodass die Regierungen von vier Bundesstaaten die Polio-Impfungen einstellten.[49] Aus europäischer Sicht eine irrationale, selbstzerstörerische Reaktion. Die Neigung islamistischer Kreise, für alles, was sie ängstigt oder belastet, fremde Mächte verantwortlich zu machen, erscheint so wahnhaft, dass wir geneigt sind, anzunehmen: Nigerias Muslime müssen ganz besonders traumatische Erfahrungen mit den Europäern gemacht haben. Doch die Annahme, dass ihr Leid ihnen von anderen zugefügt wurde, ergibt sich einfach aus der Logik religiöser Prinzipien, die von ihrem Denken Besitz ergriffen haben. Wenn sie die orthodoxe Lehre ernst nehmen und davon ausgehen, dass es einen Schöpfergott gibt, der alles, was geschieht, so gewollt hat, dann müssen sie in den politischen Krisen der Gegenwart den Widerstreit religiös bestimmter Mächte erkennen. Auch die Annahme, dass die verschiedensten sozialen und ökonomischen Probleme in allen Teilen der Welt stets von demselben satanischen Feind verursacht sind, wird ihnen durch elementare Lehrsätze ihres Glaubens nahe gelegt.[50] Die Neigung, den politischen Gegner zu dämonisieren, führt zu Handlungsstrategien, die in einem multireligiösen Land wie Nigeria die Verständigung auf demokratische Spielregeln erschweren, wenn nicht unmöglich machen: „a satanic enemy cannot be transformed; it can only be destroyed".[51]

Europäer haben wenige Möglichkeiten, solche Weltbilder zu entzaubern und ein realistischeres Verständnis der eigenen Zivilisation zu wecken. Aus der Flut von Bildern und Informationen, die durch CNN, Internet und andere Kanäle nach Afrika strömen,

---

46 Murray LAST: La charia dans le Nord-Nigeria, in: Politique Africaine 79 (2000), S. 141-152, hier S. 141; Hotline [eine Zeitschrift aus Kaduna], 26.3.2000, S. 32f.
47 Vgl. Steve BRUCE: Fundamentalism, Cambridge 2000, S. 110.
48 Tell, 5.2.2001, S. 40.
49 Economist [London], 10.1.2004, S. 32. Newswatch, 16.8.2004, S. 54f.
50 BRUCE: Fundamentalism, S. 112, 116.
51 Mark JUERGENSMEYER: Terror in the Mind of God. The Global Rise of Religious Violence. Third Edition, Berkeley / Los Angeles / London 2003, S. 220.

fügen sich die Menschen, je nach ihrer lokalen Interessenlage, ihre eigene globale Realität zusammen. Dabei vermischen sich religiöse und säkulare Deutungsmuster: Für Inflation und Massenarbeitslosigkeit werden oft internationale Einrichtungen verantwortlich gemacht, die Weltbank, die Strukturanpassungsprogramme usw. Aber Begriffe wie *World Bank* oder *SAP* sind nicht viel mehr als Chiffren für eine dämonische Verschwörung. Ähnlich wie in vorkolonialer Zeit werden politische Geschehnisse in mythischer Form erinnert und mitgeteilt. In den Erzählungen der Menschen sind sie verwoben mit okkulten Spekulationen und Gerüchten, die Glauben finden, weil sie disparate Details sinnvoll miteinander verknüpfen. Was ethnische oder religiöse Gruppen über sich und ihre Gegner memorieren, bezieht sich nicht mehr auf eine gemeinsame, objektive Geschichte, d. h. auf eine Chronologie von Ereignissen, die unabhängig von all den konfligierenden Mythen schriftlich fixiert und damit überprüfbar wäre. Christen und Muslime, Hausa und Igbo, Tiv und Jukun spinnen sich in ihre eigenen Realitäten ein, sodass die politische Verständigung zwischen ihnen schwieriger wird. Der Verfall der Schriftkultur lässt sich an vielen Symptomen ablesen: In den ‚Nationalen' Archiven werden Akten gestohlen oder vernichtet; staatliche Bürokratien produzieren kaum noch verlässliche Schriftstücke über ihr Handeln und die politische Elite bevorzugt ohnehin, sich informell zu verständigen, ohne schriftliche Dokumente.[52]

Für Muslime, mehr noch als für Christen, ist es die Religion, die festlegt, was erinnert und was vergessen wird.[53] Rückbesinnung auf den Koran bedeutet, dass das Muster von Dschihad und Kreuzzügen in die eigene afrikanische Geschichte hineingelesen wird. Die Begegnung mit den Europäern war, nach dieser Lesart, von Anfang an eine religiöse Konfrontation: „the British imperialists were infidels and grandsons of the crusaders whose aims and objectives were to wipe out Islam from the face of the earth."[54] Solche Mythen lassen sich kaum widerlegen, weil sie durch aktuelle Geschehnisse immer wieder bestätigt werden. Der Staatsbesuch von Bill Clinton z. B. wurde als ein Versuch gedeutet, die Christianisierung Nigerias zu vollenden.[55] Dass die USA und ihre Verbündeten in den drei Kriegen auf dem Balkan stets aufseiten der Muslime intervenierten, konnte die Gläubigen in Nordnigeria wenig beeindrucken. Eine Verständigung über das, was geschah, ist schon deshalb kaum möglich, weil sich Imame in Kano, Wunderpastoren in Lagos und Sozialwissenschaftler in Hamburg nicht mehr auf eine gemeinsame Realität beziehen. In Nordnigeria können selbst Intellektuelle unwidersprochen behaupten, dass der Westen auf dem Balkan Millionen von Muslimen ermordet hat.[56]

---

52 ELLIS / TER HAAR: Worlds of Power, S. 183-186.
53 Ebd., S. 184.
54 Hotline, 7. 5. 2000, S. 33.
55 The News [Lagos], 25.9.2000, S. 52.
56 Abu Yakub Yunus SAPKE: Who is a Terrorist? [gedruckt in Nigeria, o.O.] 2001, S. 11, 40, 56.

Johannes Harnischfeger

Rückkehr der Dämonen:
Wandlungen des Christentums in Afrika und Europa

Abstract

Return of the Demons: Transformations of Christianity in Africa and Europe. African mass media are producing a bewildering variety of ideas and speculations about destructive spiritual forces, without providing a reliable, generally accepted interpretive model which could reduce the complexity of the spirit world. So the popular fear of demons, witches and sorcerers is aggravated by intense uncertainty about the nature and the rules of the occult universe. In pre-colonial times, the spiritual landscape was probably less confusing. At least people could agree on certain mediators to the realms of gods and demons, like diviners, sacred kings or shrine priests who were authorised to identify witches and protect the society as a whole, whereas today, there are no institutions with a mandate to identify and eliminate evil. Everybody has to organise his spiritual protection by himself, without much guidance. One may turn to traditional healers or Pentecostal pastors, to Indian gurus (or their 'medicine'), to the Ogboni cult or a Freemasonry lodge: anything goes. Africans are participating in a global market of magico-religious objects and services. Choices are made individually, not on the basis of entrenched beliefs, but rather pragmatically following the principle of trial and error. This does not imply, however, that magic and religion will be confined to the private sphere (as would be necessary in order to maintain secular western-style constitutions). People living in panic about uncontrolled spiritual forces may join religious movements or communities which embark on crusades, exorcisms or other collective endeavours of confronting evil. African churches have become deeply involved in spiritual warfare. This is, however, not just an African phenomenon; it seems to be part of a global process of re-enchantment. Believers in Africa, Asia and Latin America, who form a majority of today's church members, are transforming Christianity into a non-European religion, with a heavy bias on miracles and demonism. Some observers have predicted that Christianity could fall apart into two opposing camps: one of them secular-minded and liberal, the other (in the southern hemisphere) steeped in mysticism, demonizing evil. But there are indications that Europe will not be left out of the spiritual revival. Its educated elites have lost faith in enlightened rationalism. Legal and educational institutions which are providing the official definitions of 'reality' still cling to a secular, 'rational' world-view. Yet in a multi-cultural environment, their influence on people's beliefs is waning. And there is not much reason to trust in the enlightening effects of other socialising agents, like internet and other electronic media. By creating fragmented virtual realities, they may encourage a belief in the existence of hidden, unexplored worlds, shaped by demonic powers and global conspiracies.

Zusammenfassung

Das Projekt der Moderne, die Entzauberung der Welt, ist in vielen Regionen gescheitert. In Afrika ließen die Kolonialmächte per Gesetz die Verfolgung von Hexen verbieten, doch nur wenige Jahrzehnte nach dem Ende der Kolonialherrschaft loderte die Angst vor Hexen, Zauberern und Dämonen wieder auf. Allein in Tansania sollen, nach Angaben der Regierung, zwischen 1994 und 1998 über 5000 Menschen den Hexenjagden zum Opfer gefallen sein.[1] Der Kampf gegen okkulte Bedrohungen beherrscht auch das afrikanische Christentum. Für europäische Beobachter, die sich an halbwegs aufgeklärte Formen des Glaubens gewöhnt haben, ist es befremdlich, dass christliche Gebete und Rituale vor allem dazu dienen, sich vor dämonischen Kräften zu schützen. Doch es gibt keinen Grund anzunehmen, dass das Christentum in Afrika weniger christlich ist als anderswo. So wie überall konnte die fremde monotheistische Religion nur deshalb heimisch werden, weil die Menschen sie in ihren eigenen spirituellen Kategorien aufnahmen. Der Wunder- und Dämonenglaube afrikanischer Christen steht dem ursprünglichen Christentum sicher näher als die ‚rationale' Weltsicht moderner Europäer, die mit vielen Passagen der Bibel nichts mehr anzufangen wissen. Charismatische Formen des Christentums dürften im Übrigen auch bei uns wieder an Einfluss gewinnen. Was sich in Afrika und Europa an postmoderner Religiosität abzeichnet, unterscheidet sich aber, in einer zentralen Hinsicht, vom doktrinären Christentum vormoderner Zeiten. Da es heute Tausende von Kirchen und Kulte gibt, die um Anhänger werben, kann niemand darauf hoffen, das eigene religiöse Weltbild gegenüber anderen durchzusetzen. Es dürfte also keine verbindliche Dämonenlehre mehr entstehen, und damit wird es schwer, das Böse einzugrenzen und kontrollierbar zu machen.

Spirituelle Unsicherheit

In Europa war einer der Gründe für die staatlich gelenkte Verfolgung von Hexen, dass sich die gebildeten Kreise vom ‚Hexenwahn' der einfachen Bevölkerung anstecken ließen. In Afrika sind die Eliten längst infiziert. Unter Richtern und Professoren, Ministern und Staatspräsidenten ist der Glaube an okkulte Kräfte ähnlich weit verbreitet wie in anderen Teilen der Bevölkerung. Trotzdem scheuen staatliche Autoritäten davor zurück, den Kampf gegen okkulte Bedrohungen aufzunehmen. Gesetzliche Handhaben wären durchaus vorhanden, denn in den meisten Ländern Sub-Sahara Afrikas ist Hexerei heute verboten. In Kamerun oder Kenia droht den Verdächtigen eine Gefängnisstrafe von bis zu zehn Jahren, und im Norden Nigerias, wo einige islamische Bundesstaaten die Scharia einführten, ist sogar die Todesstrafe vorgesehen.[2] Das Problem ist nur, dass der Gesetzgeber nicht sagt, wie man Hexen erkennen soll. Richter, die Verdächtigungen prüfen und okkulte Straftaten bewerten sollen, können auf keine klare Regeln zurückgreifen. Es fehlt also an einer verbindlichen Dämonologie, und es ist keine politische oder re-

---

1   Die Zeit, 4.1.2001, S. 28.
2   ZAMFARA STATE OF NIGERIA: Gazette No. 1, 15th June, 2000. Vol. 3. Shariah Penal Code Law, Zaria 2000, § 406.

ligiöse Autorität in Sicht, die diesen Mangel beheben könnte. Eine Regierungskommission in Südafrika, die Hexerei und Ritualmorde untersuchte, bestätigte zwar, was die große Mehrheit der Bürger immer schon angenommen hatte: Dass Hexen töten können, fügte aber hinzu, dass die aggressiven Kräfte, die von einer Hexe ausgehen, unsichtbar sind: „The most vexing problem surrounding witchcraft is that the activities of a witch cannot be witnessed by naked eyes. This means that one cannot be in a position to say that a witch has done this and that".[3]

Trotz der Schwierigkeit, die Täter zu identifizieren, plädierte die Kommission dafür, das alte koloniale Gesetz, das Hexerei-Anklagen zu unterdrücken suchte, abzuschaffen und Hexerei unter Strafe zu stellen. Doch worauf soll sich ein Gerichtsurteil gründen, wenn niemand das Verbrechen beobachten kann? Der Gesetzentwurf behilft sich hier mit einer ausweichenden Formulierung, die allen möglichen Formen der Beweisführung den Weg ebnet: „Any person who [...] does any act which creates a reasonable suspicion that he is engaged in the practice of witchcraft [...] shall be guilty of an offence and liable on conviction [...] to imprisonment for a period not exceeding four years".[4]

Ein Verdacht soll ausreichen, um Menschen ins Gefängnis zu bringen. Die Frage ist nur, wie die Richter beweisen wollen, dass dieser Verdacht 'vernünftig' ist.

Der Mangel an einer verbindlichen Dämonologie beschäftigt nicht nur Juristen und Regierungsethnologen, er ist auch für einfache Bürger ein Problem. Wenn es unsichtbare Kräfte gibt, die sich manipulieren lassen, um andere Menschen zu töten, ist nichts wichtiger, als geeignete Gegenmittel zu finden. Doch wie will man sich schützen, wenn die Art der Gefährdung nicht klar ist? Jeder Erwachsene in Kenia oder Nigeria weiß, dass die meisten seiner Mitmenschen sich an Schreinpriester wenden und das Bündnis mit mächtigen Geistern suchen oder dass sie Zauberer konsultieren und sich mit Magie beschäftigen (d. h. mit Riten oder Zaubersprüchen, die durch sich selbst, ohne die Anrufung von Geistern oder Gottheiten, unsichtbare Kräfte entfalten). Nur lässt sich nicht abschätzen, welche Kraft diese Geister haben und an welchen Symptomen fremde magische Einflüsse zu erkennen sind. Da okkulte Bedrohungen im Grunde nicht fassbar sind, werden sie in immer neuen bizarren Fantasien imaginiert. Die Gespräche kreisen um Ritualmorde und satanische Banknoten, um Kinderhexen und Wassergeister. Auch die Medien produzieren ständig neue Bilder des Bösen, sodass die Menschen mit okkulten Theorien und Spekulationen überhäuft werden. Gerade diese Flut von widersprüchlichen Informationen aber trägt zur Verunsicherung bei: Früher hatte man angenommen, dass magische Kräfte nur über eine begrenzte Distanz hin wirksam sind. Wer einem unheilvollen Zauber entgehen wollte, hatte also die Möglichkeit, sich von der Gefahrenquelle zu entfernen und an einem entlegenen Ort Zuflucht zu finden. Heute dagegen befürchten viele, dass sich feindselige Kräfte mithilfe elektronischer Medien über jede Entfernung hinweg aussenden lassen. Wie in den Nachrichten der BBC zu hören war, verbreitete sich im Sommer 2004 in Nigeria die Furcht vor einer völlig anonymen, will-

---

[3] V. RALUSHAI: Report of the Commission of Inquiry into Witchcraft Violence and Ritual Murders in the Northern Province of the Republic of South Africa. Submitted to the MEC for Safety and Security, Northern Province [unveröffentlicht] 1996, S. 57, 61.

[4] RALUSHAI: Report, S. 54f.

kürlichen Form der Magie. Die Gefahr ging von dem Anruf einer gewissen Handy-Nummer aus. Wer den Anruf entgegennahm und die Botschaft abhörte, war innerhalb von zehn Minuten tot.

Um die Gefahren richtig einzuschätzen, wäre es wichtig zu wissen, von welchen Personen Hexerei ausgehen kann. Ist die Fähigkeit zu hexen erblich bedingt, oder kann sie auf andere Weise übertragen werden, etwa durch den Genuss von Lebensmitteln? Hält man sich an Berichte der nigerianischen Presse, muss man mit dem Schlimmsten rechnen. Bei einem öffentlichen Geständnis in einer Pfingstkirche berichtete eine Frau, wie ihre Tante ihr ein gekochtes Ei in die Hand gedrückt habe. Es war ein Entenei. Nach seinem Verzehr verwandelte sie sich, gegen ihren Willen, in eine Hexe. Selbst Kinder wurden auf ähnliche Weise infiziert.[5] Die Fähigkeit zur Hexerei, die manche Menschen plötzlich mit Schrecken an sich entdecken, wird von anderen angeblich auch mit Bedacht erworben. Sie schließen sich einem Hexenkult an, weil ihnen ein Unrecht widerfahren ist und sie nach Möglichkeiten suchen, sich zu rächen. Das behauptet jedenfalls der Vorsitzende der *World Association of White Witches and Wizards*. Nach seiner Aussage sind nicht alle Hexen gefährlich. Vor schwarzen und roten Hexen müsse man sich hüten, die weißen dagegen würden den Menschen im Kampf gegen destruktive Kräfte beistehen. Er selbst sei, so wie andere weiße Hexen, ein „Engel Gottes".[6] Doch wer soll entscheiden, ob dieser Anspruch berechtigt ist? Ein Experte aus Lagos, der sich als „professor of mental arts" bezeichnet, vertritt eine ganz andere Form der Klassifikation: Hexen lassen sich nicht nach Gut oder Böse unterscheiden, sondern nur danach, wie viel Macht sie haben. Vertreter christlicher Kirchen heben demgegenüber hervor, dass Hexerei in jedem Fall verwerflich ist. Unterschiede zwischen weißen, roten und schwarzen Hexen seien frei erfunden. Warum sollte Gott weiße Hexen benötigen, um seinen Willen Geltung zu verschaffen? Nur Gott selbst biete Schutz gegen gefährliche Geister, meint etwa der Pastor des *World Harvest Evangelical Ministry*, und dieser Schutz sei in seiner Kirche erhältlich.[7]

Der Wunsch, sich vor Hexen, Zauberern und Dämonen abzuschirmen, treibt den Kirchen Millionen von Gläubigen zu. „Christen sind Feiglinge", erklärte mir eine Bekannte in Zimbabwe: „Warum rennen sie in die Kirche? Weil sie Angst vor Hexen haben." Aber sind sie im Schoß der Kirche sicher aufgehoben? Ist der Anschein christlicher Frömmigkeit, den die Kirchenbesitzer sich zulegen, nicht einfach eine Maske, hinter der sich der alte Zauber von Hexenbannern verbirgt? In Onitsha, nicht weit von meiner damaligen Universität entfernt, brannten aufgebrachte Demonstranten mehrere Kirchen nieder, nachdem dort Menschenschädel und andere verdächtige Gegenstände entdeckt worden waren.[8] In Nigeria kann jeder seine eigene Kirche eröffnen und spirituelle Dienstleistungen anbieten. Keine andere Wirtschaftsbranche verzeichnete in den letzten Jahren ähnlich hohe Wachstumsraten, denn wer sich als Prophet oder Wunderpastor etablieren

---

5   Tell [ein Nachrichtenmagazin aus Lagos], 22. 4. 2002, S. 12.
6   Tell, 22. 4. 2002, S. 13.
7   Tell, 22. 4. 2002, S. 13-14.
8   Johannes HARNISCHFEGER: Unverdienter Reichtum. Über Hexerei und Ritualmorde in Nigeria, in: Sociologus 47 (1997), S. 129-156, hier S. 149-152.

will, kommt mit einem Minimum an Startkapital aus. Kirchen sind *Low-Budget-*Unternehmen mit hohen Gewinnspannen. Geschäftsleute, die in anderen Branchen gescheitert sind, etablieren sich als traditionelle Heiler oder machen sich zum Besitzer einer Kirche.[9] Eine theologische Ausbildung ist dabei nicht vonnöten; es reicht der Anspruch, erwählt zu sein und über charismatische Kräfte zu verfügen.

Vertreter der großen Missionskirchen, denen die Gläubigen davonlaufen, forderten die Regierung auf, in den ungehemmten spirituellen Wettbewerb einzugreifen und das Land von „Schundkirchen" und „pfingstlerischer Hexerei" zu reinigen.[10] Nur: Mit welchem Recht werfen sich christliche Autoritäten zu Richtern über andere auf? Greifen sie nicht ebenfalls auf obskure Riten zurück? Katholische Geistliche verkaufen nicht nur geweihte Kerzen, sondern auch Pülverchen, um Hexen und Dämonen zu vertreiben, ja sie sind direkt an der Jagd auf Hexen beteiligt.[11] Die Prophetin Ngozi, deren Kirche ich anderthalb Jahre lang angehörte, ging sogar noch einen Schritt weiter. Es hieß, sie habe den „Präsidenten" des lokalen „Hexenclubs" und andere Gegner ihrer Mission getötet. Ihre Anhänger versicherten mir jedenfalls mit triumphierender Geste: „Sister Ngozi killed them with Holy Spirit."

In einer Welt, die von Zauber und Gegenzauber beherrscht ist, sind mehr und mehr Menschen bereit, mit allen verfügbaren Mitteln zu kämpfen. Warum sollten sie sich in der Wahl ihrer Waffen mehr Zurückhaltung auferlegen als ihre Feinde? Die Unterscheidung von Weißer und Schwarzer Magie wird aus ihrer Perspektive hinfällig, und damit verlieren auch moralische Distinktionen an Bedeutung. ‚Gut' bedeutet einfach nur: gut für mich, und ‚böse' bedeutet: schlecht für mich.

Traditionelle Gesellschaften in Afrika kannten keinen Unterschied zwischen wahren und falschen Göttern. Sie entwickelten auch keine Glaubenssysteme oder Dämonologien, wie wir sie von den großen Schriftreligionen kennen. Trotzdem war die spirituelle Welt überschaubarer als heute, denn der Zugang zu ihr war institutionell geregelt. Mit der Initiation in die Welt der Erwachsenen wurden die Menschen zugleich in die Geheimnisse des Okkulten eingeweiht, und diese Begegnung mit dem gefährlichen Reich der Geister gestaltete sich als ein kollektiver Erfahrungsprozess, der durch Männerbünde, Geheimgesellschaften oder Besessenheitskulte organisiert wurde. Heute dagegen ist es weitgehend dem Einzelnen überlassen, seine Beziehung zur spirituellen Welt zu organisieren. Er kann sich an traditionelle Heiler wenden oder an islamische Marabouts, an Geheimgesellschaften oder Wunderpastoren, an Rosenkreuzer, Freimaurer oder die Gesellschaft vom Heiligen Gral. Auf der Suche nach einem spirituellen Obdach sind die Menschen in Lagos oder Nairobi ähnlich frei und ungebunden wie Esoterik-Liebhaber

---

9   Gerrie TER HAAR: Spirit of Africa. The Healing Ministry of Archbishop Milingo of Zambia, London 1992, S. 114. Da Industrieunternehmen aus Nigeria und den Nachbarstaaten abwandern, finden talentierte junge Leute kaum andere Beschäftigungen: „Christian missions are now (…) perhaps the biggest single industry in Africa": Paul GIFFORD: African Christianity. Its Public Role, Bloomington / Indianapolis 1998, S. 315.

10 The Week [Lagos], 9. 12. 1996, S. 10, 12.

11 Mary DOUGLAS: Sorcery Accusations Unleashed: the Lele Revisited, 1987, in: Africa 69 (1999) 2, S. 177-193, hier S. 184-186. Heike BEHREND: 'Satan gekreuzigt'. Interner Terror und Katharsis in Tooro, Westuganda, in: Historische Anthropologie 12 (2004) 2, S. 211-227, hier S. 221-223.

in Kalifornien: *anything goes*. Das Sichauflösen alter Gewissheiten wird jedoch nicht als Befreiung erlebt. Das Nebeneinander widersprüchlicher Theorien und Spekulationen, die sich nicht zu einem konsistenten Bild okkulter Kräfte runden, steigert eher das Gefühl, unkontrollierbaren Mächten ausgeliefert zu sein. Es schafft Unsicherheit, die sich bis zu „moralischer Panik" steigern kann.[12] Mir scheint, es gibt ein starkes Bedürfnis nach einer Autorität, die verlässliche Auskunft gibt und die den Kampf gegen das Böse in geregelte Bahnen lenkt. Dennoch glaube ich nicht, dass sich Institutionen herausbilden werden, die eine verbindliche Dämonologie durchsetzen können. Die Verfolgung von Hexen lässt sich nicht monopolisieren; sie dürfte auch in Zukunft von rivalisierenden Gruppen, von Kirchen, Kulten und Milizen, betrieben werden. Für diese Vermutung möchte ich vier Gründe nennen.

1. Staatsverfall und soziale Desintegration

In vorkolonialer Zeit, als die Igbo, Yoruba oder Kikuyu in relativ geschlossenen lokalen Gemeinschaften lebten, war die spirituelle Welt nicht nur überschaubarer; der Zugang zu ihr ließ sich auch besser kontrollieren. Im Kreis der Familie war es in der Regel das Familienoberhaupt, das den Kontakt zu den Ahnen aufrechterhielt. Und die Kommunikation mit den Clan-, Dorf- und Stadtgottheiten wurde meist von Priestern reguliert. Wer sich gegen die spirituelle Autorität der Ältesten auflehnte, gefährdete den Zusammenhalt der Gemeinschaft und riskierte damit, von seinen Angehörigen verstoßen zu werden. Ohne den Rückhalt der eigenen Gruppe aber war es kaum möglich, Leben und Freiheit zu verteidigen. Erst die Kolonialherrschaft hat den Zusammenhalt der traditionellen – durch Nachbarschaft oder Familienbande gestifteten – Gruppen dauerhaft geschwächt. Unter der *Pax Britannica* waren Familien, Clans oder Dorfgemeinschaften nicht länger gezwungen, als geschlossene politische Einheiten aufzutreten, die ihre Mitglieder gegen Übergriffe anderer Gruppen schützten. Von diesem Wandel profitierten all jene, die nicht gewillt waren, sich der Autorität der Ältesten zu unterwerfen, also vor allem junge Leute und zum Teil auch Frauen. Sie konnten sich nun dem Zwangszusammenhang der Dörfer und Familien entziehen und in die Anonymität der Städte abwandern, wo sie sehr viel freier waren zu entscheiden, welche sozialen und religiösen Beziehungen sie eingehen.

Ein halbes Jahrhundert nach der Kolonialzeit sind die wichtigsten Errungenschaften der Moderne, der Staat und sein Gewaltmonopol, verfallen, sodass die Menschen sich wieder selbst um ihre Sicherheit kümmern müssen. Viele klammern sich, so wie früher, an ihre Familienangehörigen, die einzig natürlichen Verbündeten. Nur ihnen gegenüber hat man grundsätzlich das Recht, Hilfe einzuklagen. Doch Verwandtschaftsgruppen bieten wenig Sicherheit, weil sich das Verhalten ihrer Mitglieder kaum noch kontrollieren lässt. Oft leben Familienangehörige weit voneinander verstreut und gehen ihren eigenen Beschäftigungen nach, sodass es ihnen leicht fällt, sich ihren traditionellen Verpflichtungen zu entziehen. Statt sich um verarmte Angehörige zu kümmern, schließen sie sich

---

12 Vgl. die Berichte von Rosalind SHAW: The Politics and the Diviner: Divination and the Consumption of Power in Sierra Leone, in: Journal of Religion in Africa 26 (1996) 1, S. 30-55, hier S. 50, und Heike Behrend: BEHREND: Satan gekreuzigt, S. 212.

christlichen Gemeinden oder Geheimgesellschaften an, vielleicht auch der Gefolgschaft von lokalen *strongmen* oder *warlords*. All diese Gruppen aber binden sich auf je eigene Weise an spirituelle Mächte. Selbst ethnische Befreiungsbewegungen oder Milizen umgeben sich mit eigenen *witchdoctors* und machen Jagd auf Hexen. Da die spirituelle Aufrüstung der Bürger die Angst voreinander nur verstärkt, dürfte die Verfolgung Unschuldiger weiter zunehmen, aber wohl in der Form von Lynchjustiz, die von ‚privaten' Akteuren betrieben wird. In der afrikanischen Postmoderne können sich Zentralgewalten offenbar nicht mehr durchsetzen. Es entstehen freie Gewaltmärkte und damit auch unkontrollierbare spirituelle Märkte.

2. Massenmedien und spiritueller Pluralismus

Als sich im Europa der frühen Neuzeit die Vorstellungen von Teufelspakt und Hexensabbat durchsetzten, hatten die gebildeten Schichten in Deutschland, Frankreich oder England einen ganz ähnlichen Bildungshintergrund. Ihre dämonologischen Debatten und Traktate bezogen sich auf einen Kanon klassischer Texte, allen voran die Bibel, die ihnen durch intensive Wiederholungslektüre vertraut war. Demgegenüber gibt es im heutigen Nigeria, mit seinen 500 verschiedenen Ethnien, keine homogene Elite, die sich durch gemeinsame Denktraditionen verbunden weiß. Man könnte einwenden, die modernen Massenmedien sorgten dafür, dass sich populäre Vorstellungen des Okkulten durch alle Segmente der Gesellschaft verbreiten. Aber gerade die Medien, mit ihren globalen Bilder- und Informationsströmen, verhindern, dass sich eine verbindliche Deutung von Magie, Hexerei und spirituellen Kräften durchsetzt. Was der Einzelne, eher zufällig, auf Dutzenden von Fernsehkanälen zu sehen bekommt, präsentiert ihm immer nur Bruchstücke der okkulten Welt, noch dazu in so disparater Form, dass sie sich nicht zu einer stimmigen Theorie zusammenfügen. Keine weltliche oder religiöse Behörde kann die Flut von wild wuchernden Fantasien und Spekulationen steuern. Eine Zensur lässt sich schon deshalb kaum durchsetzen, weil all die rivalisierenden Anschauungen auch über das Internet zugänglich sind. Durch seine egalitäre, angeblich demokratische Struktur erlaubt dieses Medium einen ungehinderten Austausch spiritueller Erfahrungen, sodass hier nicht nur die Gegner der Hexen frei zu Wort kommen, sondern auch die Hexen und Teufelsanbeter selbst.

Für Afrikaner, die den *Links* im Internet folgen, ist es faszinierend zu sehen, dass okkultes Wissen gerade dort angehäuft wird, wo sich auch technologisches *Know-how* konzentriert: in den USA. Satanskirchen und Vampir-Kulte, die ihre Praktiken aus Angst vor Strafverfolgung früher geheim gehalten hatten, nutzen den Trend westlicher Gesellschaften, kulturelle Vielfalt zu fördern, um auf Tausenden von *Websites* Anhänger zu werben oder Nachahmer zu finden. Esoterische Lehren, Zaubersprüche und Rituale sind dadurch so frei zugänglich wie nie zuvor. Auf der *Website* einer Satanisten-Gruppe, Order of the Nine Angles, findet sich z. B. eine Anleitung zu Ritualmorden.[13] Vieles, was sich an Rezepten für okkulte Gewalt nachlesen lässt, ist traditionellen Hexe-

---

13 Dawn PERLMUTTER: The Forensics of Sacrifice: A Symbolic Analysis of Ritualistic Crime, in: Anthropoetics 9 (2003/2004) 2, S. 1-32. www.anthropoetics.ucla.edu/ap0902/sacrifice.htm, hier S. 2, 15.

rei-Vorstellungen, wie Afrikaner sie aus ihren eigenen Kulturen kennen, verblüffend ähnlich. Durch ‚magnetischen Vampirismus' etwa soll sich lernen lassen, seinen Astralkörper auszusenden, um andere Personen anzugreifen oder ihnen die Lebenskräfte auszusaugen. Gut möglich, dass einige dieser spirituellen Vampire sich einbilden, Mörder zu sein, so wie sich Hexen in Afrika, auch ohne äußeren Druck, monströser Verbrechen bezichtigen. Die Beschäftigung mit Okkultem spielt sich jedoch nicht nur in der Sphäre des Imaginären und Virtuellen ab. Afro-karibische Religionen, mit ihren elaborierten Zauberriten und Geisterbeschwörungen, haben in Nordamerika Millionen von Anhängern. Bizarre Rituale finden hier tatsächlich statt und hinterlassen gespenstische Spuren: Kadaver von geopferten Tieren, die an Flüssen, Stränden oder Bahngleisen zurückbleiben, zuweilen auch geschändete Friedhöfe und aufgewühlte Gräber. Für Anhänger des Palo Mayombe, einer düsteren Abart des Voodoo, spielen Leichenteile eine wichtige Rolle. Indem sie Knochen und Schädel eines Menschen in einem Kessel kochen, rufen sie den Geist des Toten herbei und verwandeln ihn in ein willenloses Werkzeug, das sich aussenden lässt, um Feinde zu vernichten.[14]

Angesichts dieser unheimlichen Praktiken sehen sich konservative, evangelikale Christen in ihrer Überzeugung bestätigt, dass von satanischen Kräften eine reale Bedrohung ausgeht. Für sie ist es empörend, dass der säkulare Staat dem düsteren Spuk fast tatenlos zusieht. Das Plündern von Gräbern ist natürlich ein strafbares Vergehen, das die Behörden zwingt, einzuschreiten. Doch ansonsten zeigt sich die Obrigkeit bemüht, das Recht jedes Bürgers, seine Religion frei auszuüben, nicht anzutasten. Juristische Klagen kommen meist nur von Tierschutzverbänden, die sich nicht damit abfinden wollen, dass Hunde, Ziegen oder Katzen auf makabre Weise zu Tode gebracht werden. Der Oberste Gerichtshof der USA hat freilich festgestellt, dass Gläubige im Prinzip das Recht haben, ihren Göttern Tieropfer darzubringen.[15] Im Übrigen gelten auch Satanskirchen als gemeinnützige Vereinigungen, mit eigenen ethischen Zielsetzungen, sodass sie Steuerfreiheit genießen.[16] Trotz dieser offiziellen Anerkennung klagen manche darüber, dass sie wegen ihrer religiösen Überzeugungen diskriminiert werden. Um gegen Vorurteile anzukämpfen, organisierten Vampir-Vereinigungen eine Kampagne unter dem Slogan „Stop Vampire Hate".[17] Die moralische Empörung, mit der sie Kritik an den eigenen Ritualen abweisen und ihren Gegnern Intoleranz vorwerfen, lässt ahnen, dass sich auch in westlichen Gesellschaften, ähnlich wie in Afrika, die Grenzen von Gut und Böse, Real und Irreal heillos verwirrt haben.

3. Legitimationsverlust der politischen Elite

Staatliche Autoritäten sind in Afrika zu sehr diskreditiert, um den Kampf gegen spirituelle Bedrohungen anzuführen. Statt das Okkulte abzuwehren, ziehen Staatsmänner es

---

14 PERLMUTTER: Forensics, S. 4, 6-8, 12, 14.
15 PERLMUTTER: Forensics, S. 13.
16 Dawn PERLMUTTER: Skandalon 2001: The Religious Practices of Modern Satanists and Terrorists, in: Anthropoetics 7 (2001/2002) 2, S. 1-40. www.anthropoetics.ucla.edu/ap0702/skandalon.htm, hier S. 13, 15.
17 PERLMUTTER: Forensics, S. 7.

in die politischen Auseinandersetzungen hinein. Sie umgeben sich mit Zauberern und Geistersehern, binden sich an Geheimgesellschaften und Schreingottheiten, sodass – nach den Worten von Peter Geschiere – Hexereivorstellungen bis in das Herz des Staates vorgedrungen sind.[18] Da Macht kaum noch institutionell geregelt ist, wird sie unberechenbar und scheint von verborgenen Kräften abhängig zu sein: „the acquisition of wealth, achievement of high office and the possession of high status consumable goods cannot be conceived without [occult powers]".[19] Politiker geben sich nicht einmal mehr die Mühe zu verbergen, dass sie in alle möglichen finsteren Praktiken verstrickt sind. Die aufwendigen okkulten Veranstaltungen dienen gerade dazu, mögliche Gegner einzuschüchtern. Schon vor Jahrzehnten machte der Präsident von Haiti, Dr. Duvalier, von sich reden, als er die Leiche eines ermordeten Oppositionspolitikers verschwinden ließ, um seine Untertanen glauben zu machen, dass er Voodoo betreibe.[20]

Nach außen hin wird oft noch die Fassade von westlicher Modernität aufrechterhalten. So wie die Kolonialmächte es verfügt hatten, treten die Staaten als säkulare Institutionen auf, die ohne das Bündnis mit spirituellen Kräften auskommen. Staatliche Gerichte fällen ihre Schiedssprüche, ohne Wahrsager oder Orakel zu befragen, und auch die Spitzen der Regierung vermeiden es in der Regel, ihre Entscheidungen mit den Anweisungen irgendwelcher Geister zu begründen. Zumindest in offiziellen Erklärungen wird so getan, als teile man jenes nüchtern-rationale Weltverständnis, mit dem die europäische Moderne ‚Realität' definiert hat. Doch die Bereitschaft, die Überlegenheit einer fremden Denkweise anzuerkennen, nimmt ab. Islamische Staaten haben bereits mit jenem aufgeklärt-säkularen Denken gebrochen, das die bürgerlichen Eliten des Westens der Staatengemeinschaft und ihren internationalen Organisationen aufgezwungen hatten.[21] Der politische Gegner wird wieder religiös bestimmt, und da liegt es nahe, ihn mit dämonischen Mächten in Verbindung zu bringen. Als Reaktion auf die politischen Ambitionen der Muslime entsteht in vielen Teilen Afrikas ein kämpferisches Christentum, das von staatlichen Autoritäten ein stärkeres religiöses Engagement verlangt, sei es im Kampf gegen Ungläubige oder gegen Hexen.[22] Gut möglich, dass einige Länder dem Beispiel Sambias folgen und sich zu christlichen Staaten erklären werden. Regierungschefs dürften versucht sein, sich durch Kampagnen gegen die Feinde Gottes Legitimität zu verschaffen, aber ob es ihnen gelingt, in der Rolle religiöser Führer anerkannt zu werden, ist fraglich.

---

18 Peter GESCHIERE: The Modernity of Witchcraft. Politics and the Occult in Postcolonial Africa, Charlottesville / London 1997, S. 200.
19 Michael ROWLANDS / Jean-Pierre WARNIER: Sorcery, Power and the Modern State in Cameroon, in: Man 23 (1988), S. 118-132, hier S. 129.
20 Robert I. ROTBERG: Vodun and the Politics of Haiti, in: Martin L. KILSON / Robert I. ROTBERG (Hg.), The African Diaspora. Interpretive Essays, Cambridge, Massachusetts / London, S. 342-365, hier S. 363-365.
21 Elizabeth SHAKMAN HURD: The Political Authority of Secularism in International Relations, in: European Journal of International Relations 10 (2004) 2, S. 235-262, hier S. 238, 246.
22 GIFFORD: African Christianity, S. 317.

4. Freie Religionsmärkte und das Werben um Kunden

Im Europa des späten Mittelalters und der beginnenden Neuzeit hatte die Katholische Kirche eine Monopolstellung. Sie konnte strikte Rechtgläubigkeit, auch in Fragen der Dämonologie anstreben, denn sie hatte die Möglichkeit, ihre Doktrin durchzusetzen. Im heutigen Afrika dagegen ist sie nur eine von vielen Tausend Kirchen; sicher die größte des Kontinents, mit mehr als 100 Millionen Anhängern, aber ohne die institutionelle Macht, abweichende Glaubensvorstellungen zu unterdrücken. Statt Häretiker zu verfolgen, muss sie um Mitglieder werben. Den potenziellen Kunden aber geht es um handfeste materielle Vorteile. Religion war für sie immer schon eine selbstsüchtige Angelegenheit: das angestrengte Bemühen, feindselige Kräfte abzuwehren, um sich Reichtum, Gesundheit und Fruchtbarkeit zu verschaffen. Seit die verschiedensten religiösen und magischen Techniken wie in einem großen spirituellen Supermarkt zur Verfügung stehen, prüfen die Gläubigen das Angebot und testen, was Wunderpastoren, indische Gurus oder esoterische Zirkel ihnen zu bieten haben: „Come and receive your miracle."[23] Manche schließen sich auch zwei oder drei Kirchen gleichzeitig an. Im Übrigen zeigen sie wenig Bedenken, die Konfession öfter zu wechseln, sodass ihre religiösen Glaubenssätze recht fluide sind.

Die Katholische Kirche ist nicht nur eine unter vielen, die weltweit um Anhänger wirbt; sie ist auch, was die Existenz von Hexen und andere Glaubensfragen angeht, tief gespalten. Ein Priester aus Südostnigeria, Rev. Dr. Akwanya, versicherte mir: Wenn der Vatikan gezwungen wäre, zur Hexerei eindeutig Stellung zu nehmen, würde die Kirche auseinanderbrechen. Deshalb sei es eine weise Entscheidung, zu diesem Thema offiziell zu schweigen. Kontroversen über dämonologische Fragen könnten, mehr als andere Antagonismen, den Bestand der Kirche als einer universalen Institution gefährden. Von den Disputen innerhalb des Klerus dringt deshalb kaum etwas nach außen. Für Aufsehen sorgte immerhin der Fall des Erzbischofs von Lusaka, Emmanuel Milingo, der durch Wunderheilungen und Geisterbeschwörungen in seiner Heimat Sambia enorme Popularität gewonnen hatte. Im Jahre 1982 wurde er nach Rom beordert, wo man ihn, zu seiner Überraschung, einer medizinischen Untersuchung unterwarf, bei der auch Psychologen über seinen Gesundheitszustand urteilten. Das Ergebnis war, dass er nicht mehr in seine Diözese zurückkehren durfte. Wir wollen den Fall Milingo etwas genauer betrachten, nicht nur, weil er uns afrikanische Formen des Christentums näherbringt, sondern auch, weil er uns einiges über die Zukunft des europäischen Christentums verrät.

Rückbesinnung auf die spirituellen Wurzeln des Christentums

Milingo hatte verlangt, dass die Europäer ihr Gefühl der Überlegenheit gegenüber den Afrikanern ablegen. Solange sie meinen, die Entwicklung des Christentums auf anderen Kontinenten weiter beaufsichtigen zu müssen, bleibe die Kirche in Afrika ein Fremdkörper. Das Zweite Vatikanische Konzil habe den Schwarzen ein Christentum verspro-

---

23 Unter dieses Motto stellte der Evangelist Reinhard Bonnke seine öffentlichen Auftritte in Nigeria. In einer einzigen Nacht kamen 1,6 Millionen Gläubige, vgl. Philip JENKINS: The Next Christendom. The Coming of Global Christianity, Oxford 2002, S. 74.

chen, das sie nicht zwingt, ihr „eigenes Selbst" zu verwerfen.[24] Was als christlich zu gelten habe, werde allerdings weiterhin in den Metropolen des Westens definiert. Das Recht, auf ihre eigene Weise Christen zu sein, können sich Afrikaner daher nur erkämpfen, wenn sie sich – auch innerlich, im eigenen Denken – von kolonialen Vorurteilen lösen und der eigenen Kultur wieder Respekt entgegenbringen. Ein integraler Bestandteil der afrikanischen Kultur aber sei der Glaube an Geister.[25]

Weiße Missionare hatten diesen Glauben als irrational abgetan. Statt die Ängste vor okkulten Kräften ernst zu nehmen, erklärten sie ihren Schutzbefohlenen, es gebe keinen Grund sich zu sorgen, da Geister nicht existierten. Erst allmählich bemerkten die Betroffenen, dass sie getäuscht worden waren, denn in der Heiligen Schrift ist recht eindeutig festgehalten, wie mit Hexen oder Zauberern zu verfahren ist. Während das moderne europäische Christentum mit solchen Bibelpassagen nichts mehr anzufangen weiß, nähern sich Afrikaner diesen Aspekten der göttlichen Offenbarung sehr viel unbefangener. Was sie in den heiligen Texten lesen, soll in der eigenen Gegenwart wieder lebendig werden. Fast alle Strömungen des afrikanischen Christentums sind, nach dem Urteil von Paul Gifford, „fundamentalistisch".[26] Dazu gehört, dass sie die Botschaft Gottes, mit ihren vielen Reminiszenzen an die Geisterwelt, wörtlich nehmen: „We do not have the same problems about the Bible as White people have with their Western scientific mentality."[27] Die Spiritualität des antiken Orients erschließt sich ihnen auf so unmittelbare Weise, weil diese verzauberte Welt ihnen sehr viel näher steht als uns. Auch in den Anfängen des Christentums lag die Anziehungskraft der Kirche darin, dass sie in einer Zeit des sozialen und moralischen Niedergangs Sicherheit versprach: „Die Menschen wurden Mitglied der neuen Gemeinschaft, um von Dämonen befreit zu werden".[28] Milingo konnte sich also auf genuin christliche Motive berufen, wenn er daran erinnerte, dass Jesus – nach dem Zeugnis der Bibel – seinen Anhängern Macht über Geister und Dämonen verliehen habe.[29]

Die heiligen Schriften sind aber nicht die einzige Quelle seiner Dämonologie. Sein Charisma, das ihn über gewöhnliche Priester erhob, speiste sich daraus, dass er in unmittelbaren Kontakt mit der Geisterwelt getreten war. Was er über Hexen, Dämonen oder Totengeister mitteilte, hatte er direkt von ihnen erfahren, durch zahllose exorzistische Sitzungen mit seinen ‚Patienten'. Bei einer dieser Geisterbeschwörungen, als sich

---

24 E[mmanuel] MILINGO: The World in Between. Christian Healing and the Struggle for Spiritual Survival. Edited, with Introduction, Commentary and Epilogue, by Mona MacMillan, London / Maryknoll, New York / Gweru, Zimbabwe 1985, S. 13. TER HAAR: Spirit, S. 159.
25 MILINGO: World in Between, S. 73. T.G. KIAGORA: Angels, Demons and Spirits in African Christianity, in: A. NASIMIYU-WASIKE / D.W. WARUTA (Hg.), Mission in African Christianity. Critical Essays in Missiology, Nairobi 1993, S. 52-66, hier S. 52, TER HAAR: Spirit, S. 174-180, 198, 235.
26 GIFFORD: African Christianity, S. 42.
27 AFRICAN INDEPENDENT CHURCHES: Speaking for Ourselves, Braamfontein 1985, S. 26, in: GIFFORD: African Christianity, S. 43.
28 Peter BROWN: Sorcery, Demons, and the Rise of Christianity from Late Antiquity into the Middle Ages, in: Mary Douglas (Hg.), Witchcraft Confessions & Accusations, London [u.a.] 1970, S. 17-45, hier S. 33.
29 Lukas 9: 1; Apostelgeschichte 5: 12-16, 19: 11.

das Antlitz einer Besessenen zu einer grotesken Fratze verzerrte, ist ihm Satan, der Anführer der Teufel, sogar persönlich erschienen. Angesichts dieser Erfahrungen beklagte er die Ignoranz westlicher Wissenschaftler, die ganze Bücher über Hexen verfassten, ohne je mit einer gesprochen zu haben. Seine Kritik galt aber auch Vertretern des kirchlichen Establishments, die davor zurückscheuten, sich mit dem Reich des Bösen auseinanderzusetzen. Um Satan zu besiegen, müsse man seine Taktiken studieren. Mit Hilfe exorzistischer Techniken habe er die Teufel oft gezwungen, die Wahrheit zu bekennen, und so finden sich in den theologischen Abhandlungen Milingos viele Zitate von Dämonen, aus denen sich das Wesen der okkulten Welt erschließt.[30]

Kritiker warfen dem Erzbischof vor, dass aus seinen Schriften der Geist des *Malleus Maleficarum* spreche. Doch seine Dämonologie trägt unverkennbar afrikanische Züge. Ahnengeister z. B. spielen eine wichtige Rolle, sei es als Beschützer der Gemeinschaft oder als friedlose Rachegeister. Dem Denken der eigenen Ngoni-Kultur ist auch die Vorstellung entnommen, dass sich an der Art, wie ein Besessener tanzt, erkennen lässt, von welchen Geistern er besessen ist: von Schlangen- oder Löwengeistern, vielleicht auch von Fremdgeistern aus anderen Kontinenten. Durch das Bündnis mit solchen Geistern, die im Grunde Teufel sind, erhalten einige der Besessenen übernatürliche Kräfte. Sie können Krankheiten heilen oder Hexen identifizieren.[31] Aus der Kommunikation mit seinen Patienten hatte Milingo erfahren, dass sich die vielen Bewohner der spirituellen Welt nicht einfach in zwei verfeindete Lager einteilen lassen. Anhänger der ‚Satanskirche', die durch einen Pakt mit dem Teufel seine ‚Agenten' geworden sind, kämpfen nicht nur gegen die Kirche und ihre Engel, sie liegen auch mit Hexen im Streit: „Those possessed by the devil will fight tooth and nail against all those human beings who are witches".[32] Solche Einsichten verdanken sich nicht der Bibel oder anderen kanonischen Texten; sie stammen aus dem Mund seiner sambischen Patienten. Das charismatische Christentum des Erzbischofs wertet damit die Adressaten der christlichen Botschaft auf; es verschafft den einfachen Gläubigen Gehör und lässt ihre Gedankenwelt in die offizielle Theologie einfließen. Darin ähneln Milingos theologische Schriften den klassischen Werken europäischer Dämonologen, die sich ebenfalls für volkstümliche Glaubensvorstellungen interessierten.[33]

Im zeitgenössischen Afrika, wo der Erfolg der Kirchen durch die Gesetze von Angebot und Nachfrage bestimmt ist, geht der Einfluss des Laienpublikums freilich viel weiter als zu Zeiten der europäischen Hexenverfolgung. Geistliche wie Emmanuel Milingo kommen den Bedürfnissen ihrer Klientel jedenfalls weit entgegen. Zu Beginn seiner Priesterausbildung, als er sich noch von europäischen Vorurteilen leiten ließ, lehnte er weite Teile der traditionellen afrikanischen Religiosität als heidnisch ab. Doch durch den engen seelsorgerischen Kontakt lernte er, dass 95% von dem, was er verworfen hat-

---

30 MILINGO: World in Between, S. 36, 41-45, 69, TER HAAR: Spirit, S. 190.
31 MILINGO: World in Between, S. 42-43, 46. TER HAAR: Spirit, S. 139-141, 148-149.
32 MILINGO: World in Between, S. 45.
33 Wolfgang BEHRINGER: Witches and Witch-Hunts. A Global History, Cambridge 2004, S. 65, 67. Pierrette PARAVY: Zur Genesis der Hexenverfolgungen im Mittelalter: Der Traktat des Claude Tholosan, Richter in der Dauphiné (um 1436), in: Andreas BLAUERT (Hg.), Ketzer, Zauberer, Hexen. Die Anfänge der europäischen Hexenverfolgungen, Frankfurt/M 1990, S. 118-159, hier S. 130, 134.

te, gut ist und sich mit dem Christentum vereinbaren lässt.³⁴ So wie Milingo hat sich offenbar ein großer Teil des Klerus damit arrangiert, dass die religiösen Aktivitäten ihrer Gemeindemitglieder, ähnlich wie in vorkolonialen Zeiten, auf ganz diesseitige, materielle Ziele gerichtet sind.³⁵ An moralischen Belehrungen ist den Gläubigen wenig gelegen. Sie wollen auch nicht, in der Nachfolge Jesu, ihr Kreuz auf sich nehmen und dem Leid der menschlichen Kreatur religiöse Würde geben. Das Bild des gekreuzigten Gottes, der Schmerzen erduldet, hat afrikanische Christen nie fasziniert, so dass es fast nirgendwo zu sehen ist. Durch die rituelle Unterwerfung unter den mächtigsten aller Götter wollen die Gläubigen, ganz im Gegenteil, diverse Wohltaten empfangen. Vorstellungen von Sünde, Reue oder Buße spielen bei diesem religiösen Handel kaum eine Rolle. Statt das Böse in sich selbst zu suchen, imaginiert man es in Gestalt äußerer Kräfte, als feindselige Geister oder fremde Magie, die dem Streben nach Glück und Erfolg im Wege stehen. Im Kampf gegen diese unheilvollen Mächte geht es nur darum, religiöse Experten zu finden, die tatsächlich über die Fähigkeit verfügen, widrige Einflüsse mit Hilfe Gottes oder des Heiligen Geistes zu vertreiben. Priester, die Gläubige an sich binden wollen, müssen also durch Zeichen und Wunder beweisen, dass sie Unglück und Krankheit besiegen und den Fluch der Armut brechen können. Erzbischof Milingo zog Tausende von Gläubigen an, nicht weil er als geweihter Priester die üblichen Sakramente spenden konnte, sondern weil er über exklusive Kräfte verfügte, die nur von seiner Person ausgingen. Deshalb wurde er Tag für Tag von Hilfesuchenden bedrängt, die mit ihm sprechen oder ihn wenigstens berühren wollten.

Wie das Beispiel Milingos zeigt, ähnelt sich die Katholische Kirche den vielen kleinen, unabhängigen Kirchen an, die mit ihrer ekstatischen, pfingstlerischen Frömmigkeit sehr viel erfolgreicher operieren. Einzelne Gemeinden verwandeln sich dadurch in lokale Kulte, die durch die charismatischen Fähigkeiten ihrer Führer zusammengehalten werden. Diese Entwicklung schwächt die Einheit der Kirche als einer Gnadenanstalt, die durch eine Hierarchie beamteter Priester die göttlichen Heilsmittel verwaltet. Statt über die Reinheit des Glaubens und der Liturgie zu wachen, wird sie zu einer Art Dachverband, der Tausende von lokalen Kulten und charismatischen Bewegungen umfasst. Eine ähnliche Entwicklung zeichnet sich bei Anglikanern, Presbyterianern oder Methodisten ab. Als multikulturelle Unternehmen verlieren weltweit operierende Kirchen die

---

34 MILINGO: World in Between, S. 102.
35 Missionare, die jahrzehntelang in Afrika tätig waren, stellten ernüchtert fest, dass die traditionellen religiösen Einstellungen ihrer Gemeindemitglieder durch die christliche Botschaft „fast unberührt" geblieben sind, vgl. Jon P. KIRBY: Cultural Change & Religious Conversion in West Africa, in: Thomas D. Blakely u.a. (Hg.), Religion in Africa. Experience & Expression, London / Portsmouth 1994, S. 57-71, hier S. 58. Auch einige schwarze Autoren sprechen davon, dass das Missionschristentum nicht viel mehr als „Pseudokonversionen" erreicht hat: Victor WAN-TATAH: Pseudo-Conversion and African Independent Churches, in: Peter B. CLARKE (Hg.), New Trends and Developments in African Religions, Westport, Connecticut / London 1998, S. 285-295, hier S. 293. „Christianity, far from being the weapon of the colonial aggressor in Africa, has been domesticated, re-appropriated and turned into the secret weapon of African people. (…) political domination did not lead to spiritual domination. (…) Christianity, the religion of the conqueror, was accepted as a strong new element to reinforce indigenous 'paganism'": Jibrin IBRAHIM: Ethno-Religious Mobilisation and the Sapping of Democracy in Nigeria, in: Jonathan HYSLOP (ed.), African Democracy in the Era of Globalisation, Johannesburg 1999, S. 93-111, hier S. 98.

Fähigkeit, einheitliche Formen der Lehre oder des Kultus durchzusetzen. Der katholische Bischof von Bloemfontein, in Südafrika, plädierte dafür, Gott durch Blutopfer zu ehren.[36] Sein anglikanischer Kollege in Kapstadt, Desmond Tutu, sprach sich dafür aus, die Polygamie einzuführen, und der Vorsitzende der Methodistischen Kirche Südafrikas verlangte, inspiriert durch islamische Vorbilder, dass man Straftätern, je nach der Art ihrer Tat, die Hände oder andere Körperteile abschneidet.[37]

Afrikanisierung des Christentums

Vertreter einer schwarzen Theologie verlangen nicht nur das Recht, ihre Kirchen nach den eigenen religiösen Überzeugungen zu führen, sie wollen auch auf die Entwicklung des globalen Christentums Einfluss nehmen. Die spirituellen Kräfte, mit denen sich Theologen wie Milingo beschäftigen, sind nach ihrer Auffassung nicht nur ein afrikanisches Phänomen; Hexen und Dämonen gebe es auch in Frankreich oder Holland. Dass Kirchenführer in Europa, aus Ignoranz oder Überheblichkeit, diese spirituellen Realitäten verleugnen, habe großen Schaden angerichtet. Der Niedergang des europäischen Christentums hänge eng damit zusammen, dass es sich von seinen spirituellen Wurzeln entfernt habe. Umso anmaßender sei es, wenn kirchliche Autoritäten, die in ihrer Heimat kaum noch Respekt genießen, anderen Christen vorschreiben wollen, wie sie die Bibel zu lesen haben. Statt sich um Afrika zu kümmern, wo die Kirche in voller Blüte stehe, sollten sie sich besser um die eigene dekadente Kultur sorgen. Nach fast 2000 Jahren christlicher Präsenz sei Europa ein irreligiöser Kontinent, ein neues „Babylon", in dem Satanskirchen sich offiziell registrieren lassen und Hexen ganz legal ihre Versammlungen abhalten.[38]

Zur Ent-Christianisierung Europas hat, nach Ansicht afrikanischer Theologen, vor allem die Aufklärung beigetragen.[39] Sie hat die Religion fast ganz aus dem öffentlichen Leben verdrängt und sie in den Bereich einer weitgehend privaten Gemeindefrömmigkeit eingeschlossen. Die Kirchen haben sich nicht nur diesem Diktat unterworfen, sie haben es auch verinnerlicht, so dass sie selbst vom aufgeklärt-säkularen Denken angekränkelt sind. Ihre Gotteshäuser sind leer, weil Priester, die sich dem rationalistischen Denken gebeugt haben und die Macht des Irrationalen verdrängten, den Menschen nichts mehr zu sagen haben. Aus eigener Kraft wird sich das europäische Christentum, mit seinem Intellektuellenglauben, nicht erneuern. Der Impuls zu einer religiösen Wiedergeburt muss von außen kommen, von einer Region wie Afrika, in der das Christentum vom Denken und Fühlen der Menschen wieder Besitz ergriffen hat. Theologen wie Milingo wollen die Spaltung zwischen dem Heiligen und Profanen rückgängig machen, damit die Religion wieder ihre führende Rolle im Kampf gegen das Böse einnehmen

---

36 JENKINS: Christendom, S. 131.
37 Mail & Guardian [Johannesburg], 9. 2. und 19. 2, 1999.
38 Emmanuel MILINGO: The Demarcations, Lusaka 1984, S. 25. TER HAAR: Spirit, S. 261.
39 Lamin SANNEH: Encountering the West. Christianity and the Global Cultural Process: The African Dimension, Maryknoll, New York 1993, S. 184, 208-212.

kann.⁴⁰ Um Europa wieder zu Gott zu führen, plädieren sie dafür, Missionare zu entsenden, die den weißen Christen „wirkliches Christentum" beibringen.⁴¹

Der Religionshistoriker Philip Jenkins hält es für wahrscheinlich, dass „sich in ein bis zwei Jahrzehnten zwei große christliche Gruppen gegenüberstehen, die ihr jeweiliges Gegenüber nicht einmal mehr als authentisch christlich ansehen".⁴² Mit einer solchen Konfrontation ist jedoch, nach meinem Eindruck, kaum zu rechnen. Die Vertreter eines aufgeklärten Christentums werden eher an den Rand gedrängt, denn auch in Europa und Nordamerika gewinnen konservative, wundergläubige Strömungen an Gewicht. Auf Kirchentagen mag es noch so aussehen, als gehöre die Zukunft jenen progressiven Gruppierungen, die gegenüber der Kirchenhierarchie auf Demokratisierung drängen. Besonders Hollands liberale Katholiken machen von sich reden, weil sie sich mit ihrem Engagement für Bürgerrechte nicht mehr von kirchlicher Orthodoxie abschrecken lassen. Doch was zählen ihre Ansichten? Den Gang der Entwicklung werden sie kaum bestimmen, schon aus demographischen Gründen. In einer Großstadt wie Manila, mit seinen elf Millionen Einwohnern, leben doppelt so viele Katholiken wie in Holland.⁴³ Noch um 1900 bildeten Christen in Europa und Nordamerika 83 Prozent der gesamten Gläubigen; heute dagegen sind sie bereits in der Minderheit, und es ist offenbar nur eine Frage der Zeit, bis in Afrika mehr Christen leben als auf jedem anderen Kontinent.⁴⁴

Im Klerus der Katholischen Kirche sind weiße Bischöfe und Kardinäle noch tonangebend. Doch afrikanische Theologen wissen, dass die Zeit auf ihrer Seite steht, und so sprechen sie selbstbewusst davon, dass das Christentum des 21. Jahrhunderts von Schwarzen geprägt werden wird. Afrika habe die Fähigkeit, das Christentum in eine nicht-westliche Religion zu verwandeln.⁴⁵ Die Kirchen, als Mittler zwischen den globalen Kulturen, würden damit eine völlig neue Funktion erhalten. In der Vergangenheit, als weiße Missionare ihren Glauben nach Afrika brachten, wollten sie damit den Menschen zugleich die Segnungen der westlichen Zivilisation nahe bringen. Demgegenüber würden die Kirchen der Zukunft dazu dienen, afrikanische Spiritualität in andere Kontinente zu verbreiten. Kwame Bediako sieht darin eine Chance, die vorherrschende, vom Westen betriebene Form der Globalisierung umzukehren und durch eine „Globalisierung von unten" zu ersetzen.⁴⁶ Damit würde sich auch die Prophezeiung Emmanuel Milingos erfüllen, dass die ganze Katholische Kirche eines Tages wieder charismatisch sein wird, so wie ihr Urbild vor fast 2000 Jahren.⁴⁷

---

40 TER HAAR: Spirit, S. 15, 156-157, 201.
41 WAN-TATAH: Pseudo-Conversion, S. 294.
42 Philip JENKINS: Das Christentum wird im 21. Jahrhundert die Welt prägen. Und es verändert sich dramatisch, in: Chrismon, August 2003, S. 36-37, hier S. 37.
43 David B. BARRETT [u.a.] (Hg.): World Christian Encyclopedia. A Comparative Survey of Churches and Religions in the Modern World. Second Edition. Volume 2, Oxford 2001, S. 589, 593-594.
44 Kwame BEDIAKO: Africa and Christianity on the Threshold of the Third Millenium: the Religious Dimension, in: African Affairs 99 (2000), S. 303-323, hier S. 305-306.
45 BEDIAKO: Africa, S. 305-306, 314. Ähnlich sehen es europäische Religionswissenschaftler, die sich mit Afrika beschäftigen: David B. BARRETT: AD 2000: 350 Million Christians in Africa, in: International Review of Mission 59 (1970), S. 39-54, hier S. 50.
46 BEDIAKO: Africa, S. 314.
47 MILINGO: Demarcations, S. 22-24.

Gegen die Ausbreitung des Geisterglaubens hatte sich im Vatikan anfangs Widerstand geregt. Dem Erzbischof von Lusaka wurden 1974 die Wunderheilungen verboten, mit der Begründung, dass die meisten seiner Patienten an psychosomatischen Störungen litten und Exorzismen deshalb nicht angeraten seien.[48] Der große Heilerfolg seiner Methode konnte die Kritiker nicht beeindrucken. Ein italienischer Kardinal meinte abschätzig, jeder könne andere Menschen in einen hysterischen Zustand versetzen.[49] Solche Skepsis ist heute selten zu hören. Die Kirche weiß, wo ihre Zukunft liegt, und so hat sie charismatischen Bewegungen innerhalb des Katholizismus weitgehende Freiheiten zugestanden. Für Milingo bedeutete diese Umorientierung, dass seine Glaubensvorstellungen und rituellen Praktiken als genuiner Teil des Christentums anerkannt wurden.[50] Wahrscheinlich wäre er heute offiziell rehabilitiert, hätte er nicht die Unvorsichtigkeit begangen, in aller Öffentlichkeit zu heiraten. Es wird geschätzt, dass bis zu drei Viertel aller katholischen Priester in Afrika in eheähnlichen Verhältnissen leben und Kinder großziehen.[51] Doch Milingo sorgte für Schlagzeilen, weil er mit seiner koreanischen Braut eine förmliche Heiratszeremonie veranstaltete und sich dabei von dem berüchtigten Reverend Moon, dem Begründer der ‚Vereinigungskirche', trauen ließ.

Die spirituelle Wiedergeburt Europas

Die Diagnose, die afrikanische Theologen dem Christentum stellen, wird von westlichen Sozialwissenschaftlern im Wesentlichen bestätigt: Bemühungen, den Glauben mit aufgeklärt-säkularen Prinzipien in Einklang zu bringen, sind weitgehend gescheitert. Erfolgreich sind heute gerade jene religiösen Bewegungen, die das Projekt der Moderne, die Entzauberung der Welt, verwerfen.[52] Die katholische Kirche kann sich diesem Trend nicht entziehen, sie öffnet sich wieder dem Glauben an Hexen und Dämonen, aber sie will nicht, dass über den langsamen Wandel ihrer Doktrin allzu offen debattiert wird. Gut möglich, dass der Vatikan die europäischen Christen, mit ihren säkularen Vorbehalten, weitgehend abgeschrieben hat.[53] An einem Bruch aber kann der Kirchenführung nicht gelegen sein. Die laxen Christen in Europa füllen zwar nicht mehr die Gotteshäuser, aber sie erbringen einen Großteil jener Budgets, mit denen die großen Missionskirchen ihre globalen Aktivitäten finanzieren. Im Übrigen können die Kirchen darauf vertrauen, dass sich die Kluft zwischen Christen im Norden und im Süden langsam einebnen wird. Denn durch die Migration aus Afrika und anderen Teilen der Dritten Welt breiten sich charismatische Formen des Christentums auch in Frankreich, Deutschland oder Holland aus. In London sind bereits mehr als die Hälfte aller Kirchgänger Schwarze oder Farbige.[54] Die meisten von ihnen haben ein intensives Interesse

---

48 MILINGO: World in Between, S. 25.
49 Kardinal Rossi, in: TER HAAR: Spirit, S. 192.
50 TER HAAR: Spirit, S. 42, 256-258.
51 Time, 25. 4. 1994, S. 68, in: GIFFORD: African Christianity, S. 312.
52 Peter L. BERGER: The Desecularization of the World: A Global Overview, in: DERS. (Hg.), The Desecularization of the World. Resurgent Religion and World Politics, Washington 1999, S. 1-18, hier S. 4, 6.
53 JENKINS: Christendom, S. 197.
54 Time [Magazine], 16.6.2003, S. 23.

an den kultischen Aspekten ihrer Religion, an geweihten Kerzen, heiligem Wasser und Exorzismen. Ihre autoritäts- und wundergläubige Frömmigkeit gibt all jenen Christen in Europa Auftrieb, die den halbherzigen Kompromiss mit der Moderne nie akzeptieren mochten. Konservative Kirchenkreise haben längst erkannt, dass sie im Bündnis mit den Migranten viele ihrer Positionen durchsetzen können. Wenn es um Abtreibung, Homosexualität oder Frauenrechte geht, sind die Gläubigen aus Kenia, Nigeria oder den Philippinen „stramm traditionell bis reaktionär".[55] Säkulares Denken ist ihnen weitgehend fremd, und so haben sie wenig Bedenken, für ihre Kirchen mehr politischen Einfluss einzufordern. Bischöfe und Kardinäle, die Europa re-christianisieren wollen, können also hoffen, massive Unterstützung zu bekommen, wenn sie sich, im Namen der Brüderlichkeit, für weitere Zuwanderung einsetzen.

Traditionelle Formen des Glaubens dringen nicht nur von außen nach Europa ein, durch die Ausbreitung der Dritten Welt nach Norden. Das Bedürfnis, sich wieder dem Spirituellen zuzuwenden, kommt auch aus der eigenen Kultur. Unter Europäern hat der Glaube an Wunder und das Interesse an Geisterheilungen stark zugenommen.[56] Dadurch konnte Emmanuel Milingo, nach der Abberufung aus Lusaka, in seiner neuen Heimat Italien bald ähnliche Erfolge feiern wie in seiner afrikanischen Diözese. Dank der persönlichen Protektion des Papstes hatte man ihm in der Nähe von Rom eine kleine Gemeinde anvertraut, mit der ausdrücklichen Genehmigung, seine Heilertätigkeit wieder aufzunehmen.[57] Der ehemalige Erzbischof trieb nun den Weißen die Dämonen aus, und sie kamen aus ganz Europa angereist: tiefgläubige Marienverehrer aus Süditalien, aber auch gut situierte Geschäftsleute aus Holland, die in teuren Limousinen vorführen. So entstand eine intensive Form der interkulturellen Kommunikation, mit Effekten, die im Konzept der Multikulti-Designer nicht eingeplant waren. Afrikanische Dämonologie fließt in die europäische Kultur ein und wird Teil unserer Lebenswelt. Um die eigene Spiritualität in Europa zu verbreiten, suchen einige afrikanische Kirchen gezielt Weiße

---

55 JENKINS: Christentum, S. 36. JENKINS: Christendom, S. 199. Auf Kirchentagen und Konferenzen, die von Europäern organisiert wurden, ließ man das Christentum der Dritten Welt am liebsten durch Vertreter der ‚Befreiungstheologie' zu Wort kommen. Aber diese sozialkritische Form der Religiosität, die ihren Ursprung in europäisch geprägten Intellektuellenzirkeln hat, findet in Afrika kaum Anklang: „LThe source of this theology is mainly the Jesuit Centre for Theological Reflection": GIFFORD: African Christianity, S. 331-332. Sehr viel leidenschaftlicher wird dagegen über den moralischen Verfall debattiert: „The primate of the Anglican Church, Archbishop Jasper Akinola had said the minds of all Nigerian Christians (…) [Homosexuality] is a perversion of Christianity and Christian Culture. (…) Anytime, we see a self confessed Gay bishop or reverend we'll withdraw. We will withdraw from World Council of Churches. It is incompatible with Christianity, especially African Christianity and time has come now when we should go and re-christianise the white people." Ola MAKINDE, Methodistischer Erzbischof von Lagos, in: Newswatch [Lagos], 3.5.2004, S. 45.
56 Dieter BAUER: Die Gegenwart der Hexen. Ein Überblick, in: Sönke Lorenz / Jürgen Michael Schmidt (Hg.), Wider alle Hexerei und Teufelswerk. Die europäische Hexenverfolgung und ihre Auswirkungen auf Südwestdeutschland, Ostfildern 2004, S. 175-191, hier S. 180. TER HAAR: Spirit, S. 252. IDEM.: A Wondrous God: Miracles in Contemporary Africa, in: African Affairs 102 (2003), S. 409-428, hier S. 411. JENKINS: Christendom, S. 136. Der Spiegel, 21 (1999), S. 188.
57 Vittorio LANTERNARI: From Africa into Italy: The Exorcistic-Therapeutic Cult of Emmanuel Milingo, in: Peter B. CLARKE (Hg.), New Trends and Developments in African Religions, Westport, Connecticut / London, S. 263-283, hier S. 277. TER HAAR: Spirit, S. 4, 256, 258.

anzuwerben, wenn auch mit bescheidenem Erfolg. Das Interesse, sich in die etwas gespenstische Welt christlich-afrikanischer Geister einweihen zu lassen, ist noch gering.[58] In den USA dagegen hat afrikanische Spiritualität bereits mehr Einfluss gewonnen. Zentren des Voodoo sind heute Miami, New Jersey und Toronto, und zu den Anhängern zählen auch Weiße. Kulte, die sich dem Schutz vor Hexerei und Schadenszauber verschrieben haben, dürften jedoch, wie in der Vergangenheit, zunächst einmal für Angehörige der Unterschicht anziehend sein.

Bürgerliche Kreise, vor allem in Europa, richten ihre okkulten Interessen eher auf harmlose Gegenstände, wie Feng Shui, Anthroposophie oder Spekulationen über den Einfluss der Gestirne. Die Beschäftigung mit Phänomenen, die in der westlichen Wissenschaft keinen Platz haben, mahnt daran, dass die Aufklärung die dunklen, abgründigen Seiten der menschlichen Existenz nicht entzaubert, sondern eher verdrängt hat. Eine Art wissenschaftlicher Exorzismus: Aus der Selbstreflexion des Menschen, so meinte Hegel, müsse man das Magische und Dämonische, überhaupt alle „Krankheiten des Geistes" „verbannen", denn in der Wissenschaft, aber auch in der Kunst sei „nichts dunkel, sondern alles klar und durchsichtig".[59] Durch die Ausgrenzung dunkler Mächte wollten aufgeklärte Denker eine Art Schutzwall errichten. Ihr Schauder vor dem ‚Irrationalen' und seiner kaum kontrollierbaren Gewalt erklärt sich vielleicht auch aus den Schrecken der Hexenverfolgungen, die ihnen sehr viel präsenter waren als uns, weil sie bis in die Zeit der Aufklärung hineinreichten. Die heutige Esoterik-Generation nähert sich dem Okkulten dagegen ganz arglos. Sie will rationalistische Tabus überschreiten und sich spirituellen Erfahrungen öffnen, um das eigene Denken zu bereichern. Meditationen über ein neues atlantisches Zeitalter oder über den Einfluss von Ahriman und Ormuzd wirken wie ein Spiel der Phantasie, von dem sich der Esoterik-Liebhaber nach Belieben lösen kann. Doch das Fremde, von dem sich die Menschen inspirieren lassen, kann sie leicht gefangen nehmen und ihre Vorstellungswelt beherrschen. Unter dem Eindruck sozialer Krisen, wenn die Sicherheiten wegfallen, die ein recht fürsorglicher Staat seinen Bürgern gewährte, dürften die Erfahrungen mit der spirituellen Welt eine eher düstere Färbung annehmen. Wie in den *low trust societies* der Dritten Welt wäre es dann vor allem die Angst vor versteckter Aggression, die dazu treibt, sich mit Okkultem zu befassen und gegen den Zauber der Mitmenschen rituelle Gegenmaßnahmen zu ergreifen.

Dass sich viele Menschen, auch im Westen, vom nüchternen Realismus der Aufklärung abgewandt haben, tritt erst seit kurzem ins Bewusstsein. Die Entzauberung der Welt ging offenbar nicht sehr tief, sie wurde im Wesentlichen nur von einer sozialen Elite getragen: „There exists an international subculture composed of people with Western-type higher education, especially in the humanities and social sciences, that is indeed secularized. This subculture is the principle ‚carrier' of progressive, enlightened beliefs and values. While its members are relatively thin on the ground, they are influen-

---

58 Nach einem Bericht der Welt am Sonntag, vom 18.1.2004, kommt es jedoch zu einer langsamen Annäherung der Kulturen: „im Millionenheer deutscher Esoterik-Freunde weicht die Schwellenangst gegenüber afrikanischer Magie langsam der Neugier".
59 Georg Wilhelm Friedrich HEGEL: Vorlesungen über die Ästhetik. Bd 1, in: DERS., Werke in zwanzig Bänden. Bd 13, Frankfurt/M. 1973, S. 315.

tial, as they control the institutions that provide the 'official' definitions of reality, notably the educational system, the media of mass communication, and the higher reaches of the legal system".[60]

In Afrika hat die Elite allerdings keine Kontrolle mehr über die Definitionen von Realität, ja sie mag das offizielle rationalistische Weltbild nicht einmal verteidigen. Das angestrengte Bemühen, sich nach westlichem Vorbild zu modernisieren, hat den Afrikanern wenig Glück gebracht, und so geben sich Politiker, Richter oder Professoren zusehends weniger Mühe, die Fassade von Aufgeklärtheit aufrecht zu erhalten.[61]

Aber auch an seinem Ursprung, in Europa, verliert das aufgeklärte Denken an Geltung. Gebildete Kreise bekennen sich heute offen dazu, dass sie okkulten Glaubensformen anhängen. An Schulen und Universitäten wird zwar weiterhin säkular-aufgeklärtes Denken vermittelt, doch die bürgerliche Bildung prägt nur noch sehr beschränkt das Selbst- und Weltverständnis der Heranwachsenden. Während die Bindungskräfte von Institutionen und überlieferter Kultur nachlassen, neigen nicht wenige Jugendliche dazu, sich in eigene Erlebniswelten einzuspinnen. Diese „Eigenwelten" sind natürlich nicht autonom, sondern sie bestehen aus einem „Mix aus Symbolen, Zeichen, Deutungsmustern und Verhaltensstilen", die der Unterhaltungsindustrie und den Massenmedien entnommen sind.[62] Die Informationsgesellschaft, mit Internet und Dutzenden von Fernsehkanälen, führt also nicht dazu, dass sich ein ‚rationales' Weltbild verbreitet, sie begünstigt eher ein Nebeneinander von Subkulturen, die sich nicht mehr auf eine gemeinsame, intersubjektiv verbürgte Realität beziehen. Es kommt hinzu, dass die elektronischen Medien den Unterschied zwischen Realem und Fiktivem einebnen, so dass sich hinter der Oberfläche der Dinge der Blick auf immer neue verborgene Wirklichkeiten auftut. Nachdem sich die Phänomene aus ihrem überlieferten Deutungszusammenhang gelöst haben, ziehen sie ganz unterschiedliche Deutungen an, ähnlich wie Michel Foucault es für die Frühe Neuzeit beschrieben hat. Er sprach „von einem flutartigen Ansteigen der Bedeutungen, von einer Multiplikation des Sinnes mit sich selbst, die zwischen den Dingen so zahlreiche, so verkreuzte und so reichhaltige Beziehungen webt, daß sie nur noch durch ein esoterisches Wissen entziffert werden können und die Dinge ihrerseits mit Attributen, Zeichen und Anspielungen überladen werden".[63]

Die postmoderne Aufbereitung des Wissens ist nur einer von vielen Faktoren, die das aufgeklärt-säkulare Weltbild auflösen. Zur Rückkehr des Okkulten trägt sicher auch bei, dass die Deutungselite das Zutrauen zur eigenen bürgerlich aufgeklärten Kultur verloren hat. Alfred Soman, ein Historiker, den ich nach den Gründen fragte, vermutete, ein einschneidendes Erlebnis sei der Erste Weltkrieg gewesen: das Erschrecken der Europäer über die dämonische Kräfte im Innern der modernen Zivilisation. Das Trauma der Krie-

---

60 BERGER: Desecularization, S. 10.
61 Ogbu U. KALU: The Religious Dimension of the Legitimacy Crisis, 1993-1998, in: Toyin FALOLA (Hg.), Nigeria in the Twentieth Century, Durham, North Carolina 2002, S. 667-685, hier S. 670, 674-675.
62 Thomas ZIEHE: Öffnung der Eigenwelten. Bildungsangebote und veränderte Jugendmentalitäten, in: Kursiv. Journal für politische Bildung 1 (2002), S. 12-17, hier S. 12.
63 Michel FOUCAULT: Wahnsinn und Gesellschaft. Eine Geschichte des Wahns im Zeitalter der Vernunft, Frankfurt/M. 1981, S. 37.

ge und politischen Massenmobilisierungen hat offenbar lange nachgehallt, ja es scheint die volle Wucht seiner verunsichernden Wirkung erst spät entfaltet zu haben. Gerade die Wohlstandsgeneration der 1960er Jahre hat sich vom Fortschrittsglauben der Aufklärung abgewandt. Susan Sontag, die später mit dem Friedenspreis des Deutschen Buchhandels geehrt wurde, schrieb damals, die weiße Rasse und ihre Zivilisation sei „das Krebsgeschwür der Menschheitsgeschichte".[64] Die Kehrseite dieser modernen Selbstzweifel ist, dass man traditionelle, vorstaatliche Gesellschaften als besonders friedlich imaginiert hat.[65]

---

64 Susan SONTAG: What's Happening to America?, in: Partisan Review 34 (1967), S. 51-58, hier S. 57f.
65 In Gesellschaften ohne staatliches Gewaltmonopol kam es „extrem häufig" zu Kriegen, und die Wahrscheinlichkeit, von seinen Mitmenschen getötet zu werden, war sehr viel höher als in den Nationalstaaten Europas, selbst wenn man zum Vergleich das 20. Jahrhundert wählt, mit seinen Weltkriegen und Massenvernichtungswaffen: Lawrence H. KEELEY: War before Civilization, New York / Oxford 1996, S. 32, 89-90. Der Kontrast wird noch deutlicher, wenn man Europa nach dem Zweiten Weltkrieg mit außereuropäischen Gesellschaften vergleicht, etwa mit Prärie-Indianern im vorkolonialen Nordamerika: „The homicide rate of the prehistoric Illinois villagers would have been 1,400 times that of modern Britain", ebd., S. 67.

Walter Bruchhausen

Repelling and Cleansing 'Bad People'
The Fight against Witchcraft
in Southeast Tanzania since Colonial Times

Zusammenfassung

Wenn die historische Entwicklung von Reaktionsformen auf Hexerei in einer Gegend Afrikas untersucht wird, so lässt dies verstehen, wie sich einschlägige überlieferte Vorstellungen und Praktiken den Modernisierungsprozessen anpassten. In Südost-Tansania haben die Auflösung traditioneller politischer und religiöser Autoritäten durch Islam und Kolonialherrschaft sowie die koloniale und nachkoloniale Gesetzgebung gegen Hexerei die Antworten verändert: von der (meist gewaltsamen) Giftprobe oder anderen Orakelformen durch die Führer der Gemeinschaften über das öffentliche Hexen-Aufspüren und -Reinigen durch auswärtige Experten bis hin zu privaten und oft eher religiösen Arten von Entdeckung, Schutz und Versöhnung durch Geistmedien.

Abstract

Studying the historical development of reactions to witchcraft in an African region enables some understanding of how the relevant inherited beliefs and practices have adapted to processes of modernisation. In Southeast Tanzania the dissolution of traditional political and religious authorities by the introduction of Islam and colonial rule as well as the colonial and post-colonial anti-witchcraft legislation changed the responses to witchcraft: from the (often violent) ordeal executed by community leaders via public witch-finding and cleansing by foreign experts to more private and often rather religious means of witch-detection, protection and reconciliation by spirit mediums.

The vast literature on witchcraft in Africa does not seem to leave much need for further studies, save for some interest in local variations. Such regional particularities in a rather under-researched region of East Africa will be one of the issues in this contribution, which at the same time aims to broaden the time perspective. As cultural and social anthropology is mainly concerned with actual meanings and functions, many studies of witchcraft in contemporary Africa do not consider the historical development in any great detail. To see the shortcomings of such an approach might seem commonplace to historians or historically minded anthropologists, but in this case neglecting the historical dimension means, in particular, that the chances for comparative studies between witchcraft in early modern Europe and in modern Africa are being missed.[1] A considerable amount of recent research on European witch-hunts clearly understands these events as corollary phenomena of modernising processes and uncertainties in political power; in Africa it was primarily the colonial conquest by European powers and the aftermath of this conquest which brought modernisation and power transitions. Therefore, an analysis of the relations between witchcraft and modernity demands a close look back to the early colonial period. As African concepts of witchcraft and colonial situations both vary considerably, such a study also has to be fairly local if it is to understand the interaction between inherited beliefs and modernisation. In the following contribution a larger research project on medical pluralism[2] provides the temporal, local and thematic focus; this also resulted in some insight into ideas and practices surrounding witchcraft. Therefore, the paper begins with a characterisation of this research project and the region where it was carried out. This is followed by an account of the concepts of witchcraft in the relevant population as compared to the more general anthropological literature on witchcraft in East Africa. The second part will describe the various responses to these concepts and situations, by individuals and local communities as well as by the colonial and, later, the national state.

The regional population and their concepts of witchcraft

Research and the population

The study of witchcraft was not a primary aim of the research project that forms the basis of the following description and analysis. Yet, whenever a comprehensive study of medical pluralism, i.e. the variety and interaction of ways of preserving health, coping with disease and procuring healing, is carried out in an East African region, witchcraft seems to be an unavoidable issue. Any thorough investigation into the explanation, prevention and treatment of illness will necessarily lead to popular assumptions of witchcraft. As the rejection of the reality of witchcraft belongs to the self-image of modern Europe, this issue has caused considerable misunderstanding between Europeans and Africans. Therefore, and because of serious social problems to be described later, it is no wonder that the government of Tanzania[3] does not want public research and publications on witchcraft. This research policy and the official prohibition of any activity related to witchcraft make ethnographic research on the dark side of magic rather difficult.[4]

---

1 For a recent review of this relationship in general see Ronald HUTTON: Anthropological and historical approaches to witchcraft: Potential for a new collaboration?, in: The Historical Journal 47 (2004), pp. 413-434.
2 Funded from 2000 to 2003 by the German VolkswagenStiftung, with field research mainly done in 2001 and 2002. This contribution is mainly based on the documented results of this project published as Walter BRUCHHAUSEN: Medizin zwischen den Welten. Vergangenheit und Gegenwart des medizinischen Pluralismus im südöstlichen Tansania, Göttingen 2006.
3 The mainland of the present United Republic of Tanzania was called *German East Africa* (and included what later became Belgian Rwanda and Burundi) until World War I, after which it became the British mandated Territory and later Republic of Tanganyika until its union with Zanzibar in 1964.
4 This demands a high level of trust between ethnographer and informant, and only two (TANZ61 and TANZ95) of the more than ninety interview partners talked about it without major restrictions,

The fear of witchcraft varies considerably in degree and form between different ethnic and social groups. Thus, the socio-cultural characteristics of the investigated groups are major factors in understanding the meaning and explaining the function of witchcraft. The region of my research in Southeast Tanzania, in the present-day regions of Mtwara and Lindi, is mainly inhabited by originally matrilineal peoples – Mwera, Makua, Makonde and Yao. The stronger economic and social position of the women who remained in their family after marriage and did not move into their husbands' clans also seems to be important in protecting them against witchcraft accusations. With the exception of the Yao, whose conversion to Islam started in the late 19th century, the majority of the population was Islamised after 1900, leaving smaller groups of Anglican and Catholic Christians around the mission stations, who have recently been challenged by a few members of Independent African Churches.

Fig. 1: The old key informant on witchcraft, demonstrating a local remedy, Mtwara Region/Tanzania.

The cultural influence of Islam, in its orthodox as well as in its Sufi and folk versions, has changed the local ways of conceptualising and fighting witchcraft considerably. Due to the smaller numbers involved, Christian influence is much less observable, patients and healers even convert from Christianity to Islam – sometimes only 'temporarily'[5] – in order to get the power of healing. Crops grown on comparatively small fields provide the main source of income, cattle are rare. The fact that, unlike nomadic people, who are often less worried about witchcraft, these small farmers cannot simply move should social tensions arise, makes them prone to witchcraft accusations. Compared to these three factors of matrilinearity, religion and residency, precise ethnic affiliation seems to be of less importance in witchcraft issues today. Members of different ethnic groups live together in the large villages that were created by force by the politics of *Ujamaa* socialism during the early 1970s to promote communal production and to make provision of transport, schooling and health care easier. Even in pre-colonial times, people of different ethnic origin were united under the leadership of the same local rulers.[6]

---

whereas the topic was touched in most interviews and noted in many observed practices, thus allowing a certain degree of triangulation. One of the two informants was a very old man (See Figure 1) beyond the actual struggles for power and the other was a young man who felt himself to be an involuntary witch and was ready to answer my research assistant's questions only in the bush far from any houses. Six long interviews (three with each of the two informants) were tape-recorded allowing further inquiries and discussions in-between the visits to them.

5   Interview TANZ6 [LR alias BK, 2.11.2001].
6   See Felicitas BECKER: Traders, ‚Big Men' and Prophets: Political continuity and crisis in the Maji Maji rebellion in Southeast Tazania, in: Journal of African History 45 (2004), pp. 1-22.

African and European perspectives on witchcraft

The ethnic differences between the researcher and the researched, however, are of the uttermost importance in questions of witchcraft. The renowned American historian of East Africa, Steve Feierman, recently remembered his early field research in the 1960s when „a traditional healer in Tanzania once asked how American healers would treat an illness caused by sorcery. 'Well, I don't know that we deal with that sort of thing,' Feierman told him. 'After all, we don't have sorcery.' 'What do you mean?' the healer exclaimed. 'Do you never get angry with one another? Do you not have enemies?'"[7]

These two fundamentally different perspectives of people from Africa and from the North Atlantic region were termed by the British social anthropologist Edward Evans-Pritchard the perspectives of the 'value system' and of 'natural philosophy'.[8] Most Europeans do not realise that, for Africans, it is the moral quality which matters, as witchcraft is about the effects of evil human intentions and practices. Many Africans are not much interested in the question of the efficacy of magical acts so that they cannot understand that Europeans doubt this efficacy, nor can they understand why, for Europeans, witchcraft should primarily be a question of the (paranormal) possibilities of nature. As 'morality' in the monotheistic and in most European philosophical traditions tends to be understood as a universal order it must be emphasised that the African witch violates a less general moral system. For we best define „witchcraft as nothing but the transgression of the code of social obligations defined by the kinship order."[9]

This is not the place to address the development of anthropological approaches to African witchcraft[10] that consecutively and, in some cases, simultaneously attributed it to the 'primitive' (Frazer)[11], the 'other' or 'foreign' (Evans-Pritchard), the 'social' (Marwick)[12], the 'religious' (Ranger)[13] and more recently the 'modern' (Jean and John L. Comaroff, Geschiere).[14] Although some of these perspectives are regarded as contra-

---

7   A Family Affair: Traditional Healing and Modern Medicine in Africa, in: Penn Arts & Sciences. Alumni newsletter of the School of Arts and Sciences, 1 July (2002), URL: http://www.upenn.edu/researchatpenn/article.php?456&hlt (14.1.2005).

8   See Edward EVANS-PRITCHARD: Witchcraft, Oracles and Magic among the Azande, Oxford 1937, shortened 1976. Tamara MULTHAUPT: Sozialanthropologische Theorien über Hexerei und Zauberei in Afrika, in: Anthropos 82 (1987) pp. 445-456.

9   Wim VAN BINSBERGEN: Witchcraft in modern Africa as virtualised boundary conditions of the kinship order, in: George Clement Bond / Diane M. Ciekawy (eds.), Witchcraft dialogues. Anthropological and Philosophical Exchanges, Athens/Ohio 2001, pp. 212-263, here p. 238.

10 See Walter BRUCHHAUSEN: Hexerei und Krankheit in Ostafrika. Beobachtungen zu einem missglückten interkulturellen Diskurs, in: Bruchhausen (ed.), Hexerei und Krankheit. Historische und ethnologische Perspektiven, Münster 2003, S. 93-124.

11 James G. FRAZER: The Golden Bough. A Study in Magic and Religion, 8 vol., London: 1914-1918.

12 Max G. MARWICK: Sorcery in Its Social Setting, Manchester 1965.

13 Terence O. RANGER / Isaria KIMAMBO (eds.): The historical study of African Religion with special reference to East and Central Africa, London 1972. Ranger did his research and teaching as a historian and not an anthropologist, but was influential in anthropology in that he pointed to the religious dimension of change in Africa.

14 Jean and John L. COMAROFF: Occult economies and the violence of abstraction: Notes from the South African postcolony, in: American Ethnologist 26 (1999), pp. 279-303. Peter GESCHIERE: The Modernity of Witchcraft: Politics and the Occult in Postcolonial Africa, Charlottesville 1997.

dictory, they all have certain undeniable traits: Witchcraft in Africa consists partly of elements inherited from much earlier times; it is based on a world view different from the mainstream of contemporary European thought, it expresses certain social tensions, it is about contingency and it is a way of coping with modernity. The challenge must be a balanced consideration of all these constituents that make up the phenomenon of witchcraft in contemporary Africa. I intend, therefore, to describe the historical origins, the basic concepts and the social and religious situation as well as the adaptation to recent changes in those rural communities where I did my field and archival research.

The independence of witchcraft from spirits

In modern Europe, especially in its early modern period, the concept of witchcraft was inescapably bound up with the idea of the demonic. As this was also taken for granted by later missionaries and colonial administrators, the question of a connection between witchcraft and spirit possession must also be asked for East Africa. The answer is quite clear and demonstrates again the grave obstacles for intercultural understanding which an unchecked transferral of European concepts poses. In many African cultures, certainly in Southeast Tanzania, magic and its destructive use as witchcraft are possible and mostly imagined to take place without any assistance by spirits. Impersonal forces are involved which often, but not always, require special knowledge and skills and can be possessed without any special relationship to non-human beings.

The basic concepts of witchcraft and spirits are, thus, not linked to one another but, in fact, several coincidences and interactions can be observed. If the question of witchcraft is – as we have seen – a matter of motives and social relations (and not so much of superior powers) possession by evil spirits can not be completely excluded as a moral source of such evil deeds as witchcraft. There also seems to be some confusion as to which group activities are directed towards spirits and which have to do with witchcraft. Whereas the practice of destructive magic is principally independent of sex or gender, the popular images of the witches' nocturnal activities remind one of predominantly female activities related to spirits: the ceremonies of possession cults also often conducted at night, which involved ecstatic dancing, drumming by (paid) men and throwing babies to each other.[15]

For Eastern and Southern Africa there is an anthropological debate on how urbanisation and colonialism have changed the quantitative distribution between witchcraft and spirit possession. Middleton believed that witchcraft was more prevalent in the more rural and African *country-towns* and belief in spirits in the more Islamic *stone-towns*.[16] Obviously, he saw the doctrines on spirits in the Koran as favouring practices related to spirits. Mitchell also saw less witchcraft in more 'modern' towns but argued that the increased social conflicts in towns are solved in other ways than by witchcraft accusations, as the common 'tribal' bond was missing here.[17] However, empirical observations

---

15 Interview TANZ95 II [Longino Livigha with JDO, 27.12.2001] p. 3.
16 John Francis MIDDLETON: The world of the Swahili. An African mercantile civilization, New Haven 1992, p. 182.
17 See James Clyde MITCHELL: The Meaning in Misfortune for Urban Africans, in: Max Marwick (ed.), Witchcraft and Sorcery. Selected Readings, London 1990, pp. 381-390.

on consultations with healers from the same ethnic group, the *Zaramo,* in Dar es Salaam and in the surrounding area led SWANTZ to the opposite conclusion: in only 10% of the analysed one hundred consultations with *waganga* ('traditional healers') in the city of Dar es Salaam were spirits diagnosed, whereas this happened in 58% of cases in the less Islamised area around the city.[18] Lloyd Swantz explained these differences by the situation that there is a lack of treatment opportunities for afflictions by spirits in the city since these require both special experts and shrines. It is simply possible to purchase counter-magic against witchcraft, whereas the satisfaction of spirits requires much more than this. Bond recently argued for Zambia that ancestor spirits, as representatives of the ancient social order, seem to be of less relevance in the present situation than witches, who pursue individual interests only.[19]

A further question regarding the relationship between spirit possession and witchcraft would be whether spirits may be of help in combating destructive magic. The answer has to be affirmative since, in addition to more technical oracles and ordeals, the spirits' assistance is the most important means of detecting witchcraft and witches. Without being called, spirits can raise the alarm when people with bad intentions are approaching.[20] A medium in spirit possession can be asked for divination in order to discover bewitchment, identify the culprits and choose measures against them.[21]

The irrelevance of the witchcraft – sorcery distinction in Southeast Tanzania

Besides contrasting the 'moral' and the 'natural', Evans-Pritchard introduced another dichotomy which he demonstrated for the South Sudanese *Zande*[22] and which other authors discussed with regard to Eastern Africa in general at a later date[23]: the distinction between witchcraft on the one and evil magic or sorcery on the other hand. The criteria for the characterisation and attribution of these different concepts comprise the dichotomies of inborn versus acquired, (potentially) unconscious versus (always) intentional, without versus with magical objects, and regarding the gender balance even female versus male. In the volume mentioned above, several authors wrote on the question of whether this distinction is of any relevance to East Africa in general. The at-

---

18 Lloyd W. SWANTZ: The Medicine Man among the Zaramo of Dar es Salaam, Dar es Salaam 1990, pp. 114 and 118, referring to Marja Liisa SWANTZ: Ritual and Symbol in Transitional Zaramo Society. With Special Reference to Women, Uppsala 1970.
19 See George Clement BOND: Ancestors and Witches. Explanations and the Ideology of Individual Power in Northern Zambia, in: Bond / Ciekawy, Witchcraft dialogues, pp. 131-57, here pp. 155-56.
20 See interview TANZ95 I [Longino Livigha with JDO, 25.12.2001].
21 One of the reasons why the consulted spirits have such abilities may be that they used to be the relevant ritual experts in their lives on earth before their death, e.g. mbandwa among the Ugandan Nyoro, see Lucy Philip MAIR: Witchcraft, London 1969, pp. 81-82 referring to John H. M. BEATTIE: Group Aspects of the Nyoro Spirit Medium Cult, in: Human Problems in British Central Africa 30 (1961), pp. 11-39.
22 Edward Evans EVANS-PRITCHARD: Witchcraft (Mangu) amongst the A-Zande', in: Sudan Notes and Records (1929), pp. 163-247, and EVANS-PRITCHARD: Witchcraft, oracle.
23 See John Francis MIDDLETON / Edward Henry WINTER (eds.): Witchcraft and Sorcery in East Africa, London 1963.

tempts, however, to demonstrate the universal or at least regionally coherent distribution of this dichotomy failed. The criteria as to how witchcraft and sorcery had to be defined for an emic distinction within different ethnic groups were too variable. Nevertheless, some distinctions do seem to make sense with respect to more than just a few groups, e.g. the difference between a practice committed out of viciousness and within the kin group (witchcraft) and a calculated act directed primarily against people outside the kin group (sorcery). Thus, this distinction remains a possible, but in no way presupposable one. For the *Swahili*, as one of the neighbouring ethnic groups influencing the research region, MIDDLETON maintained the existence and importance of the distinction. *'Mwanga'* embodied, as a woman active during the night, the 'witch'-type, whereas *'mchawi'* and *'mlozi',* as people who used substances, corresponded to the 'sorcerer'. This could not be demonstrated for other ethnic groups, the *Swahili* word *mchawi* (plural *wachawi*) being widely used for any person who does secret damage to other people in whatever way.[24]

The classical witchcraft-sorcery distinction does not seem to play a role for Southeast Tanzania either. It has no linguistic equivalent,[25] and in *Swahili* the unspecific words *watu wabaya* (bad or evil people) and *kuteswa* (to be teased) are used more often than the feared words *uchawi* (witchcraft), *wachawi* and *kulogwa* (to be bewitched), in order to avoid the proper terms. Nevertheless, different attributions to male and female witches can be observed. According to these popular views, women have their secret substances, called *uchawi*, in shells (see figure 2) which are hidden in the vagina, whereas men carry them in calabashes *(ndumba)* openly hanging from their waist belt. The sexual connotations of these attributes are obvious and related to other traits of the witches referring to issues of sexuality, e.g. cheating the husband, interfering with virility and committing adultery. Thus, the female witches hide the shell from their husbands by removing it secretly before sexual intercourse and are generally involved in causing impotence. Among the male witch's alleged activities figures the narcotising of women for sexual intercourse without their will.[26] With the substances in shell or calabash both sexes use

---

24 Whereas the Swahili as an ethnic group comprise some million inhabitants along the Tanzanian and Kenyan coast and islands only, the language (Ki-)Swahili is spoken as a national language (in Tanzania) and lingua franca by about 70 million East Africans, even in the Eastern Congo.

25 The only terms relevant for a linguistic distinction are kulogwa und uchawi. In some places, such as Pare in North Tanzania, these word stems are strictly distinguished into the meanings 'physically or spiritually induced (Kuoghwa)' and 'sourcery [sic!] (Vuthavi)', see Rogate R. MSHANA: Insisting upon People's Knowledge to Resist Developmentalism. Peasant Communities as Producers of Knowledge for Social Transformation in Tanzania, Frankfurt/M. 1992, p. 121. In the Southeast, however, as probably in most Tanzanian regions today, the two words figure as synonyms for destructive magic. It is remarkable, however, that the local languages of Southeastern Tanzania, i.e. of the Mwera, Yao and Makonde, all have the cognate stem *-cábí for their terms of (abstract and substantial) witchcraft and (personal) witches, in common with the Swahili (-chawi), see Malcolm GUTHRIE: Comparative Bantu. An introduction to the comparative linguistics and prehistory of the Bantu languages, vol. 3, Hants/England 1970, p. 74, C.S. [cognate stem] 240. For the verb, however, they use – like the Swahili - a stem which corresponds to inland Banto groups with *-dòg-, *-dògá, *-dògi or *-dògò respectively, see GUTHRIE: Comparative Bantu, p. 176, C.S. 644-647. Thus, one could speculate on whether the concepts of the persons and their activities had different origins.

26 See interview TANZ95 I [Longino Livigha with JDO, 25.12.2001] p. 7.

Fig. 2: Painting by H. M. Manoli, Mkalapa/Tanzania: Many healing offers.

magical objects which would mean 'sorcery' in the classical definition. The greater secrecy and association with existing relationships in the case of the women, however, make their acts more 'private', i.e. more in the way of Evans-Pritchard's definition of witchcraft in contrast to more open and even 'professional' sorcery.

The relation between witchcraft and healing

Outside the academic discussion, the English terms 'witch' or 'witchcraft' are not reflected or defined but applied quite indiscriminately. My research assistants and the rare English speaking informants regularly used the word 'witch-doctor' as it is taught in English at school for *mganga* (translated as 'traditional healer' in official documents). A strict Muslim research assistant with a university degree even spoke of 'witch' only. Thus they reproduced a term which could and still can name an important task of the *waganga* (plural of *mganga*), i.e. fighting diseases caused by witchcraft. Yet as this understanding is uncommon and the spontaneous misunderstanding that the witch-doctor himself practices witchcraft is too evident, one has to agree with John Mbiti's often quoted recommendation, „'witch-doctors' – a term which should be buried and forgotten forever".[27]

However, the question of the connection between the words 'witch' and 'doctor' is more than just a terminological one. In Southeast Tanzania, and probably many other places, combating witchcraft has more in common with practising witchcraft than many *waganga* like to admit for fear of damaging their public reputation. Often, the means for fighting witchcraft and the means employed by the witches are not only similar, but

---

27 John S. MBITI: African Religions and Philosophy, London 1982, p. 218.

even identical. Counter-magic against destructive magic is equally harmful, the only difference being that, according to the *mganga* and to society at large, it affects a culprit and thus justly causes damage.[28] In order even to acquire the relevant skills, the *mganga* has to commit the horrible acts of the *wachawi*, especially the murder of relatives and the consumption of human flesh; however, this is only required once, for the initiation procedure.[29]

With such acts, the borders between *mganga* and *mchawi* become blurred. It is only the intentions or even the position taken in conflicts which determine what an expert is called and how he or she is regarded.[30] Healers tend to emphasise this boundary and hence the difference between the two roles. The general population, however, and also my young informant who regards himself as *mchawi* stress the similarity between both roles: 'some *waganga* are arch-witches *(wachawi wa wachawi)*'.[31] When, in 1973, the Tanzanian government banned the healers' association *UWATA,* one of the arguments was that ritual objects for *uchawi* had been found with some members in the Kilimanjaro region.[32] Similarly, popular paintings and drawings like to present the *waganga* as witches: naked, with a calabash for medicines around the waist, with a small beard and the skull shaved apart from a small curl (see figure 2). Although I observed the shaving, save the curl, as part of a *mganga*'s staged initiation ceremonies, calabashes used for medicines and a male *mganga* taking off his shirt before dancing and entering a possession state, I have never encountered or been told of any *mganga* of such description treating a patient.

Witchcraft and the causes of affliction, illness and death

For Africa the term 'magic' is of very limited use as there are no local equivalents for this term nor is there any other neutral word with the general meaning of secret effects.[33] In a system of thought without a fundamental ontological distinction between

---

28 For the logical, but actually often impossible distinction between uchawi and uganga, see Peter LIENHARDT (ed): Hasani bin Ismail, The Medicine Man. Swifa ya Nguvumali, Oxford 1968, pp. 52-53.

29 A Benedictine missionary, Fr. Benno Heckel, wrote in 1935 of the Yao that at night a student of witchcraft has to go together with his master to a grave of a recently dead baby of his kin in order to dig out the corpse, eat heart and liver cooked with roots and then cover up the traces, see Benno HECKEL: The Yao tribe, their culture and education, London 1935, p. 15. As Heckel does not use a local word and as at that time, missionaries often identified both, one cannot exclude the possibility that he is referring not to the witch-doctor, but to the actual witch.

30 See Diane M. CIEKAWY: Utsai as Ethical Discourse: A Critique of Power from Mijikenda in Coastal Kenya, in: BOND / CIEKAWY: Witchcraft dialogues, pp. 158-189, here pp. 164-165.

31 Interview TANZ95 I [Longino Livigha with JDO, 25.12.2001] p. 3.

32 See Ulrich SCHULZ-BURGDORF: Aspekte der Swahili Volksmedizin im Lamu-Archipel Kenyas, Münster 1994, p. 53, referring to the annotated collection of newspaper articels Vincent van AMELSVOORT: Medical Anthropology in African newspapers, Nijmwegen 1976, pp. 71-72.

33 See CIEKAWY: Utsai, p. 165. Cosmas HAULE'S attempt (Bantu „witchcraft" and Christian morality. The encounter of Bantu uchawi with Christian morality. An anthropological and theological study, Schöneck-Beckenried 1969, especially pp. 38-51) to establish 'uchawi' as not always reprehensible, but as a morally neutral generic term, in the sense of 'mysterious power', comprising both 'good-uchawi' for protection, healing and promotion of human activities and 'bad-uchawi' as anti-social

different hidden effects, e.g. between the Western categories of poisoning and of bewitching, such secondary distinctions as 'public' and 'secret' knowledge or 'good' and 'evil' use are of importance, and not the distinction between 'natural' and 'supernatural' effects. While Europeans are used to distinguishing only these two categories, African ideas on the causes of affliction tend to be tripartite, seeing affliction as caused by spirits, by fellow human beings, and by God or nature. 'By God' and 'natural' are synonymous here as God, who created nature, is the last cause of all that happens naturally. Anything else would be unnatural; this would include the effects of the doings of spirits, who may in the past have been either human or other spiritual beings, and the effects of human activity, be it by poison or magic ('witchcraft'), breaking of taboos and other negligence or violence. This view can, perhaps, be understood better when we consider the central idea of a vital force that does not know any distinction between the natural and the supernatural. This is a well-established model that was developed in European religious and missionary studies and well received by some African academics, but may be debatable due to its origin in vitalistic European thought.[34] The explanation runs as follows: God is the ultimate, though distant source of the vital force which reaches the individual in three ways. Firstly, the ancestors have given life to their progeny and continue to support them even after their death. Secondly, human beings are dependent on others for their survival, thus fellow human beings are a source of life. And thirdly, plants – for nurture as well as for remedy – are an indispensable source of life. The same three secondary sources of the vital force can be perverted and thereby turn from life-supporting to life-destroying factors. Spirits may trouble or even kill, fellow human beings may act as witches or other enemies, and plants may be used for poisoning or destructive magic.

---

    use is not convincing, considering the unambiguous local evaluation in all relevant practical uses. Wherever HAULE tries to prove a morally good 'uchawi' by pointing to local examples and to other authors, these do not use uchawi, but either the Swahili word 'nguvu' (power) or the English term 'power' bzw. power can this be omitted?, see p. 30. Similarly, the argument that 'dawa ya uchawi' ('medicine of witchcraft') implies a benevolent use, pp. 38-47, results from an uncritical confusion with 'medicines' in general. The fact that the word uchawi can be used for an 'unaccountable skill' such as walking the tightrope or artistic car driving (see p. 21 and 26, respectively) does not indicate a neutral core meaning, but similarly to European languages, it is rather a metaphorical use which plays down the originally feared word. Against the background of the undifferentiated colonial denunciation in which all local ritual practice was indiscriminately called 'witchcraft', Haule's inconsistent attempt to reinterpret the meaning of uchawi could be seen as an equally undifferentiated attempt to rehabilitate local practice.

34 The expression life force or vital force, force vitale, which played a central role in several European medical theories, namely those problematically labeled as animism and vitalism, see Wolfgang U. ECKART: Geschichte der Medizin, Berlin 52005, pp. 150-154 and 158-161, was introduced by Placide TEMPELS: Bantu-Philosophie. Ontologie und Ethik, Heidelberg 1956 [Original: La philosophie Bantoue, Elisabethville 1945], into the description of African thought. As an obviously useful concept it has been, and still is, applied in medical anthropology as well as religious studies on Africa, e.g. Gabriele LADEMANN-PRIEMER: Heilung als Zeichen für die Einheit der Welten, Marburg 1988, p. 109. Gotthold HASENHÜTTL: Schwarz bin ich und schön. Der theologische Aufbruch Schwarzafrikas, Darmstadt 1991, pp. 32-36.

Who are the wachawi *and what do they commit?*

In Southeast Tanzania, as presumably in most other regions, precise ideas about the staff and the activities of witchcraft do not seem to be consistent or widely disseminated.[35] Anybody, man or woman, child or elderly, could be somebody who damages others by destructive magic. On the other hand, it is also held that there are closed groups which hold nocturnal meetings and have conditions of admission which consist mainly of crimes agreed upon and committed by all members. *Wachawi* have to fly not only to their gatherings in the night, but also to the places of their crimes. Flying and intrusion through locked doors belong to their arts. For this reason, the distinction between thief *(mwizi)* and *mchawi* also becomes blurred.[36] However, their reason for secretly entering huts tends not to be theft but the administration of the harmful substance through the mouth or the nose of the sleeping victim. The idea that they cannot simply kill or damage from a distant place is proof of the remarkably materialistic understanding of witchcraft and effective means in general that is found in Southeast Tanzania; this belief that the witch must have physical contact with the victim is somehow reflected by the fact that murder by poison is common in this region.

Once again, this confirms the central moral meaning of *uchawi*. As poisoning of members of the kinship or even beyond the kinship who refuse to do their duties or even act contrary to them is widely accepted, the general repugnance felt for *uchawi* is not so much related to the means themselves as to the anti-social, fundamentally evil character of the *wachawi*. This evil character is especially expressed in the one deed which, as mentioned above, is also a precondition for successful witch-fighters: cannibalism. In 1921 an entry in a mission chronic mentioned a medicine called *Mmandu* which contains human flesh or bones and which, when consumed, makes people conscious *wachawi*.[37] The idea of becoming *mchawi* or strengthening one's disposition to evil by swallowing a medicine is still virulent.[38]

Even if the accusation of cannibalism obviously embraces various European anxieties, projections and fantasies regarding primitivism, there cannot be any reasonable

---

35 The precise descriptions of the sorcerers ('Zauberer') given by Benedictine missionaries for the Mwera ca. 1930 could not be confirmed in my interviews; see Meinulf KÜSTERS: Die Wamuera, unpublished typescript 1931, pp. o.3.-q.9., and Joachim AMMANN: Sitten und Gebräuche bei den Wamwera, unpublished typescript 1955 [both provided and to be edited by Maria KECSKÉSI]. KÜSTERS who did not live among the Mwera for long based his account largely on AMMANN's notes.

36 See Interview TANZ61 II [JN, 21.11.2001].

37 See Masasi Log books 3.7.1921, in: Rhodes House Oxford [RHO], Ranger Archive (17).

38 Interview TANZ95 II [Longino Livigha with JDO, 27.12.2001], p. 4. JDO: 'A mchawi certainly eats human flesh, but it depends of what and in which condition a man died [...] Wachawi eat humans, whether you believe it or not, a mchawi eats human beings. On the day of their funeral they take him/her away, they do not want the head, they do not want the hands, also not the legs.' LL: 'What do they take?' JDO: 'They take brain, and they eat the soft parts like lungs, they do not like the bones. Yet it depends on how you had lived.' LL.: 'Whether you had been well nourished?' JDO.: 'They do not eat you if you have lost weight.' LL.: 'What about e.g. somebody who died of AIDS?' JDO.: 'They want somebody like you, Longino, they only take what is safe, they eat it, they really eat it."

doubt that human body parts are used. The ritual meal of human flesh was proven for many regions in colonial times.[39] The same might be true for Southeast Tanzania[40] for, as it accords to widespread customs and beliefs it would not be an inconceivable action. Eating human body substances, e.g. the chief's son's prepuce chopped up and mixed with a meal during the puberty rites, can be a public ritual and is an example of the local concept of *ntela,* the vital force which can be acquired by incorporation. Theft of corpses and even ritual murder are also known in Tanzania, though the latter is much rarer than in South Africa. Since it is assumed that powerful medicine requires parts of a body, it is not astonishing that medicine from Europe also acquired this reputation. The preparation of corpses for anatomical education, pathology and forensic purposes aroused the suspicion that biomedical staff practice witchcraft.

The hunger for human flesh which stems from exhumed corpses as well as from members of their own family or circle of friends killed specifically for this purpose[41], expresses what the *wachawi* go for: to profit from the life force of others. Destructive magical objects hidden in the roof of the victim's hut, dug into the earth or scattered along the way can suck the victim's vital force, although it is not always clear how the witch profits from this. Therefore, some emphasise the fact that this is viciousness with no reason behind it. The informant, who sees himself as *mchawi,* calls witchcraft a 'useless science of the Africans', but mentions at the same time the pursuit of a selfish interest, namely sexual intercourse with women against their will[42], while the other key informant sees intrusion into houses as also being committed for theft.[43]

Counteractions by individuals, society and state

The manifold aspects of witchcraft in the region led to an even greater variety of reactions. The African and the European views see competing functions and interpretations of witchcraft, considering it as social or religious, causing or solving tensions, outmoded or up-to-date, rational or irrational, a fact which has prompted very different, often even opposing measures with which to handle the perceived problem. Therefore, a history of the counteractions is as informative with regard to the development of the political situation as to the varying opinions on the nature of and reasons for witchcraft.

The older public ways: poison ordeal and naming the culprits

Reports on practices of witchcraft-fighting that should correspond to those of pre-colonial times can be found in early writings by Anglican and Catholic missionaries of Southeast Tanzania. In 1883 the Anglican mission complained that the local ruler Matola I. who would have liked to become a Christian convert encountered major obstacles

---

39 See Travers A. LACEY (Director of Education, Nyasaland Protectorate): Notes on a recent Anti-Witchcraft Movement in Nyasaland. A Dissertation submitted for the Diploma of Anthropology at the University of Cambridge (May 1934), pp. 17-19, in: RHO, Ranger Archive (16).
40 See KÜSTERS: Wamuera, p. q.7.
41 See HAULE: Bantu witchcraft, pp. 23 and 52-55.
42 Interview TANZ95 I [Longino Livigha with JDO, 25.12.2001] p. 7.
43 See Interview TANZ61 II [JN 21.11.2001].

on one point. The population demanded that he should continue to submit a subject accused of witchcraft by a diviner to the often lethal ordeal.⁴⁴

Benedictine missionaries' ethnographic accounts of other ethnic groups in the region can be found for the interwar period, although the age of the reported practices does not become sufficiently clear. The *Mwera* spoke of the burning of detected witches or sorcerers (*'Zauberer'*), but obviously this was not observed by the ethnographer.⁴⁵ Poison ordeal and burning, however, were not the only solutions for the suspicion of witchcraft in this region. Another Benedictine missionary reported on an option for a Makonde group that was slightly more favourable for the accused. Here, in a case of illness presumed to have been caused by witchcraft, the village head together with the whole village community, implored and increasingly threatened the unknown person who was thought to have been the origin of the illness to give up the bewitchment. Only when the condition of the sick person remained unchanged was the diviner (*'Wahrsager'*) or 'expert for catching witches' (*'fundi ya kuwakamata wachawi'*) called,

„When this diviner comes, all inhabitants gather. They sit on the ground in rows. The men, women, young men and girls. The expert [*„Meister"*] fills a small leather bag with magical medicine and holds it with both hands, then his whole body starts trembling and he passes along the rows beating the culprits on their foreheads. He also tells who the chief sorcerer [*„Hauptzauberer"*] is and who his assistants are. In the past, somebody who was repeatedly accused of witchcraft, especially if he was a slave, was bound, led aside and struck dead with the axe. If some were accused of sorcery for the first time, they were brought into the sick person's house and bound to the beams with the cord not to be released before they released the sick. If the *Humu* [village head] intercedes on behalf of the imprisoned he can arrest them in their own houses saying that if the patient dies they have to die, too. Even this death sentence can be lifted by the *Humu* if advocates for the accused are found. Most often there is dispute: the relatives of the dead refuse to wash and bury the dead; this is your prey (nyama yenu), they accuse the accused sorcerers, take it with you and bury it yourself. Then it is again up to the *Humu* to reconcile all concerned".⁴⁶

The report demonstrates that it was the aim even of the pre-state leadership to avoid and deescalate conflicts wherever possible. Other than under the rule of law in the modern state, it was even more important to remove the cause of the trouble than it was to impose punishment.

Early intervention by the colonial administration

Despite the fact that some local practices had this deescalating tendency the fight against witchcraft became the battle field of a severe conflict between African and colonial law which the European side would have preferred to avoid. Colonial administrators presumed the African and the European sense of justice shared a good deal of common ground as far as jurisdiction was concerned, whereas missionaries initially saw a fundamental contradiction between African religion and Christianity. The application of local law in as many cases as possible, with the exception of certain capital crimes,

---

44 See UMCA, Annual Report 1882-83, 31, File: UMCA Annual Reports [Extracts 1876-1918], RHO Ranger Archive (22).
45 See KÜSTERS: Wamuera, p. q.6-q.7.
46 Gerfried LINDER: Unyago des Mwenye, pp. 2-3, typescript n.d., Abbey Library Ndanda.

was the declared aim of many German and, later, British law experts. However, witchcraft accusations regularly transgressed this principle of the compatibility of the two judicial systems as they fundamentally contradicted the European idea of having the opportunity to present one's case.

After German judges had only dealt with witchcraft as trouble-making and – if proven in an animal experiment – poisoning offences, the British introduced, as a result of their experience in other territories, anti-witchcraft legislation, the witchcraft ordinances. According to these ordinances the following were punishable: claiming to practice witchcraft, proven practice of black arts as well as witchcraft accusations and even persecution of people as witches. Some Europeans were also aware of the contradiction inherent in these laws in which one offence seems to presuppose the existence of witchcraft and at the same time the other presupposes its non-existence.[47] The European sense of justice considered the local punishment of witches to be lynching; however, at the same time they could not dismiss any threat that witchcraft would be used as a mere joke and hence, this seemingly contradictory regulation remained in place in all the many amendments to the witchcraft ordinances.

The witch-doctor became the most common victim of colonial anti-witchcraft legislation although, as explained above, his task had been to fight and not to practise witchcraft. However, whereas witchcraft itself is practised secretly, witch-finding by the witch-doctor took place in public and was, thus, easily proven. Therefore, in many African eyes the evil people were spared and even protected while their opponents, i.e. the good, were punished. The influence which this African view had on the evaluation of the European intentions during colonial rule can not be overestimated. European superiority in telecommunication, transport and weapons had already aroused the suspicion of occult forces, and now the Europeans seemed to take the witches' side. Besides fighting the belief in witchcraft by means of the penal law, the colonial administration also opted to change the Africans' minds by education and by demonstrating that non-magical means, such as European medicine, could be even more efficient. Yet, as medicine is always prone to magical interpretation, these attempts might even have contributed to the fact that magical skills and intentions were ascribed to Europeans.

Personal defence and removal of witchcraft

It is remarkable that there is no mention of any kind of ritual form of removing witchcraft either from the victim or the culprits in the older descriptions of poison ordeals and witch-detecting by Anglican and Catholic missionaries. For today, in all ethnic groups in Southern Tanzania, people employ many means to protect themselves against the continuous effects of witchcraft or to get rid of such effects, this involving the healing of complaints even when the witches have not given up their doings.[48] This might indicate that, due to pressure from the colonial state and the dissolution of the previous social

---

47 For a description by an African intellectual see Cuthbert K. OMARI: The Role of Witchcraft and Sorcery in Society, in: Psychopathologie Africaine 8 (1972), pp. 115-125, here pp. 120-121.

48 See, for example, the many recipes in the notes of the Mwera healer Vitus MBINGA, copy in the Archive of the Abbey Ndanda/Tanzania.

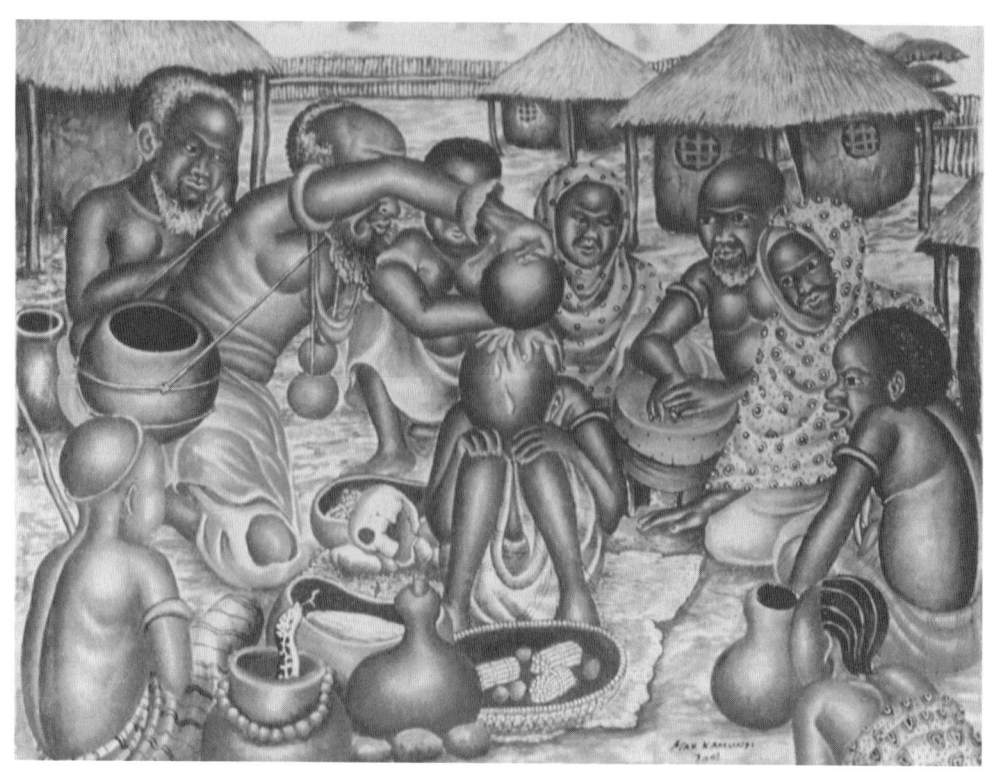

Fig. 3: Painting by Max Kamundi, Njenga/Tanzania: Ablution (kuoga).

order, a privatisation of the counteractions against witchcraft took place. Forms of defence, magic and counter magic are various in Southeast Tanzania and were obviously used before colonial rule. *Zindiko* or *kinga*[49], protection against evil influence, can be found in the repertory of nearly all healers. Special expertise is needed for the vulnerable periods of pregnancy, birth and early childhood, but also for puberty rites *(unyago)* involving circumcision of boys, in the past for hunting and war, today for travel and school, times at which death and other affliction are more likely. In addition to mixtures of various substances conserved in calabashes, amulets *(hirizi)* and objects with a special symbolism are applied: these might be, for example, a sickle neutralised by a large shell or bottles dug into the ground at the threshold of a house with the open end pointing outwards to the feared evil influence from outside. Some measures do not actually repel witchcraft themselves but serve to alarm the potential victims when witches are

---

[49] According to Hildegard HÖFTMANN / Irmtraud HERMS: Langenscheidts Handwörterbuch Swahili-Deutsch, Berlin 2000, p. 400; zindiko means in anthropology 'Schutzzauber' ('protective magic'), in medicine 'Antikörper' ('antibody'). In GUTHRIE: Comparative Bantu, p. 281, C.S. 1068 *-kíng, , has the basic meaning 'protect by screening'. The implied indication of a differentiated response for defence might have prompted the medical use of this word (which also has military connotations) for prevention and protection, but also for immunization and the immune system, as in the official Swahili term for AIDS: ukosefu wa kinga mwilini (UKIMWI), 'weakening of the defense in the body'. Such magical connotations of modern scientific terms and other neologisms are probably unavoidable, given the fact that previous concepts and their words did not distinguish between 'natural' und 'supernatural'.

approaching, which gives potential victims the opportunity to prevent witches from administering their substances or hiding their objects.

When the evil influence is already at work there are various means of removing it. The most important external ways of doing so are ablutions with specially prepared solutions and shaving of hair (see figure 3 and 4). In Southwest Tanzania 'shaving' is even the technical term used for the removal of witchcraft and is often performed at the same time on both the victim and the person causing the trouble so as to remove the evil completely.[50] Ablutions are practised in a more Islamic and a more traditionally African way. The tional African method is to place roots in water for some time and then to use the water for washing *(kuoga)*. Today nearly all healers use the Islamic way, independent of their other preferred practices. Alleged or genuine Koran verses and Islamic symbols are written on a white plate (kombe) in red ink. The water in which this writing is dissolved can be administered by drinking or ablution. This custom can also be found in other Islamic regions of the world, and in similar forms in other religions based on holy writings.

Fig. 4: Ablution of witchcraft influence from a child, Nachingwea / Tanzania.

For stronger physical complaints the suspected witchcraft substance may be removed by inducing vomiting or diarrhoea with herbal remedies. Even boiling the evil substance out of the victim by seating him or her in water heated as hot as bearable has been practised traditionally[51], as one patient I interviewed reported[52]; this is also depicted in popular drawings (see figure 5).

The new local ways: self-denunciation and cleansing of villages

Besides these rather private counteractions and the conservation or even extension of purely defensive means, new public and active ways of fighting witchcraft also developed as a consequence of the colonial witchcraft ordinances. As a result of these laws the witch-finders no longer actually accuse anybody themselves. This role is either taken by the victim or by the perpetrator, or the counteraction, i.e. the removal of witchcraft or the punishment takes place quasi-automatically without a culprit being identified or confessing. These rituals may take place either in private or in public. When the procedure takes place in public the aim is to make the alleged witches themselves confess, whereas

---

50 See Maya GREEN: Shaving witchcraft in Ulanga: Kunyolewa and the Catholic Church, in: R. G. ABRAHAMS (ed.): Witchcraft in contemporary Tanzania, Cambridge 1994, pp. 23-45.
51 See KÜSTERS: Wamuera, pp. o.3-o.4.
52 See TANZ89 (TM, 21.1.2002).

Fig. 5: Painting by H.M. Manoli, Mkalapa / Tanzania: Boiling (kuchemsha) *evil substances.*

in the private forms of the procedure the presumed victims also get the chance to identify the perpetrator themselves. As the law no longer allowed violence for the punishment and extinction of the culprit, these had to be substituted by cleansing and reconciliation when the measures were applied publicly. The private forms did not require the alleged witch to be present, thus direct violent revenge was not possible and therefore practical interference by the government unlikely, although the resulting reaction could be poisoning or beating, even beating to death, at a later date.

Only three years after the first witchcraft ordinance in Tanganyika, one of these new means of discovering witches appeared in the Anglican mission area of Masasi at Easter 1925. The inhabitants of a village were forced to prove, by taking a medicine, that they were not *wachawi* or forced to have their witchcraft removed.[53] In the public form, violence is no longer used once the witches have been named, but is only employed to enforce detection, in itself a harmless act, whereafter the identified witches can be cleansed of witchcraft. Equally new is the fact that the expert comes from outside, mostly from another ethnic group, and fills the gap that resulted from the loss of the old authorities previously responsible for such ordeals. At least initially, the old means of the veneration of ancestors were still used during this witch-cleansing as, for example, the use of flour as a sacrifice and as a device for divination.[54] At the same time, the newly imported forms are described when 'a man called Ngoja'[55] 'shaved and vaccinated with bush medicine' [= rubbed substances into superficial incisions].[56] During the following years these witch-finders were a recurrent phenomenon in the Lindi area, and were usually reported to the colonial authorities, arrested, expelled and fined.[57] When the mainly African clergy of the Anglican mission, supported by their church elders, discovered the secret gatherings of the witch-cleansing ceremonies, the witch-finders were expelled in all cases noted in the reports. Obviously, they feared the alliance between church and colonial state.

A movement which had spread from Nyasaland, now Malawi, and Portuguese East Africa, now Mozambique, to Tanzania in the 1930s achieved greater publicity, reaching as far as Dar es Salaam. The movement initiated a series of ethnographic studies which still influence anthropology and witchcraft studies today. Four young men introduced the *mchapi* movement[58], which became well-known in anthropological circles as *Bamucapi* when it appeared in North Rhodesia (now Zambia) in 1934[59], into Southern Tanga-

---

53 See entry 12.4.1925, Log book Masasi 102-1952, RHO, Ranger Archive (17).
54 See entry 9.3. 1927 (Diarist Obed KASEMBE), Log books Chiwata 1912 to 1962, RHO, Ranger Archive (20).
55 For Ngoja bin Kimeta and mchape see John ILIFFE: A Modern History of Tanganyika, Cambridge 1979, pp. 367-368.
56 Entry 24.2.1927, Log book Mapale (near Kanyimbi), RHO, Ranger Archive (22): 'mtu mmoja jina lake Ngoja [...] amekwisha nyoa na kuchanja dawa hii ya Kishenzi'.
57 Entry 24.5.1928, Log book Masasi 1902-1952, RHO, Ranger Archive (17).
58 See Richard G. STUART: Mchape and the UMCA, 1933, SOAS, Conference on the History of Central African Religious Systems, Lusaka, 30.8.-8.9.1972, RHO, Ranger Archive (17).
59 See Audrey I. RICHARDS: A modern movement of witch-finders, in: Africa 8 (1935), pp. 448-461.

nyika in 1933.⁶⁰ They summoned the whole village for the ordeal and received large sums for detecting the hidden alleged witchcraft medicines of which many, if not most, were in fact protective medicines installed by people for their own protection.⁶¹ Characteristically, the *Bamucapi* used small mirrors by which they identified the culprits from among the villagers passing behind them. In addition to being summoned to cleanse whole villages when cases of affliction had increased to an unbearable degree, the experts could also be called in for an individual sick person or for a suspicion.

That witch-finding was replacing older ways of solving problems becomes clear from the reaction of the population when the rains failed in 1942.⁶² When the expert *(fundi)* WAHAMU recommended sacrifices of flour on the graves of the ancestors, the crowd demanded 'divination' for identifying the culprit. Typically enough, the *fundi* who had made himself suspect by showing his repugnance of witch-finding was found to be the perpetrator. It is also common in other regions of present-day Tanzania that ritual experts for rain are themselves accused of being rain witches, i.e. the cause of failing rains.⁶³

The ambiguity of the late colonial administration

In Southeast Tanzania there were several differences in the way the witchcraft ordinance on witch-finding was applied. Initially, the British administration of the Lindi district did not feel that punishment was absolutely necessary in order to prevent the exploitation of the credulous population. Some years later, and contrary to the witchcraft ordinance⁶⁴, however, the provincial government was inclined to distinguish between 'benevolent witchcraft' or 'benevolent removal of witchcraft' or *'uganga'* on the one hand and *'uchawi'* as 'black art' on the other⁶⁵, for which the culprit was only expelled, but not taken to court. It was requested that a therapeutically acting 'witchdoctor' should not be imprisoned, even if a lethal outcome could be attributed to his practice, as long as he did not cause any social trouble.⁶⁶ Some years later, even the Colonial

---

60 See Ann BECK: Medicine, Tradition and Development in Kenya and Tanzania 1920-1970, Waltham/MA 1981, pp. 63-64.
61 See BECK: Medicine, p. 103, note 8.
62 See entry Masasi Log book 20.1.1942, RHO, Ranger Archive (17).
63 See Todd SANDERS: Reconsidering Witchcraft: Postcolonial Africa and Analytic Uncertainties, in: American Anthropologist 105 (2003), pp. 338-352, here pp. 345-346. For an analysis of precolonial rainmaking see Gloria WAITE: Public Health in Precolonial East-Central Africa, in: Steven FEIERMAN / John M. JANZEN (eds.), The Social basis of health and healing in Africa, Berkeley 1992, pp. 212-231.
64 See J. S. R. COLE / W. N. DENISON: Tanganyika. The Development of its Laws and Constitution, London 1964, pp. 254-255.
65 See Acting Provincial Commissioner [PC] O. Guise Williams to Chief Secretary [CS], 25.9.1933, TNA [Tanzanian National Archives] 16/5/7, p. 229, and report PC A. E. KITCHING, Lindi, to CS, 22.7.1937, TNA 16/5/7, p. 284.
66 See letter to District officer [DO] Kilwa, 23.4.1933, quoted after Ann BECK: A History of the British Medical Administration in East Africa, Cambridge/MA 1970, p. 140.

Office in London inquired into the necessity of a distinction between allegedly benevolent and destructive 'witchcraft'.[67]

The 'Native Authorities' in Tunduru favoured another option for handling the problem. They demanded by-laws under the 'Native Authority Ordinance' which would make it permissible to fine a perpetrator, prohibit witch-finding in the area and to punish a village head who invited a witch-finder.[68] Obviously there was a struggle for power between the various local elites. After World War II the British administration of the South-east even employed paid experts for witchcraft such as the famous NGUVUMALI in order to detect witchcraft objects and thus to calm down the population.[69]

Detecting and treating witchcraft in independent Tanzania

After independence in 1961 the new political leadership was also confronted with the problem of public witch-finding. A witch-finder who, like the *Bamucapi*, practised outside his home region was arrested by the black administration, whereas a white anthropologist emphasised that such activities could solve the increasing problems of fear and suspicion.[70] Below the more Europeanised level of the central government many voices demanded a change in the colonial witchcraft ordinances as a last act of liberation from white domination. They wanted the reality of destructive magic to be acknowledged by law. In the Southeast in 1972 a local administrative officer stated to the ethnographic interviewer, „I emphasize the same thing, that the peoples [sic!] government (i.e. Tanzania Government), must now understand that these things are true and do exist [...]. The colonialists deceived us that such things were not existing. But we here have proved these things, (and) those who made them have themselves confirmed this".[71] Many requested that witch-finding should be legalised and witchcraft be listed in the code of penal law with punishment according to the damage it caused.

It was not by accident that such a demand arose at that particular point in time. In the early 1970s the great fear of witchcraft in the newly imposed *Ujamaa* villages led to increased witch-cleansing.[72] The closer settlements and uncertainties regarding land ownership aroused the fear of bewitchment, as we know from the comparison of resident with nomadic peoples. In 1972 in a village of my research region close to Luatala the local representatives of the ruling party, among them an Anglican church elder, in-

---

67 See Memorandum J. L. KEITH, 21.11.1939, Public Record Office in Kew/London [PRO] CO 847/13/11 Laws relating to witchcraft (1938), p. 2.
68 See Acting DO Tunduru to PC Lindi, 9.11.1933, TNA 16/5/7, p. 233.
69 See J. Gus LIEBENOW: Colonial rule and political development in Tanzania: The case of the Makonde, Nairobi 1971, pp. 61-62; for the famous person NGUVUMALI see LIENHARDT: Hasani.
70 See James Lewton BRAIN: More modern witchfinding, in: Tanganyika Notes & Records 62 (1964), pp. 44-48.
71 Quoted after John A. R. WEMBAH-RASHID: The Traditional Religion of the People of Masasi District. Ethnographic Field Research Report = National Museum of Tanzania. Occasional Papers No. 1, Dar es Salaam 1974, reprinted 1977, pp. 18-19; original quotation in: Katibu Tarafa Otto Leo MROPE. Ethnographic Research Notes. National Museum, Dar es Salaam 1972, p. 1
72 See James Lewton BRAIN: Witchcraft and Development = University of Dar es Salaam Inaugural Lecture Series 31, Dar es Salaam 1981.

vited a woman from Mozambique to administer for payment to the whole village population a medicine which would kill anybody attempting witchcraft.[73] The government's hopes that the *Ujamaa* villages would bring 'progress' were rather disappointed by such widespread reactions to the enforced villageisation.[74]

Even in present-day Tanzania there are many instances where the village heads call witch-finders for assistance. In Liputu, another village in my research region, the last time this happened, to my knowledge, was in 1998: because of increasing damage attributed to witchcraft, the village secretary invited the itinerant witch-finder Lukemo from the Makonde plateau. This woman gave all suspected persons an obviously intoxicating drink. Under its influence some confessed to the use of witchcraft, demonstrated their medicines, had to pay compensation and were ritually cleansed. Some Christians refused to participate, and the Catholic parish priest stepped in. Obviously, no physical force was employed to make the villagers undergo the ordeal. Similar expulsions of witch-finders by church elders which turned out peacefully in the end, also occurred in other places.[75] In Michenga in the neighbouring region Lindi, however, the village witch-cleansing resulted in violent riots, as not all the summoned inhabitants were prepared to participate. In the end, the special police force from the regional capital even had to be brought in. The famous witch-finder who earned high sums from this business was imprisoned, but released later and practises as a famous healer in a settlement further north today.

The non-public, and therefore under certain circumstances even more dangerous way of detecting witches in East Africa, often makes use of a mirror which had been introduced by the *Bamucapi* for public witch-finding. In this contemporary private mode of fighting witchcraft not only the *waganga*, but also the victims themselves, often after the administration of intoxicating substances, detect the culprits, i.e. the causes of the bewitchment, by looking into the mirror (see figure 2 and 6). Thus, the responsibility for the identification of witches may be transferred to the client, and the *mganga* escapes the legal liability for accusing people of witchcraft, which his legal license to practise 'traditional medicine' forbids him to do.

In addition to witch-detection, there are the above mentioned options of protection and cleansing which are employed in order to help victims of bewitchment without identifying the personal cause. Many of these rituals have an obvious, mostly Islamic religious appearance with prayers and songs directed to godly powers, religious symbols and holy water. Sometimes, more or less official Christian rituals are even used in the fight against witchcraft, e.g. the prayer and signs of charismatic groups, medals of saints and blessed water among Catholics, as well as the Sunday services of Pentecostal or Independent African Churches.

---

73 See Interview Terence O. RANGER with Bishop Hilary CHIGUNDA, Masasi, 21.8.1975, Masasi Medical, RHO Ranger Archive (22).
74 Terence O. RANGER, Development policies in colonial and post colonial East Africa, unpublished Paper, Postgraduate Seminar University of London (CEH/76/4) 18.3.1976, 11, Masasi Seminar Economic Data, RHO Ranger Archive (22).
75 See Interview Abbot Dionys, 20.1.2002; TANZ89 (TM, 21.1.2002).

Fig. 6: Drawing by Steven Lucas, Mkalapa/Tanzania: Detecting the witch in the mirror.

The quantitative development of public witchcraft-related activities in East Africa is difficult to judge. Serious methodological problems make it impossible to investigate whether the well-known increase in social conflicts as a result of processes of modernisation also actually causes an often presumed increase in witchcraft accusations. Certainly in the towns, where a more Europeanised system of law rules, witch-hunts are considerably rarer than in many rural areas, such as the notorious Sukumaland of Northwest Tanzania. The more Europeanised the media are, for example, journals in colonial languages and especially their readers' letters, the less witchcraft is mentioned.[76] Nevertheless, in 2003 even the Speaker of the Ugandan parliament Edward SSEKANDI proclaimed publicly, 'when Aids struck us in the 1980s, we believed it was witchcraft. When we eventually discovered the source of the scourge, we opened up and

---

76 See Karl PELTZER: Psychology and Health in African Cultures, Frankfurt/M. 1995, p. 98, for the letters in a Nairobi journal. The opposite is reported from West Africa where Geschiere, according to van Binsbergen: Witchcraft, p. 245, noted that Cameroonians often prefer to discuss witchcraft matters in French or English.

today the difference can be easily discerned'.[77] With this statement, the initial attribution of Aids to witchcraft as well as – by the allegedly easy distinction – the causation of disease by witchcraft is acknowledged. For even when witchcraft is excluded, this is done against the background of its assumed reality. The reality is not officially recognised by the Tanzanian government. According to studies by researchers from the University of Dar es Salaam, however, there can be no doubt that destructive magic plays an important role in politics, especially in the competitive climate of the new multiparty system after the decades of one party rule, and that magical means have been applied by the majority of parliamentary candidates, from whatever faith.[78] Witchcraft is only mentioned publicly in connection with a great, perhaps increasing problem for a state under the rule of law: lynching – often of those suspected of witchcraft.[79]

Despite these public and political aspects of witchcraft, in East Africa the main tendency – if compared with the pre-colonial and early colonial situation – seems to be the demonstrated individualisation, privatisation and more religious contextualisation of the measures against witchcraft. Thus, central features of modern society, i.e. the rise of the individual, the separation between a private and a public sphere and the compartmentalisation of religion as a distinct system in society, have changed the conceptualisation and control of witchcraft decisively. This conclusion certainly differs from recent research on urban and cosmopolitan witchcraft in West or South Africa where a more violent struggle for power and more advanced globalisation might have moved the location of witchcraft further to a national and international level. In any of these perspectives, however, witchcraft is neither simply a brake on nor a motor for modernisation but just one of the many aspects of African life that had to be adapted to the multiple transfers from the North Atlantic region – with more or less success.

---

77 Quoted after Mike MUSISI-MUSOKE: Mutale Sacking Good, Danish Envoy Says, in: The Monitor, Kampala 5.11.2003.
78 See Alfred MBOGORA: Verhexte Demokratie, in: Der Überblick. Zeitschrift für ökonomische Zusammenrbeit und internationale Begegnung 38, 2 (2002), p. 14.
79 See Benjamin William MKAPA: Hotuba ya Rais wa Jamhuri ya Muungano wa Tanzania, Mheshimiwa Benjamin William MKAPA, kwenye Sikukuu ya Wafanyakazi, Dar es Salaam, Mei mosi, 2001 [Speech of the President of the United Republic Tanzania, The Honourable Benjamin William Mkapa, on Labour Day, Dar es Salaam, 1 May 2001] URL: http://www.tanzania.go.tz/hotuba.htm, 1.10.2002; see Lilian LUGAKINGIRA: Wananchi watakiwa kutochukua sheria mkononi [Citizens take the law into their own hands], in: Mwananchi 02.07. 2002.

Katrin Pfeiffer

Buwaa: Cannibals of supernatural power and changing appearance.[1] A term from the Mandinka language (Gambia, Senegal, Guinea-Bissau)

Zusammenfassung

Im Vordergrund dieses Überblicks stehen Begriffe aus der westafrikanischen Sprache Mandinka aus dem Kontext des Übernatürlichen. Ausgehend von Wörterbucheinträgen, die zum Teil höchst widersprüchlich sind, wird auf die Problematik der Übertragung derartiger Begriffe in europäische Sprachen hingewiesen. Insbesondere wird die Frage erörtert, was das Mandinka-Wort *buwaa* bedeutet und ob Übersetzungen wie 'Hexe', 'witch' oder 'sorcier' gerechtfertigt sind.

Abstract

This overview focuses on terms of the supernatural in the West African language of Mandinka. Proceeding from entries in dictionaries, which are highly contradictory in part, problems in translating such terms into European languages will be referred to. Special attention will be paid to the question what the Mandinka word *buwaa* means and whether translations such as 'witch' or 'sorcier' are justified.

Introduction

A thorough competence in the language and some linguistic knowledge are imperative for the understanding of the supernatural in a given society. Understanding the 'undertones', 'reading – or rather 'hearing' – between the lines' help us to better understand the commonness and permanent presence of the supernatural in a society such as the Mandinka in West Africa.

Whoever makes an attempt to find out from Mandinka dictionaries what the word 'witch' means in Mandinka, or – one step further – knows the word *buwaa* already, (which at least partially covers the semantic content of 'witch'), and who wants to investigate the different meanings of this word, does not get far. Quite the opposite, at the end one is puzzled: a jumble of different lexemes buzzes around the semantic field 'supernatural' and does not help to understand the difference between human and non-human, between dangerous and harmless, between socially acceptable and unacceptable.

After an overview of the Mandinka language I will introduce some of the Mandinka words for 'supernatural' on the basis of explanations from migrants from The Gambia

---

1 My special thanks to Rita Wöbcke for helping me to prepare the English version of this article. Likewise I would like to thank my husband, Sulayman Marong, for his patience in discussing the meanings of Mandinka words referred to in this text.

who live in Hamburg, but who were socialised in a Mandinka surrounding. Then I will discuss the respective entries in dictionaries with regard to translations of such terms from Mandinka into and from a European language.

This stock-taking will be illustrated by language examples which contain the term *buwaa*: the usage of *buwaa* in everyday language and its occurrence in narratives.

I. Mandinka – language and speakers

Mandinka[2] is a West African language as well as a people. It is spoken by more than 1.7 mill. people, of which about 40% are the Mandinka population of the Gambia.[3] The Mandinka language, which is also spoken in the Casamance/South-Senegal and in Guinea-Bissau, is a Mande language. The Mande languages form a subgroup of Niger-Congo, one of the four African language families. The Mandinka are organised patrilinarly and 99% of them are Muslims. 'Mandinka' means 'somebody from Manding'[4], the heartland and area of origin of the empire of Mali located at the boarder between modern Guinea and Mali. The empire gained strength and expanded in the 13th and 14th centuries due to the trade with gold.

In African linguistics the term 'Manding' denotes a language (or dialect) cluster, among which Mandinka is classified together with Bamana, Jula, Maninka and others.

Manding variants – the main portion of the Mande languages – are spoken in The Gambia, Senegal and Guinea-Bissau as well as in Guinea, Côte d'Ivoire, Mali and Burkina Faso – which were all part of the empire of Mali in the Middle Ages.

The position of the Mandinka area was at the periphery of the Mali empire. Therefore some particularities developed concerning the language. For example the term *buwaa* is used only in Mandinka, whereas in other Manding languages they say – with the same connotation – *subaga*.

Mandinka is written in Latin letters with two graphs taken from the International Phonetic Association. One has to be careful with the following graphems:

    ŋ (Ŋ) = si<u>ng</u>   ñ (Ñ) = Espa<u>ñ</u>a
    c = Ka<u>tj</u>a   j = dy
    r is pronounced rolled

Short vowels are written single, long vowels are written doubled. Mandinka is a tonal language. An *accent grave* on the first syllable points to a tonal movement within a word which normally runs from down to up.

---

2   In the literature about Mandinka the terms 'Mandingue', 'Mandingo' and 'Malinke' are all word inventions by Europeans.

3   About 45% of the 1.5 mill. Gambians are Mandinka, a further 25% speak this language as a second language. In Senegal (particularly in the Casamance) 3% of the all together 10 mill. inhabitants and in Guinea-Bissau 13% of the 1.4 mill. inhabitants are Mandinka. In both countries there are some ten thousand second language speakers to be added.

4   -(n)ka = somebody from.

II. Connotations and attitudes of the Mandinka regarding the treatment of different forms of supernatural action and being

In the following I shall try to describe what some of the Mandinka terms connected to the supernatural mean. *Buwaa, moori* and *saabutii* are the figures, together with some verbs, and the term *nasi* which are, – according to the English-Mandinka dictionaries – connected with 'witch' or 'witchcraft'. The opponents of *buwaa, kùmfanuntee* and *fambondi,* will be described, too, although there is no connection between these words and the words for 'witch' or 'witchcraft' mentioned in the dictionaries.

BUWAA

Buwaa are basically looked upon as human-beings who can change their appearance and can loose their *buwaa*-power as well. At the same time the *buwaas*' being human is the best camouflage for them to live among and profit from human-beings. *Buwaa* are extremely dangerous. *Buwaa* can appear in male or female form, irrespective of age. They are invisible for average human-beings. They can change their appearance particularly into owls, red monkeys, cats, horses, also into fire or a single spark which flies from one compound over to the next one. Fast flying is another ability of *buwaa*. They are active especially at night, therefore there is the synonym *suutonka*, 'person from the night'.

What makes *buwaa* so dangerous? *Buwaa* kill people from among their own human clan making use of undefinable diseases. Then, after the burial, they convert the corpses into animals, invite other *buwaa* and together eat these single animals. As *buwaa* expect a re-invitation, it is just the others' duty to sacrifice somebody from time to time in return for these invitations – even if the chosen one is one's only child. If a *buwaa* dies before they have been able to reciprocate, the others themselves are allowed to take the sacrifice from the clan of the dead *buwaa*. The *buwaa* society is organised after human criteria: with a *buwaa-mansa* (-ruler) as well as representatives from each profession and all tasks. However, single *buwaa* seem to be very lonely creatures.

Initiates (*ŋànsiŋ*) are particularly endangered to be attacked by *buwaa* in the initiation camp (*kàsayi*). The young stay in the bush without protection by the community for weeks. At the same time they are the pride of their families and clans. That is why they are particularly vulnerable and an easy prey. Perhaps it is the injuries through the circumcision which allure the *buwaa*?

Protection against *buwaa* – *KÙMFANUNTEE* and *FAMBONDI*

There are no general means of protection against *buwaa* (one could think of certain plants or actions and gestures everybody could carry out). The so-called *kànkuraŋ*-masks serve as general protection of the initiates. The masks are normally worn by men and seldom by women, but cannot do anything against *buwaa*. *Kànkuraŋ* wear a body mask, which consists of bark and leaves.[5]

---

[5] An anticipation to the entries in dictionaries: *kànkuraŋ* is just translated with 'mask', 'masked dancer' or 'masquerade'.

If somebody in the initiation camp falls seriously sick, the best thing to do is to call a *kùmfanuntee* [6] or *fambondi* [7] to identify the responsible *buwaa* and fight them with the help of special means, called *jaburundirilaŋ*. A *jaburundirilaŋ*, which deprives the *buwaa* of their power, can also made by a *moori* ('marabout', see below).

A *kùmfanuntee*, the only effective opponent of *buwaa*, will be engaged to keep the *buwaa* away from the initiation camp. The *kùmfanuntee* can do this irrespectively of the place of attendance. The extended masked form of *kùmfanuntee* is the *fambondi*: the one who prepares himself – in opposition to *kànkuraŋ*, who needs help to put on his mask.

A *kùmfanuntee* knows everything a *buwaa* does and plans. In addition a *fambondi* can fly. Both a *kùmfanuntee* and a *fambondi* are authorised to impose a night curfew during the time of initiation.

If the *kùmfanuntee* or *fambondi* succeed in identifying the *buwaa* and to treat them with *jabundirilaŋ*, the *buwaa* get beside themselves, take off their cloths in public, reveal what they did themselves and betray other *buwaa*. The *buwaa* have revealed their secret and have lost their fatal power. In Mandinka this is: *buwaa jaburuta*. *Jaburu* is no permanent condition and *buwaa* convert into 'normal' human-beings during the *jaburu-*phase. The verb *jaburu* is exclusively used in connection with *buwaa*. Possibly *jaburu* is an Arabic loan-word from *ǧafr* meaning 'art of predicting'.[8]

In general *buwaa* are not persecuted. But single persons can be suspected to be a *buwaa* on the ground of their behaviour or by a *moori*'s indication. Questions which help with the identification can be: „Who was the last person to touch you before your disease started?" „Who gave you food?" According to the decision of a village community, a *kùmfanuntee* can be engaged to remove the *buwaa*. Special drums, *buwaa-tantaŋ* [9], can be played as well in order to chase *buwaa* away or to destroy them. They are used according to the advice of a *kùmfanuntee* and in accordance with the mayor of the village, in the event of many sudden deaths. Then the *buwaa* become nervous and are in danger of having to reveal their true nature. This kind of drum is produced by a *moori* or a *kùmfanuntee* and must be played exactly according to their orders. (The knowledge about how a *buwaa-tantaŋ* is played is disappearing nowadays.)

---

6   *Kùmfanuntee* = sb. with a wide head; Denis CREISSELS / Sidia JATTA / Kalifa JOBARTHE: Lexique Mandinka-Français, Mandenkan No 2. Paris 1982 give 'personne qui jouit de pouvoirs surnaturels'; only one entry occurs in Peace Corps The Gambia (1995): Lexique Mandinka-français, Mandenkan No. 2, Paris, concerning the verb form *kuŋofanuta*: 'mystically sighted, can see the unseen'.

7   *Faŋ-bondi* = to take oneself out = sb. who prepares/masks themselves without help. In W.E.C. W[orld] E[vangelium] C[hrist] International: Mandinka English Dictionary, Banjul 1990, one finds the entry *fambondi*: 'mask dancer, super-human being (it is believed that he appears from nowhere through the air and harasses people, when the word spreads that 'fambondi' is coming no-one would leave the compound out of fear), loner, versatile person'. In Peace Corps you only find the reference: 'see „kankuraŋo"'.

8   Gundula MOTSCH: Arabische Lehn- und Fremdwörter im Mandinka – Eine linguistische und historische Untersuchung. Unveröffentlichte Magisterarbeit, Hamburg 1994, p. 81.

9   Entry in W.E.C. 1990 for *buwaa-tantaŋ*: 'witch drum (the alikaaloo [mayor] will only allow it to be played when many deaths have occurred caused by witches. When played, witches come and dance saying whom he/she killed or implicate other witches not present.)'.

It can also happen that somebody who lost their child through a *buwaa*, want to take revenge and engage a *moori* to kill the *buwaa*-being by special means.

MOORI

A *moori* is a learned Muslim, a scholar who has studied the Qur'an and, at the same time, he is a healer who is consulted about different social problems and about somatic or psychic suffering.[10] These healers identify the cause of the problem by seeing (*jùubeeri*): Often they would diagnose a misfortune (*sètaani*), which was caused by the activities of another *moori* or a *buwaa*.

A *moori* heals by prescribing certain sacrifices and prepares certain objects for protection: *safe* or *balandaŋ* to be tied, *nasi* to be applied to the body or to drink and *tawuŋ* to be burried or to be hanged somewhere. All of these objects have to be used exactly according to the *moori*'s orders. Extracts from roots, bark or leaves can also be administered.

A *moori* is also responsible for his clients' wishes concerning a positive change of their lives. He can influence (*kùŋoduŋ*) in favour of his customer, too. He can bring about uncontrollable movements (*sitikoŋ*), e.g. in the opposing team during a football match. If a *moori* causes a disease without administered drugs, this is called *dàbari*[11], or, with poison, *kor(i)tee*. Generally speaking, *moori* 'work on' others: *I ye a dookuu le* 'he/she was worked on'.

Female *moori* (*musu-moori*) are seldom, but there are some and they can perform the same tasks like their male collegues. Healing and seeing are predominant in their activities. All *moori* are specialised in certain fields they are particularly good at: for example healing of sprains and fractures by chiropractic and splints or healing of skin diseases or identifying *buwaa*.

Not to be classified as *moori*, but worth to be mentioned are the mothers of twins who can heal sprains, strains, joint pains etc.

SAABUTII

Saabutii, owner of a *saabu*, (synonym: *daliilatii* 'owner of a *daliila*')[12] are often disabled persons who were taken away from human society by the spirits (*jina*) for one or more years, deformed and equipped with a prophetic eye for a limited time. Sometimes this special power consists only of single words. The result: *A ye saaboo/jina-londoo soto* 'he has a *saabu*/knowledge from the jinn'. A *saabutii* has similar abilities like a *moori*, only that he does not use any Islamic religious means, but only works with what he re-

---

10 From Arabic *mu'addib* teacher in a Qur'anic school; s. Gundula MOTSCH: Lehn- und Fremdwörter, p. 91.
11 From Arabic *dabbāra* means, way out, strategy, trick, magic; IDEM, p. 73.
12 On one hand *saabu* and *daliila* mean 'reason' or 'result', on the other hand 'gift', 'talent', 'special skill'; *saabu* is possibly derived from Arabic *siǧr* = magic, spell, conjuration; IDEM, p. 94. Entry for *saabu* in CREISSELS et al. 1982: 'amulette, incantation'; in:W.E.C., Mandinka English Dictionary: 'recitation, formula, curse, spell; in Peace Corps: charm, cause'.

ceived from the *jina*: an object, an instruction, a word, a special term or sign, which nobody else knows. Some *saabutii* got their knowledge from other persons, for example from a *kùmfanuntee*. The special gift of a *saabutii* can be to detect *buwaa* and render them harmless. But also among *saabutii* are such who are devoted the negative powers.

The difference between *kùmfanuntee*, *moori* and *saabutii* consists of the fact that a *saabutii* got his abilities from the *jina* or from somebody else, a *kùmfanuntee* has had his gift naturally since he was born and a *moori* achieves or – if he is a *kùmfanuntee* – enforces it through the study of the Qur'an. *Moori* should always work in connection with God and Islam, whereas there are also those who can contact negative powers in order to do harm to others.

As a summary here is a table with information about the degree of the dangerousness of the figures introduced above:

Table 1

	human	harmless, helpful for human-beings	dangerous, requires protection
buwaa/suutonka	-/+		XX
moori	+	x	x
saabutii / daliilatii	+	x	(x)
kùmfanuntee / fambondi	+	x	

III. Entries in dictionaries

In the everyday life of the Mandinka we find many more figures, creatures and beings which are connected to the supernatural. In the course of this overview, however, this discussion about *buwaa*, *moori* und *saabutii* shall be sufficient.

There are four useful Mandinka dictionaries:

1. Creissels et al.
    Creissels, Denis, Sidia Jatta, Kalifa Jobarthe (1982): Lexique Mandinka-Français, Mandenkan No 2. Paris.

2. W.E.C. 1984
    W[orld] E[vangelium for] C[hrist] International (1984): English-Mandinka Dictionary, Banjul.

3. W.E.C. 1990
    W[orld] E[vangelium for] C[hrist] International (1990): Mandinka English Dictionary, Banjul.

4. Peace Corps
    Peace Corps The Gambia (1995): Mandinka-English Dictionary (S. 1-108 Mandinka-Englisch, S.109-159 English-Mandinka), Banjul.
    http://www.africanculture.dk/gambia/ftp/mandinka.pdf

English-Mandinka

In W.E.C. 1984 and Peace-Corps 1995 one reads the following entries for the nouns 'witch', 'witchcraft', 'witch(craft) doctor', 'wizard' and the verbs 'bewitch', 'hex':

Table 2

NOUNS	W.E.C. 1984	Peace Corps
witch	buwaa male: buwaa-kewo female: buwaa-musoo	buwaa, suutonkoo[13]
witchcraft (to drink or smear)	buwaa-kuwo nasoo	buwaayaa
witchcraft doctor (making jujus with writings in leather bag) (**making witchcraft** from trees)	mooroo saabutiyo	-/-
wizard	saabutiyo	-/-

VERBS

bewitch	dooku	sitikoŋ
hex	-/-	dabari, dookuu, kuŋoduŋ

According to the entry in Peace Corps, *buwaa* and *suutonka* mean 'witch'. In fact these are synonyms for the same phenomenon and *suutonka* means literally 'person from the night'. This entry is problematic because a 'witch' does not have exactly the same properties as those referred to as *buwaa*. The suffixation of *kèe* (man) and *mùsu* (woman) to names of any kind of creature in order to mark the male or female form is, however, usual.

Moori and *saabutii,* according to W.E.C. 1984, are those who use 'witchcraft' – one prepares 'jujus'[14], the other one 'witchcraft' from trees. At the same time *saabutii* is supposed to mean 'wizard'.

According to W.E.C. the word composition *buwaa-kuu* means 'witchcraft', as does the derivation *buwaayaa* according to Peace Corps. According to W.E.C. there is a third 'witchcraft' – to drink or to smear: *nasi*. The last named is a liquid, which is prepared by *moori*. *Buwaa-kuu* denotes everything *buwaa* can do: to transform, to kill etc. *Buwayaa* is literally the 'being a *buwaa*', but it does not have any other particular connotation and is thus absolutely false as a translation for 'witchcraft'.

Not a single of the Mandinka verbs mentioned is used in connection with *buwaa*. *Dòokuu, sitikoŋ, dàbari, kùŋoduŋ* denote, what a *moori* can do besides healing: to influence the will of another person or to do him harm.

W.E.C. gives the form *dooku*. The missing second '-u' at the end is obviously meant to point at a difference between this word and *dòokuu* meaning 'work'. This differentiation is wrong: The word *dòokuu* means 'to work' as well as 'to be worked on by a *moori*'. The differentiation in Peace Corps between 'bewitch' and 'hex' is not understandable at all.

Mandinka-English/-French

By looking at the Mandinka-English rsp. Mandinka-French dictionaries and by comparing the denotations given, the entries from table 2 concerning nouns are generally confirmed. But W.E.C. have introduced a number of changes in their Mandinka-English

---

13 In most cases there is an /o/ suffixed to Mandinka nouns within a sentence which is comparable to an article in English. Therefore entries in dictionaries should appear without the 'o', but W.E.C. and Peace Corps neglect this system.

14 Religious verses written in Arabic, usually wrapped in a little leather bag; in Mandinka: *safe*.

edition compared to the English-Mandinka dictionary. Creissels et al. succeed best in trying to approach the correct meanings. This Mandinka-French dictionary is unfortunately not very extensive and many words are missing completely.

Table 3

NOUNS	Creissels et al.	WEC 1990	Peace Corps
buwaa	sorcier censé „manger" les personnes par le moyen de pratiques magiques	witch	witch, man's name
buwaa-kee (-kewo)	-/-	wizard, male witch	-/-
buwaa-kuu (-kuwo)	-/-	witchcraft	-/-
buwaa-musu (-musoo)	-/-	witch	-/-
buwaayaa	-/-	-/-	witchcraft
moori (mooroo)	marabout	marabout	fortune teller, a „marabout"
nasi (nasoo)	amulette fabriquée par les marabouts avec l'eau ayant servi[15] à laver les tablettes coraniques	liquid charm for drinking or washing	charm (in liquid form)
saabutii (saabutiyo)	feticheur	witch-doctor	one who posesses and makes charms
sabutii (sabutiyo)	-/-	person who establishes himself as an authority in the secret arts of the Mandinka society	-/-
suutonka (suutonkoo)	-/-	-/-	witch

Verbs	Creissels et al.	WEC 1990	Peace Corps
dàbari	nuire à quelq'un au moyen de pratiques magiques	to bewitch, use a juju to harm s.o., use a juju to influence s.o.'s behaviour	to witch, to hex
dòokuu	(V) travailler (y compris au sense de jeter un sort à quelqu'un) (N) travail (et aussi: pratique magique)	1. to work, cultivate 2. to bewitch	to make, hex, work on
kùŋoduŋ	-/-	to persuade s.o. by witchcraft (mostly done to get s.o.'s love)	to hex
sitikoŋ	-/-	to persuade by witchcraft or by some secret verses	bewitch, hypnotize

---

15 In French it should read grammatically correctly: 'l'eau ayant servie'.

It is interesting to note that W.E.C. adds 'wizard' to the entry *buwaa-kewo* 'male witch'. To my opinion, this is an unnecessary addition, or else one would expect the entry 'female witch' for *buwaa-musoo*.

Creissels et al. talk about a 'witch, who eats human-beings through magical means', which is quite close to the meaning of *buwaa*.

Concerning *moori* W.E.C. (1990) is in accordance with the others by translating 'marabout'. However, the meaning of 'marabout' is only understandable, if one knows already what he can do and does. Peace Corps adds the meaning 'fortune teller'. Of course *moori* can do prophecy, but this activity is only one small part of what *moori* (can) do. In the English-Mandinka part of the Peace-Corps dictionary you find *juubeerilaa*, which means 'seer', and *mooroo* under 'fortune teller'. If one neglects the sentence example given for the verb *sitikoŋ* (*Mooroo ye a sitikoŋ ne.* The marabout hypnotized him.), the meaning and function of *moori* is hereby reflected in a very reduced form by Peace Corps.

For unknown reasons the translation 'witchdoctor' for saabutii appears in Peace Corps only in the Mandinka-English part: 'one who possesses and makes charms', a connotation, which is also true for *moori*! In W.E.C. 1990, besides *saabutiyo* with the translation 'witch-doctor' a second, unnecessary entry in different writing exists – *sabutiyo*: 'person who establishes himself as an authority in the secret arts of the Mandinka society'. According to Creissels et al. *saabutii* is simply a 'feticheur', obviously meant to mark off 'marabout', but this is not very helpful.

Only Creissels et al. explain what *nasi* is made of: 'amulet of water produced through washing Qur'anic black-boards'.

For the verbs the picture is much less obvious:

Creissels et al. translates dàbari with 'to harm somebody by magical means'. W.E.C. 1990 say even less clearly: 'to bewitch, use a juju [s. footnote 14] to harm s.o., use a juju to influence s.o.'s behaviour'. In none of these two dictionaries it is mentioned that these are the possible activities of a *moori*.

Apart from the double entries in W.E.C. 1990 dookuu/dooku, all authors agree insofar as the verb 'work' is also used in the context of magic or witchcraft. Nobody mentions that this is the general term for the work of a *moori*.

For *kùŋoduŋ* W.E.C. 1990 mentions, that it means influencing somebody concerning respective love; in Peace Corps it is translated simply as 'to hex'. In reality *kùŋoduŋ* can aim at any kind of not self-motivated action caused by a *moori*.

The least agreement between the authors is found in translating the verb *sitikoŋ*. W.E.C. 1990 translates more generally: 'to persuade by witchcraft or by some secret verses'. Peace Corps propose, *sitikoŋ* would not only mean 'bewitch', but also very concrete 'hypnotize'. This is also confirmed in the English-Mandinka part of the dictionary. In addition there is another entry with the noun *sitikoŋo*: 'charm for bewitching, charm for hexing, hypnotizing with magic'. Once again I would like to emphasise that all of the four verbs – *dòokuu, sitikoŋ, dàbari, kùŋoduŋ* – do not have anything to do with the acts of a *buwaa*, but to the activities of *moori* only.

Here are further entries which are connected to *buwaa* and which give a clear idea about the difficulties to offer intelligible translations in dictionaries:

Table 4

	Creissels et al.	WEC 1990	Peace Corps
buwaa jaburiŋ / jafuriŋ (jaburiŋo / jafuriŋo)	-/-	crazy witch	-/-
jaburu, jafuru	se réfère à d'état (délire?) dans lequel le sorcier mangeur d´âmes révèle ses activités[16]	to be suddenly mad (used only for witches)	insane, crazy because of guilt
jaburu (jaburoo)	-/-	-/-	insanity, madness caused by guilt

According to W.E.C. 1990 and Peace Corps the word *jaburu* is a kind of being crazy or mad, whereas W.E.C. mentions, that this condition concerns only 'witches'. Peace Corps mention 'guilt' as a reason for *jaburu*, which could theoretically apply to everybody. Only Creissels et al. try to understand what it means: 'to be in a condition (lunacy?), in which a cannibal-witch reveals her activities'.

IV. Usage of *buwaa* in everyday language

Examples where *buwaa* appears in the everyday language are:

The physical features of a certain object is connected to *buwaa*: *nèe-buwaa* = iron-*buwaa* = magnet.

As Peace Corps mention correctly, 'Buwaa' is also used as a personal name. Women who have difficulties in giving birth, can join the so-called *kañeleŋ* groups. This requires an initiation as well as the courage for spectacular, loud and obscene behaviour. Whenever a *kañeleŋ* woman gives birth to a child, the group chooses a special name for the baby. This name is usually a Mandinka word which means something ugly or intimidating, so that the evil powers loose the interest to take the child away. 'Buwaa' as a name for a girl or a boy fits this purpose very well: It does not pay to take such a creature away from the human-beings.

Buwaa is also used a term of abuse for somebody who bites or pinches during a row or becomes dangerously brutal in any other way. If somebody stares at another person, he could be asked: *I ka n juubee ñaadii? Fo ite mu buwaa le ti baŋ*? 'How are you looking at me? Are you a *buwaa*?'

None the verbs *dòokuu*, *sitikoŋ*, *dàbari* and *kùŋoduŋ* apply to the activities of witch/sorcier in the sense of *buwaa*. Here the verbs *maa* 'to touch' or *domo* 'to eat' are used instead:

buwaa le ye a maa = a *buwaa* touched him/her
buwaa le ye a domo = a *buwaa* ate him/her

---

[16] In French it should read grammatically correctly: 'se réfère à l'état dans lequel le sorcier est mangeur d'âmes...'

V. Appearance of *buwaa* in narratives

In the first text, narrated by a *jàli*[17], a *buwaa* appears, whereas the *buwaa* characteristics 'changing' and 'eating human-beings' are accentuated.

In the second, very short, but well-known narrative – a *taaliŋ* – 'eating human-beings' is in the foreground, but also the element 'victim from one's own family'.

Jali account

This narrative is about General Tiramakang and his conquests in the 13th century, which led to the expansion of the Mali empire to the west. In the beginning the narrator, a *jàli* called Sana Kuyate (75 years old) from the Casamance, describes how two young hunters succeed to find, as predicted, the mother of the next king of Mali, Sunjata Keeta. (Recorded in Saare Lawo, Departement de Welingara, Cassamance, Senegal, 8.6.1979.)

In order to do a favour to the ruler of the region, Sankarang Konte, (grandfather of the unborn king) the hunters first have to free the land from a horrible plague. As a reward they are to receive presents: among other things the prospective mother of Sunjata Keeta. The names of the two hunters are Daamansa Wulanding and Daamansa Wulambaa.

I cite from my translation into English:

> (When) those ones had left, it happened that there was a woman in the land of Sankarang, by the *tilibonka*s called '*suba*'.
> The Mandinkas say '*buwaa*', a great *buwaa*.
> Because the people she used to eat in a single year were more numerous than one thousand.
> The eldest of the Kontees, he came to say: „Who kills that Duu Kamisa [the *buwaa*'s name], whatever he wants in the world, I will pay him with that.
> Whatever is under my control, I will give him a hundred of all of it."
> Daamansa Wulanding and Daamansa Wulambaa, finally they left.
> When they left, they threw the *jabaa*s (they consulted the oracle/the diviners) and went to the *moori*s.

The prediction points to the fact that they will meet Duu Kamisa doing heavy work, but she would not let them help her and be altogether very unapproachable. They were not to give up.

> They walked and walked until they had done twelve days of walking through the bush.
> Where they finally found her, (that was) where she had built a house of leaves, where she usually slept in the bush, where she lived.
> It was deep in the bush, no settlement was close by. (...)
> She was all alone there, only she and God.

Actually they meet the woman in the strenuous search for firewood. She does not respond their greetings, but denounces both of them. She refuses their help.

> They argued with her until they had persuaded her.
> She said to them: „Bisimilayi, it is me whom you are after."
> They divided her firewood into two.

---

17 *Jàli*: master of the word; expert in the oral tradition of historical events, genealogies and praise names of the Manding clans; s. Katrin PFEIFFER: Mandinka Spoken Art. Folktales, Griot Accounts and Songs, Köln 1997, pp. 155ff.

The younger brother loaded one up, the elder brother loaded the other one up.
They went with all of it up to the place where she had built her big house of leaves.
If she had killed anybody, where she dried the meat, that is where she took the firewood to; she smoked human meat to eat them there, that is what she usually ate.
When they had arrived they let the loads down. She asked them: „Have you had the midday meal?"
They said to her: „Today it is twelve days, apart from our water *sumalle*s, we have not seen any cooked rice with our eyes." (…)
She said to them: „It is human meat which is here, all of this is human meat, I am a *buwaa*, I eat only human beings!"
They said to her: „We know you do."
She said to them: „If you come, you can eat human meat.
Look at it, if you won't eat human meat, hn, that is with me here as food."
They said to her: „No problem, we are hippopotamus killers, we ourselves can look for our own evening meal." (…)

Three days later:
They said to her: „Before we came to greet you, and now we want to seek permission (to go), we will go."
She said to them: „Bisimilayi, you came after me, my life.
But because of your good manners, children, I will give myself to you, my time has come, but you will be the reason for it."

Duu Kamisa's exact orders follow, how the two young men can kill her. They should offer certain sacrifices and get an egg, a cotton seed and a stone for their own protection.
They said to her: „We have given out those things as charity."
She said to them: „I know.
The day when you were giving out the things as charity, I knew it."
She said to them: „Now, you will stay her until day after tomorrow, Thursday, (then) you can leave.
When you have gone, when you are going, you will meet me somewhere, I will be black.
I will be black, a blackness of any kind, if you know it is blackness.
And the extent of my size also, you will not see it towards the sky.
The extent of my width on these two sides, you will not be able to see it.
But don't be afraid, don't shoot me!
When you kill me at that moment, whomever I get (hold of) among you, I will kill him.
If I get both of you I will kill both of you."

After that she was to get horribly red, then terribly white, high and broad. This would be the right time for them to kill her. Things happen exactly to Duu Kamisa's predictions: she dies and Daamansa Wulanding and Daamansa Wulambaa receive their reward.

Taaliŋ

These kinds of narrative, called *taaliŋ*, are narrated by the grandmothers in front of their grandchildren. Then we are given the summary of a short tale:

A woman entrusts her children to her own mother. Right at the beginning the grandmother is introduced as a *buwaa*. When the mother wants to pick up her children again, the older woman repeatedly tells her to wait by telling her the children were busy with different home chores, such as finding firewood and fetching water. This dialogue is repeated several time in the form of a song.[18]

1* *N naa Suluŋ nee, Suluŋ nee, Suluŋ Salaŋ nee.*
  My Mummy, where is Sulung, where is Sulung Salang?
2* *Saara lee, Saara Fula lee.*
  Where is Saara, where is Saara Fula?
3* *Ɖansumaane lee, Kundoo Fula lee.*
  Where is Ngansumaane, where is Kundoo Fula?
4* *Suluŋ loo-ñinoo, Suluŋ Salaŋ loo-ñinoo.*
  Sulung is finding firewood, Sulung Salang is finding firewood.
5* *Saara loo-ñinoo, Saara Fula loo-ñinoo.*
  Saara is finding firewood, Saara Fula is finding firewood.
6* *Ɖansumaane loo-ñinoo, Kundoo Fula jii-biyo.*
  Ngansumaane is finding firewood, Kundoo Fula is fetching water.

The old woman has eaten the children long ago, leaving nothing but their heads. It is only in the last stanza that the father points out what happened to the children.

4* *M bitaŋ, Suluŋ kuŋo fele, Suluŋ Salaŋ kuŋo fele.*
  My son in-law, look at Sulung's head, look at Sulung Salang's head.
5* *Saara taa fele, Saara Fula taa fele.*
  Look at Saara's, look at Saara Fula's.
6* *Ɖansumaane taa fele, Kundoo fula taa fele.*
  Look at the one of Ngansumaane, look at Kundoo Fula's.

Finally she is killed by the father.
Ntaaliŋ ntaaliŋ konkorondiŋ kos.

Ntaaliŋ is an older form of *taaliŋ* meaning 'fictitious narrative' and together with *konkorondiŋ kos*, which only appears in the context of *taaliŋ*, it is the formula to end every fictitious narrative in Mandinka.

VI. Final remarks

The above mentioned attitudes of the Mandinka concerning phenomena like *buwaa* or *kumfanuntee* are not shared by all the individuals of this people. Some do not believe in the existence of *buwaa* due to religious convictions, to social experience outside of the Mandinka context or due to people's own reflections. Doubters also take the activities of *moori* – including the prescribed means and sacrifices – to be ineffective and even discourage the consultation of a *moori*. It is, however, not very much in doubt that there are persons who can 'see' further than others – e.g. in dreams or through the gift of providence.

It is difficult to evade believing in such occurrences because people's habit of making use of related customs and convictions is omnipresent. Hardly anybody will openly discuss the existence or non-existence of such occurrences or creatures – due to the fact that the non-existence of the supernatural cannot be conclusively established. Discussions of these matters in public may lead people to be caught in a dangerous and most fearful situation in which *buwaa* or the like might very well be involved.

---

18 This *taaliŋ* originates from a recording with Kasamanding Jaabi (f, 40J.) in Salikenye/The Gambia, 1994; s. Katrin PFEIFFER: Sprache und Musik in Mandinka-Erzählungen, Köln 2001, pp. 216f.

The Mandinka dictionaries only tell us about a group of figures and activities which have to do one way or the other with supernatural power, magic etc. We are told nothing about differences of meaning, let alone about the psychological, social and religious backgrounds. The translations given by Creissels et al. are correct but vague enough as to leave much room for interpretation. The entries in W.E.C. as in Peace Corps are not only wrong in part, they also fail to differentiate between the different areas of supernatural acting and existence.

The greatest challenge in compiling a bilingual dictionary are the words used and understandable only in a well defined social, psychological and religious context. We must keep in mind who compiles the dictionaries and for whom they are written. W.E.C. writes mostly for Christian missionary use. Detailed information from the Mandinka informants is available to the mostly European staff. Both dictionaries, the one by Creissels et al. as well as the one by Peace Corps, were compiled by Mandinka speakers.

In both cases there are difficulties of religious limitations to overcome.

1. Christian missionaries are prone to negate any understanding of supernatural incidents, or at least to describe them in a very demeaning way. This has to be kept in mind when considering and working with the entries in W.E.C. and particularly with those in Peace Corps.

2. The same applies to Muslim informants: May a Muslim mention and talk about his/her knowledge of *buwaa* and *kùmfanuntee*? And if he/she is writing about supernatural instances, will he/she be able to distance himself/herself from any close knowledge without getting into conflict with his/her belief?

We also have to keep in mind that authors as well as informants might come under the spell of taboo when relating magic, revelations and secret knowledge.

I have not managed to solve all the problems concerning the meaning of certain terms and their exact definition and their intersection with other semantic properties. Clarifying those would demand broader research.

It would be helpful to supply an encyclopaedia of the supernatural for the African continent with as many African-language terms as possible on the supernatural. These terms are to be drafted and to be explained as correctly and as precisely as possible. This would evade, when compiling dictionaries, the danger of judging phenomena in a given culture according to European values. It often happens that, instead of describing African phenomena in an unprejudiced way, the Western scholar looks upon African phenomena in a Western eye: thus African cultures are stripped of most of their wide range of meanings, easy to handle by a European mind, from European point of view.

When translating texts from African languages or describing phenomena of a culturally different society from the researcher's own, one should avoid word-to-word translations and leave words in their original language and then explain these words in special chapters or glossaries. In the case of dictionaries the authors – if they have any interest of transmitting culturally specific knowledge at all – have to make an effort to look for appropriate characteristics by giving short descriptions for the words to be translated.

My suggestion for a short translation for *buwaa* is: 'person who is said to be a cannibal of supernatural power and changing appearance'.

Rolf Schulte

Okkulte Mächte, Hexenverfolgungen und Geschlecht in Afrika

Abstract

The belief in witches and the reality of witch-hunts in African societies are a consequence of structural conflicts in the network of relatives and neighbours. The gender dimension is only one variable in this network, in which a broad variety of patterns are formed. Although conflicting gender relations can lead to brutal consequences during times of crisis, the gender aspect isn't the magic key to find causes and functions of witch-hunts monocausally. South of the Sahara, age is an important variable, as well as economical, political and other cultural or social factors. While gender specific factors played an important role in Europe, there is a wide variation in the proportion of male to female witches in Africa: Within the big ethnic, regional, economical and cultural differences of this continent a homogeneous and, most importantly, a constant female stereotype of a witch is nowhere to be found. In Europe, gender specific images of magic formed women-discriminating outlines, but in Africa images of witches and witch-hunting are mostly gender-inclusive or gender-overlapping. Previous approaches to explain African witch-paradigms, no matter if they are feministic in the meaning of gender conflicts, ethnologic in the meaning of a worldwide anthropologic constant or cognitive in the meaning of a reaction to the modernisation and globalisation, can only offer partial interpretations, because they generalize and explain the reality in the respective African societies too limitedly. Although the preoccupation with this topic leads to more questions than answers, a comparison to European witch-hunts is very informative, as it allows to question the long time predominating theories and to view European witch-hunts in a more different aspect. The very complex relation of ascriptions to occult forces, witch-hunts and gender will stay open to further approaches and explanations.

Zusammenfassung

Ein Blick auf das Verhältnis von okkulten Vorstellungswelten und ihrer Geschlechtsdimension zeigt, dass der Hexenglaube wie auch die Hexenverfolgungen in afrikanischen Gesellschaften an strukturelle Konflikte im Verwandtschafts- bzw. Nachbarschaftsgeflecht gebunden sind. Der Gender-Aspekt bildet nur eine Variable in diesem Spannungsfeld, in dem vielfältigen Muster entstehen. Auch wenn konflikthafte Geschlechterbeziehungen sich in Krisenzeiten mit brutalen Konsequenzen spiegeln können, ist die Kategorie des Geschlechts nicht der magische Schlüssel, der Ursachen und Funktion von Hexenverfolgungen monokausal erschließt. Im südlich der Sahara gelegenen Afrika spielt das Alter als eine Variable in Krisenzeiten ebenfalls eine wichtige Rolle. Wirtschaftliche, soziale, politische und kulturelle

Faktoren könnten gleichfalls genannt werden. Während in Europa geschlechtsspezifische Faktoren einen hohen Stellenwert einnahmen, lässt sich Ähnliches für Afrika nicht feststellen: Hier existiert innerhalb der großen ethnischen, regionalen, wirtschaftlichen und kulturellen Differenzen kein homogenes Hexenbild und vor allem kein durchgängiges weibliches Hexenstereotyp. Geschlechtsspezifische Magiebilder hatten zwar in Europa klare Frauen diskriminierende Konturen, nicht aber zwingend in Afrika. Bisherige Erklärungsansätze des Gender-Aspekts afrikanischer Hexenparadigmen und -verfolgungen, seien es „feministische" im Sinne eines Geschlechterkonflikts, ethnologische im Sinne einer weltweiten anthropologischen Konstante oder kognitive im Sinne einer Reaktion auf die Modernisierung und Globalisierung, bieten lediglich Teildeutungen: Sie systematisieren und erklären zu eingeschränkt die Realität in den jeweiligen Gesellschaften Afrikas.

„We, in Tonga manner, our women use witchcraft only a little. It is the men who do witchcraft. But Goba women use witchcraft greatly, and their men too."[1]

Die Tonga in Sambia bringen demnach hauptsächlich Männer in Verbindung zu okkulten Kräften, dagegen übernehmen bei den benachbarten Goba beide Geschlechter diese Funktion.

Für einen Historiker, der sich mit Hexenverfolgungen in Europa beschäftigt hat, sind diese geschlechtsspezifischen Zuschreibungsmuster ungewöhnlich: Hexerei galt in Zentraleuropa der Frühen Neuzeit als frauenspezifische Aktivität – und schließlich als frauentypisches Delikt. Schon der Begriff „H e x e n - Verfolgung" verweist durch den Gebrauch des femininen grammatischen Geschlechts auf eine Zuspitzung auf Frauen als Zielgruppe gesellschaftlicher Sanktionen. Über drei Viertel aller Hexenprozesse richteten sich gegen Angehörige des weiblichen Geschlechts.[2] Auch wenn Studien inzwischen für Europa nachgewiesen haben, dass jede vierte verfolgte Hexe ein Mann war, bleibt das Übergewicht der Frauen innerhalb der Gruppe von Verfolgten unstrittig.[3]

Wer sich mit magischen Vorstellungen in Afrika beschäftigt, stößt im Vergleich zu Europa auf nicht wenige Inkompatibilitäten.

Zum Einen umfasst dieser Kontinent eine ausgedehnte politische, ökonomische und ethnisch-kulturelle Vielfalt, die es nur sehr bedingt erlaubt, einen geografischen Sammelbegriff für diese heterogenen Gesellschaften mit rund 2000 Sprachen zu verwenden. Eine historisch-kolonialherrschaftliche Periode wie eine strukturelle Unterentwicklung bilden lediglich den kleinsten gemeinsamen Nenner. Deswegen wird dieser Begriff hier aufgelöst beziehungsweise nur differenziert angewendet.

Zum Zweiten unterscheiden sich afrikanische Gesellschaften innerhalb dieses riesigen Kontinents unabhängig von der sozialen Schichtung durch ihren Glauben an die Wirkungs-

---

1 Aussage eines Shopkeepers aus Sambia, zitiert nach Elisabeth COLSON: The father as a witch, in: Africa 70 (2000), S. 336.
2 Wolfgang BEHRINGER: Hexen. Glaube, Verfolgung, Vermarktung, München 1998, S. 67.
3 Rolf SCHULTE: Hexenmeister. Die Verfolgung von Männern im Rahmen der Hexenverfolgung von 1530-1730 im Alten Reich, Frankfurt u. a. 2000; besonders S. 83-86. DERS: „Man as Witch", Basingstoke 2008.

mächtigkeit von okkulten Kräften. Während in nicht wenigen Ethnien[4] die Existenz von okkulten Kräften abgelehnt wird, spielt sie in anderen eine untergeordnete Rolle. Bei zahlreichen und häufig zugleich benachbarten Gesellschaften mit vergleichbarer Organisation und materieller Produktion ist sie dagegen fester Bestandteil von Sinn- und Weltdeutung.[5]

Zum Dritten hat die ethnologische Forschung der letzten 50 Jahre zwar die Hexereivorstellungen und Hexenverfolgungen bei zahlreichen Ethnien bzw. Gesellschaften untersucht und die Ergebnisse in vielen Studien veröffentlicht. Ihr Hauptinteresse lag jedoch seit der richtungsweisenden Studie von Evans-Pritchard darin, die Funktion des Hexenglaubens zu erklären. Die Zuweisung okkulter Fähigkeiten an das jeweilige Geschlecht wurde zwar thematisiert, dennoch nahm sie in den Studien nicht den Platz ein wie Untersuchungen zu anderen Fragestellungen. Der Gender-Aspekt magischer Praxis wie der Hexenbilder erscheint häufig als untergeordnetes Phänomen, das in zahlreichen Fällen zur Kenntnis genommen, in wenigen Studien jedoch eingehend diskutiert wird.

In diesem Aufsatz werden daher zuerst Vorstellungen der geschlechtsspezifischen Konturen okkulter Macht in afrikanischen Gesellschaften aus der bisherigen Forschung vorgestellt und dann einzelne Erklärungsansätze erörtert.

1. Hexenbilder, „day-to-day-accusations" und geschlechtsspezifische Zuschreibungen

Hexereianklagen treten in Afrika häufig in Gestalt so genannter „day-to-day-accusations" auf. Sie entstehen meistens aus privaten und interpersonalen Konflikten, dienen zur Deutung persönlichen Unglücks und umfassen nach ethnologisch-soziologischer Definition bis zu zehn Hexereibeschuldigungen in einem Kalenderjahr innerhalb eines definierten Raums.[6] „Day-to-day-accusations" enthalten spontane Hexereibeschimpfungen privater Art, öffentlich wiederholt vertretene Hexereiverdächtigungen, aber auch öffentlich verfolgte Hexereibeschuldigungen in begrenztem Umfang. Wie sahen solche Beschuldigungen, die auch in informellen wie formellen Verfolgungen enden konnten, aus?

Uganda ca. 1960: Ein Vorarbeiter im öffentlichen Dienst im Territorium von Bunyoro trennt sich von seiner Frau wegen vermeintlichem ständigen Ehebruch. Als nach den Besuchen der Frau im ehemaligen Haus die gemeinsam beim Vater verbliebenen Kinder

---

4 Der noch häufig in der älteren Literatur verwendete Begriff „Stamm" entspricht als Konstruktion der Kolonialzeit nicht der Realität und Komplexität afrikanischer Gesellschaften und wird hier nicht übernommen.

5 Mathias G. GUENTHER: "Not a Bushman Thing" – Witchcraft among the Bushmen and Hunt-gatherers, in: Anthropos 87 (1992), S. 83ff.. Tamara MULTHAUPT: Hexerei und Anti-Hexerei in Afrika, München 1989, S. 96-99. Daniel E. OFFIONG: Social Relations an Witch-Beliefs among the Ibibio in Nigeria, in: Journal of Anthropological Research 39 (1983), S. 81-95. P. T. W. BAXTER: Absence makes the heart grow fonder. Some suggestions, why witchcraft accusations are rare among East African Pastoralists, in: Max GLUCKMAN: The allocation of responsibility, Manchester 1972, S. 163-187. G. J. JONES: A Boundary to Accusations, in: Mary DOUGLAS (ed.): Witchcraft confessions and accusations, London 1970, S. 321-331.

6 R. G. WILLIS: Kamcape: An Anti-Sorcery Movement in Southwest Tanzania, in: Africa 38 (1968), S. 1-12. Daniel E. OFFIONG: Witchcraft among the Ibibio of Nigeria, in: African Studies Review, 26 (1983), S. 107, COLSON, Father, S. 336.

immer wieder erkranken, deutet der Ex-Ehemann diese körperlichen Beschwerden als okkulte Vergiftung durch die Mutter. Doch der Frau gelingt es erneut, das Vertrauen des Mannes zu erringen, sodass sich das Paar versöhnt. Als der Vorarbeiter erblindet, vermutet er erneut einen Racheakt seitens seiner Frau. Der Mann konsultiert einen Heiler und erhält dort die Bestätigung, dass sein Verdacht auf magische Aggression gerechtfertigt und die Urheberin der Misere seine eigene Frau sei. Der Vorarbeiter äußert seine Hexereiverdächtigungen öffentlich, verzichtet aber auf eine öffentliche Anklage. Er bleibt blind, weist seine Frau erneut aus dem Haushalt und lässt sich scheiden.[7]

Uganda ebenfalls ca. 1960: Ein Soldat heiratet nach Ende seiner Dienstzeit in einem Dorf im Nordosten des Landes. Als er sich durch Alkoholmissbrauch verschuldet, greift der Schwiegervater ein und fordert seine Tochter auf, in den väterlichen Haushalt zurückzukehren. Der nun allein lebende Ehemann kündigt daraufhin an, sich an der Familie seiner Frau rächen zu wollen. Als die Schwiegereltern plötzlich an heftigem Durchfall leiden, deuten sie diese Erkrankung als magische Attacke und klagen den Schwiegersohn vor dem örtlichen Dorfchef wegen vermeintlicher Hexerei an. Eine angeordnete Hausdurchsuchung ergibt, dass der Schwiegersohn tatsächlich verschiedene als Zaubermittel geltende Flüssigkeiten und Instrumente benutzt hatte. Das Dorfgericht verurteilt den angeblichen Hexer zu einer Gefängnisstrafe von sechs Monaten, in einem zweiten Verfahren wegen wiederholter okkulter Aggression zu zwei Jahren. Der Kläger vor Gericht stirbt in dieser Zeit an einer unerkannten Krankheit.[8]

Südafrika 1990: Eine Markthändlerin und ihre unmittelbaren Nachbarn beschuldigen sich nach einem Streit gegenseitig der Hexerei. In beiden Häusern waren zuvor Menschen krank geworden oder gestorben. Beide Parteien sind überzeugt, dass die Gegenseite durch magische Manipulationen dieses Leid beim anderen verursacht hat. Die alleinstehende Witwe gilt im Dorf als auffällig, weil die Beziehungen, in der ihre erwachsenen Kinder leben, immer wieder zerrütten. Gerüchte und Verdächtigungen steigern sich schließlich, als der Marktvorsteher des Ortes plötzlich stirbt und angeblich Schlangen und so genannte ‚Zombies' im Garten der Beschuldigten beobachtet werden. Mitglieder des afrikanischen National Congress beginnen sich für den Fall zu interessieren und suchen nach Zeugen der Vorfälle in der Ansiedlung. Sie finden im Ort zahlreiche Einwohner, die die Marktfrau wegen ihrer vermeintlichen okkulten Kräfte als Hexe belasten und die ihr Neid auf höheres Einkommen als Motiv unterstellen. Möglicherweise griff man jetzt zu massiven Maßnahmen gegen die Bezichtigte. Die weiteren Ereignisse bleiben jedoch im Dunkeln, da die Informationen aus dem Dorf zu diesem Zeitpunkt abbrechen.[9]

Benin 1998: Nachbarn bezichtigen einen in Tebu in Nordbenin lebenden Bauern wegen nicht erklärlicher Vorfälle der Hexerei. Der Dorfvorsteher weigert sich allerdings, gegen den Beschuldigten vorzugehen und fordert Polizeischutz für den inzwischen in der Dorfgemeinschaft isolierten Mann an. Einwohner beiderlei Geschlechts erstürmen und

---

7   John BEATTIE: Sorcery in Bunyoro, in: John MIDDLETON / EDWARD H. WINTER (eds.): Witchcraft and Sorcery in East Africa, London 1963, S. 33.
8   BEATTIE 1963, S. 34f.
9   Isak NIEHAUS: Witchcraft, Power and Politics. Exploring the Occult in the South African Lowveld, London / Cape Town 2001, S. 118-121.

verwüsten daraufhin die Hütte des Bauern. Selbst als ein herbeigerufener „witch-doctor" den Bezichtigten entlastet, klingen die Zaubereiverdächtigungen nicht ab. Der Beschuldigte resigniert und lässt sich endgültig in einem entfernten Dorf nieder. 2001 wird er tot – wahrscheinlich gelyncht – außerhalb der Ansiedlung aufgefunden. Die Täter bleiben unerkannt.[10]

Die vorstehenden Fallbeschreibungen zeigen, dass der Geschlechterbezug magischer Aktivitäten in afrikanischen Gesellschaften variieren kann: Während in den Beispielfällen Südafrika Frauen angeklagt werden, steht in Benin ein Mann im Zentrum der Verdächtigungen. In Uganda trafen die Bezichtigungen dagegen beide Geschlechter.

Diese Hexereianklagen der verschiedensten Art sind nur auf dem Hintergrund der ihnen zugrunde liegenden Hexenbilder, zu der auch der Gender-Aspekt gehört, zu verstehen. Die Forschungen in der Afrikanistik haben sich diesen Vorstellungen zwar meistens nur peripher gewidmet, haben sie jedoch auch regelmäßig ermittelt. Die ältere, koloniale und unmittelbar nachkoloniale Ethnologie bzw. Anthropologie arbeitete hier vielfach mit den Methoden der qualitativen Sozialforschung, vorzugsweise der teilnehmenden Beobachtung nach Bronislav Malinowski innerhalb zwei- oder dreijähriger Feldforschungsaufenthalte. Gelegentlich scheinen auch Informationen, die nicht nur von der Forschungskraft selbst, sondern von den Untersuchten aus Befragungen und aus Interviews stammen, eingearbeitet worden zu sein. Da die angewendeten Methoden häufig nur indirekt aus der Literatur erschließbar sind und nicht explizit thematisiert werden, fehlen in den meisten Fällen Angaben zur Erhebung von Daten. Mögliche Fehlerquellen, wie der bekannte Halo-Effekt bzw. wie mögliche Verzerrungen aufgrund von Vorkenntnissen von Befragungspersonen oder die Hinterfragung potenzieller Überidentifikationen werden leider kaum in der älteren Literatur diskutiert. Angaben zu Überprüfungsverfahren wie Reliabilität und Validität fehlen in den Studien weitgehend, eine Erörterung der Repräsentativität und der Auswahl von Informanten sucht man ebenfalls vergeblich. Neuere Feldforschungen haben allerdings die bestehenden Schwächen in der Methodik aufgearbeitet und sich aus der rein qualitativen Analyse verabschiedet.

Vorstellungen über geschlechtsspezifische Zuweisungen okkulter Kräfte in afrikanischen Gesellschaften wurden somit durch Erforschung magischer Vorstellungen mittels Befragung oder durch Beobachtung alltäglicher Hexereiverdächtigungen gewonnen.

Die folgende Tabelle stellt unterschiedliche Hexenbilder wie Zuschreibungen von okkulten Fähigkeiten konstruktiver u n d destruktiver Art vor, die wegen des ambivalenten Hexereibegriffs in Afrika nie getrennt werden dürfen:[11]

---

10 Erdmute ALBER: Hexerei, Selbstjustiz und Rechtspluralismus in Benin, in: Africa Spectrum, 1/2 (2001), S. 145-154.
11 Peter GESCHIERE: Sorcellerie et Politique en Afrique. La viande des autres, Paris 1993, S. 21.

Gesellschaft / Region / Land	GZ*	Quelle
Gonja/Burkina Faso	♀	Goody 1979
Akan/Ghana	♀ (♂)	Schönhuth 1989
Bakweri/ Kamerun	♀ ♂	Ardener 1970
Amba/Kenia	♀ (♂)	Winter 1963
Gusii/ Kenia	♀	LeVine 1963, Ogembo 2006
Nandi/Kenia	♀ ♂	Huntingford 1963
Lele/Kongo	♂	Douglas 1963
Yao /Malawi	♂	Mitchell 1956
Gwari/Nigeria	♀ ♂	Nadel 1970
Nupe/Nigeria	♀	Nadel 1970
Tonga/Sambia	♂	Colson 2000; Luig 2000
Shona/Simbabwe	♀	Colson 2000; Schmidt 1992, Skønsberg 1989
Pondo/Südafrika	♂	Wilson 1970
Lovedu/Südafrika	♀ ♂	Krige 1947/1970
Zulu/Südafrika	♀	Gluckman 1972
Mesakin/Sudan	♂	Nadel 1970
Kaguru/Tansania	♀	Beidelman 1963
Mbugwe/Tansania	♀	Gray 1963
Mwera, Makua, Makonde/Tansania	♀ ♂	Bruchhausen 2005
Gisu/Uganda	♀ (♂)	Heald 1986, La Fontaine 1963
Lugbara/ Uganda	♂	Middleton 1960/1999

Tabelle 1: Geschlechtsspezifische Vorstellungen von Personen mit okkulten Kräften in afrikanischen Gesellschaften[12] (Auswahl aus der ethnologischen Forschung 1950-2005). Geschlechtsspezifische Zuschreibung: ♀=Vorstellungen von Frauen als Hexen, ♂= Vorstellungen von Männern als Hexen.

---

12 Esther GOODY: Legitimate and Illegitimate Aggression in an West African State, in: Mary DOUGLAS (ed.): Witchcraft confessions, S. 210f.. Michael Schönhuth: Das Einsetzen der Nacht in die Rechte des Tages. Hexerei im symbolischen Kontext afrikanischer und europäischer Weltbilder, Münster 1992, S. 111- 123. Edwin ARDENER: Witchcraft, economics and the continuity of belief, in: DOUGLAS (ed.) Witchcraft confessions, S. 145. Edward H. WINTER: The Enemy within: Amba witchcraft and Sociological Theory, in: MIDDLETON/ WINTER (eds.): East Africa, S.279. Robert LEVINE: Witchcraft and Sorcery in an Gusii Community, in: MIDDLETON / WINTER: East Africa, S.225. Justus M. OGEMBO: Contemporary Witch-Hunting in Gusii, Southwestern Kenya, London 2006. G.W.B. HUNTINGFORD: Nandi Witchcraft, in: MIDDLETON / WINTER: East Africa, S. 175. Mary DOUGLAS: The Lele of Kasai, Oxford 1963, S. 229. J. Clyde MITCHELL: The Yao Village, Manchester 1956, S. 153. Siegfried F. NADEL: Witchcraft in Four African Societies, in: Max MARWICK (ed.): Witchcraft and Sorcery, Harmondsworth 1970/1982, S. 264-279. COLSON: father, S. 336. Ute LUIG: Der Kampf der Regenmacher: Macht und Magie in einer Tonga-Familie (Zambia), in Günther BEST/ Reinhart KÖßLER (Hg.): Subjekte und Systeme: Soziologische und anthropologische Annäherungen, Frankfurt 2000, bes. S. 26f. Elisabeth SCHMIDT: Peasants, Traders and Wives. Shona women in the history of Zimbabwe 1870-1939, London 1992, S. 18. Else SKØNSBERG: Change in an African Village, Kefa speaks, West Hartford 1989, S. 167. Mary HUNTER-WILSON: Witch-Beliefs and social Structure, in: Max MARWICK (ed.): witchcraft, S. 253. E. JENSEN / J.D. KRIGE: The Realm of the Rain Queen, Oxford 1947/1970, S. 239-257. Max GLUCKMAN: Moral Crisis: Magical and Secular Solutions, in: Max GLUCKMAN (ed.), Allocation, S. 12-16. Thomas. O. BEIDELMAN: Witchcraft in Ukaguru, in: MIDDLETON / WINTER (eds.), East Africa, S. 34, 48, 61, 74, 86-94. R. F. GRAY: Structural Aspects of Mbugwe Witchcraft, in: MIDDLETON / WINTER (eds.) East Africa, S. 152f. Walter BRUCHHAUSEN: Repelling and Cleansing: 'Bad People'. The Fight against Witchcraft in Southeast Tanzania since Colonial Times (hier im Band). Suzette HEALD: Witches and Thieves, in: Man 21 (1986), S. 65-78. Jean LAFONTAINE: Witchcraft in Bugisu, in: MIDDLETON / WINTER (eds.), East Africa, S. 194f. John MIDDLETON: Lugbara Religion, Oxford 1960/1999, S. 239f.

Die Hexenparadigmen in afrikanischen Gesellschaften umfassen unterschiedliche geschlechtsspezifische Zuweisungen und unterscheiden sich quer durch den Kontinent in mannigfaltiger Weise: Während einige Gesellschaften sich ausschließlich Männer als Hexen vorstellen, sind es in anderen hauptsächlich Frauen, denen die Macht zu erfolgreichen magischen Handlungen unterstellt wird. Nicht wenige Gesellschaften kennen auch beide Geschlechter in jeweils unterschiedlichen bzw. ähnlichen Relationen als Personen mit magischen Fähigkeiten. Ein weiblicher Hexenstereotyp, wie er oft für Europa konstatiert wird, existiert in zahlreichen Regionen Afrikas südlich der Sahara nicht: Die Fähigkeit, okkulte Kräfte aggressiver Natur zu mobilisieren, stellt keine frauentypische Eigenschaft dar, sondern gehört in vielen Gesellschaften auch zu Merkmalen des männlichen Geschlechts.

2. „Social conflict accusations" und Geschlecht

Seit etwa 1900 organisieren sich im subsaharischen Afrika immer wieder periodisch Anti-Hexerei-Bewegungen, die entweder durch einen Propheten, ein spirituelles Medium oder von traditionellen Geheimgesellschaften initiiert werden. Die Giriama-Bewegung in Kenia, die Bamucapi- oder Mchape-Bewegung in Sambia und Rhodesien, die Mpulumutsi-Bwanali- Bewegung in Malawi, die Kamcape-Bewegung in Tansania bzw. die Kabuga-Benga-Bewegung im Kongo zielten allerdings nicht auf die physische Liquidierung von Hexen und Hexern. Sie beabsichtigten lediglich, magische Aggressionen in den betroffenen Regionen zu eliminieren. Derartige Reinigungsbewegungen führten daher nicht unbedingt zu massenhaften Tötungen, sondern versuchten die angeblichen magisch agierenden Kriminellen nach deren Reuebekenntnis im Sinne des traditionellen Ideals von sozialer Einheit und Harmonie wieder zu reintegrieren. Diese traditionellen Anti-Hexerei-Bewegungen entsprechen daher in ihrer Zielsetzung und ihrem Verlauf nicht klassischen europäischen Mustern. Bei einem Teil dieser Kampagnen stellten sich aber nach deren Erfolglosigkeit oder durch eine Eskalationsdynamik bedingt – wie zum Beispiel in der Atinga-Bewegung in Westafrika – neue und gewalttätige Formen heraus. Ab 1990 nahmen diese, jetzt mit europäischen Mustern teilweise ansatzweise vergleichbaren Verfolgungen besonders in Teilen Südafrikas, Tansanias, des Kongos und Westafrikas zu. Im letzten Jahrzehnt des 20. Jahrhunderts sollen über 20.000 Menschen wegen vermeintlicher Hexerei in afrikanischen Gesellschaften umgebracht worden sein. Diese Hexenverfolgungen sind mit Ausnahme Kameruns meist durch Bewegungen „von unten" bzw. nicht-institutioneller Träger gekennzeichnet, d. h. große Teile der Bevölkerung tragen bzw. akzeptieren sie und führen sie auch aktiv durch.[13]

Die folgenden Fallbeispiele dienen der exemplarischen Veranschaulichung dessen, was Hexenverfolgungen für verdächtigte Männer und Frauen in Afrika bedeuten können.

---

13 Siehe die Zusammenstellung von Informationen verschiedener Nachrichtenagenturen bei: Richard PETRAITIS: The Witch Killers of Africa, 2003, http://www.infidels.org/library/modern/richard_ petraitis/witch_killers.shtml (besucht am 17.11.2007). Andrew APTER: Atinga Revisited, in: Jean COMAROFF / John COMAROFF (eds.), Modernity and its Malcontents. Modernity, Ritual and Power in Postcolonial Africa, Chicago 1993, S. 111-128. Bryan R. WILSON: Magic and Millenium. A Sociological Study of Religious Movements of Protest among Tribal and Third-World Peoples, London 1973, S. 86-95.

Ost-Kamerun 1982: Nachbarn bitten einen Dorfvorsteher, aufgrund ungeklärter Todesfälle und immer wieder auftretender Hexerei-Verdächtigungen gegen einen männlichen Dorfbewohner vorzugehen. Sie fordern eine Untersuchung durch einen bekannten Hexenfinder. Nach seinem Eintreffen lässt dieser alle im Dorf magisch besetzten und instrumentalisierbaren Gegenstände einsammeln. Als sich drei Personen dieser Maßnahme widersetzen, erscheint der Hexenfinder in Begleitung der Dorfältesten zu einer Hausdurchsuchung. Tatsächlich finden sie in den Häusern mehrere Panther-Haare und identifizieren sie als Zaubereimittel. Der Besitz dieser Haare wie auch die Aussage des „witch-doctors" genügen für ein Gericht, die drei Männer wegen Hexerei bis zu fünf Jahren Gefängnis und 70.000 CFA-Francs zu verurteilen. Ein Revisionstribunal bestätigte dieses Urteil ein halbes Jahr später.

Diese strafrechtliche Ahndung reihte sich in eine Justizkampagne ein, die in den 80er-Jahren des 20. Jahrhunderts in Ostkamerun wegen vermeintlicher magischer Aggression geführt wurde.[14]

Südafrika/ Lebowa 1990: In einem Dorf begehen drei Menschen Selbstmord. Zahlreiche Einwohner führen diese Suizide auf magische Eingriffe zurück und suchen nach den angeblichen Initiatoren. Schließlich treiben sie 30 verdächtige Mitbewohnerinnen und Mitbewohner in der Ortschaft zusammen und bezichtigen sie der Hexerei. Besonders Mitglieder der Jugendorganisation des African National Congress spielen bei dieser Aktion des Hexentreibens eine führende Rolle. Sie beschuldigen zum Beispiel eine Frau, den Uterus der Schwiegertochter bezaubert zu haben, um damit eine gewünschte Schwangerschaft zu verhüten. Andere werden verdächtigt, schwere Erkrankungen von Nachbarn magisch initiiert zu haben. Auch an den drei Selbstmorden sei diese destruktive Gruppe beteiligt gewesen. Die Ankläger beginnen, die Beschuldigten zu steinigen. Als die Polizei eintrifft, haben sich bereits über 1.000 Menschen in dem Dorf eingefunden, sodass die Beamten angesichts der aufgeheizten Stimmung nur durch den Einsatz von Tränengas und Gummigeschossen eine mögliche Lynchung der vermeintlichen Hexen und Hexern verhindern können. Als ältere ANC-Mitglieder schließlich in das Geschehen eingreifen, die Lage beschwichtigen und für den Schutz der Angeklagten eintreten, beruhigt sich die Stimmung wieder. Die vermeintlichen Hexen und Hexer finden in einer Polizeistation Unterschlupf und entgehen so einer möglichen Ermordung. Auch wenn in diesem Dorf die Hexenverfolgungen keinen tödlichen Ausgang nahmen, wurden in anderen Ortschaften der Region zu diesem Zeitpunkt zahlreiche Menschen, insbesondere Frauen, von einer aufgebrachten Menge umgebracht, da staatlicher Schutz nicht erreichbar war oder zu spät kam.[15]

Während die Hexenvorstellungen in „day-to-day-accusations" je nach regionaler und ethnischer Ausprägung geschlechtsspezifisch variieren, wenden sich Anschuldigungen in den oben geschilderten massiven Formen der „social conflict accusations" und der

---

14 Peter GESCHIERE: Sorcellerie et modernité.Les enjeux des nouveaux procès de sorcellerie au Cameroun. Approches anthropologiques et historiques, in: Annales E.S.C. 53 (1998), S. 1256-1259.
15 Isak A. NIEHAUS: Witch-hunting and political legitimacy: continuity and change in Green Valley, Lebowa 1930-91, in: Africa 63 (1993), S. 518-526.

damit verbundenen Ahndung vermeintlicher Zauberei oft gegen Frauen und weisen damit einen signifikanten Gender-Aspekt auf.

Eine Auswahl von Hexenverfolgungen, für die das geschlechtsspezifische Profil überliefert ist, zeigt folgende Zusammenstellung:

Gesellschaft-Region/ Land	Anteil Frauen an Opfern	Quelle
Bertoua/ Kamerun (1981-84)	16%	Geschiere 1995
Limpopo/Südafrika (1971-84)	40-60%	Niehaus 2001
Kongo (1958)	mehrheitlich	Vansina 1969
Benin, Ghana, Nigeria (1950)	mehrheitlich	Apter 1993
Sukuma/Tansania (1970-84)	62%	Mesaki 1994
Transkei/Südafrika (1990-95)	80%	Kohnert 2003
Shinyanga/Tansania (1990-92)	96%	Miguel 2003
Mamprusi/Ghana (ca.1990)	98%	Drucker-Brown 1993[16]

Tabelle 2: Hexenverfolgungen in afrikanischen Gesellschaften (Unter „Hexenverfolgungen" werden im Gegensatz zu „day-to-day-accusations" unabhängig von ihrer Gestalt Massenverfolgungen mit mehr als 100 Todesopfern in einem nationalstaatlichen Raum verstanden).[17]

Massive Hexenverfolgungen Afrika sind nicht immer, jedoch in der Mehrheit signifikant geschlechtsbezogen: Während sie sich in Kamerun mehrheitlich gegen Männer richten, wenden Sie sich in zahlreichen anderen afrikanischen Ländern zu größeren Teilen gegen Frauen.

Für einige Regionen des Kontinents liegen genauere Beobachtungen über Status und Schichtzugehörigkeit der Verfolgten vor: In der Provinz Shinyanga in Tansania gehören sie in den neunziger Jahren zu 96% dem weiblichen Geschlecht an, zu 90% der Ethnie Sukuma, zu 55 bis 69% der unteren Unterschicht. Zu 98% haben sie Verwandte im gleichen Dorf. Im Nordosten Südafrikas entstammen die Beschuldigten überrepräsentativ älteren Generationen (mit einem deutlichen Übergewicht bei Männern), sind arbeitslos oder mit Gelegenheitstätigkeiten beschäftigt und stammen überdurchschnittlich aus dem Milieu der traditionellen Heilerinnen und Heiler. Männliche Jugendliche oder junge Erwachsene treten häufig als Ankläger hervor. In Kamerun dagegen richten sich die Verfolgungen auffällig gegen allein stehende Männer mittleren und höheren Alters, die zu den sogenannten „nouveaux riches" oder den „nouvelles élites" des Landes zählen.[18]

---

16 GESCHIERE: Sorcellerie et Politique, S. 224f. Isak NIEHAUS: Witchcraft 2001, S. 202. Jan VANSINA: The Bushong Poison Ordeal, in: Mary DOUGLAS / Phyllis M. KABERRY (eds.), Man in Africa, London 1969, S. 246. APTER: Atinga, S. 111-128. Simeon MESAKI: Witch-Killing in Sukumaland, in: Ray ABRAHAMS (ed.), Witchcraft in Contemporary Tanzania, Cambridge 1994, S. 47-60. Dirk KOHNERT: Witchcraft and transnational social spaces, in: Journal of Modern African Studies 41 (2003), S. 1-29. Edward MIGUEL: Poverty and Witch Killing, in: Review of Economic Studies (2005) 72, Berkley 2003 / 2005, pp. 1153–1172 (http://elsa.berkeley.edu/~emiguel/miguel_witch.pdf). Susan DRUCKER-BROWN: Mamprusi witchcraft, subversion and changing gender relations, in: Africa 64 (1993), S. 537. Justus M. OGEMBO: Contemporary Witch-Hunting in Gusii, Southwestern Kenya, London 2006.

17 Wolfgang BEHRINGER: Witches and Witch-Hunts. A Global History, Cambridge 2004, S. 49.

18 MIGUEL: Poverty, table 2 (im Anhang). NIEHAUS: Witchcraft, S. 165-178. GESCHIERE: Sorcellerie 1993, S. 223-225.

3. Erklärungs - A n s ä t z e

Die anthropologische und ethnologische Forschung hat der geschlechtsspezifischen Dimension okkulter Aktivitäten in Afrika bislang wenig Beachtung geschenkt. Im Zentrum des Interesses stand die Funktion, nicht die Trägerschaft angeblich magischer Tätigkeiten. In diesem Fokus stellte sich die Frage nach der Bedeutung von Gender-Aspekten nur am Rande. Die strukturfunktionalistische Schule in der Tradition von Evans-Pritchard und die hieran anknüpfende soziologische Manchester-School in Großbritannien behandelte geschlechtsspezifische Ausprägungen magischer Lebenspraxis nicht analytisch im Sinne einer systematischen Erklärung eines Phänomenenkomplexes. Erst Arbeiten, die ab 1950 Erkenntnisse der Psychologie integrierten und die Schwächen der klassischen Ethnologie zu überwinden versuchten, thematisierten das Verhältnis von Gender und vermeintlichen zaubererischen Fähigkeiten in einem theoretischen Zusammenhang. Dennoch bleiben die Erklärungen, die aus regionalen Untersuchungen entwickelt wurden, disparat und können wegen ihres lokalen Bezugs keinen Anspruch auf allgemeine Gültigkeit erheben. Sie bieten folglich nur erste Erklärungs-Ansätze.[19] Die ethnologische Forschung befindet sich in damit in guter Gesellschaft mit der historischen Wissenschaft: Anders als in Afrika lässt sich die geschlechtsspezifische Asymmetrie in der Hexenverfolgungen nicht übersehen, doch die Diskussion über Ursachen und Funktionen dieser Ausrichtung ist nicht abgeschlossen, so dass auch hier Erklärungsansätze in Konkurrenz oder in Koexistenz zueinander stehen: Die Forschung hat sich von den Erklärungen wie der frauenfeindlichen Ausrichtung der elitären Schrift- und Gelehrtenkultur oder der männerdominierten Besetzung der frühneuzeitlicher Gerichte abgewendet. Angesichts des Faktums, dass Hexenverfolgungen in Europa „von unten" aktiv initiiert wurden und auch Frauen in diesen Bewegungen eine nicht unbeträchtliche Rolle spielten, werden heute soziale wie anthropologische Ursachen erörtert: Die geschlechtsspezifische Dimension der europäischen Hexenprozesse wird auf die frühneuzeitliche Arbeitsteilung in bäuerlichen Haushalten zurückgeführt, in denen die für Schadenszauber anfälligen Bereiche wie Kind, Haus und Vieh zum Tätigkeitsfeld von Frauen gehörten. Eine andere Interpretation geht von unterschiedlichen geschlechtstypischen Konfliktslösungsmustern aus, nach denen Männer eher zur physischen Gewaltanwendung, Frauen zum Gebrauch von Magie neigten. Wiederum andere Deutungen meinen, dass durch die Nähe von Frauen als Gebärende dem weiblichen Geschlecht ein engeres Verhältnis zu den Tabubereichen Leben und Tod und damit eine offenere Verbindung zum Übersinnlichen zugewiesen wurde.[20] Während zahlreiche Untersuchungen zu Hexenverfolgungen in verschiedenen Regionen Europas vorliegen, mangelt es allerdings nach wie vor an einer

---

19 Z. B. findet der Gender-Aspekt in dem Sammelband mit über 400 Seiten von Marwick bis auf einen Aufsatz kaum Beachtung, schon gar nicht in einer Kapitelüberschrift. Auch im dem von Douglas herausgegebenen Werk, in dem zahlreiche Autorinnen und Autoren sich zum Thema „witchcraft" in Afrika äußerten, werden geschlechtsbezogene Aspekte lediglich in einem Aufsatz thematisiert. Coquery-Vidrovitch beschäftigt sich lediglich auf drei Seiten innerhalb einer umfassenden Darstellung mit diesem Thema, s. Catherine COQUERY-VIDROVITCH: African Women. A Modern History, Oxford 1997.
20 Ingrid AHRENDT-SCHULTE u.a. (Hg): Geschlecht, Magie und Hexenverfolgung, Bielefeld 2002.

neueren Studie, die Zuspitzung auf Frauen umfassend diskutiert.[21] Vermutlich fehlt auch der Mut, sich in einer Monografie einem derartigen komplexen, aber zentralen Thema zu stellen und einer interessierten Öffentlichkeit Antworten auf immer wieder gestellte Fragen zu geben.

Sozialpsychologische Erklärungen: „sex antagonism"

Als Vertreter der soziologischen Konflikttheorie widersprach der australische Ethnologe Siegfried F. Nadel in einem zuerst 1952 veröffentlichten Aufsatz der Behauptung der Funktionalisten, Hexereiverdächtigungen leisteten einen Beitrag zur Stabilität afrikanischer Gesellschaften. Hexereianklagen entstehen seiner Auffassung nach auf Grundlage von Angstgefühlen in Folge nicht gelöster Konflikte, die dann auf vermeintliche Feinde der Gesellschaften projiziert werden.

In seiner empirischen Forschung stellte Nadel fest, dass sich Hexenbilder bei den Nupe in Nigeria ausschließlich auf Frauen, bei den benachbarten Gwari jedoch auf beide Geschlechter beziehen. Der Ethnologe erklärte diesen unterschiedlichen Gender-Aspekt aus der Diskrepanz zwischen Rollenerwartungen und tatsächlichem Rollenverhalten. Bei den Nupe hatten zur Zeit der Untersuchung zahlreiche Frauen als Händlerinnen eine starke ökonomische Position inne, so dass nicht wenige Männer – auch Ehemänner – bei ihnen verschuldet waren bzw. in finanzieller Abhängigkeit lebten. Frauen – und nicht Männer – bestritten daher Brautpreise, Schulgeld und die Kosten von Festlichkeiten für die Kinder. Mit dieser sozialen Funktion verkehrten zahlreiche Frauen die ihnen zugeschriebene Rolle als abhängige und untergeordnete Gattinnen ins Gegenteil. Die Dominanz des weiblichen Geschlechts spiegelt sich nach Nadel auch auf der Ebene der kulturellen Symbole und Mythen, da in der Folklore immer wieder von abhängigen Söhnen und reichen Müttern bzw. Frauen die Rede ist. Männer bei den Nupe brächten somit Rollenerwartungen und Rollenverhalten von Frauen im Gegensatz zu den Gwari nicht in Deckung und versuchten diese Spannung durch Hexereianklagen zu ventilieren:[22] Dieser „sex antagonism" gilt nach Nadel als Hauptursache für die geschlechtsspezifische Ausrichtung von Hexenbildern und -verfolgungen. Die Ethnologin Susan Drucker-Brown folgte diesem Ansatz in einer Untersuchung über die Mamprusi in Ghana. Frauen hatten hier nach den Hungerkrisen ab 1980 durch Anbau von Getreide selbstständig ihre ökonomische Stellung ausgebaut und brachen damit in bisherige männliche Domänen ein. Sich anschließende Hexenbeschuldigungen von Mamprusi-Männern hätten daher die Funktion, die verlorene Kontrolle über die Aktivitäten und das Verhalten von Frauen zurück zu gewinnen.[23] Als Auslöser von Hexenverfolgungen erkennt Esther Goody den Konflikt zwischen den Geschlechtern in einer Untersuchung zu den Gonja in Burkina Faso. Magische Aktivitäten von Männern gelten in dieser Gesellschaft als legitim und statuserhaltend. Bei Frauen werden sie hingegen als illegitim

---

21 BEHRINGER: Witches, S. 31-43, der diesem Thema nur sechs innerhalb von 337 Seiten widmet.
22 SIEGFRIED F. NADEL: Witchcraft in Four African Societies: An essay in Comparison, in: Africa 54 (1952), S. 18-29; ähnlich für die Mpondo in Südafrika: HUNTER-WILSON: Witch-beliefs, S. 256.
23 DRUCKER-BROWN: Mamprusi, S. 531-549.

und destruktiv angesehen, da aggressive Impulse generell nicht in das feminine Rollenbild passten und über Hexereianklagen gesellschaftlich sanktioniert würden.[24]

Der Geschlechterkonflikt sowie strikte Verhaltensnormen und die Sanktionierung weiblichen abweichenden Verhaltens stellen nach diesen Erklärungsansätzen die Grundlage für Hexenverfolgungen in afrikanischen Gesellschaften dar.

Zu Recht wird dabei auf den Zusammenhang zwischen negativ besetzten normativen Frauenbildern und der Zuspitzung von Hexereiverdächtigungen auf das weibliche Geschlecht verwiesen. Die beobachtete Diskrepanz zwischen faktischer ökonomischer Dominanz und der von Männern gewünschten Unterordnung der Frauen als Ursache für Hexenverfolgungen lässt sich jedoch nur teilweise auf andere als die untersuchten afrikanischen Gesellschaften übertragen. Verdächtigungen wegen schädigender okkulter Fähigkeiten richten sich nicht nur gegen privilegierte, sondern auch gegen sozial deprivierte Frauen. Während in Teilen Westafrikas wirtschaftlich unabhängige Frauen zur Zielgruppe von Hexenverfolgungen werden, gehören vermeintliche Hexen in Süd- aber auch Ostafrika zu den sozialen Unterschichten mit geringen Einkommen und niedrigem Status an. Dieser Ansatz erklärt auch nicht, warum Frauen in nicht unbeträchtlicher Anzahl andere Frauen der magischen Aggressionen bezichtigen – einen Sachverhalt, den Nadel gerade für die von ihm untersuchten Nupe beobachtete. Gegenläufige Entwicklungen im ländlichen Raum Nigerias stellen zudem die These des ökonomischen Aufstiegs von Frauen in Frage.[25] In afrikanischen Gesellschaften lässt sich außerdem der Hexenbegriff auch auf Männer anwenden, ein Faktum, das dieser sozialpsychologische Ansatz ignoriert.

Der Ansatz des „sex antagonism" in der Tradition von Nadel erklärt somit nur partiell geschlechtsspezifische Hexenbilder in afrikanischen Gesellschaften und kann wegen seines regionalen Bezugs nicht verallgemeinert werden.

„Kultur versus Natur"- anthropologische Erklärungsansätze

Die amerikanische Anthropologe James L. Brain setzte dieser sozialpsychologischen Erklärung eine differente Deutung gegenüber. In der Denktradition des französischen Philosophen Lévi-Strauss behauptete Brain eine grundsätzliche Spaltung der menschlichen Wahrnehmung in komplementäre beziehungsweise konträre Pole, eine Beobachtung, die schon auf den griechischen Mathematiker Pythagoras im sechsten Jahrhundert v. Chr. zurück geht. Durch diese Konzeptionalisierung von Wirklichkeit unterschiede die Menschheit allgemein auch die Kategorie „Natur" von der Kategorie „Kultur". Während „Kultur" prinzipiell in vielen Gesellschaften als Reich der Ordnung gelte, verbinde sich „Natur" mit Assoziationen der Unordnung, der unkontrollierten Kräfte und der Sphäre der Gefahr und des Todes. Viele Gesellschaften konnotierten aber Kultur mit dem männlichen, Natur dagegen mit dem weiblichen Geschlecht und brächten somit hauptsächlich Frauen mit okkulten Fähigkeiten in Verbindung.[26]

---

24 GOODY: Aggression, S. 207-244.
25 Dirk KOHNERT: Klassenbildung im ländlichen Nigeria. Das Beispiel der Savannenbauern im Nupeland, Hamburg 1982, S. 232-242.
26 JAMES L. BRAIN: Witchcraft and development, in: African Affairs 81 (1982), S. 371-384.

Zu Recht verweist Brain auf die Annahme einer Dichotomisierung der Wirklichkeitswahrnehmung in der europäischen Philosophie der Frühen Neuzeit, die zur Erklärung der Hexenverfolgungen in England Frankreich und Deutschland erhellend gewirkt hat.[27] Es stellt sich jedoch die Frage, ob ein Transfer auf afrikanische Gesellschaften mit ihren unterschiedlichen Denkstilen und Wahrnehmungen zulässig ist. Diese Erklärung geht zudem von dem Grundaxiom einer anthropologisch konstanten Zuschreibung zauberischer Potenz an das weibliche Geschlecht aus – eine Verbindung, die gerade für Afrika nicht zutreffend ist: Weder existiert für das gesamte Afrika ein weiblicher Hexenstereotyp, noch ist hier die Verbindung von Geschlecht und Magie zwingend, noch ergeben sich geschlechtsspezifische Konturen bei Verdächtigungen magischer Aggressionen so eindeutig, wie sie der amerikanische Anthropologe sehen möchte.

Der Erklärungsansatz „Natur versus Kultur" kann daher wegen seiner eingeschränkten Reichweite ebenfalls nicht verallgemeinert werden.

Modernisierung und Geschlecht: politisch-ökonomische Erklärungsansätze

In ihrer Kritik älterer Studien hat sich die neuere ethnologische Forschung bewusst über die Mikroebene hinaus bewegt und magische Praktiken im Rahmen von Modernisierung und Globalisierung reflektiert. Sie bezieht daher nicht nur die Bedingungen von Produktion, Austausch und Konsum ein, sondern auch die Sphäre politischer Macht. Der niederländische Anthropologe Peter Geschiere stellte Hexereivorstellungen in den Kontext der Spannungen zwischen Staat und Gesellschaft, zwischen Dorfeinwohnern und neuen städtischen Eliten und ihren unterschiedlichen Zugängen zu Kapitalbildung und politischer Herrschaft. Am Beispiel Kameruns zeigte Geschiere auf, dass die Verlagerung von Konflikten auf die politische Ebene eine Änderung der Geschlechtsbezogenheit von Hexenbildern nach sich zieht. Hexereivorwürfe, die in Beziehung zur Machtausübung stehen, werden mit dem männlichen Geschlecht in Verbindung gebracht, andere Konflikte im magischen Kontext würden mit dem weiblichen Geschlecht assoziiert.[28]

Geschieres hoher Verdienst besteht darin, magische Vorstellungen aus dem Dorfzusammenhang herausgelöst, neue Fragestellungen entwickelt und die Dynamik von modernen Hexereidiskursen in Afrika thematisiert zu haben. In dieser Makroperspektive kann er auch veränderte geschlechtsspezifische Zuschreibungen feststellen, die er durch empirische Untersuchungen bei Feldforschungsaufenthalten verifizierte.

Politische Konflikte werden auch ebenfalls in anderen als westafrikanischen Gesellschaften über Hexereibeschuldigungen ausgetragen. Doch auch hier stellt sich die Frage nach der Übertragbarkeit derartiger Konzepte: Die Normen verletzende und die in den Augen zahlreicher Afrikanerinnen und Afrikaner ebenso unmoralische wie faszinierende Ansammlung politischer Macht und ökonomischen Reichtums spielt auch in anderen Teilen des großen Kontinents eine Rolle, ohne zu einer geschlechtsspezifischen Asymmetrie von Hexereiverdächtigungen wie in Kamerun oder im Kongo geführt zu haben. Zudem ist es schwierig, bei gleichförmigen Beschuldigungen wegen Hexerei, in denen

---

27 Stuart CLARK: Thinking with Demons. The Idea of Witchcraft in Early Modern Europe, Oxford 1997.
28 GESCHIERE: Sorcellerie, S. 183 und 264 (Fußnote). Peter GESCHIERE: Witchcraft and Sorcery, in: John Middleton (ed.), Encyclopedia of Africa South of the Sahara, New York 1997, Vol. IV, S. 378.

in Afrika oft Krankheiten eine wichtige Rolle spielen, auf unterschiedlich gelagerte Spannungen im Hintergrund von Gesellschaften empirisch valide zurück zu schließen. Dieser Ansatz kann zwar die Revitalisierung des Hexenglaubens in Afrika erklären, die Gründe für Geschlechtsspezifik in den massiven Hexenverfolgungen in Tanzania ab 1980, in Südafrika ab 1990, und die Ausgrenzung von Jugendlichen im Kongo als Hexenkinder ab 2000 bleiben aber in diesem politisch-ökonomischen Ansatz im Dunklen.

Bisherige Erklärungsansätze des Gender-Aspekts afrikanischer Hexenparadigmen und -verfolgungen, seien es „feministische" im Sinne eines Geschlechterkonflikts, ethnologische im Sinne einer globalen anthropologischen Konstante oder „politisch-ökonomische" im Sinne einer Reaktion auf die Modernisierung und Globalisierung, bieten lediglich Teildeutungen: Sie systematisieren zu stark und erklären und zu eingeschränkt die Realität in den jeweiligen unterschiedlichen Gesellschaften Afrikas.

Männliche „sorcery" und weibliche „witchcraft"?

In seiner Studie über die Azande hat der englische Ethnologe Evans-Pritchard einen entscheidenden Unterschied beobachtet und gab hierdurch für lange Zeit wichtige Impulse für die Erforschung magischer Vorstellungswelten. Die Azande unterschieden nämlich zwischen „sorcery" (häufig übersetzt mit „Zauberei"), verursacht durch bewusst erzeugte Manipulationen durch physische Mittel, und „witchcraft" (häufig übersetzt mit „Hexerei"), geschöpft aus einer der Person innewohnenden, meistens erblichen Kraft.[29]

Diese Einteilung spiegelt eine traditionelle Auffassung europäischer Provenienz wider, nach der die Hexe mit einer Mischung von vererbten, persönlichen und angelernten Fähigkeiten (in Verbindung mit übermenschlicher Macht) arbeitet. Der Zauberer hingegen erlernt seine magischen Aktivitäten aus Büchern oder von Lehrmeistern und beherrscht nur okkulte Techniken. Während im Rahmen der europäischen frühneuzeitlichen Hexenverfolgungen hauptsächlich Frauen der „witchcraft" und damit einer dämonischen Verbindung bezichtigt wurden, blieben die Zauberer als gelehrte Magie der Renaissance nicht nur physisch unversehrt, sondern lebten meistens als geachtete Intellektuelle ihrer Zeit.[30]

Eine Verallgemeinerung dieser Einteilung ist sowohl für Europa als auch für Afrika jedoch nicht haltbar[31] – auch wenn Ethnologen für einzelne Gesellschaften einen solchen Zusammenhang festzustellen meinten. „Sorcery" und „witchcraft" bezeichnen zwar unterschiedliche Qualitäten okkulter Macht, sind aber in den verschiedenen Gesellschaften Afrikas nicht genau definiert, so dass das Zeichen für das Bezeichnete zwar variiert, das Bezeichnete aber oft ähnlich aufgefasst wird. Die nicht vereinheitlichten Begriffe führen zur Konfusion: Ein prominenter Altmeister der Hexenforschung in Afrika wie Marwick

---

29 Edward EVANS-PRITCHARD: Witchcraft, Oracles and Magic among the Azande, Oxford 1937, S. 29-34.
30 Zu Zauberern in der europäischen Renaissance, die ihre Naturmagie auf wieder entdeckte klassische Texte stützten: Anthony GRAFTON / Moshe IDEL (Hg.): Der Magus. Seine Ursprünge und seine Geschichte in verschiedenen Kulturen, Berlin 2001. W. SHUMAKER: The Occult Science in the Renaissance, Berkeley 1972, S. 108-159. GENE A. BRUCKER: Sorcery in Renaissance Florence, in: Studies in the Renaissance, 10 (1963), S. 7-24.
31 Victor W. TURNER: Witchcraft and Sorcery, in: Taxonomy versus Dynamics, in: Africa 34 (1964), S. 314-324.

übernimmt Kategorien von Evans-Pritchard als „sorcery" für bestimmte Handlungen, obwohl sie für seine Untersuchungsgruppe längst zur Kategorie von „witchcraft" zählen.[32] Wenn schon der Unterschied in der Nutzung okkulter Optionen sich nicht für afrikanische Gesellschaften halten lässt, dann können sie erst recht nicht geschlechtsspezifisch zugeordnet werden: Die Beobachtung, dass „Zauberei" männlich und „Hexerei" weiblich konnotiert ist,[33] lässt sich nicht generalisieren. Männern und Frauen in Afrika werden sowohl erlernte bzw. ererbte, innewohnende magische Fähigkeiten als auch die erfolgreiche Verwendung manipulativer Techniken zugeschrieben. Zudem stellt man sich in zahlreichen afrikanischen Gesellschaften vor, dass sowohl Männer als auch Frauen den destruktiven bzw. dämonischen Part als Verkörperung des kosmologisch Bösen in okkulten Beziehungen übernehmen können. Männer gelten somit nicht als das in Hexereikrisen harmlosere Geschlecht.

Patrilineare Gesellschaften und Virilokalität - „Residenztheorien"

Die ethnologische Forschung hat seit langem herausgearbeitet, dass gerade in Afrika Hexerei zur dunklen Seite der Verwandtschaft gehört. Mitglieder einer Verwandtschaftsgruppe, dem vorwiegenden Strukturprinzip gesellschaftlicher Organisation in weiten Teilen des Kontinents, kommen unter Bedingungen ökologischer als auch ökonomischer Krisen häufig in „kinship-stress". Auf der einen Seite bestehen Normen von Harmonie und Einheit, auf der andern Seite treten gerade in schwierigen Zeiten Spannungen auf, die aber aufgrund der gesetzten Ideal-Norm nicht artikuliert werden dürfen. Schließlich äußern sich Konflikte auf indirekte Art: Aggressionen münden in Hexenbeschuldigungen. Einprägsam formuliert, lassen sich derartige soziale Beziehungen mit folgendem Satz charakterisieren: „Witches and their accusers are individuals who ought to like each other but in fact do not."[34]

Je nach Abstammungs- und Verwandtschaftssystem erfolgt in ländlichen afrikanischen Gesellschaften die rechtliche Zuweisung einer Person zur Familie des Vaters (Patrilinearität), der Mutter (Matrilinearität) oder beider Eltern (Duolinearität). Aus dieser Einteilung ergeben sich nicht nur ein unterschiedlicher persönlicher und rechtlicher Status, sondern auch Zugangsrechte zu wichtigen Ressourcen wie Besitz und Wohnung, zu Erbfolge wie zu politischer Herrschaft. Eheschließungen betreffen nicht nur zwei Partner, sondern wirken sich immer auf gesamte soziale Gruppen aus. Frauen genießen in matrilinearen Gesellschaften größere Rechte: Kontrolle über Vieh und Land stellen für sie eine große ökonomische Sicherheit dar, sodass sie sich auch in Konflikten ohne weiter reichende Restriktionen von der Verwandtschaft trennen können, was in patrilinearen Gruppen weniger gebräuchlich ist.[35] Matrilinear organisierte Gesellschaften finden sich in einem breiten Gürtel des Kontinents, der sich quer über das südliche Zentralafrika, von Angola bis zum Kongo am Atlantik nach Tansania und Mosambik am indischen Ozean erstreckt.

---

32 Alan HARWOOD: Witchcraft, Sorcery and Social Categories among the Safwa, London 1970, S. 140.
33 J. R. CRAWFORD: The Consequences of Allegation, in: MARWICK (ed.), Witchcraft, S. 314f.
34 Philip MAYER: Witches, in: MARWICK (ed.), Witchcraft, S. 55.
35 Jack GOODY: Kinship and marriage, in: Middleton, Encyclopedia, Vol. II, S. 459. Michael KEVANE: Women and development in Africa, London 2004, S. 31-33. Mary DOUGLAS: Is Matriliny Doomed in Africa, in: DOUGLAS / KABERRY (eds.), Man.

Patrilinearität herrscht nördlich und südlich dieses Gebietes mit Ausnahme einiger Inseln wie in Ghana oder von Duolinearität in Städten vor.

Anthropologen wie Middleton und Winter stellen nun Beziehungen zwischen den Residenzregeln, der Linearität und den Hexereiverdächtigungen fest.[36] Interessant ist es nun in Fortführung und Erörterung dieser These, unterschiedliche soziale Organisationsformen mitsamt des veränderten gesellschaftlichen Status bzw. der Rolle mit der Gender-Dimension in magischen Vorstellungswelten in Verbindung zu bringen.

Region/Land	Geschlechtsbezug	Organisation	Quelle
Akan/Ghana	♀ (♂)	matrilinear	Schönhuth 1989
Yao/Malawi	♂	„	Mitchell 1956
Tonga/Sambia	♂	„	Colson 2000
Mesakin/Suda	♂	„	Nadel 1970
Kaguru/Tansania	♀	„	Beidelman 1963
Mbugwe/Tansania	♀	„	Gray 1963
Lele/Kongo	♂	patrilinear	Douglas 1963
Amba/Kenia	♀ (♂)	„	Winter 1963
Nupe/Nigeria	♀	„	Nadel 1970
Shona/Simbawe	♀	„	Schmidt 1992, Skønsberg 1989
Pondo/Südafrika	♂	„	Hunter-Wilson 1970
Lovedu/Südafrika	♀♂	„	Krige 1947/1970
Zulu/Südafrika	♀	„	Gluckman 1972
Gisu/Uganda	♀ (♂)	„	LaFontaine 1963
Lugbara/Uganda	♂	„	Middleton 1960/1999

Tab. 3: Hexenbilder, Geschlecht und Organisation[37] *(Auswahl aus der ethnologischen Forschung).*

Zwar lässt sich in patrilinearen Gesellschaften ein Übergewicht eines weiblichen, in matrilinearen die Herausbildung eines männlichen Hexentyps beobachten, dennoch ist der Zusammenhang zwischen Geschlecht und Zuweisung von okkulten Kräften nicht eindeutig. Auch in Gruppen mit weiblicher Besitz- und Erbfolge gelten Frauen als Hexen, während bei Patrilinearität auch Männer der okkulten Schädigung bezichtigt werden. Kein Wunder, denn unter dem Begriff der Linearität verbergen sich sehr unterschiedliche und flexible Möglichkeiten sozialer Beziehungen und keinesfalls einheitliche Normen für die Handlungsräume beider Geschlechter. Matrilinearität kann z. B. nur zu neuen Hierarchien innerhalb von Frauengenerationen führen, kann veränderte soziale

---

36 MIDDLETON / WINTER: East Africa, S. 14f.
37 Eigene Zusammenstellung: SCHÖNHUTH: Akan: 152-160. MITCHELL: Yao, S. 153. COLSON: Father, S. 336. NADEL: Witchcraft in four societies, S. 269f. BEIDELMAN: Ukaguru, S. 90. GRAY: Mbugwe, S. 152-160. DOUGLAS: Lele, S. 222-229. WINTER: Amba, S. 279. NADEL: Witchcraft in four societies, S. 270f. SCHMIDT: Shona women, S. 18. SKØNSBERG: Kefa, S. 167. WILSON 1970 / 82. KRIGE: Rain Queen, in: E. JENSEN / J. D. KRIGE: The Realm of the Rain Queen. A Study of the Lovedu Society, Oxford 1947/1970, S. 239. GLUCKMAN: Allocation, S. 12-16. LAFONTAINE: Witchcraft in Bugisu, S. 203-208. MIDDLETON: Lugbara, S. 239f.

Rollen durch sogenannte „männliche Töchter" und „weibliche Ehemänner"[38] zur Folge haben, aber auch politische Autorität in die Hände von Frauen legen.[39]

Nicht Fragen nach der Deszendenz, sondern nach der Residenz ergeben eindeutigere Zusammenhänge zwischen magischen Vorstellungen und Gender-Dimension in magischen Vorstellungswelten. In viri- bzw. patrilokalen Mustern siedelt die Frau nach Eheschließung zum Wohnsitz des Mannes oder beide zum Wohnsitz des Vaters um. In uxori- bzw. matrilokalen Mustern zieht der Mann zum Wohnsitz der Frau beziehungsweise das Ehepaar zum Domizil der Mutter der Frau um.

***Residenzregeln, Geschlecht und Hexenbilder*[40]**

viri-/patrilokale Gesellschaften

"Shinyanga", Kaguru, Mbugwe (Tansania)
Zulu (Südafrika), Shona (Simbabwe), Gusii (Kenia), Bunyoro (Uganda), Mamprusi (Ghana), Mpondo (Südafrika), Yoruba (Nigeria)

Hexenbild = ♀

uxori-/matrilokale Gesellschaften

Chewa/ Sambia-Simbabwe-Malawi; Chiawa / Sambia, Yao / Malawi

Hexenbild = ♂

Frauen und Männer, die nach Eheschließung in Höfe oder Dörfer der nicht-eigenen Verwandtschaftsgruppe einheiraten, gelten als Menschen mit hohen Ambivalenzen und ungeklärten Loyalitäten, denn sie stammen von fremden Clans ab, mit denen man in offenen oder verdeckten Konflikten lebt oder lebte. Nur selten können dann die Partner bei Spannungen zur eigenen Verwandtschaftsgruppe zurückkehren, deswegen schließt man sie in der Regel vom Ahnenkult aus. Fremde bleiben so Fremde, die die Einheit und den Zusammenhalt bedrohen.[41] Ehepartner schirmen sich rituell ab, um die vermeintlichen negativen okkulten Kräfte, die in die eigene "lineage" eindringen, zu neutralisieren.

---

38 Ifi AMADIUME: Männliche Töchter, weibliche Ehemänner. Soziale Rollen und Geschlecht in einer afrikanischen Gesellschaft, Zürich 1996, S. 39-61.

39 COQUERY-VIDROVITCH: African Women, S. 16.

40 Eigene Zusammenstellung: MIGUEL: Poverty, S. 8. BEIDELMAN: Ukaguru, S. 58. GRAY: Mbugwe, S. 157. GLUCKMAN: Allocation S. 11. CRAWFORD: Consequences, S. 314. LEVINE: Gusii, S. 222-234. BEATTIE: Bunyoro, S. 27-32. DRUCKER-BROWN: Mamprusi, S. 537f. HUNTER-WILSON: witch-beliefs, S. 256. Peter G. MORTON-WILLIAMS: The Atinga-Cult among the South-Western Yoruba: A Sociological Analysis of a Witch-finding, in: Bulletin de l'Institut Français d'Afrique Noire 18 (1956), S. 326. Max MARWICK: Sorcery and its Social Setting, Manchester 1965, S. 103. C. Bawa JAMBA: Cosmologies in Turmoil: Witch-finding and AIDS in Chiawa, Sambia, in: Africa 67 (1997), S. 200-223. MITCHELL: Yao, S. 153f. u. S. 264.

41 Rita SCHÄFER: Frauen, Männer, Kinder, Familienalltag im ländlichen und städtischen Afrika, in: Katja BÖHLER / Jürgen HOEREN (Hg.): Afrika, Mythos und Zukunft, Bonn / Freiburg 2003, S. 74f. Johannes HARNISCHFEGER: Rivalität unter Frauen. Häusliche Gewalt und Hexerei in einer Erzählung der Jukun, Nigeria, in: Fabula 45 (2004), S. 33-54. Susan RASSMUSSEN: Betrayal or affirmation. Transformations in witchcraft technologies of power and agency among the Tuareg of Niger, in: Henrietta L. MOORE / Todd SANDERS (eds): magical interpretations and material realities, London 2001, S. 136-159.

Für Frauen haben die mehrheitlichen virilokalen Residenzregeln erhebliche Konsequenzen. Ihr Status als Außenseiterinnen fällt oft mit einem niedrigen sozialen Status und geringem eigenem ökonomischen Vermögen zusammen. Befinden sich allerdings Frauen in einer stigmatisierten und marginalisierten sozialen Stellung, bildet sich in afrikanischen Dörfern häufig eine Abhängigkeit zu eigenen und damit blutsverwandten Söhnen heraus, denn nur männliche Kinder können die labile Situation der Mutter stützen. Schwächt sich diese Beziehung ab, weil die Söhne entweder den Wohnsitz wechseln oder in eine entfernte Stadt ziehen, versuchen Mütter nicht selten ihre Kinder unter Loyalitätsdruck zu setzen. Während die Söhne sich Schuldgefühlen zu entziehen suchen, geraten die Mütter häufig in Rivalität zu Schwiegertöchtern: Der Konflikt wandelt sich schnell zu einer Krise, an deren Ende eine Hexereivorwurf gegen die Mutter, eine ältere Frau und Verwandte, steht.

Die Außenseiterstellung verstärkt sich auch in den nicht wenigen polygynen afrikanischen Gesellschaften, die immerhin 35% des subsaharischen Afrikas ausmachen, in denen verschiedene Frauen eines Mannes miteinander rivalisieren. Auch hier münden Konflikte in Hexereibezichtigungen wegen angeblicher magischer Aggression. Bei gleichmäßiger Verteilung des Eigentums des Mannes auf verschiedene Frauen, dem so genannten „house-property-complex", eskalieren Spannungen zudem schneller und werden gegebenenfalls auch auf Kinder übertragen.[42]

Matri-/Uxorilokale Gesellschaften hingegen, in denen Frauen bei der eigenen Verwandtschaft leben, kennen keine deprivilegierten allein stehenden Witwen, die in patrilokalen Gruppen oft zum Ziel von Hexenverfolgungen werden. Zu beobachten ist, dass sich der „kinship-stress" in einigen Regionen Afrikas zu einem „neighborhood-stress" umwandelt und die Nachbarn die Rolle der früheren Verwandtschaft in Sachen Hexenverdächtigung übernehmen.

Hexenanklagen hängen mit dem Grad der Integration von Individuen in lokalen Gemeinschaften zusammen und wenden sich in Krisenzeiten schnell gegen als Außenseiter gesehene Mitglieder anderer Gruppen. Fremde oder marginalisierte Frauen in krisengeschüttelten bäuerlichen Gruppen werden zu Hexen, weil ihnen eine indirekte Aggression unterstellt wird und sie über keine legitimen Mittel verfügen, ihre Position im ländlichen Kontext zu behaupten.

Die Reichweite a u c h dieses Erklärungsansatzes ist jedoch begrenzt: Zum einen erfasst sie manche Konfliktarten nicht, aus denen Hexereiverdächtigungen entstehen. Zum anderen sind die Residenzregelungen in afrikanischen Gesellschaften wenig erforscht und so können daher nur in geringem Maße matri- oder uxorilokale Muster herangezogen werden. Patrilokalität stellt die vorherrschende Wohnsitzregel dar, die jedoch in den letzten Jahrzehnten zunehmend an Bedeutung verliert.

Der Erklärungsgrad für die Analyse geschlechtsspezifischer Zuweisungen okkulter Fähigkeiten bleibt auch deswegen eingeschränkt, weil die Residenzregelungen sich nur auf bäuerliche Gesellschaften beziehen und hier ein Afrikabild zu Grunde liegt, dass der

---

42 Johannes HARNISCHFEGER: Rivalität unter Frauen. Häusliche Gewalt und Hexerei in einer Erzählung der Jukun, Nigeria, in: Fabula 45 (2004), S. 33-54. MULTHAUPT: Hexerei, S. 121.

Gegenwart immer weniger entspricht. Während 1970 jeder vierte Afrikaner in einer Stadt wohnte, ist der Verstädterungsgrad inzwischen weiter angestiegen, sodass zum Beispiel in Südafrika inzwischen fast jeder zweite Einwohner in urbanen Zentren lebt. Der rapiden Urbanisierung trägt der Theorieansatz der Ausgrenzung durch Wohnsitzveränderungen keine Rechnung. Dennoch lösen sich ländliche Familienstrukturen und Wahrnehmungsmuster in den städtischen Gebieten nicht auf, sondern die Stadt-Land-Verbindung bleibt nach wie vor bestehen.[43] Moderne Entwicklungen werden in den Städten noch häufig aus der Perspektive von Verwandtschaftsordnungen betrachtet und lokale „kinships" prägen noch immer die sozialen Beziehungen – auch in städtischen Milieus.[44] Die eigene dörfliche Abstammung spielt für die Identitätsbildung eine große Rolle, sodass trotz höherem Urbanisierungsgrad die Verbundenheit mit Wertorientierungen und Lebenspraxis in den ländlichen Regionen aufrechterhalten bleibt.[45] Magische Vorstellungswelten und geschlechtsspezifische Zuschreibungsmuster erhalten sich in dieser Traditionskette trotz des erheblichen gesellschaftlichen Wandels.

Für die als Hexer verfolgten Männer liegen allerdings so wenige Daten vor, dass eine genauere Analyse nicht möglich ist. Generationenkonflikte scheinen dabei gleichfalls eine große Rolle bei der Entstehung und Entwicklung von Hexereiverdächtigungen gegen Erwachsene männlichen Geschlechts zu spielen.[46]

4. Geschlecht und okkulte Kräfte – Ein Fazit

Ein Blick auf das Verhältnis von okkulten Vorstellungswelten und ihrer Geschlechtsdimension zeigt, dass der Hexenglaube wie auch die Hexenverfolgungen in afrikanischen Gesellschaften an strukturelle Konflikte im Verwandtschafts- bzw. Nachbarschaftsgeflecht gebunden sind. Der Gender-Aspekt bildet nur eine Variable in diesem Spannungsfeld, in dem vielfältigen Muster entstehen. Auch wenn konflikthafte Geschlechterbeziehungen sich in Krisenzeiten mit brutalen Konsequenzen spiegeln können, ist die Kategorie des Geschlechts nicht der magische Schlüssel, der Ursachen und Funktion von Hexenverfolgungen monokausal erschließt. In Afrika südlich der Sahara spielt das Alter als eine Variable in Krisenzeiten ebenfalls eine wichtige Rolle. Wirtschaftliche, soziale, politische und kulturelle Faktoren könnten gleichfalls genannt werden. Während im frühneuzeitlichen Europa geschlechtsspezifische Faktoren einen hohen Stellenwert einnahmen, lässt sich Ähnliches für Afrika nicht feststellen: Hier existiert innerhalb der großen ethnischen, regionalen, wirtschaftlichen und kulturellen Differenzen kein homogenes Hexenbild und vor allem keinen durchgängiges weibliches Hexenstereotyp.

Geschlechtsspezifische Magiebilder hatten zwar in Europa klare Frauen diskriminierende Konturen, nicht aber zwingend in Afrika. Bisherige Erklärungsansätze des Gen-

---

43 SCHÄFER: Frauen, Männer, Kinder, in: BÖHLER / HOEREN (Hg.), Afrika, S. 74f.
44 Siehe den Aufsatz der Ethnologin Bettina VON LINTIG: Der Glaube an Hexerei und Zauberkraft in der afrikanischen Moderne, in: Neue Züricher Zeitung vom 6.7.2004.
45 Peter GESCHIERE: The Urban-Rural Connection: Changing issues of belonging identification, in: Africa 68 (1998), S. 309-318. Lilian TRAGER: Home town. Linkages and local development in South-West Nigeria. Whose agenda? What impact?, in: Africa 68 (1998), S. 380-382.
46 J. STADLER: Witches and Witch-hunters. Witchcraft generational Relations and the Life-cycle in a Lowveld village, in: African Studies 55 (1996), S. 87-110.

der-Aspekts afrikanischer Hexenparadigmen und -verfolgungen – seien es „feministische" im Sinne eines Geschlechterkonflikts, ethnologische im Sinne einer weltweiten anthropologischen Konstante, kognitive im Sinne einer Reaktion auf die Modernisierung und Globalisierung oder „Residenz-Theorien" – bieten lediglich Teildeutungen: Sie systematisieren zu sehr und erklären zu eingeschränkt die Realität in den jeweiligen Gesellschaften Afrikas.

Auch wenn bei der Beschäftigung mit diesem Thema mehr Fragen als Antworten auftreten, ist der Mehrwert, den die Berücksichtigung der Kategorie „Geschlecht" für den Erkenntnisgewinn der wissenschaftlichen Forschung mit sich bringt, sehr hoch: Eine komparative Betrachtung der frühneuzeitlich-europäischen und der gegenwärtigen afrikanischen Verhaltensmuster erlaubt es, lange vorherrschende Sichtweisen und Erklärungen zu relativieren und darüber hinaus nicht nur die afrikanischen, sondern auch die europäischen Hexenverfolgungen differenzierter zu betrachten. Das Verhältnis von Zuschreibungen okkulter Kräfte, Hexenverfolgungen und Geschlecht bleibt im modernen Afrika auf jeden Fall hochkomplex. Es ist und bleibt für weitere Erörterungen offen.

Oliver G. Becker

„Muti Morde" in Afrika: Töten für okkulte Medizin

Abstract

The following contribution is based on the results of almost three years research and a series of interviews with anthropologists, ethnologists, religious studies experts, members of the medical profession and criminal prosecutors, which were primarily intended for the production of a documentary film. The film deals critically with the complex reasons for and background to an extreme form of occult aggression in Sub-Saharan Africa. Criminologists have come to see the psychological motivation behind and the nature of certain murder cases – known as 'muti murders' – as belonging to a distinct category of crime, although in sociological and anthropological research these murders are subsumed, together with the exorcism and subsequent killing of witches, under the term "witchcraft violence". The results of our research studies show that both these forms of murder must be regarded and treated as related aspects of one and the same problem.

Zusammenfassung

Der vorliegende Beitrag basiert auf den Ergebnissen einer knapp dreijährigen Recherche sowie einer Reihe von Interviews mit Anthropologen, Ethnologen, Religionswissenschaftlern, Medizinern, Psychologen und Strafverfolgern, die im Wesentlichen der Produktion eines Dokumentarfilms dienten.[1] Der Film setzt sich mit den vielschichtigen Gründen und Hintergründen einer extremen Form okkulter Aggression in Afrikas Sub-Sahara-Zone kritisch auseinander. Bestimmte Mordfälle, sog. „Muti Morde", sind Verbrechen, deren psychologische Motivation und Ausführung von Kriminologen, Anthropologen und anderen Wissenschaftlern inzwischen als eigene Kategorie bewertet wird, obwohl sie in der Forschung zusammen mit der Ver- oder Austreibung und der anschließenden Tötung von Hexen unter der Bezeichnung „witchcraft violence" subsumiert werden. Die Resultate wissenschaftlicher Untersuchungen zeigen, dass beide Formen in ein und derselben Publikation als zusammenhängende Problematik begriffen und behandelt werden. Stellvertretend für diese gemeinsame Analyse unterschiedlicher Verbrechen („witchcraft related crimes") sei hier auf den Bericht der Le Roux Commision (1988), den sog. „Ralushai Report" (1996) und die Untersuchung von Lars Buur (2004) hingewiesen.[2]

---

1 „Muti Mord – die Schattenseite okkulten Glaubens in Afrika", Ausstrahlung in Deutschland / Frankreich am 07.10.2004 bei ARTE sowie am 22.11.2004 und 12.01.2005 im US Dokumentationskanal „Sundance Channel" („Muti Murder – the dark side of occult belief systems in Africa").

2 LE ROUX COMMISSION: Report of the Commission of Inquiry into unrest and ritual murders in Venda during 1988. Victor N. RALUSHAI (Hg.) u.a.: Report of the Commission of inquiry into witchcraft violence and ritual murders in the Northern Province of the Republic of South Africa,

Muti Mord – eine extreme Form okkulter Gewalt

Obwohl Muti Morde ebenfalls zu den „witchcraft related crimes" in Afrikas Sub-Sahara zählen und sie ebenso wie die genannten Formen der Hexenverbrennung Teil des gleichen Problemkreises sind, stellen sie aus kriminologischer Sicht einen völlig unterschiedlichen Typ von Verbrechen dar. Muti Morde unterscheiden sich nicht nur erheblich in ihrer psychologischen Motivation, der Ausführung der Tat, der Anzahl der Täter sowie der Auswahl der Opfer gegenüber den Hexenverbrennungen.[3] Während die Tötung von Hexen von öffentlichen Anschuldigungen begleitet wird, die den angeblichen Grund ihrer Verbrennung für die Bevölkerung klar ersichtlich machen, sind Muti Morde auf den ersten Blick motivlos. Die Angehörigen der Opfer schweigen in diesen Fällen meist ebenso hartnäckig wie mutmaßlich verhaftete Täter, und zwar aus Angst vor der Rache der Hexen. Im Unterschied zur Tötung von Hexen werden Muti Morde bei Dunkelheit und an einsamen Orten begangen. Außer dem Umstand, dass der Täter die Aufklärung des Mordes so zu verhindern sucht, sind Zeitpunkt und Tatort nach Kriterien des Mörders ausgewählt, auf die im Folgenden gesondert eingegangen wird.

Muti Medizin, okkulte Gewalt und Verbrechen

Sobald man sich in einem Fall von Muti Mord mit der schlichten Frage nach dem „Warum?" zu beschäftigen beginnt, wird man schnell auf eine Reihe komplexer gesellschaftlicher Zusammenhänge stoßen, die eine einfache Beantwortung aus rein westlich-pragmatischer Sicht sehr schwierig machen.

> „Die Regierung Südafrikas muss sich mit dem Phänomen „Muti Mord" und rituellen Tötungen auseinandersetzen, auch wenn einige hier dieses Problem lieber verbergen möchten. In unserem Land scheuen wir uns offensichtlich davor, offen über diese Vorkommnisse zu sprechen. Wir wollen der Welt zwar zeigen, dass wir es in den letzten zehn Jahren geschafft haben, eine Demokratie aufzubauen, aber hinsichtlich der Muti Morde weigern wir uns eine öffentliche Diskussion anzustoßen, denn diese Verbrechen repräsentieren einen sehr düsteren Teil unserer Kultur."[4]

Vorausgegangen war die Beerdigung des zehnjährigen Schülers Sello Chokwe, dessen Leichnam man wenige Tage zuvor in der Limpopo Province im Norden Südafrikas entdeckt hatte. Warum wurde der Junge getötet? Warum hatten der oder die Täter dem Opfer die linke Hand, die Genitalien und das linke Ohr entfernt?

Es geht bei solchen Muti Morden um weit mehr als „nur" eine bestimmte Form von Gewaltverbrechen. Die Antwort auf die nur anscheinend einfache Frage nach dem „Warum?" berührt vielmehr ganz verschiedene Lebensbereiche der Menschen im südlichen Afrika: Ein vermuteter Zusammenhang zwischen traditioneller afrikanischer Religion und Medizin, aber auch und vor allem der ökonomische Niedergang vieler Regionen in

---

1996. Lars BUUR: Everyday Policing and the Occult: Notions of witchcraft, Crime and the people, in: African Studies, 63 (2004), S. 193-211. Auch: Anthony MINNAAR: Witchpurging and muti murders in South Africa with specific reference to the Northern Province, Pretoria 1998.

3   Allgemein: Gérard LABUSCHAGNE: Muti Murder: the challenges facing Psychological Investigators, Head of Investigative Psychology Unit, South African Police Service, Pretoria 2004.

4   Thias KGATLA: „Confront Ritual Crimes – Expert", Südafrika, in: News 24, South Africa Politics, 17. August 2004.

Afrikas Sub-Sahara-Zone sind oftmals als Hintergrund des Tatmotivs ebenso bedeutend wie der Glaube an Magie und okkulte Mächte.[5]

Welche bizarren Auswirkungen dieser ökonomische Niedergang der Region haben kann, zeigt sich in verdeckter Form in vielen Fällen von Muti Morden. Der Anthropologe Victor N. Ralushai, der 1995 im Auftrag der Regierung Südafrikas zusammen mit einer Wissenschaftskommission den sog. „Ralushai-Report" zusammenstellte, wies im Herbst 2003 nochmals darauf hin, dass die Untersuchung zahlreicher Muti Morde im Norden der Republik Südafrika gezeigt habe, dass z. B. Händler und Geschäftsleute, die in Muti Morde verwickelt waren, sehr oft bereits vorher in großen finanziellen Schwierigkeiten steckten.

> „Solche Ritualmorde wurden in präkolonialer Zeit aus drei Gründen begangen. Erstens konnte es sein, dass ein neuer Chief oder junger Mann, der Herrscher werden sollte, mehr Macht brauchte. Mit anderen Worten – man glaubte damals daran, dass durch die bestimmten Körperteile eines getöteten Menschen, einer kräftigen Person also, die Macht auf den jungen Chief überging. Aber das kam nicht regelmäßig vor. Oder zweitens, das Fett eines Menschen. Es konnten damals auch menschliche Körperteile zum Schmelzen von Eisenerz benutzt werden. Man glaubte, dass das Erz mit menschlichem Fett schneller schmelzen würde. Und drittens wurden menschliche Körperteile, bestimmte Körperteile eines getöteten Menschen verwendet, um eine erfolgreiche Ernte zu garantieren.
>
> In der Vergangenheit haben also traditionelle Herrscher zum Nutzen ihrer Gemeinschaft und in ganz bestimmten Ausnahmesituationen solche Morde begangen. Heute ist eine ganz neue Gruppe in Muti Morde verwickelt; oft sind es Gewerbetreibende oder Geschäftsleute. In vielen Fällen, in denen Geschäftsleute wegen Muti Morden verurteilt wurden, muss man sich nur ihre geschäftliche Situation ansehen. Fast immer waren sie bereits vorher in großen finanziellen Schwierigkeiten. Sie gingen zu bestimmten Leuten und diese rieten ihnen: `Sieh' mal, wenn du unbedingt wieder erfolgreich sein willst, werden wir dir ein menschliches Körperteil besorgen und durch diese Körperteile in der ‚Muti' (-Medizin) wirst du wieder ein erfolgreicher Geschäftsmann werden.' In anderen Worten: Die heutige Form der Muti Morde wird nur noch zum Nutzen Einzelner begangen, die unbedingt reich werden wollen."[6]

Ein Zusammenhang zwischen der ökonomisch prekären Lage des Auftraggebers und dem Mordfall des 10-jährigen Schülers scheint sich zu bestätigen. Am 17. September, also genau einen Monat nach dem Interview des Religionswissenschaftlers Thias Kgatla in den Lokalnachrichten, gibt der Police Commissioner der Limpopo Province, N. C. Sengani, bekannt, dass den Behörden in diesem Fall der Durchbruch bei der Ermittlungsarbeit gelungen sei. Man habe soeben zwei Männer verhaftet, die des Mordes an dem Jungen dringend verdächtigt werden. Es handelte sich um einen 55-jährigen Geschäftsmann sowie um einen 73-jährigen traditionellen Heiler.

---

5 Ernesto HERNÁNDEZ-CATÁ: World Economic Forum: Africa Competitiveness Report 2004, Executive Summary, S. 1, vorgelegt auf der Konferenz in Maputo / Mocambique vom 2.-4. Juni 2004. Der Bericht stellt unter anderem fest, dass das Pro-Kopf-Einkommen in Afrika südlich der Sahara seit 1974 um 11% gesunken sei.

6 Eigenes Interview mit Prof. Victor N. Ralushai, Thohoyandou, Limpopo Province, Rep. Südafrika, 01. November 2003.

> THE OFFICE OF THE PROVINCIAL COMMISSIONER OF THE SOUTH AFRICAN POLICE SERVICE IN LIMPOPO, COMM. N. C. SENGANI
>
> Police in Limpopo made a breakthrough when they arrested two suspects in connection with the murder of 10 year old Sello Chokwe of Moletji about two months ago. Sello was brutally murdered when several of his body parts were severed. He died in hospital approximately 10 days after the incident.
>
> Members of the Serious and Violent Crime Unit arrested the suspects at Ga-Maleka at Moletji, the same village where Sello lived. They appared in the Seshego Magistrates Court today and were formally charged with murder. The case was remanded to 29 September 2004. They are Moses Mmko, a 55 year old businessman and 73 year old Petrus Kgabe, a local traditional healer. They did not receive bail and will remain in custody.
>
> Contact Person
> Sr. Supt. Motlafela Mojapelo

Diese Morde geschehen aber weder im Affekt noch trachtet der eigentliche Mörder dem gezielt ausgesuchten Opfer tatsächlich nach dem Leben, weil er sich dessen materiellen Besitz anzueignen sucht. Die folgende Fallbeschreibung der südafrikanischen Polizei geht auf einen Fall aus dem Jahr 1999 zurück, der die typischen Charakteristika eines Muti Mordes aufweist und sich in Südafrikas Gauteng Province (Johannesburg / Pretoria / Soweto) zutrug.

Fallbeschreibung eines prototypischen Muti Mordes

Am Sonntag, dem 30. Mai, verlässt der elfjährige Lungelo D. gegen 13.00 Uhr das Haus seiner Mutter, um in der Nähe Fußball zu spielen. Als er um 18.00 Uhr noch nicht zu Hause ist, bittet die Mutter die Jungen der Nachbarschaft, nach Lungelo zu suchen. Kurz darauf finden sie in einem nahe gelegenen Feld die Leiche eines Kindes, die anschließend als die des gesuchten Lungelo identifiziert wird. Kopf und äußere Geschlechtsorgane wurden mithilfe eines scharfen Gegenstandes entfernt, der Leichnam war vollständig bekleidet. Am folgenden Tag fand man den Kopf in einer Plastiktüte auf dem Dach eines Hauses, das zum örtlichen Tennisverein gehörte. Innerhalb der nächsten vier Tage wurde ein Verdächtiger verhaftet. Der 17-jährige Johnson B. wurde von Zeugen am fraglichen Tag mit einem Messer und blutbefleckter Kleidung in der Nähe des Fundorts der Leiche gesehen. Nach seiner Verhaftung gestand er im Rahmen der Vernehmung durch die Polizei, den Jungen getötet zu haben. In seinem Geständnis berichtet Johnson B. ferner, dass er zwei Tage vor dem Mord von einem Mann und einer Frau aufgesucht worden sei, von zwei traditionellen Heilern (Sangomas), die ihm Geld geboten hätten, wenn er ihnen einen männlichen Kopf, die Zunge, die Augen und die Genitalien bringe. Nachdem am Samstag ein erster Versuch gescheitert war, stieß Johnson B. am Sonntag auf Lungelo, das elfjährige Opfer. Als Tatwaffe benutzte er ein sogenanntes „Okapi Knife", ein einfaches Klappmesser mit einer 13 cm langen Klinge und hölzernem Griff. Am Montag brachte er den beiden Sangomas die Genitalien, nachdem er gehört hatte, dass der Kopf, den er auf dem Dach der Hütte versteckt hatte, entdeckt worden sei. Die beiden Sangomas zeigten sich enttäuscht darüber, dass er ihnen nicht auch die anderen Körperteile mitgebracht hatte und fragten, ob er sie von einem weiteren Opfer besorgen könne. Johnson behauptete am Tag der Tat eine Mischung aus Marihuana und zerkleinerten Mandraxtabletten geraucht zu haben, eine laut Polizei in Südafrika gebräuchliche Droge. Dennoch wurde er für zurechnungsfähig erklärt und anschließend verurteilt. Die beiden Sangomas wurden ebenfalls zu Haftstrafen verurteilt, doch kurze Zeit später wieder auf freien Fuß gesetzt, denn Johnson B. widerrief und weigerte sich später, aus Angst vor Vergeltung durch die Sangomas, gegen die beiden auszusagen. Das ist bis auf den heutigen Tag der Fall. Die Körperteile, die Johnson ihnen übergeben hatte, blieben ebenfalls verschwunden. Dieser gut dokumentierte Fall ist bei Weitem kein Einzelfall und weist die typischen Merkmale eines Muti Mordes auf: Der Täter selbst war kein traditioneller Heiler, wurde aber von Sangomas (oder von Personen, die sich als solche ausgaben!) aufgesucht und hat gegen Bezahlung die menschlichen Körperteile geliefert. Diese „traditionellen Heiler" hatten den Täter zuvor genau instruiert, welche Körperteile (Kopf, Zunge, Augen, Genitalien) sie von welchem Opfer (männlich) benötigten. Der Täter kannte sein Opfer nicht, es gab keine Anzeichen sexueller Aktivität oder Vergewaltigung; dem Körper des Opfers fehlten bestimmte Körperteile, das Opfer war bekleidet und wurde schließlich direkt am Tatort zurückgelassen, ohne irgendwelche Anstrengungen zu unternehmen, seinen Leichnam zu verbergen.[7]

> „Typischerweise fehlen Muti Mord Opfern bestimmte Körperteile. Das ist unser erstes Indiz, um festzustellen, ob es wirklich ein Muti Mord ist. Oft fehlt der ganze Kopf oder der sogenannte „Atlas", der erste Halswirbel unterhalb des Schädels, er ist ein wichtiges Indiz. Wenn wir also einen Kopf oder einen Körper finden, dem genau dieser Knochen fehlt, ist das ein wichtiges Merkmal. Ebenso fehlen manchmal die Geschlechtsorgane, männliche wie weibliche oder Brüste. Und dann fehlen manchmal die Hände oder Augäpfel. Das sind charakteristische Merkmale. Wenn den Leichen diese Körperteile fehlen, beginnen wir die ersten Überlegungen anzustellen, ob es ein Muti Mord ist.
>
> Ein weiteres typisches Merkmal, das wir im Verlauf unserer Ermittlungen festgestellt haben, ist, dass Muti Opfer selten vollständig entkleidet sind. Oft haben sich die Täter also durch die Kleidung hindurch nur Zugang zu dem gewünschten Körperteil verschafft. In einer Reihe von Fällen finden wir die Opfer an Gewässern. Der Grund ist, dass die Täter sich von den Spuren der Tat reinigen können. Offenbar hat Wasser auch eine symbolische Funktion, es soll die Schuld der Täter wegspülen."[8]

Was ist „Muti Medizin"? Was sind „Muti Morde"?

Nehmen wir an, ein Klient würde einen solchen traditionellen Heiler oder „Sangoma" mit einem bestimmten Anliegen aufsuchen. Die Gründe hierfür könnten vielfältiger Natur sein. Neben den zahllosen alltäglichen, ausdrücklich nicht kriminellen Konsultationen, in denen die Klienten eines traditionellen Heilers um spirituellen Beistand oder um einen einfachen medizinischen Rat bitten, gibt es auch immer wieder Vorfälle, die mit Muti Morden in Verbindung stehen.

Ein Sangoma (oder eine Person, die sich als solcher ausgibt) wird nach der Kommunikation mit den Geistern der Ahnen entscheiden, ob und wie das gewünschte Ziel des Klienten erreichbar ist, die Geister der Ahnen durch das Opfern eines Tieres oder durch

---

7 LABUSCHAGNE: Muti Murder, S. 19f.
8 Senior Superintendent Dr. Gérard Labuschagne ist Leiter des Investigative Psychology Unit des South African Police Service. Die Interviews mit ihm wurden im September 2002 und Oktober 2003 in Pretoria sowie im Mai 2004 in Paris aufgezeichnet.

andere Möglichkeiten der Kontaktaufnahme zufrieden zu stellen. Wenn er dem Klienten allerdings eine „extrem starke Muti Medizin" empfiehlt, impliziert das unter Umständen die Verwendung menschlicher Körperteile.

> „Was wir vor allem in Südafrika seit 1995 feststellen konnten, sind regelmäßigere Berichte über Muti Morde. Die Medien hier (in Südafrika; Anm. des Autors) haben versucht, die Zusammenhänge herauszufinden und die Täter wurden einfach nachlässiger. Diese Verbrechen geschehen inzwischen nicht mehr ausschließlich in ländlichen Gegenden, sondern wandern in die Städte. Und das hat mit der Migration von Arbeitern aus schwach entwickelten Gebieten zu tun, die die traditionellen Glaubenssysteme mit in die Townships von Johannesburg mitbringen. Die Polizei vermutet, dass viele Personen, die in den Townships Woche für Woche verschwinden, für Muti Medizin getötet werden. Die Polizei glaubt das, weil sie mehr Körper finden und weil sie mehr Leute verhaften, die gerade versuchten, menschliche Körperteile an traditionelle Heiler zu verkaufen. Das ist ein Grund, warum die Zahl der angezeigten Muti Morde in den letzten 10 Jahren gestiegen ist."[9]

Analysiert man die näheren Umstände von Muti Mordfällen und fragt nach den Beteiligten dieser Verbrechen, so zeigt sich, dass die Mitglieder dreier Personengruppen offenbar häufiger in Muti Mordfällen auftauchen: Es kann ein Geschäftsmann sein, der den ökonomischen Erfolg eines künftigen Unternehmens sichern will oder ein Krimineller, der sich um Schutz vor potenziellen „Angreifern", d. h. in aller Regel der Polizei bemüht oder auch eine Person des öffentlichen Lebens, die ihre Macht oder Einflusssphäre erweitern will. Es gibt immer wieder Gerüchte, dass gerade Politiker in solche Muti Morde verwickelt sein sollen, da in einigen Ländern südlich der Sahara der Anstieg der Mordrate vor Wahlen zu verzeichnen war.[10]

Wesentliche Merkmale, Motivation und Ausführung eines Muti Mordes

Das wichtigste Merkmal eines Muti Mordes ist, dass den Opfern ein bestimmtes Körperteil gewaltsam in der Absicht entfernt wird, daraus eine deviante Form der traditionellen afrikanischen Medizin herzustellen. Das Fehlen von Körperteilen einer Leiche lässt jedoch nicht automatisch den Umkehrschluss auf einen Muti Mord zu.

Die folgenden vier Hauptkategorien krimineller Verstümmelung lassen sich grob unterscheiden in:

---

9 Eigenes Interview mit Prof. Anthony Minnaar, Senior Crime Researcher, Technikon SA , Pretoria, 23. Oktober 2003.

10 Vgl. Ruth Franziska HOFFMANN: „Zwischen Wahn und Wirklichkeit. Amnestie für Hexenmörder, Konjunktur für Zauberer: In Afrika breitet sich ein zerstörerischer Irrglaube aus", in: DIE ZEIT, 04. Januar 2001 sowie Johannes DIETRICH: „Töten im Wahlkampf verboten. Der König von Swaziland spricht ein Machtwort", in: Frankfurter Rundschau, 21. Juni 2003. Der Autor erhielt ferner im August 2004 einen entsprechenden Report des National Police Director aus Monrovia / Liberia. Col. Joseph C. Kekula nennt darin drei konkrete Mordfälle, in deren Verlauf einerseits den Opfern Körperteile entnommen wurden und andererseits liberianische Politiker oder Personen des öffentlichen Lebens zumindest als Auftraggeber in Erscheinung getreten zu sein scheinen: „Besides these infamous incidents of ritualistic killings, there were a lot more that occured in several parts of the country that went with impunity by intervention of some powerful or invincible hands."

- **defensive Verstümmelung:** Dabei werden vor allem Kopf und / oder Hände des Opfers werden entfernt, um seine Identifizierung durch Finger- oder Gebissabdrücke zu verhindern oder wenigstens zu verlangsamen.
- **aggressive Verstümmelung:** Das Motiv ist Zorn / Wut; im Verlauf eines Mordes kann der Körper spontan verstümmelt werden, vor allem Geschlechtsorgane oder Teile des Gesichts können entfernt werden.
- **offensive Verstümmelung / offensive mutilation:** oft in Zusammenhang mit lust- oder nekrosadistischen Morden. Die Motivation des Täters entspringt dabei

    a) Nekrophilie, d. h. einem krankhaft triebgesteuerter Zwang, zu töten und / oder sexuelle Handlungen an der Leiche vorzunehmen, bei vorhergehender oder anschließender Verstümmelung, oder

    b) sexual-sadistischen Aktivitäten, d. h. dem Opfer während sexueller Kontakte Schmerz zuzufügen, es zu demütigen oder zu töten. Die Verstümmelung beginnt, noch während das Opfer lebt, kann nach dem Tod fortgesetzt werden oder mit dem Todeszeitpunkt enden.
- **nekromanische Verstümmelung:** wird an Leichen begangen, der Täter will eine „Trophäe" seines Opfers.

Ein Muti Mord stellt eine eigene Kategorie dar und folgt in Motivation und Ausführung keinem der oben genannten Verhaltensmuster. Für gewöhnlich sind vier Parteien[11] in einen Muti Mord verwickelt: a) Klient, b) traditioneller Heiler (Sangoma / Inayanga) oder jemand, der sich als solcher ausgibt, c) Mörder und d) Opfer.

Die Art und Anzahl der Wunden geben in Fällen von Muti Mord weniger Auskunft über die psychosoziale Struktur des Täters als über den Hintergrund der Tat. Im Gegensatz zu Mordopfern von Satanisten, Serienmördern und den oben genannten Hauptkategorien krimineller Verstümmelung, weisen die Opfer von Muti Morden weniger Wunden auf; dafür werden diese mit funktionellem Hintergrund beigebracht. Opfer von Satanisten hingegen weisen viele Wunden auf, die aber weniger schwerwiegend sind. Dem Opfer werden Schmerzen zugefügt; sexuelle Motive und Fantasien werden am Tatort ausgelebt. Einziges Ziel eines Muti Mordes ist die Entnahme des Körperteils. Diese ist weder durch die Fantasie des Täters gesteuert noch geschieht dies aus sexuellen Motiven.

Die Opfer werden daher selten vollständig entkleidet aufgefunden. Die Täter verschaffen sich lediglich Zugang durch die Kleidung, um an das benötigte Körperteil zu gelangen.

Die Opfer werden oft in oder in der Nähe fließender Gewässer gefunden. Das hat einmal einen praktischen Nutzen, denn der Täter kann sich von der Tat reinigen, das Wasser hat zudem auch symbolische Bedeutung: Es soll die „Schuld" des Täters davonspülen.

---

11 In Ausnahmefällen verübten traditionelle Heiler den Mord selbst. 1994 wurde im Boystown Squatter Camp in Kapstadt ein 30-jähriger Sangoma mit seinem 18-jährigen Komplizen verhaftet, die gestanden hatten gemeinsam einen Muti Mord begangen zu haben, um dem Opfer beide Hände und Unterarme zu entfernen. H. J. SCHOLTZ / V. M. PHILLIPS / G. J. KNOBEL: Muti or Ritual Murder, in: Forensic Science Journal (1997), S. 119f.

Die Opfer werden meist direkt am Tatort zurückgelassen und nicht verborgen; je mehr Passanten das Opfer sehen, desto größer ist dieser Vorstellung folgend die Wirkung der aus den Körperteilen gewonnenen Medizin.

Die Opfer sind selten älter als 40 Jahre, da dann die Lebenskraft nachzulassen beginnt. Eine Medizin aus Körperteilen älterer Menschen würde als „schwach" gelten.[12]

Muti Mord oder Ritualmord?

Während bei einem klassischen Ritualmord der Tod des Opfers im Mittelpunkt steht, denn das Leben des Menschen wird einem Ritual folgend einem bestimmten Zweck geopfert, geht es bei einem Muti Mord ausschließlich um die Entnahme eines bestimmten Körperteils eines Menschen. Die dem Mordopfer fehlenden Körperteile lassen Rückschlüsse auf die Bedürfnisse des Klienten zu, da sie seinen bestimmten „Wunsch" oder ein „Problem" als Tathintergrund reflektieren.

Die Antwort auf die Frage, ob ein Muti Mord den Ritualmorden zugerechnet werden kann oder nicht, ist bislang strittig und wird von Ermittlern, Kriminologen und Psychologen unterschiedlich bewertet: Dagegen spricht, dass vor, während und nach der Tat keine kultischen Handlungen an der Leiche durchgeführt werden und dass das Leben des Menschen bei einem Muti Mord keinem bestimmten Zweck geopfert wird. Im Gegenteil, das bestimmte Körperteil soll dem gezielt ausgesuchten Opfer sogar „prae mortem" entnommen werden. Dahinter verbirgt sich allerdings nicht etwa die Absicht, dem Opfer zusätzlich Schmerz zuzufügen, sondern durch das Schreien des Opfers soll die gesamte Lebenskraft des Menschen („life essence") in den vom Täter gesuchten Körperteil gelangen und so die Wirkung der Medizin verstärken. Die Effizienz der (Muti-) „Medizin" soll durch die Entdeckung des Leichnams durch Passanten nochmals gesteigert werden. Deshalb werden die Opfer von Muti Morden charakteristischerweise am Tatort zurückgelassen und nicht versteckt oder vergraben. Andererseits spricht für die Klassifizierung „Ritualmord", dass diese Verbrechen einem bestimmten Schema unterliegen.

> „Ein Muti Mord ist ein einzigartiges Verbrechen, verübt mit einem ganz bestimmten Motiv und begangen, aus einem ganz bestimmten Grund. Diese Morde folgen einem rituellen Muster, denn für gewöhnlich werden die Opfer mit dem Kopf nach unten gehalten, besondere Schnitte werden gemacht, die Körperteile sind nicht einfach abgehackt. Sie werden einem Ritual folgend abgetrennt. Normalerweise an einem einsamen Ort, z. B. im Wald, und die Opfer wurden gezielt ausgesucht. Ein Klient kommt zu einem traditionellen Heiler und sagt, ich brauche eine sehr starke Muti Medizin, womit er möglicherweise implizit menschliche Körperteile meint."[13]

In dieser devianten Form der „Muti Medizin" wechseln für dortige Verhältnisse sehr große Summen Geldes ihre Besitzer. Der Anziehungskraft dieser enormen Summen erliegen manche Heiler. Auf einem sogenannten „Muti Markt" verkaufen Händler, Heiler oder Gehilfen eines Heilers[14] für gewöhnlich vor allem die Wurzeln und Rinden beson-

---

12 LABUSCHAGNE. Muti Murder, S. 191-206.
13 Eigenes Interview mit Anthony Minnaar. Pretoria, Rep. Südafrika 23. Oktober 2003.
14 Tshigomamutanda ist eine Person, die sich als Heiler in einem Vorstadium befindet und ihrerseits für einen oder mehrere traditionelle Heiler Pflanzen in freier Natur sammelt. Vgl.: Frank MAVHUNGU: Controversial healer a Child-killer? in: THE MIRROR, Rep. of South Africa, 27. Februar 1998.

Menschliche Körperteile / Anwendungsgebiete	
(weibliche) Brust:	Quelle von Mutterglück; um ein Geschäft für weibliche Kunden attraktiver zu machen, wurde das Fettgewebe weiblicher Brüste in die Wand von Läden eingemauert; menschliches Fett symbolisiert ganz allg. „Glück";
Genitalien:	männl. / weibl.; durch die Verwendung erhoffen sich Männer die Behebung ihrer Potenzprobleme;
Kehlkopf / Adamsapfel:	Kriminelle, die vor Gericht stehen, versuchen durch deren Gebrauch als „Muti Medizin" Zeugen zum Schweigen zu bringen;
Atlasknochen:	letzter Knochen am unteren Schädel; sehr wertvoll, denn er stellt die Verbindung zwischen „Körper und Geist" dar, da sowohl die Aorta als auch das Nervensystem von diesem Atlasknochen umgeben sind;
Hände:	werden unter Türschwellen vergraben, sie sollen Kunden hereinwinken und / oder ihnen symbolisch das Geld aus der Tasche ziehen; in anderen Fällen berührten die Ladeninhaber ihre Waren mit einer abgetrennten menschlichen Hand, um sie für Kunden attraktiver zu machen;
Muskeln:	Bizeps / (Ober-)Schenkelmuskulatur;
Fettgewebe:	Magenhaut, die Nieren oder die Leber sollen „Glück bringen", in Venda eine „gute Ernte" sichern helfen;
Urin / Sperma:	allg. Glück / Erfolg;
Gliedmaßen, Arme / Beine:	sollen Waren / Geschäft für Kunden attraktiver machen; für ein Bein wurde in Lesotho 500$ bezahlt;
Schädel:	entweder als Ganzes vergraben, um sich vor einer gegnerischen Gemeinschaft (Clan, Ethnie) zu schützen oder das Gehirn und / oder der Atlas werden entfernt und anschließend der Kopf weggeworfen;
Zunge:	in sog. „Liebesmedizin", soll den Weg zum Herzen einer Frau ebnen;
Augen:	ermöglichen, zu „Medizin" verarbeitet, den Blick in die Zukunft; (Sie werden aber auch oft ausgestochen, da sie den Mörder „gesehen haben" und ihr „Geist" den Täter identifizieren könnte).[15]

derer Bäume sowie Kräuter, Heilpflanzen und Körperteile bzw. Knochen bestimmter Tiere, die den Hauptbestandteil der traditionellen Medizin ausmachen. Neben den Vorderbeinen von Huftieren findet man dort z. B. auch die Köpfe oder Pfoten von Affen, die Klauen von Krokodilen, ganze Schlangen, Vögel oder einzelne Organe. Auf solchen Märkten tauchten in unregelmäßigen Abständen immer wieder auch menschliche Körperteile auf, die freilich nur unter der Hand veräußert wurden, da schon der Besitz menschlicher Körperteile einen Straftatbestand darstellt.[16]

---

15 Quelle: Investigative Psychology Unit, SAPS Pretoria.
16 Auf dem Muti Markt in Johannesburg, unter dem Highway M1, zwischen Hauptbahnhof und Faradaystreet verhafteten im Mai 2001 als Kunden getarnte SAPS Detectives einen Mann, der ihnen den

Abb. 1: Der Muti Markt in Johannesburg zwischen Hauptbahnhof und Faraday Stree, unter dem Highway M1. Hier arbeiten je nach Saison zwischen 60-200 Menschen an der Herstellung und dem Verkauf von Tier- und Pflanzenteilen für Muti Medizin. Die Händler kommen aus dem Norden Südafrikas, der Grenze zu Zimbabwe bzw. Mosambik oder aus dem Krüger-Nationalpark. Foto: Becker / occasione documentaries.

Arbeitslosigkeit und Perspektivlosigkeit vieler Menschen vor allem in den ländlichen Regionen, verbunden mit der enormen Anziehungskraft solcher Summen Geldes führten dazu, dass sich Scharlatane, die weder die tatsächliche Berufung noch die Qualifikation eines echten Sangomas besitzen, in dieser Szene breitmachen. Der Sprecher einer Vereinigung von 25.000 Sangomas im südlichen Afrika, der sich wie die allermeisten traditionellen Heiler scharf von jeder Verwendung menschlicher Körperteile in der traditionellen Medizin distanziert, nennt sie „hidden", also „versteckte" Sangomas. Den Ermittlern blieb bislang unklar, wie man einen solchen Sangoma identifiziert, der bereit ist, eine Muti Medizin herzustellen, die menschliche Körperteile enthält.

Weder der Sangoma noch der Klient tritt bei dem Mord selbst in Erscheinung. In einen Muti Mord sind für gewöhnlich vier Parteien verwickelt: Ein Klient oder Kunde, der einen traditioneller Heiler (Sangoma / Inyanga) mit einem Wunsch oder Problem aufsucht. Der / die Sangoma beauftragt den tatsächlichen Mörder, ihm bestimmte Körperteile eines Opfers zu besorgen. Der Mörder erhält im Gegenzug sein Geld bei Übergabe der Körperteile. Diese würde der Sangoma möglicherweise und je nach Art des Anliegens seines Klienten mit anderen Pflanzen, Tierteilen oder auch kleinen Gegenständen mischen und dem Klienten, der unter Umständen nicht weiß, dass seine Muti Medizin menschliche Körperteile enthält, verkaufen.

Kopf eines Menschen für 1.000 US$ verkaufen wollte. Der Mann gestand im Rahmen der Vernehmung, dass er die männliche Leiche nur gefunden und ihr den Kopf entfernt habe, um ihn anschließend zu Geld zu machen. Eigenes Interview mit Col. Kobus Jonker, Head of Occult Related Crimes Unit, SAPS, Pretoria, 02. Oktober 2002.

Diese Verbrechen sind ausgesprochen schwer zu ermitteln: Der Mörder sagt im Fall seiner Verhaftung, er habe auf Anweisung des Sangomas gehandelt oder schweigt aus Angst vor den okkulten Fähigkeiten seines Auftraggebers wie in der konkreten Fallbeschreibung. Der traditionelle Heiler streitet seinerseits jede Beteiligung an einem Verbrechen ab. Werden bei ihm im Rahmen einer (Haus-) Durchsuchung durch die Polizei menschliche Körperteile entdeckt, gibt er sich ahnungslos, allerdings kann er für den Besitz dieser Körperteile belangt werden. Der Klient ist entweder unauffindbar oder bestreitet den Sangoma und / oder den Mörder jemals gesehen zu haben.

Einem Geschäftsmann würde ein Sangoma beispielsweise empfehlen, eine kleine Menge dieser „Medizin" auf seine Waren[17] zu schmieren, um sie für Kunden „attraktiver" zu machen. Den Kriminellen würde er instruieren, seine Waffe oder die Kugeln in der Muti Medizin zu tränken, damit er bei seinen anstehenden kriminellen Aktivitäten vor der Polizei oder rivalisierenden Gangstern geschützt sei.

Ethymologie und verengter Bedeutungsschwerpunkt

Die vor allem von den Medien sogenannte „Muti Morde" repräsentieren die Extremform eines wenig bekannten Phänomens südlich der Sahara, in dem der okkulte Glaube an „Medizin" aus Körperteilen, der Haut oder Blut eines Menschen und Mord in Zusammenhang stehen. Die Bezeichnung „Muti" ist zwar heute durch diese Morde stark verengt auf das gleichlautende Verbrechen, sie ist aber dennoch keine verkürzte Form des englischen Wortes „mutilation", also „Verstümmelung" sondern entstammt ursprünglich einem Begriff aus der Sprache der Zulu. „Umu thi" bedeutet etwa Baum, giftiges Gebräu oder auch einfach „Medizin".[18] Wenn also von „Muti Medizin" die Rede ist, hat das nicht notwendigerweise einen kriminellen Aspekt.

Trotzdem taucht heute in der Berichterstattung westlicher, aber auch (süd-) afrikanischer Medien, der Begriff „Muti" fast ausschließlich in Zusammenhang mit Verbrechen auf, d. h. dem kriminellen Gebrauch menschlicher Körperteile als „traditionelle Medizin", obwohl der Begriff „muti" eine viel umfangreichere, ausdrücklich nicht kriminelle Bedeutung hat. Die Verbreitung dieser Meldungen via Fernsehen, Radio, Zeitung und Internet hat inzwischen dafür gesorgt, dass man nun auch in Nigeria „Muti" (neben dem in Nigeria bekannten Begriff „Juju") oft genug als eine kriminelle Art „okkulter Medizin" kennt, obwohl die ursprüngliche Bezeichnung „Muti" aus dem Zululand, also der heutigen Republik Südafrika stammt.[19]

---

17 Ein Lebensmittelhändler in der Gauteng Province (RSA) soll auf Anweisung eines traditionellen Heilers seine Waren morgens – vor der Öffnung seines Ladens – mit einer abgetrennten menschlichen Hand berührt haben, um diese „schmackhafter" und für seine Kunden „attraktiver" zu machen. Eigenes Interview mit Col. Kobus Jonker, Occult related Crimes Unit, SAPS, Pretoria, 02. Oktober 2002.

18 Anthony MINNAAR / Dirk OFFRINGA / C. PAYZE: To live in fear. Witchburning and medicine murder in Venda, in: Human Science Research Council, Pretoria, 1992, S. 19.

19 Zitat: „Muti ist ein Begriff aus Südafrika, der eine enorme Weite von Bedeutungen hat, nicht nur das Töten eines Menschen für seine Körperteile. Es sieht so aus, als würde der Begriff „Muti" auf eine bestimmte Bedeutung verengt werden; auf die schrecklichen Szenarien, die beschrieben werden. Wir sehen das jetzt auch in Nigeria, was sehr verwirrend ist. Es ist klar, dass die Leute in Nigeria

Insofern hat sich der Begriff nicht nur in anderen Nationen Afrikas ausgebreitet, sondern auch verselbstständigt und steht oft *per se* für diese Form ritualisierten Verbrechens. Nicht nur in Südafrika, auch in anderen Staaten der Sub-Sahara-Zone, tauchen immer wieder Mordfälle auf, in deren Verlauf den Opfern Körperteile entnommen wurden, um daraus „okkulte Medizin" herzustellen.[20] Dieses Phänomen ist unter verschiedenen Bezeichnungen bekannt, von Nigeria im Westen, bis Tansania im Osten des Kontinents.[21]

Muti Mord und Tötung von Hexen: „Witchpurging" und „Necklacing"

Dass die Austreibung und Verbrennung vermeintlicher Hexen, zusammen mit bestimmten Formen des Schadenszaubers und eben auch den Muti Morden in der Kategorie „okkulte Gewalt" zusammengefasst und analysiert wird, geschieht mit einiger Berechtigung, wenn man als eine der gemeinsamen Hauptursachen den Glauben an die „Begrenztheit kosmischer Güter" anerkennt.[22]

Unter „Witchpurging" kann man sowohl die Aus- oder Vertreibung einer oder mehrerer Hexen aus einer lokalen Gemeinschaft verstehen, als auch ihre tatsächliche Verbrennung. Der vermeintlichen Hexe oder auch dem Hexer – das Englische nennt beide Geschlechter „a witch" – wird dabei die Behausung über dem Kopf angezündet. Die Täter beabsichtigen durch den Brandanschlag mindestens die Vernichtung des materiellen Eigentums, um das Opfer zur Flucht aus der Region zu zwingen. Kann das Opfer den Flammen aus eigener Kraft nicht entfliehen, wird auch die vollständige Vernichtung von Leib und Leben des Opfers selbst von den Tätern zumindest billigend in Kauf genommen. Zahlreiche Wissenschaftler verweisen inzwischen auf die verschärfte Hexenverfolgung in Afrika. Früher habe man sich oft mit der lokalen Vertreibung der Hexe begnügt. Inzwischen sei eine Hexe unschädlich zu machen, indem man ihren Körper völlig zerstöre und am besten auch gleich ihr Haus anzünde, damit alle Paraphernalien mit ihr verbrennen.

---

diese Praktiken aus Südafrika kennen, doch meiner Ansicht nach bezieht sich das alles grundsätzlich auf okkulte Aggression insgesamt, „Hexerei", wenn sie so wollen. Es überrascht mich sehr, welche verschiedenen Formen das heute angenommen hat, obwohl es in gewisser Weise logisch ist, denn sie wollen ihren Gegner mit einem „Zauber" überraschen, einem, der neu ist, um seine Verteidigungsmechanismen zu umgehen ... alles was neu ist, scheint erfolgversprechend zu sein, weil es erschreckend ist, weil es den Schutz des Gegners entfernt oder ihn überrascht. Okkulte Gewalt ist eine Welt, in der die Menschen ständig etwas Neues erfinden." Eigenes Interview mit Peter Geschiere, Leiden, Niederlande, 25. November 2003.

20 Vgl. Zitat: „A Zambian national whose private parts were severely mutilated after he was attacked by three men at Katimo Mulilo last week may have been a target for a ritual „muti killings". Petros KATEEUE: Muti Hunters go for the genitals, Zeitungsartikel, in: THE NAMIBIAN, Windhuk, Namibia, 20. Februar 2004. Dayo AIYETAN: „Many more Nigerians than ever before are declared missing, just as the incedence of ritual killings attains worrisome dimensions. Yet the authorities appear helpless". Bildunterschrift des Special Report / Tell Magazine (Nigeria) vom 29. Dezember 2003, S. 25-29.

21 Vgl. Jeremy EVANS: Where can we get a beast without hair? Medicine Murder in Swaziland from 1970 to 1988, in: African Studies 52 (1993), S. 27-42.

22 George D. SPINDLER: Peasant Society and the Image of Limited Good, in: American Anthropologist 67 (1965), S. 293-315.

Ein noch höheres Maß an krimineller Energie entfalten die Täter beim sog. „Necklacing" von Hexen. Dem Opfer wird dabei ein mit Benzin gefüllter Autoreifen als Brandbeschleuniger um den Hals gehängt und anschließend angezündet. Beiden Formen der Hexenverfolgung ist gemein, dass sie für gewöhnlich gemeinschaftlich begangen werden, d. h. in aller Öffentlichkeit und oft auch bei Tag. Die Opfer, oft ältere, alleinstehende und verarmte Frauen, wurden und werden in solchen Fällen meist von mehreren Mitgliedern einer Gemeinschaft verdächtigt, der Hexerei beschuldigt, für einen Missstand oder Unglück verantwortlich gemacht und öffentlich und „zum Wohl der Gemeinschaft" verbrannt. Solche Verbrennungen deklarieren die Täter als „reinigenden Akt", der die Allgemeinheit vom „Bösen" befreit.

Zahlreiche Afrikanisten weisen auch auf den politischen Zusammenhang hin, der zwischen den Hexenverfolgungen der 90er Jahre in der Republik Südafrika und der zum Befreiungskampf mobilisierten ANC Jugend bestand. In der Beseitigung von Hexen sehen sie, neben der Ausrottung „des Bösen" an sich, die gewaltsame Abrechnung mit der in den Augen der „Comrades" untätigen Elterngeneration, die sich dem Apartheidsregime weitgehend widerstandslos ergeben hatte.[23] Mitunter dienten Hexereianschuldigungen auch als bloßer Vorwand, um sich einer Person auf bequeme Art und Weise zu entledigen. Schließlich wurden auch Fälle bekannt, in denen ökonomisch erfolglose Mitglieder einer Gemeinschaft als Ursache eines Unglücks oder Missstands gemeinschaftlich identifiziert und als Hexe verbrannt wurden.

Kolonialgesetzgebung, traditionelle Religion und Medizin in Afrika

Für das Verständnis und eine angemessene Darstellung des Zusammenhangs von traditioneller Religion, -Medizin und bestimmten Formen okkulter Aggression ist die Gesetzgebung der Kolonialmächte Afrikas von großer Bedeutung.

„In den meisten Ländern südlich der Sahara ist bis heute die Ausübung von Magie und Hexerei durch verschiedene Gesetze verboten. Eine große Anzahl der Menschen begreift aber die Anwendung von Magie noch immer als ein durchaus normales Ereignis und als Bestandteil ihres täglichen Lebens. Insofern leuchtet es ein, dass die meisten Menschen hier diese Gesetze nicht ohne Weiteres anerkennen."[24]

Bereits 1891 verboten die britischen Kolinialbehörden, ihrer eigenen christlichen Herkunft und Vorstellung folgend, im „Natal Code of Native Law" (Sektion 268, Gesetz 19) den afrikanischen Wahrsagern (engl. Diviner / „Sangoma") ausdrücklich die Ausübung ihres Berufs. 1895 erließen die britischen Kolonialbehörden schließlich den sogenannten „Witchcraft Suppression Act" (WCSA), durch den sie den Glauben an und die Ausübung von Magie und Hexerei unter Strafe stellten und qua Gesetz endgültig auszurotten versuchten. Von einigen Änderungen in den Jahren 1957, 1970 und 1997 einmal abgesehen, ist dieser „Witchcraft Suppression Act" bis heute in der Republik Südafrika gültig.

---

23 Siehe zusammenfassend: Johannes HARNISCHFEGER: Witchcraft and the State in South Africa, in: Antropos 95 (2000), S. 104.
24 Eigenes Interview mit Prof. Victor Ralushai, Thohoyandou, Limpopo Province, Rep. Südafrika, 01. November 2003.

Wenn man also dementsprechend annimmt, dass die Mehrheit der Bevölkerung in den Staaten südlich der Sahara noch heute an etwas wie Magie oder Hexerei glaubt, die Organe des (südafrikanischen) Staates aber deren Existenz aufgrund der alten, kolonialen Rechtsprechung schlichtweg abstreiten, prallen hier nicht nur die Rechtsvorstellungen zweier Kulturen aufeinander. Diejenigen im Süden Afrikas, die sich auf spiritueller Ebene bedroht fühlen, werden demnach gezwungen, ihre eigenen Verteidigungsmechanismen gegen die Auswirkungen von Magie und Zauberei zu organisieren, wenn der Staat sie davor nicht bewahrt und sie nicht schutzlos ausgeliefert sein wollen. Hierin liegt vermutlich einer der wesentlichen Gründe, warum die Anziehungskraft traditioneller Heiler ungebrochen scheint.

Wenn der südafrikanische Staat den „Witchcraft Suppression Act" abschaffte, und damit die Existenz von Geistwesen und okkulten, möglicherweise „bösen", übernatürlichen Mächten anerkennen würde, (spiritueller Kräfte also, die außerhalb christlicher Glaubensvorstellungen liegen) wäre das ein Signal, dass er die Ängste vieler Menschen ernst nähme. Gleichzeitig müsste er dann eine Instanz schaffen, die juristisch zweifelsfrei beurteilt, ob es sich im Streitfall um „bösen Zauber" eines Hexers, Geistes oder eines menschlichen Individuums handelt, durch die jemand geschädigt werden sollte oder, ob die Ursache des Schadens einen „natürlichen" Hintergrund hat. Wer oder was sollte aber diese Instanz sein? Und wer sollte, im Fall, dass nach Auffassung der Instanz übernatürliche Kräfte verantwortlich sind, die Ordnung wieder herstellen?[25]

Traditionelle Heiler der Zulu-Kultur und die britische Kolonialgesetzgebung

In der Zulu-Kultur gibt es unterschiedliche Formen traditioneller Heiler, die zwar untereinander in Verbindung stehen, aber nicht identisch sind. Die bedeutendsten im Süden Afrikas sind *Inyanga* und *Sangoma*. Sie haben neben der rein medizinischen eine spirituelle Funktion und sind angesehene Mitglieder der Gesellschaft. Ein *Inyanga* („inyanga yokwelapha", also ein „Doktor, um zu heilen") ist ursprünglich eine Art Homöopath, ein Kenner der Heilpflanzen und der Tierwelt, der seine Kenntnisse und Fähigkeiten erst erlernen muss. Am Ende seiner Lehrzeit kennt ein *Inyanga* im Durchschnitt die Anwendungsgebiete und Wirkung von über 240 Heilpflanzen. Mehr als die Hälfte der traditionellen Heiler kommt durch die Großeltern zu diesem Beruf, wie eine Untersuchung von G. L. Chavunduka in Zimbabwe zeigte.[26]

Nach einem Initiationsritus lernt ein *Inyanga* nicht nur die Bestandteile und Funktion von Muti Medizin, sondern auch, Hexen und Zauberer „auszuriechen", also Menschen mit okkulten Fähigkeiten zu identifizieren. *Inyanga yokwelapha* diagnostizieren für gewöhnlich keine Krankheiten und sind in der Regel männlich.

Ein *Sangoma* („Inyanga-yokubhula") dagegen ist ein „Doktor zum Wahrsagen", der durch den Ruf seiner Ahnen bestimmt wird. Im meist noch jugendlichen Alter wird sie / er

---

25 Vgl. Peter GESCHIERE: Witchcraft and the limits of law. Cameroon and South Africa, in: Jean & John COMAROFF (Hg.): Law and Disorder in the Postcolony, Chicago 2006, S. 219-246.
26 Gordon L. CHAVUNDUKA: Traditional Medicine in modern Zimbabwe, Harare 1994, S. 48f. Tabelle 7.

Abb. 2: Dreharbeiten / Interview mit einem Inyanga in Kwazulu Natal / Südafrika, Oktober 2003. Er trägt Frauenkleider, ein in der Szene verbreitetes Phänomen. Die Bestandteile seiner Medizin reichen vom Fett eines Löwen bis zu geschredderten und zu Asche verbrannten Autoreifen, die er zu einer Paste verrührt. Daneben arbeitet er auch mit tatsächlichen Heilkräutern. Foto: Becker / occasione documentaries.

von einer Krankheit („thwasa") befallen, die durch die westliche Medizin nicht diagnostiziert werden kann. Man könne sich gegen den Ruf seiner Ahnen nicht wehren, man müsse in diesem Fall dem Ruf der Ahnen folgen und *Sangoma* werden, anderenfalls stürbe man an dieser Krankheit, berichteten einige *Sangomas* im Interview. In dieser Zeit, für gewöhnlich einige Jahre, wird der / die angehende *Sangoma* allein durch die Natur streifen. Die Träume und die Kommunikation mit den Geistern werden ihm den Weg zu bestimmten Pflanzen weisen. Anschließend wird er von einem erfahrenen Lehrer die Zubereitung von Medizin aus verschiedenen Pflanzen, die Interpretation von Träumen und die Kommunikation mit Geistern ebenso erlernen und entwickeln wie Geschichte, Mythologie und Opferzeremonien seiner Ethnie.

Einige Zeit wird sich ein *Sangoma* aber auch über die medizinische Bedeutung von Heilpflanzen hinaus mit dem Gebrauch von Flüchen, Schadenszauber und anderer okkulter Praktiken beschäftigen, weshalb ihn die Menschen auch „Hexendoktor" (engl. „witch doctor") nennen. Ein *Sangoma* berät die Menschen, die zu ihm kommen, weil sie sich von „Zauber" oder okkulten Mächten bedroht fühlen. Jeder *Sangoma* ist also auch ein *Inyanga*, aber nicht umgekehrt. In dieser personifizierten Überschneidung des *Sangomas* von Ahnenkult und Heilverfahren sehen Kritiker auch eine der größten Gefahren der traditionellen afrikanischen Medizin, denn hier ist der Arzt gleichzeitig auch Priester. Krankheit ist in diesem System nicht einfach die Abwesenheit von Gesundheit. Wenn jemand krank wird kann das, dieser Vorstellung folgend, einen spirituellen Grund haben. Um den Grund der Krankheit zu erfahren, kontaktiert ein *Sangoma* die Geister der Krankheit oder die Ahnen eines Patienten. Das kann durch ein Tieropfer geschehen oder das

Werfen und Interpretieren kleiner Knochen oder durch die Deutung eines Traumes. Durch diese Prozedur „vergeistigt" ein *Sangoma* den physischen Zustand des Patienten, oder er stellt einen Zusammenhang zwischen gegenwärtigen Ereignissen und längst Vergangenem her. *Sangomas* in Südafrika seien fast ausschließlich weiblich, männliche *Sangomas* ihr Leben lang Transvestiten, behaupten die Autoren des Essays „Muti- oder Ritualmord".[27]

Als die britische Krone am Ende des 19. Jahrhunderts den „Witchcraft Suppression Act" erließ, um – die Absicht verrät schon der Titel – den in ihren Augen heidnischen Glauben an Hexerei und Magie bei der indigenen Bevölkerung Afrikas zu unterdrücken, konnten sich vermutlich weder die Lordrichter in London noch die britischen Kolonialbeamten in Afrika vorstellen, welche Folgen diese Gesetzgebung bis heute haben würde: Indem sie diese zwei Arten traditioneller Heiler, also *Inyanga* und *Sangoma*, ausschließlich aus ihrer westlich-abendländischen Perspektive unterschiedlich bewertete und behandelte, trennte die Kolonialverwaltung zwei respektierte und nach indigener Vorstellung zusammenhängende Vertreter der Zulu Medizin.

Der *Inyanga* war nach Ansicht der Briten ein Arzt, zwar ohne akademische Ausbildung im europäischen Sinne, aber ein Heilkundiger, dessen umfangreiches Wissen im Wesentlichen auf der erworbenen Kenntnis der Heilpflanzen und seiner persönlichen Erfahrung im Umgang mit diesen beruhte. Art des Personals und Form dieser medizinischen Versorgung war den Europäern nicht unbekannt: Auch in England gab es zu dieser Zeit z. B. Heiler, Bader und anderes, nicht aus dem akademischen Umfeld stammendes, aber durchaus medizinisch geschultes Personal.

Ein *Sangoma* dagegen ist ein Wahrsager (engl. „diviner"), dessen Beruf auf der Kommunikation mit den Geistern einer Krankheit oder seiner Ahnen basiert, wofür man im Europa am Ende der Aufklärung nur wenig übrig hatte. Man fand dort zu diesem Beruf des *Sangoma* kein entsprechendes Pendant mehr. Während sich in der zweiten Hälfte des 19. Jahrhunderts in Europa, durch die Fortschritte in der medizinischen Forschung allmählich die Erkenntnis durchsetzte, dass die Ursache vieler Krankheiten biomedizinischer oder bakteriologischer Natur sein müsse, vermutete man in der Zulu-Medizin als Ursache mancher Leiden spirituelle Kräfte, wie Hexerei oder die Unzufriedenheit der Ahnen mit einem Patienten. Die spirituellen Fähigkeiten eines *Sangoma* wurden von der Kolonialverwaltung nicht anerkannt. Seine Qualifikation und Profession brachten die Briten, mit dem ihrer Ansicht nach rückwärts gewandten Glauben an okkulte Mächte, Zauberei und Hexerei – kurzum nicht aufgeklärtem Aberglauben – in Verbindung, und verboten deshalb diesen Berufszweig kurzerhand.

Durch dieses Verbot unterschieden die Gesetzgeber und die Organe der Strafverfolgung fortan nicht mehr zwischen dem einerseits von der Bevölkerung geachteten Wahrsager oder „Hexendoktor" (Sangoma), der einzelnen Mitgliedern oder ganzen Gemeinschaften bei Bedarf eben genau gegen die Bedrohung dunkler Mächte hilft, und andererseits tatsächlich „bösen" Zauberern und Hexern, durch die sich die Bevölkerung – bis heute – zumindest zeitweise bedroht fühlt.

---

27 SCHOLTZ / PHILLIPS / KNOBEL: Muti- or Ritual murder, S. 122.

Der Beruf des *Sangoma* wurde und wird aber nicht nur durch den „Witchcraft Suppression Act" ins Abseits gedrängt. 1931 haben sich die *Inyangas* selbst sogar in einem eigenen Berufsverband organisiert, der „Natal Native Medical Association" und sich freiwillig von den wahrsagenden Kollegen, „deren Wissen nur auf Aberglaube beruht", abzugrenzen versucht.

Traditionelle Heiler früher und heute

Viele Heiler der Republik Südafrika lassen sich inzwischen zwar als Inyanga registrieren, denn das ist nicht illegal. Sie arbeiten aber nicht nur als „heilender Inyanga", sondern gleichzeitig als Sangoma, also zusätzlich als Wahrsager. Denn das Bedürfnis vieler Menschen in dieser Region nach Erklärung okkulter Phänomene und spirituellem Beistand im Sinne traditioneller afrikanischer Religion ist immer noch ungebrochen. Das führt mitunter dazu, dass ein und derselbe traditionelle Heiler zwei Dienstleistungen ausführt, die ursprünglich von zwei verschiedenen Vertretern indigener Medizin getrennt voneinander durchgeführt worden sind, nämlich „heilen" und „wahrsagen". Im schlimmsten Fall sind manche Heiler heute in beiden Berufen mangelhaft oder gar nicht von ihrerseits inkompetenten Tutoren ausgebildet worden.[28]

Doch allein die Selektion eines / einer Sangoma selbst ist nicht unproblematisch: Wie sollte man überprüfen, beweisen oder gar abstreiten, wenn jemand behauptet, ihm sei im Traum der Geist eines Vorfahren erschienen, der ihm / ihr befohlen habe, er oder sie müsse eine Sangoma werden? Ist es nur der einfache aber umso verständlichere Wunsch ein finanzielles Auskommen zu haben? Einen weithin respektierten Beruf auszuüben und geachtetes, ja zum Teil gefürchtetes Mitglied der Gesellschaft zu sein? Oder ist derjenige tatsächlich von Geistwesen aufgefordert worden, Sangoma zu werden?

„Ich sprach mit einigen traditionellen Heilern im Norden Südafrikas und die sagten mir, dass sie es sich nicht aussuchen konnten, diesem Ruf der Ahnen zu folgen. „Wir haben es uns nicht ausgesucht, Sangomas zu werden, wir wurden von den Geistern ausgesucht. Sie sagten uns, dass es für uns keine andere Möglichkeit gebe. Wir wurden ausgesucht und sogar durch die Geister gezwungen, Sangomas zu werden.

---

28 „With respect to traditional healers, I would say most people in Maryland (Liberia) saw traditional healers before coming to the western-trained medical system. Much of that was because of a lack of access. In Monrovia, where there was much more access to western medical care, many fewer people seemed to make use of traditional cures. In Maryland county, I feel that much of the possibly beneficial knowledge of traditional healers has been lost. It seemed many of the traditional healers had very little training and instead just „took up the business" and started prescribing this or that herb to people who came to them. With such a low level of basic education, people didn't seem to ask too many questions. In our hospital we saw a lot of cases of poisoning from herbal medicines, many that people self-prescribed and many that were prescribed by traditional healers. As a Western doctor who appreciates some of the incredible potential of herbal medicines, I was disappointed that most of the traditional healers in Liberia right now seem to be hacks. One form of traditional healer – the bone setter – was very well respected. In six months in Harper I didn't see any patients with broken bones. They all went to the traditional bone setter instead. I saw their handy work once or twice and it was a disaster that likely results in bad outcomes for the patients. Still, when better alternatives are so often unavailable as they were in most of Liberia, having someone to go to for help makes sense." Aussage des Arztes Andrew Schechtman, Field coordinator, MSF France, J. J. Dossen Memorial Hospital, Maryland County, Liberia, 31. Juli 2004.

Ohne die Hilfe der Geister zu beschwören, wären sie auch nicht in der Lage, den Grund eines Übels oder einer Krankheit zu diagnostizieren oder zu entscheiden, welche Kräuter in einer Medizin zu verwenden sind. Durch Träume und andere Methoden der Kommunikation mit den Geistern werden sie erfahren, wo in der Natur sie bestimmte Wurzeln und Pflanzen finden, die sie dann der Anleitung der Geister entsprechend, als Medizin benutzen."[29]

Es wurden einige Fälle bekannt, in denen man später medizinisch nachgewiesene Verhaltensstörungen junger Menschen zunächst als Ruf der Ahnen fehlinterpretierte. Familienmitglieder brachten einen Angehörigen zu einem traditionellen Heiler, weil sie bestimmte „Auffälligkeiten" seines Verhaltens nicht mit einem Krankheitsbild in Verbindung brachten, sondern glaubten, dass der / die Angehörige dazu bestimmt sei, ein traditioneller Heiler oder Wahrsager zu werden. Interessanterweise soll in einigen Fällen sogar eine Besserung des Gesundheitszustands eingetreten sein, nachdem der Patient als traditioneller Heiler initiiert worden ist.[30]

Krankheit und die Bedeutung traditioneller Medizin

In ihrer Studie „Bringing Epilepsy out of the shadows in Africa"[31] veröffentlicht die Genfer Weltgesundheitsorganisation WHO, dass die konservativ geschätzten drei bis vier Millionen Menschen, die in Afrika an Epilepsie erkrankt sind, oft zusätzlich unter sozialer und kultureller Stigmatisierung leiden. Bis zu 80% der epileptischen Erkrankungen blieben in Afrika unbehandelt. In sehr vielen Fällen liegen die Gründe hierfür nicht nur im ökonomischen, sondern auch im sozialen Bereich. Mythen und Aberglauben umgeben die Krankheit Epilepsie, denn in vielen afrikanischen Kulturen wird sie mit „bösen Geistern" in Verbindung gebracht. In Kamerun z. B. glaubt man noch heute, dass Menschen, die unter Epilepsie leiden, vom Teufel besessen sind. Nicht die Menschen selbst seien „böse", sondern ein Teufel fahre von Zeit zu Zeit in sie und verursache so die krampfhaften Zuckungen. In Liberia, wie auch in vielen anderen Teilen Afrikas, bringt man Epilepsie mit „Hexerei" und bösen Geistern in Verbindung. Die meisten der traditionellen Heiler Swazilands nannten Zauberei als Grund dieser Erkrankung. Ein Feind des Patienten sende Geister, um in den Körper einzudringen und die Krämpfe zu verursachen. Solche Missinterpretationen führten dazu, dass die Mehrheit der Afrikaner, die die Symptome der Krankheit zeigten und eigentlich eine solide Diagnose und Behandlung benötigten, keinen (schul-) medizinischen Beistand suchten. Vielmehr würden die meisten einen traditionellen Heiler aufsuchen, der ihnen aber weder helfen könne die Krankheit loszuwerden noch sie zu kontrollieren.

---

29 Interview mit dem Arzt Frikkie Kellerman, der 10 Jahre als District-Doctor in einem Krankenhaus in Venda arbeitete. Durban, Rep. Südafrika, 04. Oktober 2002.

30 Interview mit Peter Geschiere, 25. November 2003 im Rijksmuseum voor Volkenkunde, National Museum of Ethnology, Leiden, Niederlande.

31 „Bringing Epilepsy out of the shadows in Africa", World Health Organization Pressreport No. 30, Genf, 4. Mai 2000, S.1. Im Report von 2004 beziffert WHO die Anzahl der in Afrika an Epilepsie Erkrankten sogar mit 10 Millionen: „Epilepsy in the African region", the cultural context, S. 10-14. In Liberia beispielsweise dürfen an Epilepsie erkrankte Frauen ihre Wäsche nicht mit den anderen Frauen gemeinsam waschen, sie dürfen nicht heiraten und werden auch von traditionellen Feierlichkeiten ausgeschlossen.

Abb. 3: Ein Experte der staatlichen Kulturbehörde für traditionelle Religion, Medizin, Alltagskultur und auch „witchcraft" im Gespräch bei Dreharbeiten in Polokwane / Limpopo Province, Südafrika, Oktober 2003. Im Film bei 13.16 ´min im O-ton sagt er: „We Africans believe in witchcraft, whether you are a christian or not ... educated or not .... very much!" Foto: Becker / occasione documentaries.

Ein weiterer Grund, der dem Renommee der traditionellen Heiler geschadet hat, ist, dass bis vor 20 oder 30 Jahren Sangomas und Inyangas für gewöhnlich an einem Ort praktizierten. Sie waren bei der Bevölkerung im Umland bekannt, genossen Ansehen und Reputation durch die Menschen in dieser Gegend. Sie wurden damals nur bezahlt, wenn ihre Vorhersage dem Klienten eine Lösung bot, oder seine / ihre Therapie die gewünschte Wirkung zeigte und wurden in Naturalien bezahlt. Heute praktizieren traditionelle Heiler oft dort, wo viele Menschen sind, um ihre Dienste möglichst gewinnbringend anzubieten. Allein in und um Johannesburg soll es 10.000 von ihnen geben.[32]

Viele traditionelle Heiler verlangen heute ihre Bezahlung im Voraus. In der Anonymität der Großstadt fliegen Scharlatane nicht so schnell auf wie in ländlichen Gegenden. Die Sogwirkung der Metropolen, verursacht vor allem durch Arbeitsmigration, sorgt dafür, dass ständig neue Kunden aus ländlichen Gegenden in die Städte abwandern. Auch und vor allem dort, d. h. in der Fremde, benötigt man spirituellen Schutz oder Beratung. Sich auf Dauer von seinem gewohnten Umfeld zu entfernen, von Menschen, Tieren, Pflanzen, der Landschaft, in der man geboren wurde, bedeutet nach traditionellem Verständnis „krank" zu werden. Um sich vor den „spirituellen" Auswirkungen, d. h. in erster Linie Gefahren zu schützen, benötigt man die Hilfe eines traditionellen Heilers, der den Schutz in gewissen Abständen erneuern muss.[33]

---

32 Dirk KOHNERT: „Magie und Hexerei in Zeiten der Globalisierung", SWR 2 Radiobeitrag vom 04. Januar 2004, Manuskriptseite 4.
33 Harriet NGUBANE: The Predicament of the sinister Healer, some Observations on „Ritual Murder" and the role of the Inyanga, in: International African Institute: Seminar on Professionalisation of African Medicine, Gaborone, September 1983, S. 3.

Isanusi – ein spirituelles Medium

Der Autor hatte im Oktober 2003 die seltene Gelegenheit, in Südafrika ein Interview mit einem Isanusi (Inyanga yezulu) einer hochrangigen Form eines Sangoma, aufzuzeichnen. Vusa' Mazulu Mutwa ist ein bekannter traditioneller Heiler, ein spirituelles Medium und religiöse Identifikationsfigur. Als Isanusi ist er ein prominenter Repräsentant indigener Medizin und Religion, seit mehr als 60 Jahren ein geachteter und von vielen verehrter traditioneller Heiler der Zulu und anderer Ethnien im Süden Afrikas. Die folgenden Auszüge eines knapp dreistündigen Interviews sollen einen Einblick in die unterschiedlichen Tätigkeitsbereiche eines Sangoma bzw. Isanusi geben. Sie dokumentieren Mutwas eigenen Selektionsprozess und seine persönliche Erfahrung mit rituellen Verbrechen.

Mutwa:

> „Ich wurde am 21. Juli 1921 geboren und bin seit 1937 traditioneller Heiler. Ein Sangoma, wie ich es bin, wird in jungen Jahren von einer einzigartigen Krankheit befallen, die wir *thwasa* nennen, die westliche Mediziner aber nicht diagnostizieren können. Sie erhalten den Ruf ihrer Ahnen. Im Verlauf dieser Krankheit werden sie Dinge „sehen", bevor sie geschehen. Wenn zum Beispiel Leute zu Ihnen kommen wollen, werden sie das spüren, bevor es ihnen jemand sagt. Diese und andere Gaben entwickeln sie im Laufe der Jahre. Sie werden Zugang zu diesem Wissen erlangen. Sie werden lernen, wie man heilende Medizin zubereitet. Ihre Lehrmeister werden ihnen zeigen, wie sie diese und andere Fähigkeiten entwickeln und verfeinern.
>
> Sir, ich weiß nicht, ob sie das wissen und welche Bedeutung es für Sie hat. Aber wussten Sie, dass ich der Anführer von 25.000 traditionellen Heilern in Süden Afrikas bin? Von Männern und Frauen, die heilen. Von Männern und Frauen, die z. B. gegen AIDS kämpfen, genauso, wie ich das auch tue? Ich möchte Ihnen das nicht in allen Einzelheiten schildern, ich möchte Ihnen nur schildern, wer ich bin und was ich tue. Wir wissen, dass es dunkle Praktiken hier in Afrika gibt, genauso wie übrigens auch in Europa und den USA. Wir kämpfen gegen diese dunklen Mächte seit vielen, vielen Jahren. Es geschieht hier sehr oft, Menschen sind besessen, werden zu wahnsinnigen Mördern oder sogar Serienkillern. Eine unserer Aufgaben als traditionelle Heiler ist es, diese Menschen zu heilen, ihnen zu helfen, wenn wir können. Manchmal können wir sie heilen, manchmal nicht. Von bösen Geistern besessen zu sein, kommt häufiger vor, vor allem in diesen Zeiten. Menschen werden aus dem einen oder anderen Grund verrückt, versuchen andere zu töten. Wir leben hier unter schwierigen gesellschaftlichen Bedingungen, mit einer hohen Verbrechensrate und großer Arbeitslosigkeit. Die Leute leiden sehr stark unter diesen Einflüssen und manche entwickeln deshalb schwere Störungen.
>
> Als Sangoma habe ich an einer Reihe von Austreibungen böser Geister teilgenommen, von denen Menschen besessen waren. Und ich sage Ihnen – ich kann solche Prozeduren noch immer nicht ausstehen! Sehen Sie, es gab z. B. diesen Mann, der von einer sehr seltsamen und bösen Angewohnheit befallen war: Er ist verhaftet worden, weil er Kinder übel zugerichtet hatte, indem er auf ihren Händen herumkaute. In einigen Fällen hatte er Kinder schwer verletzt durch diese gefährliche Angewohnheit, die Hände der Kinder essen zu wollen. Ich wurde zusammen mit anderen Sangomas gerufen, um mit dieser Person den Grund für sein Verhalten herauszufinden.
>
> Wir entdeckten, dass er von einem kannibalischen Geist besessen war, dem bösen Geist eines weit entfernten Vorfahren, der mehrere Generationen vor ihm gelebt haben muss. Es war genau diese gemeine Kreatur, die das Problem dieses Mannes verursachte, denn dieser böse Geist wollte sich noch immer an menschlichem Fleisch weiden. In einer Zeremonie entfachten die anderen sieben Sagomas und ich um uns herum viele Feuer. Wir brachten den Geist des Vorfahren zum Vorschein, um festzustellen, wer in dem Mann sei und trieben ihn an-

schließend aus. Eine dunkle Wolke und ein entsetzlicher Gestank stiegen aus dem Mann auf, den wir dann seiner Wege schickten. Er war danach völlig normal.[34] Oft sind wir mit unserer Arbeit erfolgreich und können einem Menschen zurück in ein normales Leben verhelfen. Das ist es, was ein Izanusi, ein Sangoma oder ein Inyanga tut, je nach Art des Problems. Manchmal können wir einer Person auch nicht helfen und sie endet in einer geschlossenen Anstalt."

Becker:

„Könnten Sie diesen Prozess noch etwas näher beschreiben? Wie helfen Sie in solchen Fällen?"

Mutwa:

„Das hängt sehr stark von der betroffenen Person ab. Lassen Sie uns annehmen, dass eine Person zu mir kommt, die besessen ist, die sich von einem bösen Geist oder Macht bedroht fühlt. Ich werde mein gesamtes Wissen zum Kampf gegen diese Macht einsetzen. Lassen sie mich noch etwas mehr berichten, von dem was wir tun: Wenn bei den Zulu ein Mörder einen Menschen getötet hat, werden wir dem Mörder, wenn wir ihn fangen konnten, die Augen verbinden und ihm mehr als zehnmal die Hände gründlich waschen. Anschließend bringen wir ihn an einen entlegenen Ort, an dem eine Frau zu Hause, auf traditionelle Weise, ein Kind zur Welt bringt. In dem Moment, in dem das Kind zur Welt kommt, werden wir sehr vorsichtig und mit allem Respekt gegenüber der Mutter und dem Kind, das Neugeborene und die Plazenta für einen Augenblick in die Hände des Mörders legen. Folgendes wird daraufhin geschehen: Wir werden sehen, dass der Mörder daraufhin sehr krank werden wird. Zunächst nehmen wir ihm das Baby aus den Händen, danach die Augenbinde ab. Er sieht die Frau, die soeben ein Kind zur Welt gebracht hat, er wird ihr Blut sehen, und schließlich wird er nach draußen rennen und sich die Seele aus dem Leib kotzen. Er wird niemals mehr einen anderen Menschen töten! Serienkiller haben sich vom Leben abgewandt, und wenn wir sie in dieser Form mit dem entstehenden Leben konfrontieren, wird das ihr Wesen verändern. Wenigstens bei einigen ist das so geschehen. Die Mehrheit derer, die ich so behandelt habe, hat sich verändert, sie wurden bessere Menschen.

Wenn ein Soldat aus dem Krieg nach Hause kommt, ich meine einen richtigen Kämpfer, ist er besessen vom Geist des Tötens. Er wird plötzlich, und manchmal ohne Grund, sehr zornig werden. Er schlägt dann seine Frau, seine Kinder oder andere in seiner Umgebung. Nun, was tun wir in einer solchen Situation mit so einem Soldaten? Auch ihn konfrontieren wir mit dem Leben! Wenn die Zulu-Krieger früher aus der Schlacht nach Hause kehrten, wurden sie an einem bestimmten Ort drei Monate lang isoliert, sie wurden von ihren Familien ferngehalten. An diesem Ort sollten sie sich innerlich vom Krieg reinigen, bevor sie zu ihren Familien zurückkehrten. Sie waren angefüllt mit dem Geist des Tötens. Das, was sie auf dem Schlachtfeld ihren Feinden angetan haben, tun manche Krieger den eigenen Familienmitgliedern an. Sehen Sie, das ist nur eines dieser sehr schwer wiegenden Probleme, mit denen wir uns als traditionelle Heiler befassen. Es ist Teil unserer Arbeit. Wenn einer dieser Menschen zu uns kommt, werden wir versuchen, ihm zu helfen, das ist unsere Pflicht. Wenn er unsere Hilfe nicht will, gut, dann lassen wir ihn in Ruhe. Ich habe diese Praktiken mit der Hilfe von Frauen durchgeführt, die ein Kind geboren haben, aber selbst mit Tieren, also Ziegen oder Schafen, die ein Junges zur Welt brachten. Ich kann ihnen jedenfalls sagen, dass ein Mörder es nicht ertragen wird, wenn in seiner Anwesenheit ein Leben zur Welt gebracht wird. Er begreift sich in diesem Moment als das, was er ist: eine schreckliche, mordende Bestie!"[35]

---

34 Vgl. Vusa Mazulu MUTWA: Sangoma´s Lore of the Soul, in: African Legal Studies, Volume II., 2001, Special Issue: Witchcraft Violence and the Law, Faculty of Law, University of the North, Rep. of South Africa, S. 64f.

35 Eigenes Interview mit Vusa' Mazulu Mutwa in Südafrikas Gauteng Province, 25. Oktober 2003.

Negative Auswirkungen der Kolonialgesetzgebung

Die britische Kolonialverwaltung versuchte, den traditionellen afrikanischen Glauben an übernatürliche Wesen, an Geister und spirituelle Kräfte – also Aberglaube, der ihrer Ansicht nach nicht mit dem spirituellen Gedankengut der Bibel übereinstimmte – durch ein Gesetz zu unterdrücken und auszulöschen. Dieses Vorhaben ist gründlich gescheitert und trug dazu bei, dass über die ursprünglich getrennte Aufgabenverteilung verschiedener traditioneller Heiler große Unklarheit herrscht. Eine „neue Art" traditioneller Heiler entstand, die durch das Gesetz nur gezwungen wurde, sich als Inyanga registrieren zu lassen, obwohl sie auch die Tätigkeit eines Sangoma ausübte. Die unterschiedslose Kriminalisierung traditioneller Heiler verkennt die deutliche Mehrheit der Inyangas und Sangomas. Der Polizeiexperte Labuschagne berichtet:

> „Die weitaus größte Mehrheit der traditionellen Heiler und auch der Bevölkerung distanziert sich strikt von dieser Abart traditioneller afrikanischer Medizin. Die Heiler, die solche Praktiken anwenden, sind nicht Teil des „main streams" traditioneller afrikanischer Medizin. Es ist aber sicher, dass die traditionellen Heiler, die in Muti Mordfälle verwickelt waren, in ihrer Umgebung als Heiler bekannt waren und auch als solche praktizierten. Muti Morde gibt es in Afrika südlich der Sahara schon seit Jahrhunderten. Aber niemand könnte wirklich den genauen Zeitpunkt nennen, wann das alles begann. Das Konzept, das hinter einem solchen Mord steckt, ist, einem lebenden Menschen Körperteile zu entnehmen, die man dann anschließend als Bestandteil für eine okkulte „Medizin" in dieser Abart der traditionellen Medizin benutzt. Ich glaube, manche Klienten wissen gar nicht, was genau in ihrer Muti Medizin enthalten ist. Oft werden natürlich sie als Erstes verhaftet, wenn sie im Besitz von „Muti Medizin" sind, die menschliche Körperteile enthält. Das lässt sich auf Anhieb nicht immer sofort erkennen, denn oft benutzen die Täter sie in pulverisierter Form oder gemischt mit anderen Bestandteilen. Es gibt aber auch Fälle, wo die Kunden eine komplette menschliche Hand erhalten haben, z. B. ein Geschäftsmann, der erfolgreich sein will, und dem gesagt wird, er solle die Hand unter der Türschwelle vergraben. Es gibt also durchaus Fälle, wo die Kunden sehr wohl wissen, dass es sich um menschliche Körperteile handelt, die ihr Schicksal beeinflussen sollen. Doch oft sind die Körperteile verarbeitet mit anderen Bestandteilen und in eine gänzlich andere Form gebracht, sodass der Kunde das nicht notwendigerweise erkennen muss.
>
> Lassen sie mich den üblichen Prozess, nach dem so etwas abläuft, einmal folgendermaßen beschreiben: Ein Klient oder Kunde hat einen präzisen Wunsch oder ein Problem. Dieser Klient geht zu einem Sangoma, sagt ihm, dass er in einem bereits geplanten Geschäft ökonomischen Erfolg garantieren will. Er wird ihm sagen, `hier ist mein Problem, was kann ich tun, damit ich in der bevorstehenden Situation z. B. wirtschaftlich erfolgreich bin?´ Der Heiler wird entscheiden, ob für diese Angelegenheit eine einfache Zeremonie reicht, also möglicherweise Pflanzen oder Tiere geopfert werden müssen, oder im Extremfall eben auch menschliche Körperteile benutzt werden. Diese Entscheidung liegt ganz im Ermessen des traditionellen Heilers oder eben eines Scharlatans, der sich nur als solcher ausgibt und auf schnellen Profit aus ist.
>
> Der Heiler geht dann zu einem seiner „Lehrlinge" oder einem, dem er vertraut, und wird ihn im schlimmsten Fall losschicken, um einen bestimmten Teil eines menschlichen Körpers auf eine klar definierte Art und Weise zu besorgen und ihm diesen unverzüglich zurückzubringen. Der Heiler / Sangoma / Scharlatan bereitet aus diesem Körperteil eines Menschen und möglicherweise weiteren Bestandteilen eine „Muti Medizin" zu und gibt sie gegen Bezahlung dem Kunden mit dem Versprechen, das bei korrekter Anwendung sein Problem gelöst werden würde oder sein Wunsch in Erfüllung gehe. Bei Übergabe wird der Heiler den Klienten

genau instruieren, wie er diese „Muti Medizin" richtig anwenden muss. Ist der tatsächliche Mörder ein Gehilfe des Sangomas, so ist dieser Mord sozusagen Teil der „Ausbildung" des Gehilfen. Andernfalls kann die Motivation des Mörders ein pures materielles Bedürfnis sein, also schnell an verhältnismäßig viel Geld zu kommen. Der eigentliche Mörder glaubt dann möglicherweise selbst gar nicht an die „Heilkraft" oder Macht menschlicher Körperteile, begeht diesen Mord nur im „Auftrag" des Heilers, seine Motivation ist rein ökonomischer Art.

Wir wissen aber inzwischen aus unserer Erfahrung, dass die Opfer oft gewisse Merkmale aufweisen oder Voraussetzungen erfüllen. In sehr vielen Fällen sind es genau diese Merkmale oder körperlichen Voraussetzungen, nach denen die Klienten der Heiler suchten. Wenn sie beispielsweise einen Muti Mordfall betrachten, in dem der Klient ein Berufsspieler war, der lange Zeit eine Pechsträhne hatte, der deshalb auf der Suche nach „mehr Glück" war, suchten die Mörder als Opfer eine Person, die viel Glück zu haben schien. In diesem konkreten Fall verhaftete man auf einer Pferderennbahn einen Mann, der einen Verwandten getötet hatte. In seiner Jackentasche trug er die Geschlechtsorgane seines Neffen. Offensichtlich erschien der Neffe dem Onkel als jemand, der viel Glück hat.

Der „traditionelle Heiler" oder Scharlatan sagt dem eigentlichen Mörder, dass er beispielsweise die Brüste oder Fettgewebe einer jungen Frau benötige oder diesen oder jenen besonderen Körperteil eines Menschen. Es gibt eine Reihe Kriterien, nach denen das Opfer ausgewählt wird. Offensichtlich wird zuerst das benötigte Körperteil definiert, je nach den Bedürfnissen des Klienten, dann versuchen die Täter ein Opfer zu finden, das dieses spezielle Merkmal aufweist. Nochmals, wir beginnen diese Fragen erst allmählich zu erforschen. Soweit wir das bislang verstehen, wird der Mörder eine bestimmte Person eine Zeit lang beobachten und im Fall positiver Übereinstimmung mit den Bedürfnissen des Klienten dieses Opfer gezielt aussuchen. Es kann jemand sein, den der Mörder bereits kennt, vielleicht sogar jemand aus dem engeren oder erweiterten Familienkreis. Vielleicht führen körperliche Voraussetzungen dazu, dass der Mörder auf eine bestimmte Person aufmerksam wurde. Oder, unter gewissen Umständen, besondere Verhaltensmuster. Jedenfalls muss ein bestimmtes Anforderungsprofil durch das Opfer erfüllt werden, das für die Belange des Klienten von einem traditionellen Heiler zuvor erstellt wurde."[36]

Welche Fähigkeiten hat ein Sangoma – oder gibt er vor zu haben?

Schon jetzt lässt sich festhalten, dass die verschiedenen Formen traditioneller Heiler offensichtlich eine Schlüsselfunktion in den Gesellschaften im südlichen Afrika einnehmen. Obwohl es südlich der Sahara sicher bedeutende regionale Unterschiede in der Klassifizierung, den Behandlungsmethoden und der sozialen Anerkennung traditioneller Heiler gibt, lassen sich einige wichtige Gemeinsamkeiten innerhalb dieser Berufsgruppe zeigen. Eine Beurteilung ihrer Fähigkeiten aus rein westlich pragmatischer Sicht scheint jedoch zumindest problematisch, denn ein traditioneller Heiler kann seine Kenntnisse und Fähigkeiten zum Wohl der Menschen einsetzen, ihnen aber auch Schaden zufügen, wie noch anhand einiger Beispiele gezeigt werden wird. Die rein medizinische Versorgung einzelner Personen kann ebenso zum Aufgabengebiet eines traditionellen Heilers gehören, wie die Beratung einer ganzen Gemeinschaft; die Behandlung körperlicher Gebrechen ebenso wie die Hilfe in schwierigen Lebensabschnitten (Geburt, Initiation, Heirat, Tod). Die Basis ihrer medizinischen und spirituellen Fähigkeiten entstammt je-

---

36 Eigenes Interview mit Dr. Gérard Labuschagne, Investigative Psychology Unit, SAPS, Pretoria 6. Oktober 2002.

doch der Kenntnis der traditionellen afrikanischen Medizin und damit eng verbunden auch der traditionellen afrikanischen Religion sowie dem außerhalb der Familie erlernten oder auch innerhalb der Familie vererbten Umgang mit „übernatürlichen Kräften".

Man könnte traditionelle Heiler vermutlich am ehesten als Vermittler oder Agenten zwischen der physischen und der spirituellen Welt definieren.[37] Da für die Heilung eines körperlichen Gebrechens oder für die Beratung einer Familie in einer kritischen Situation die Kommunikation mit Geistern oder den Geistern ihrer Ahnen notwendig werden kann, steht man ihnen im Westen im günstigsten Fall nur skeptisch gegenüber. Die Verständnislosigkeit mancher Afrikaner gegenüber dieser Skepsis oder gar schroffen Ablehnung gegenüber dem traditionellen Heiler seitens der Europäer wird in diesem Vorwort deutlich:

> „Der Begriff *Hexendoktor* wird (von Europäern, Anm. des Autors) oft sehr frei benutzt, fast synonym mit dem `Hexe´ oder dem `Zauberer´. Das ist etwa so, als würde man den Polizisten oder den Detektiv mit dem Kriminellen gleichsetzten. Es mag Hexendoktoren geben, die Scharlatane sind, so, wie es auch unehrenhafte Beamte oder korrupte Polizisten gibt. Aber alles in allem ist der Hexendoktor eine Kraft, die auf der Seite des Gesetzes steht. Es ist unverständlich, warum in einem Glaubenssystem, bei dem der Glaube an `Hexerei´ fest im Bewusstsein der Bevölkerung verankert ist, der Hexendoktor überflüssig sein sollte. Seine Aufgabe ist es Verbrechen herauszufinden und zu verhindern, die Täter vor Gericht zu bringen. Kein Afrikaner würde jemals diese beiden Figuren durcheinanderbringen: den Hexendoktor – also einen Inyanga / Sagoma – und den Hexer oder Zauberer `Mchawi´ oder `Umtagati´."[38]

> „Es hängt davon ab, was Sie mit dem Zauber erreichen wollen. Lassen Sie mich von etwas berichten, etwas, was ich selbst getan habe. Vor vielen Jahren gab es in Soweto eine Reihe schlimmer Unruhen. Meine Frau wurde damals von neun jungen Männern vergewaltigt! Ich werde ihnen die Wahrheit nicht verschweigen, ich werde ihnen jetzt sagen, was ich damals getan habe. Ich habe damals diese neun Männer verhext. Sie sind anschließend gestorben! Alle, einer nach dem anderen. Ich verhexte sie durch den Körper meiner Frau, und sie starben alle daran. Sie brauchen die Einzelheiten nicht zu wissen, aber ich habe Puppen angefertigt, bildhafte Darstellungen, die diesen verhassten Personen in Gestalt und Aussehen sehr ähnlich waren. Ich sagte meiner Frau, nachdem ich die Puppen verhext hatte, sie solle diese Puppen mit Honig einschmieren und sie anschließend vergraben. Alle neun Männer starben daraufhin, einer nach dem anderen. Alle starben sie, und sie verdienten es so! Das ist es, was wir Sangomas tun können, wenn es notwendig ist."[39]

Diese Beispiele mögen als Hinweise dienen, welche Rolle traditionelle Heiler im Zusammenhang mit Berichten über okkulte Gewalt und bestimmten Verbrechensformen spielen. Warum ließ Mutwa damals seine Frau auf die von ihm angefertigten Bildnisse der Täter Honig schmieren, nachdem er die Puppen „verhext" hatte und bevor seine Frau

---

37 „A traditional healer is defined as an educated or lay person who claims an ability or a healing power to cure ailments, or a particular skill to treat specific types of complaints or afflictions and who might have gained a reputation in his own community or elsewhere. They may base their powers or practice on religion, the supernatural, experience, apprenticeship or family heritage. Traditional healers may be males or females and are usually mature." In: World Health Organization: Characteristics of visitors to traditional healers in central Sudan, International Publication Vol. 5, Issue 1, Genf, 1999, S. 79.
38 Alice WERNER: Myths and Legends of the Bantu, Chapter XVI: Doctors, Prophets and Witches, 1933.
39 Eigenes Interview mit Vusá Mazulu Mutwa, Gauten Province, Rep. Südafrika, 25. Oktober 2003.

die Puppen vergrub? Die Verwendung bildlicher Darstellungen oder Puppen, die von einer Person angefertigt werden, um dem betreffenden Opfer durch Magie aus sicherer Distanz zu schaden, hat in Afrika eine lange Tradition. Man verwendet für diese Form des Schadenszaubers noch heute z. B. eine Haarsträhne, abgeschnittene Fingernägel, im Falle einer Vergewaltigung auch die Samenflüssigkeit des Vergewaltigers oder auch Exkremente derer, denen man schaden will. Bildliche Darstellungen oder Puppen von Personen, die man durch solche Formen okkulter Aggression angreifen will, werden mit biologischen Abfällen des Betreffenden versehen, um die Objekte zu personifizieren. Anschließend belegt man diese Objekte mit einem Fluch, der durch das Symbol der personifizierten Puppe auf den realen Feind übertragen werden soll.

> „Die klare Reinheit, Natürlichkeit und Süße des Honigs solle den Fluch, der auf den Puppen liegt, verbergen. Gegnerische Geister sollten so vom eigentlichen Ziel, d. h. dem Tod der Vergewaltiger aus der Entfernung durch Magie, abgelenkt werden" [40]

„Hexer" und „Hexendoktor" sind Protagonist und Antagonist des gleichen Systems: Beide haben sie, dieser traditionellen Vorstellung folgend, vergleichbare Fähigkeiten. Doch der eine nutzt sie zum Heilen, während der andere sie einsetzt, um jemandem zu schaden oder ihn sogar zu töten. Das Zulu-Wort „Inyanga" kann viele verschiedene Bedeutungen haben. Es bezeichnet eine Person, die mit besonderem Wissen oder Fähigkeiten ausgestattet ist. Ein Schmied z. B. wäre demnach ein Inyanga yensimbi, ein „Doktor des Eisens". Ein Inyanga kann also ein Wahrsager (engl. „diviner"), ein Heilkundiger (engl. „herbalist") oder beides zur gleichen Zeit sein, möglicherweise auch ein Seher oder Prophet. Aus dieser Perspektive lässt sich bereits erahnen, warum traditionelle Heiler insgesamt und oft zu Unrecht mit Muti Morden in Verbindung gebracht werden.

Die Auseinandersetzung mit Muti Morden: ein statistisches Problem oder Panikmache der Medien?

Wann immer die Auseinandersetzung mit Muti Morden in Afrikas Sub-Sahara erfolgt, stellt sich unmittelbar auch die Frage nach der Häufigkeit dieser Verbrechen. Sorgen die Berichte sensationslüsterner Medien für eine Überbewertung von „Einzelfällen"?

Offizielle Schätzungen gehen von 70 bis 100 Muti Morden pro Jahr allein in der Republik Südafrika aus. Gemessen an den knapp 20.000 Morden[41], die pro Jahr in diesem Land verübt werden, sind das nur ca. 0,5% aller Morde. Doch Experten[42] der Polizei (SAPS) und südafrikanische Verbrechensforscher lieferten gleich mehrere Argumente, warum man vermutlich von einer höheren Dunkelziffer ausgehen muss:

In der Vergangenheit, d. h. bis in die 80er Jahre, tauchten Muti Morde nicht gesondert in der Mordstatistik auf. Das ist offiziell zwar immer noch der Fall, doch existieren inzwischen die Berichte verschiedener Wissenschaftskommissionen, die sich im Auftrag der Regierung Südafrikas ausschließlich der Erforschung von Verbrechen mit okkultem

---

40 Eignes Interview mit Anthony Minnaar, Pretoria, Rep. Südafrika, 23. Oktober 2003.
41 South African Police Service, Official Crime Statistic 2003/2004.
42 Interviews zwischen 2002-2004 mit A. Minnaar, G. Labuschagne, K. Jonker.

Abb. 4: Masken vor dem Haus eines Muti Mörders in der Limpopo-Provinz. Der Fall ist insofern einzigartig, da der Mörder die Tat selbst gestanden hat und bis heute nicht leugnet. In diesem Ausnahmefall war der traditionelle Heiler auch der eigentliche Mörder. Foto: Becker / occasione documentaries.

Hintergrund widmeten.[43] Die klimatischen Bedingungen in diesem Land sorgen dafür, dass Leichen schnell verwesen. Wilde Tiere in den ruralen Gebieten verschleppen gelegentlich Teile von Mordopfern. Sollten Leichen am oder im Wasser liegen, können sie durch das Wasser selbst oder den Befall von Fischen und Krebsen entstellt werden. Schon nach kurzer Zeit lässt sich in diesen Fällen anhand der Begutachtung des Leichnams nicht mehr zweifelsfrei beurteilen, ob ein Muti Mord vorliegt oder nicht.

Hinzu kommt der Umstand, dass Angehörige in ländlichen Regionen ihre Verwandten der Polizei nicht unbedingt als vermisst melden, auch wenn diese sich ein oder zwei Jahre nicht bei ihnen melden. Es ist nicht ungewöhnlich, dass junge Männer und Frauen, z. B. aus dem schwach entwickelten Norden in die großen Städte des Südens reisen, um dort auf Arbeitssuche zu gehen.[44]

Schließlich gab es in der Vergangenheit Fälle, in denen Polizeioffiziere der ländlichen Regionen Muti Mordfälle nicht als solche auswiesen, die Ermittlungen nur zögernd betrieben oder gar nach kurzer Zeit einstellten, aus Angst in okkulte Zusammenhänge verwickelt zu werden und anschließend von der Vergeltung eines traditionellen Heilers in Form von Schadenszauber in ihrer Region betroffen zu sein.

Muti Morde erscheinen aus heutiger Sicht besonders grausam und sind doch weder „gewöhnliche" Verbrechen noch die Taten Wahnsinniger. Die extremste Form okkulter Gewalt repräsentiert auf drastische Weise den Konflikt von Markt und Moderne mit der Schattenseite traditioneller Glaubenssysteme im Süden Afrikas.

---

43 Der Le Roux Report und Ralushai Report gehören zu derartigen Berichten (wie Anm. 2). Nicht zuletzt als Antwort auf die gestiegenen Anzahl der Muti Morde ab Mitte der 80er Jahre wurde 1992 die „Occult related Crimes Unit" gegründet, eine Einheit der Polizei SAPS, die sich sowohl mit der Aufklärung von „witchcraft related crimes" als auch „occult related crimes" befasst.

44 Im Sommer und Herbst 2003 vergewaltigte und tötete ein Serientäter in der Gauteng Province 13 junge Frauen. Elf von ihnen wurden nicht identifiziert, da sie vermutlich aus der Grenzregion im Norden stammten oder aus Simbabwe eingewandert waren und ihre Verwandten dort glaubten, sie seien auf Arbeitssuche.

Joan Wardrop

"The witch. She is in her house" – „We don't have witches here. Not in Soweto"

Soweto witchcraft accusations in the transition from apartheid through liberation to democracy[1]

Zusammenfassung

1994 und 1995 registrierte und diskutierte die Polizeieinheit von Soweto („Soweto Flying Squad"), die zur Aufklärung von Schwerverbrechen im größten schwarzen Township in Südafrika eingesetzt war, einen Anstieg der Zahl der Anklagen, Vorfälle und Hilfeersuchen von auf Hexerei bezogenen Delikten. In dieser Zeit des Übergangs und der tiefen kulturellen Verunsicherung tauchten in dieser Atmosphäre in Soweto oft Konflikte und Anliegen auf, die während der Apartheid-Zeit unterdrückt worden waren, nun aber häufig auf unerwarteten Wegen an die Oberfläche hochkochten. Sie sind in den zwei widersprüchlichen Aussagen im Titel dieses Aufsatzes enthalten, die von einer Frau mittleren Alters im Abstand von zwei Tagen in der Umgebung des Townships gemacht wurden. In dieser erweiterten Feldforschung mit der „Soweto Flying Squad" nahm die Autorin die Erklärungen und Schilderungen auf, die die örtliche Bevölkerung über die Existenz von ansonsten unerklärlichen Phänomenen und über die Antworten von Nachbarn, Familien, Freuden und Feinden gegenüber den Anklagen gegen bestimmte Personen (größtenteils Frauen)gemacht wurden. Diese Schilderungen beinhalten detaillierte Erklärungen des vielschichtigen Verständnisses des schnellen politischen und sozialen Wandels, denen verschiedene verbundene und oft widersprüchliche Glaubenssysteme zugrundeliegen. Durch die sehr nahe Erfahrung und die hochgradig kontextualisierte ethnographische Untersuchung einiger Ereignisse von 1994-95 erforscht die Autorin die miteinander verschränkten Rollen der Beschreibung, des Geschlechts und der sozialen Schicht in den Hexereiklageprozessen von Soweto.

Abstract

During 1994 and 1995 major-crime emergency response police (Soweto Flying Squad) in the largest black township in South Africa noticed and frequently discussed a rise in the number of witchcraft-related complaints, incidents and requests for assistance. In that time of transition and deep cultural anxiety, the at-

---

[1] The quotations are from two female participants in one of two witch hunting episodes in Soweto, South Africa, explored in more detail below. My own participation occurred as a consequence of extended participant observation fieldwork with the major-crime emergency-response policing unit for the township, the Soweto Flying Squad. I began fieldwork with the unit on 21 March 1994 (Sharpeville Day), before the first democratic election, and continued „to work outside" „in the area" intermittently until July 1998, working just over 250 of their 12-15 hour shifts „on the vehicles" in that time.

mosphere in Soweto was often seething with resentments and concerns which had been suppressed during the apartheid years of oppression but which now bubbled to the surface in often-unexpected ways, exemplified in the two contradictory statements in this paper's title, each made by a middle-aged woman, two days apart in contiguous areas of the township. In doing extended fieldwork with Soweto Flying Squad, the author listened to the explanations and narratives that local people were constructing, both about the existence of otherwise unexplainable phenomena, and about the responses of neighbours, families, friends and enemies, to the accusations made against particular people (most often women). In these narratives lie detailed accounts and understandings of the complex travails of rapid political and social change, underscored by the interwoven and often-contradictory expressions of multiple belief systems. Through an experience-near, highly-contextualised ethnographic examination of several accusatory events from 1994 and 1995, the author explores the interlocking roles of narrative, gender and class, in processes of accusation in Soweto.

The topography of „old Soweto", through Orlando East, Orlando West, Mzimhlope, Dobsonville and Meadowlands, where the displaced communities from Sophiatown were relocated in the 1950s, is hilly, main roads winding round the contour lines, some running down into the valleys of the Klip River and up the other side, wide dusty verges, row after row of low-ceilinged one-storey houses set back from the road, huge Highveld[2] skies, a bare landscape conjuring an overwhelming sense of space. In the mid-1990s trees were few: riding in the back seat of Soweto Flying Squad vehicles I internalised my first way points of the police geography of Soweto by learning to recognise the tall old gum trees on the *dubbelpad*[3] of Mooki Street and up past the Meadowlands[4] hostel, the willows down through Dube and Mofolo, towards the geographical centre of the township and, in individual yards, the odd scraggly, wind-blown trees for which no one could tell me names. The trees, like the street signs, had disappeared during the hard years of the 1976 student uprising and the states of emergency of the 1980s: the trees for fuel and road blocks, the street signs to confuse the Security Forces as they tried to impose control over the township.

To the explicit relief of Flying Squad members and local residents alike, road works signalled one of the first visible changes in Soweto's physical landscape in the weeks and months after the April 1994 elections which brought formal democracy[5] to South Africa: within days piles of sand and stones appeared and road gangs began to tar and

---

2 Soweto lies between 1,600 and 1,700 metres altitude on the open high plain called the Highveld.
3 lit. double road (Afrikaans), road with a wide median strip.
4 Officially known as the Mzimhlope hostel, but more often called (by residents and police) simply Meadowlands.
5 As opposed to the „informal" democracy of the period from about 1985, during which, following the ANC -in-exile's call to „make the townships ungovernable", the formal authority of the apartheid state had largely broken down in many townships, including Soweto, replaced by unofficial local structures such as the „civics" (informal local governance structures), block and street committees, and so forth.

seal some of the dirt or gravel side roads. But street signs were not high on anybody's agenda, certainly not that of the new local government: it had much else to consider as the enormity of the backlog of services such as water and electricity delivery became apparent. Not the police. Members of Soweto Flying Squad prided themselves on „knowing their area," navigating the streets by cataloguing and memorising hundreds and thousands of house numbers, of local landmarks and the locations of previous complaints and significant events in their working lives (such as major vehicle accidents or chases). And not local people, many of whom were vocally expressing continuing uncertainties about „government" and its capacity to misuse power, even though „apartheid has gone" and the new ANC-dominated government promised change.[6]

These uncertainties, intertwined with a pervasive historical sense of insecurity, persisted as an underlying trope: few people, even long-term ANC activists, were confident about what the inauguration of the new government would mean for life in the township. What impact would it have on 40% unemployment rates, on people living eight or ten to a small house, on a welfare/social support system confined essentially to a minuscule old age pension? In „town" (Johannesburg) lifestyle convergences blurred these issues: already in the early 1990s, for some at least, socio-economic status had replaced race as the determinant of job and residence preferences, and a migration of the wealthy and of the well-connected from the township to the formerly-white suburbs had begun. The „tourists" (as they came to be called), detached from „township life," returned perhaps for weddings and funerals, driving BMWs and Mercedes which were noticeably too clean and unscratched to have been long on potholed township roads.

What implications did liberation have for the culture of violence[7] in the township? What did it mean for the tens of thousands of Soweto youth who had been characterised by Nelson Mandela as „the lost generation"[8], who had learned their politics on the streets, in running battles with the Security Forces, stones and sticks against long guns and tear gas? And, after four years of violent contestation between the ANC and the IFP[9], focussed around the huge single-sex migrant-labour hostels, what did the new democracy mean for residents in Meadowlands and Dube, Jabulani, Diepkloof, Merafe and other Soweto locations which bordered on the hostels, who still spent anxious

---

6   African National Congress, the largest of the liberation organisations, and the major partner in the Government of National Unity that was formed in May 1994. A number of police remarked to me that I was lucky („had a luck") to be researching at that time, rather than a year or more earlier because local people were much more willing to express opinions to me at incidents and on the streets.

7   A description that came to be much used from about 1991 onwards, probably coined by Lloyd Vogelman, then Director of the Centre for the Study of Violence (as it then was).

8   See Nancy SCHEPER-HUGHES: Children without childhoods, in: New Internationalist 295 (1995): http://www.newint.org/issue265/children.htm. Also Colin BUNDY: At war with the future? Black South African youth in the 1990s, in: Southern Africa Report Archive Vol 8 No 1 http://www.africa files.org/article.asp?ID=4716

9   Representing the Zulu-based Inkatha Freedom Party's bid for national power in the wake of the unbanning of the ANC in February 1990, this was officially brought to an end in mid-1992 but continued on a lesser, and largely unreported, scale until some months after the 1994 election.

nights in darkness, listening for any sound that might mean that the hostel dwellers were coming, armed with *pangas* (machetes) and *knobkieries* (cudgels)?

As power shifted, new ascriptions unfolded of how „community" might be explicated and new inscriptions emerged of the relationships between the stalwarts of the civics and the street committees (the core structures of the street democracy inculcated by the liberation movement in the 1980s) on the one hand and the rearticulated authority of what township argot continued to refer to as „Pretoria" or „GA" („Government Agent", any government official). New expressions of anxieties and fears about what taxes might now be imposed became apparent; worries about the service charges and rents which few township residents had paid for nearly a decade;[10] new imaginings of what „liberation" might mean for the individual or the community. Indeed, what now was the „community"? In „the old times," when the lines of struggle were clearly delineated, the identifications of „them" and of „us" more precisely perceived, when „enemies", „traitors", *mpimpi* („spies") could be recognised, made known, accused, destroyed, social understandings had been more certain, more clearly defined. In the new South Africa the boundaries had been disturbed, and blurred, made dangerously ambiguous.

The stresses of change

In the search for ways to contextualise outbreaks of witch hunting, accounts and understandings about imaginings of community have provided us with windows through which we can discern the lineaments of cultural expression and cultural anxieties. The literature on the relations between imaginings of community and witchcraft accusations is extensive, and much can be gained by reading across disciplines, regions and periods. The research of Anne Reiber DeWindt, for example, deals with a cultural environment far distant from Soweto in both time and geography, but perhaps not in spirit: the village of Warboys in England's Huntingdonshire in the very late 16th century, a period of substantial social change in outlying rural areas. De Windt describes a rapidly-changing „social landscape" which she argues was a precondition for accusation: „in this case at least, a witchcraft accusation was nurtured within an environment in which neighbours held incompatible expectations about how best to share their community."[11]

While Warboys was subject to an in-migration of gentry which disturbed the village's delicately-balanced class and economic structures, in the 1990s Soweto too was dealing with greatly-increased in-migration, not of the well-to-do but of the poor, landless and workless. Since 1986[12] people had been coming to eGoli (Johannesburg/Soweto: the city of gold), searching for work and for places to stay. In 1994 and 1995, the influx from the former „homelands", from the grinding rural poverty of the former KwaZulu, Transkei and Ciskei[13], was unstoppable. Many Soweto residents took advantage of the de-

---

10 A significant element of the „Struggle" and of the ANC's policy of „making the townships ungovernable" had been the boycott of payment of rent and service charges.
11 Anne REIBER DEWINDT: Witchcraft and conflicting visions of the ideal village community, in: The Journal of British Studies 34, 4 (Oct. 1995), p. 435.
12 When the apartheid Influx Control legislation was repealed, allowing freer movement.
13 Now reshaped and renamed as KwaZulu-Natal, and the Eastern Cape.

mand for living quarters: if they had space and could afford to, they built solid concrete structures in their backyards and rented them to incomers. Others allowed incomers to erect shacks in their yards for a monthly rent. This infill development facilitated very rapid population increases, as did the shack settlements which sprang up on unoccupied land, almost overnight, in many areas of the township. To revisit new shack areas such as Snake Park in the north of the township or the „Chris Hani shacks" behind the Chris Hani Baragwanath Hospital in the south after an absence of only a few days was often a disorienting experience, so many new shacks and alleys would have appeared.

A significant proportion of requests for police assistance in 1994 and 1995 came from „the shacks" and from contiguous areas. At times of tension police often were called to arbitrate disputes between shack dwellers and nearby residents. Police from the four reliefs that made up Flying Squad consciously shared knowledge of such incidents and disputes between the reliefs, reflecting their common understanding that the shacks or areas of high infill were particularly susceptible to violent outbreaks of social tension. But even a „safe" area such as Mzimhlope which was not directly affected either by a large new shack settlement in its immediate area or by large numbers of backyard shacks of the type that were integral to the new social environments of neighbouring Orlando East or Orlando West, could suddenly become a hotbed of localised violence. By late 1994 and early 1995, Mzimhlope residents were articulating a concern that social stability was being threatened: „We never had to call 10111", a woman in some distress at a witchcraft complaint in the area[14] said to me, and a policeman standing nearby agreed: „We never had to come here." Flying Squad police recognised that the changes in Mzimhlope had occurred remarkably rapidly. On three occasions in January and February 1995 when I was „riding on" Flying Squad vehicles which had been called to fighting complaints at local schools I recorded that police had expressed concern and bemusement that something was seriously wrong in this area which, even though it was very close to one of the biggest hostels in the township, previously had been „quiet quiet".[15] What was particularly bewildering for some police was that no one, even local residents, could articulate an explanation which made sense.

Imagined equilibria were precipitously unbalanced, political power had shifted: for residents and for emergency personnel such as police and paramedics who worked in the township alike, the ambiguous, constantly renegotiated lines of social power were now even more difficult to read. Despite the widely-shared expectation that once liberation was achieved the „old problems," of inequitable access to resources, of lack of respect for human dignity, of arbitrary government, would be minimised or even eliminated, in practice finding paths through the maze of newly reshaped relationships was turning out to be just as difficult as deciphering the surreal realities of apartheid had been. As Adam Ashforth recognises: „With the ending of apartheid, profound transformations in everyday life in Soweto began" yet:

14　The complaint is analysed in more detail below; „10111" was the emergency phone number which connected directly with the Soweto Flying Squad radio control room in Protea, in the west of Soweto.

15　The doubling of the word is a common Afrikaans and Zulu usage and indicates emphasis.

Despite the dawning of democracy, then, people were still suffering. Yet the task of interpreting the meaning of misfortune was becoming more complex. Hitherto, the misfortunes of individuals and families in a place like Soweto could be reckoned not only by reference to particular causes by also to a general name hanging over the suffering of all black people - Apartheid. Now, with apartheid gone, the sorrows of an unfair fate could only be measured, case by case, against the conspicuous „progress" and good fortune of particular relatives, colleagues, and neighbours, not to mention the ubiquitous images in the media of black people who had made it, and advertisements tailored to their desires.[16]

As Flying Squad policemen constructed their narratives of their working environment, they traced a reduction in the violent intensity and numbers of the types of confrontations and street clashes they had monitored and policed in the early years of the 1990s. The big street battles, the „war" between the ANC and the IFP, and the mass action demonstrations of anti-apartheid activists had come to an end, but now, in the new democratic South Africa, violent crime rates were escalating rapidly: crimes against property (vehicle hijackings, home invasions, armed robberies) and crimes against people (rapes, assaults, murders).[17] In the police narratives, some criminal acts were understood as deriving from frustrated expectations, from a disappointed „culture of entitlement". Others flowed more directly from the the ready availability of the rapidly-increasing numbers of firearms, both legal and illegal, being carried in the township.[18] Yet local residents and police alike were adamant that although the economic situation played a part in the crime rate, it was not a specific trigger for events such as the two witchcraft accusations on which I focus here. These social and economic circumstances were quite unlike those that Edwin Ritchken deciphers in the northern rural area of the Brooklyn Trust Land in Pedi-speaking Mapulaneng, where „Neighbourly harmony turns to neighbourly conflict as competition over scarce resources increases. In a situation where migrants are losing their jobs or simply not returning to the countryside, access to rural resources becomes a life and death issue."[19] I suggest that the events in Soweto, at least in the explanations developed by local residents and police, resonate more strongly with Max Marwick's „social strain gauge" theory,[20] used to telling effect by Isak Nie-

---

16 Adam ASHFORTH: Madumo: a man bewitched, Chicago, University of Chicago Press 2000, p. 8-9.
17 Crime statistics in South Africa have been and continue to be problematic but those quoted here illustrate the levels of violence in the township. The official SAPS figures for Soweto for the period April 1994-March 1995 (followed for comparison purposes by the 2002-2003 figures in parentheses) indicate: murder: 1,164 (614); attempted murder: 1,523 (990); culpable homicide: 305 (202); aggravated robbery: 5,826(6,501); public violence: 45 (26); rape: 2,525 (1,779); childabuse: 111 (248); kidnapping: 323 (242); abduction: 86 (186); assault (grievous bodily harm) : 7,528 (8,376); common assault: 4,733 (8,972); malicious damage to property: 3,993 (4,891); illegal firearm: 580 (664).http://www.iss.org.za/CJM/stats0903/gtsow2.htm.
18 Under apartheid law before 1994, township residents found obtaining a firearm licence comparatively difficult but this changed after April 1994. Illegal firearms were the most common weapons however, many were police issue which had been stolen from police, and many more were entering the country across the porous Mozambican border.
19 Edwin RITCHKEN: The meaning of rural political violence: the meaning of the anti-witchcraft attacks, Johannesburg, Centre for the Study of Violence and Reconciliation, seminar no. 5 (1989) http://www.csvr.org.za/papers/papritch.html.
20 Max MARWICK: Witchcraft as a social strain gauge, in: Max MARWICK (ed), Witchcraft and sorcery, Harmondsworth 1970, pp. 280-295.

haus in his study of witchcraft on the Lowveld,[21] and more recently by Riekje Pelgrim in a study of witchcraft accusations in South Africa's Northern Province,[22] and in particular to its emphasis on the stresses of constant social change and on the significance of social instability, which in the accounts of both Pelgrim and Niehaus is a more significant factor.

Many policemen had stories to tell of women accused of witchcraft, particularly women living alone in standard four-room houses.[23] The stories followed a stereotypical pattern of transient accusation, usually by neighbours, generating some heat (often called in to the 10111 emergency number as a „fighting complaint") but rarely taken seriously, even by close neighbours for more than a day or two. Such episodes were read by almost everyone concerned, including the police, as half-baked attempts to acquire a house that was considered by others as too large for one person (in an overheated and crowded housing environment) or as temporary explosions of social tension. Police and street committee representatives often collaborated closely in handling such incidents, combining to unravel the origins of the accusations. In my fieldnotes I have recorded stories dating back decades in some cases, including one of a family feud involving four generations for which no agreement about its cause could be found. A member of a street committee in Diepkloof zone four summed up one such incident as „too many people, too much history".

Often the witchcraft accusation seemed to have been thrown into the mix of allegations and insinuations almost as an afterthought, without any serious attempt to demonstrate that a particular person either was a witch or had misused his or her powers. In the nearly twenty such complaints I attended between March 1994 and July 1998, I saw no severe physical violence.[24] Some women had been assaulted and most had been threatened with violence but only one of those required hospital treatment and none needed protection in the next hours and days. In almost all of these complaints, police and/or ANC/civic street leaders were able to negotiate through the situation and to find older community mediators who would continue the process of finding more permanent solutions. While on some occasions these complaints represented long-standing frustrations or resentments, the lack of violence and the lack of prolonged emotional intensity was significant. The resources were scarce but the contestation was even more limited.

Even in the febrility and violence of the transition period, many of the streets of Soweto were *still still*[25], quiet, orderly, untroubled, or at least so they appeared on the

---

21 Isak NIEHAUS: Witchcraft in the New South Africa, in: African Legal Studies (2001), pp. 116-148.
22 Riejke PELGRIM: Witchcraft and policing: South Africa Police Service attitudes towards witchcraft and witchcraft-related crime in the Northern Province, in: Research Report 72 (2003), pp. 61-64 (= Leiden African Studies Centre, 2003).
23 These „matchbox" houses usually housed many more people, from eight to ten adults and children, sometimes more.
24 Such incidents do not show up as a separate category in South African Police Service statistics or even in the police reports made in pocketbooks, the Occurrence Book and shift records. Rather, they are subsumed under a variety of headings such as fighting complaints, burglary (housebreaking), assault, etc.
25 lit. quiet (Afrikaans), commonly used descriptor on Flying Squad.

surface: the task for police was to decipher what the quietness actually meant, what it might be hiding. The stillness could be deceptive, a marker of something menacing: „If there's no children, some shit is going to happen".[26] Driving the many side streets of the township[27] was often a slow progress, held up by informal road blocks (rocks and stones placed across the road and the wide verges), and by children playing street cricket, soccer, skipping games, complicated hopping games (requiring chalked/painted patterns of squares and circles), marbles, games involving wire replicas of vehicles, helicopters and planes; and reenactment and chasing games (hide and seek and its variants, including a „hiding from the police" game that was popular at that time in Rockville and Moroka in the south of Soweto and a more widely-spread game involving homemade replica wooden firearms and knives).

But, as the police had learned to know, if the streets were quiet at a time when usually the children would be everywhere, then something was happening nearby, or was planned to happen very soon: the children had been hustled inside, out of potential lines of fire. In „the old days", as police who had been in Soweto in the 1980s and early 1990s, often referred to them, the absence of children was often preceded by the loud banging of broomsticks on metal rubbish bin lids; the warning signal. I had heard and watched this myself many times in earlier years. By 1994 the signal had changed, equally loud but somehow more penetrating than the brooms and the rubbish bin lids: whistling in rising tones, passed from one block to another, warning that police were entering the area, warning that trouble of some sort was on its way, warning local *tsotsis*[28] „working"[29] robbed (hijacked) or stolen vehicles in the neighbourhood that they should be ready to run, or perhaps to fight.

„I feel violence all around us"[30]

The culture of violence permeated much of Soweto life, leaving indelible imprints on Soweto people and their daily lives, and even on the streetscapes. The newly-ubiquitous walls (locally called „stop nonsenses") around houses, even ordinary matchbox houses, represented a new manifestation of a deep-seated need for security in the midst of pervasive vulnerability. A small but telling signifier: after nearly ten years of rent boycotts, and the consequent decision by the former apartheid government to limit services in the township, rubbish collection occurred only sporadically so any vacant piece of land (no matter how small) was liable to be turned (sometimes overnight) into an informal impromptu rubbish dump. Residents made their own signs against the practice:

---

26 A quote from a young policeman in the first week that I was allowed „to work with" members of Soweto Flying Squad.

27 At that time about 15 kilometres east-west and about 11 kilometres on the north-south axis, Soweto's population size was a guessing game. No accurate census had measured it, and the inflow of migrants simply exacerbated the situation.

28 Criminals, almost always male, usually a member of a gang.

29 „Chopping" the vehicles, changing engine, registration, window and chassis numbers, repainting to change the colour, etc.

30 Said to me by an older man, a resident of Diepkloof Zone 3, after an incident in which two women had been „robbed" of their car.

„NO DUMPING HERE PLEASE"
„NO DUMPING RESPECT"

or more directly to the point:

„NO MORE DUMPING HERE. YOU WILL BE MARKED FOR DEATH"
„PLEASE NO DUMPING HERE. YOUR HOUSE WILL BE BURNED"

Dumps often smouldered for weeks, the moisture in the rubbish damping down open flames: foul smoke drifted through neighbourhoods, aggravating eye, skin and respiratory conditions. Some police read rubbish dumping and its texts as emblematic of what they perceived as the rottenness of Soweto, of a place consumed by a culture of violence, „no-rules Soweto", where „nothing works", a „shit place", the language used implying (without specification) that almost everyone in Soweto, almost without exception, was somehow complicit in crime. Another reading (sometimes, paradoxically, articulated by the same policemen) explicated a more polarised view that recognised difference: that not all (in fact comparatively few) of „the people" were likely to be engaged in the types of criminal activity in which the police were interested – crimes against property, as well as major crimes of violence (murder and assault), possession of illegal firearms and other weaponry, and so forth. Some police indeed expressed complex understandings that the violence of the threats in such signs was an indication of a sense of helplessness, and of a disbelief that „the government" or „the police" would be able to act in any decisive or longlasting way.

The ubiquitous anti-dumping graffiti, much of it redolent of an implied violence, was mirrored by the even larger numbers of struggle graffiti left over from the 1980s and early 1990s:

„NO TO CURFEW"
„IF YOU SEE SAP[31] PLEASE CONTACT A.P.L.A."[32]
„ARM THE PEOPLE"
„ONE SETTLER ONE BULLET"
„KILL THE COP ADVANCE THE STRUGGLE"

By late 1994 the tone changed, to:

„PEACE MAGENTS[33] PEACE"

or the infinitely sad:

„BLACK PEOPLE UR STILL ON YOUR OWN AZAPO"[34]

These visible signs of the culture of violence, of the ready turn to threats or actual violence, represented significations of a more inchoate violence that lurked just below the conscious surface of Soweto life in those months and years of transition from the massive state violence of the previous apartheid era. That state violence constructed and conditioned the culture of violence which felt to one Sowetan in early 1995 like „a flood"

---

31 South African Police.
32 Azanian People's Liberation Armywhose armed wing was popularly supposed to be particularly violent.
33 Magents, from gentlemen, township slang for the gangsters who dominated much of the township.
34 Azanian People's Organisation, Black Consciousness liberation organisation.

Fig. 1: Smoke drifting out of an informal rubbish dump close to houses in Meadowlands in the 1990s.

Fig. 2: Graffiti in Orlando West: the 1990s political slogan of the Pan Africanist Congress (PAC): „One settler one bullet".

Fig. 3: Protective animal skulls, horns and skins, over the doorway of a Diepkloof house (photo taken in the 1990s).

and to another recalled „what the Bible says about brother against brother".[35] Here I seek to position threats against witches within that normative culture of violence, both the verbal culture of threats, graffiti, and common speaking, and the physical culture of weapon carrying, crimes of violence, and the instrumental uses of violence for revenge, or reinstatement of the moral order. While burning witches has not been a common phenomenon in Soweto, the beliefs that underlie the practice, the understandings that the witch has brought disharmony to the society, that *muti*[36] is a powerful and genuine force, are ubiquitous.

„Kill the witches"

In February 1995, an elderly woman in the Soweto area of Orlando East was accused by a crowd besieging her house, described by the *Sowetan* as „a frenzied and berserk mob of youths who indicated in no uncertain terms that they wanted the old woman dead", of having variously kidnapped or bewitched young girls, and forced them to drink human

---

35 Both people spoke to me at the scene of a violent robbery in Orlando West in January 1995. Biblical references often came readily to Sowetans.

36 Muti is a fundamental component of traditional healing, of prophecy and the manipulation of the future. It is medicine, talisman and protection (for example, playing a substantial role in the preparations to launch an attack, on a hostel, from a hostel, by izinkabi (Zulu, hitmen, men of violence).

blood.[37] She and her husband escaped, rescued by police who gave them refuge at Orlando SAP, but the house was burned down. During a search of the site, reportedly for „a monkey",[38] the crowd found a body in the ashes. Seizing the body they carried it more than three kilometres to the SAP, dumping it inside the station „upon which a number of police ran away".[39] They demanded that the elderly couple be handed over to them. Some days later police revealed that the body was that of the couple's son, who had been sleeping and had failed to escape the burning house. While the police were hopeful of being able to charge the ringleaders, the reality of the situation, both politically and socially in terms of the potential consequences of such arrests, mitigated against any retribution by the state for the offences.

Lloyd Vogelman has argued that the witch burnings which have plagued rural areas of South Africa are an extension of „the 1980s murders of informers at the hands of militant youths in urban centres"[40] and this connection has not been lost on township residents. During the weeks following the Orlando „house of horrors" incident, a number of people raised this issue with me as I talked with Sowetan contacts and with participants and bystanders at other incidents. The accusations against the old woman focussed a sense of helplessness in many people; a sense that despite the political success of achieving a new government that nothing had changed.[41] And more, that the „culture of struggle" was still so powerful that the township would never be „safe", that the „youth", or groups of people swept away by emotion and the intoxication of collective action, would always find a way to hold the real power. Embedded in this notion was an historical understanding of the state as weak (paradoxical as that might sound in the face of the historical reality of the apartheid state). Flowing from this, or at the least running alongside it, was the expression by many Sowetans of concomitant anxieties arising from intergenerational tensions (also dating from the struggle years), and the more subterranean but ubiquitous fears swirling around male violence against women. Others however argued vehemently that the episode represented the new community policing as it should be done: the community acting to police itself, restoring the moral order, recovering social harmony.

This Orlando East incident closely followed another, in Mzimhlope, which had gone unreported in the media (and indeed unlike the Orlando East complaint was not widely known or discussed outside the small area in which it occurred). Orlando East had the

---

37 Sowetan (7 Feb., 1995) 1; (8 Feb., 1995) 1, 4; (23 Feb., 1995) 1, 8. I was not present at the incident itself, but was able to observe and talk to people involved, both police and residents, during the following night and days.

38 Explained to me in much graphic detail by an onlooker as a search for a tokolosh, a diminutive humanoid creature, found in the northern and eastern sections of the country. It takes possession of both men and women through the act of rape during sleep and is widely recognised in the anthropological literature.

39 Sowetan (7 Feb., 1995) 1.

40 Quoted in The Star (9 Feb.,1995) 10.

41 See June NASH's analogous situation in: Death as a way of life: the increasing resort to homicide in a Maya Indian community, in Thomas Weaver (ed.), To see ourselves: anthropology and modern social issues, Glenview, Illinois 1973, pp. 346-354.

reputation among the police of being difficult in which to work. One of the oldest areas of Soweto, originally it consisted of very small houses constructed on comparatively large plots of land. The combination was irresistible: by 1994 the infill development of backyard rooms and *zozos* (shacks) was already extensive. Police answered many calls in this area to shooting or fighting complaints, particularly on weekend nights, many of them understood by police to be a direct consequence of a much-expanded population, of whom a number were illegal aliens (predominantly Mozambicans). As I have indicated above, however, complaints of any kind in Mzimhlope were much rarer. As a consequence police „knew the area" in a different way; even finding a house number in Mzimhlope took longer than in Orlando East, because few police had any deep acquaintance with the area and the institutional topographic memory was minimal.

So it was that in the middle of the afternoon of a Sunday day shift, a Flying Squad vehicle with three policemen and myself working on it took a radio complaint of a witchcraft accusation in progress in Mzimhlope. We were in the process of booking a rape suspect into the Diepkloof SAP when the call came, the product of an earlier incident which had distressed all of us on the vehicle: a girl of five had been raped by a seventeen-year old boy. That incident had originally been called over the radio as a street justice in progress complaint: the boy was holed up in the house of his uncle in Meadowlands zone 8 with a large crowd outside intent on killing him. We managed to enter the house, through a crowd which was exhorting all of us to „discipline" the young man, and only then were able to work out why he was the potential target of „street justice". The policemen took him out through the crowd, a difficult exercise and one fraught with the potential for massive violence. We then went in search of the young girl, who had been taken to her mother's house some kilometres away in Diepkloof, receiving a radio call as we did so, since the girl's family had decided, somewhat against the odds, to lay a complaint. The little girl was able to walk but was clearly in distress, the mother and the mother's sisters were frozen in anger and shock. The young man meanwhile sat beside me in the vehicle, telling me that he had given the child sweets so „it wasn't rape", and explaining that sex with „the virgin" meant that he would not become „positive", infected with HIV.[42]

The complaint took several hours and was emotionally exhausting even for experienced policemen. The call to another potentially difficult complaint came just when all of us on the vehicle needed some downtime, at least time for a cool drink and to regroup emotionally. Instead, we came flying down the hill and across the valley of the Klip River at high speed, the police driver one of the most experienced on the unit. On the video tape that I kept running from the back seat, the tension in the vehicle is evident as all three passengers, crew, third crew and myself, „spotted" house numbers left and right, down streets and from corners, and called them to the driver, who was throwing the vehicle almost sideways into the curves.

After some minutes of searching, as we rocketed up an unmade road between two rows of houses with the stereotypical curved concrete slab roofs of Mzimhlope, brightly

---

42 The first occasion that I or the many police I talked to about this heard this explanation, which was later to become ubiquitous in cases of child rape.

coloured and appealing, the third crew locked his R5 automatic long gun into firing position and the crew and the driver both leant forward suddenly, drawing their 9 mill. pistols from their belt holsters. The noise of the crowd had guided us the last four hundred metres, people milling in the street, others moving in and out of a side path alongside the house. The third crew took up a position by the front gate, R5 cradled, the crew banged on the front door, as both he and the driver tried to make sense of what was being shouted at them by several women simultaneously.

Round the back, that was where „the witch" was, standing in her back door (the Mzimhlope houses are duplexes, one-storey houses sharing a common wall) with two other women visible at her side and behind her. An older woman, tall, slim, almost gaunt, not well nourished, long hair tied back, a patient almost resigned demeanour. Several young men were leaning over the rickety wooden fence that separated her small yard from her neighbour's to the west, shouting targeted abuse and threats, threatening to kill her. Numbers of women stood shouting in her yard, incited by a small woman in her thirties who was the principal accuser. Others came and went from the yard, along the path, over the fences at both sides and at the rear. From time to time the noise levels became deafening: the two policemen at times struggled to hear and to make themselves heard as they tried to disentangle what was being said by whom and for what reason.

At one point during the several hours we were there, I was taken out to the street by a young woman who lived at the end of the street: a policewoman, she worked at the Protea police base and knew us all by sight. She had called the complaint in, having spent several hours trying to talk the incident down, but realising finally that it was spinning out of her capacity to control it. She wanted me to meet the members of the street committee, three older women, formally dressed, each with a small ribbon of office pinned to her dress. They more quietly narrated the story, which they wanted me to relay to the two policemen at the back of the house. The „witch" was accused of four acts: of dancing naked on her neighbour's lawn in the early hours of the morning (three to four am); of going naked into the houses of other women and disturbing them; of bewitching „the child," the small principal accuser whose mother also lived in the street; and, a final accusation that once the episode had begun, the previous night, „the witch" had phoned several friends of her son to come and protect her. Her son, I was told, was in Sun City, the ironic name for the main prison for the Johannesburg area, and his friends had recently been released. They had arrived with firearms and had shot into the air to warn the neighbours of what would follow any attempt to burn the woman. When I remarked that I had stood close to the woman a few minutes before and had seen her trembling and had noticed marks on her arms and the side of her face that looked as though they would turn into bruises, the three women explained, matter of factly, that „the witch" had been chased along the street and had been „disciplined" in her back yard. That had been the trigger for the policewoman to call for police assistance.

The police slowly cooled the situation down, sending as many people as they could away from the house, listening to participants who seemed to have something to say, and talking and listening to the principal accuser (although this to little avail since she became increasingly distressed that her other complaints, to do with a house she had lost the right to live in and a husband who had left, were not being given as much consideration, she thought, as her complaint about the witch). The women from the street committee eventually agreed that they would listen to the young policewoman and allow her to speak and to negotiate if the incident reignited. The senior policeman, the driver, called in the Dog Unit to make a pass in their vehicle through the street, and radioed a friend who was on duty in the Public Order Policing Unit, so that as well as being officially aware, the POP unit was also on unofficial alert. Finally, as the situation calmed down sufficiently for him to contemplate leaving the scene, he called a senior policeman from the Flying Squad relief that was about to take over for Sunday night shift so that he could be sure that the patrols would be aware and attentive, and could overtly circle around the area through the night. The „witch" had nowhere else to go, this was the best he could manage in terms of state protection for her for the critical next few hours.[43]

Understandings

Beyond the functional, instrumentalist explanations, redolent of a modernist understanding within which the structures of state and party and police somehow would, or at least should, dominate the situation, other understandings and accounts were being constructed and circulated in the township. These construed what had occurred in the context of older beliefs, those that were often defined locally as more „traditional" or more „rural". For some residents and police with whom I discussed what had happened, these explanations were visibly comforting, marking out and delineating a set of links which grounded the events in „custom", in what „my fathers" had done, constructing a sense that, even though change was happening much too fast, the world could still be set to rights, could still make sense. For others, these older beliefs were part of what they had moved away from, indeed in some cases had fled from, when they had migrated from the rural areas to the urban township: in assuming „modern"[44] modes of thinking, in reconstructing both their world views and their senses of self, in reshaping rural „unsophisticated" identities, they had actively rejected these pasts and these beliefs. Or at least (since the nature of social realities is always that the caveat must apply), some had rejected what they perceived as negative elements of those beliefs, while retaining other elements, so that some of my participants wholeheartedly endorsed a belief in witchcraft but saw it as a purely rural phenomenon, while still others acknowledged the belief in witchcraft as being omnipresent in the township, yet denied the presence of witches.

The percipient Norman Cohn, writing of the development in medieval Europe of a persecuting society (to use R I Moore's terminology)[45] defined the onset of heresy and

---

43 Months later I was at a housebreaking complaint in the next street and enquired about the „witch". I was told that she was alive and that after her son was released from prison she went with him to „another township".

44 „Modern" was a much-used word in Sowetan discourse in the transition years. Many residents and police were articulating a self-conscious need to modify or break with the past, the „traditional" past of the rural areas in some instances, the distorted unequal separatist past of the apartheid government in others.

45 R. I. MOORE: The formation of a persecuting society: power and deviance in Western Europe, 950-1250, Oxford 1987.

witchcraft accusations as „a fantasy"[46], emphasising the psychological disturbances that surrounded and enabled the construction of wild accusations of deviance: „In pursuing its history one is led far beyond the confines of the history of ideas and deep into the sociology and social psychology of persecution".[47] For a later period, Robin Briggs also has used, tellingly, this discourse of what he calls „collusive fantasies".[48] Clearly though, for many Soweto residents a belief in witchcraft and in the existence of witches living among them is not a fantasy: such beliefs are totally integrated into the total world view of individuals, but the expression, intensity and representation of these beliefs varies from one person to another.

The existence of a belief in witchcraft is not what is most interesting here. Rather, the compelling facet of these new public accusations of witchcraft is their timing. As Ashforth too showed in *Madumo,* many private accusations of witchcraft are made in Soweto, and understandings that witchcraft is causative of specific negative events in the life of an individual or a family are commonplace. On the basis of local responses during and around the two witchcraft accusations in early 1995 that I describe here, I argue that new cultural patterns emerged in the period of transition. These patterns shifted the location of the boundaries between the formerly almost-exclusively private domain, a domain of reticence and individual struggle against the forces of spells on the one hand, and the public sphere, a newly-opened arena within which overt accusations could be voiced on the other. In this arena, I suggest, the local understandings of the witch/es and their powers differed from those expressed in *Madumo* (for example) since they were both highly specific (forcing young girls to drink human blood, „bewitching the child") yet had effects which impacted on whole communities, rather than on individuals or families. Individuals had literally come to be seen by large numbers of their neighbours as archetypal „troubling figures". To be sure, specific individuals brought the original accusations, but quickly these became elaborated and disseminated through the respective local communities, taking on fantastical elements, yet elements which did not transgress existing sets of beliefs about how witches might be identified, how they operate, what their ends and purposes might be.

Not a fantasy then, but perhaps both fantastical and nightmarish, the narrative, like the old game of Chinese Whispers, born out of some misconstrued word or action, gathering strength, transmogrifying, drawing on those beliefs that lie just below the surface of consciousness, pushed forward from idea to praxis.

> "Normally strange things circulate discreetly below our streets. But a crisis will suffice for them to rise up, as if swollen by flood waters, pushing aside manhole covers, invading the cellars, then spreading through the towns. It always comes as a surprise when the nocturnal erupts into broad daylight. What it reveals is an underground existence, an inner resistance that has never been broken. This lurking force infiltrates the lines of tension within the society it threatens. Suddenly it magnifies them; using the means, the circuitry already in place,

---

46 Norman COHN: Europe's inner demons: the demonization of christians in medieval christendom rev ed Chicago 2000, p. ix.
47 Ibid.
48 Robin BRIGGS: Witches and neighbours: the social and cultural context of European witchcraft, London 1996, p. 381.

but re-employing them in the service of an anxiety that comes from afar, unanticipated. It breaks through barriers, flooding the social channels and opening new pathways that, once the flow of its passage has subsided, will leave behind a different landscape and a different order.

Is this the outbreak of something new, or the repetition of a past? The historian never knows which. For mythologies reappear, providing the eruption of strangeness with forms of expression prepared in advance, as it were, for that sudden inundation. These languages of social anxiety seem to reject both the limits of a present and the real conditions of its future. Like scars that mark for a new illness the spot of an earlier one, they designate in advance the signs and location of a flight (or return?) of time."[49]

Here Michel de Certeau, writing of the accusations of demonic possession in 17th century Loudun, vividly evokes those inchoate subterranean „strange things" whose presence we ignore in our ordinary lives, but whose tense existence becomes manifest in times of crisis, „strange things," understandings, accounts, beliefs, conduits for the re-ignition of „languages of social anxiety," mining the old in order to express the anxieties and fears of the new. This notion of languages of social anxiety allows us to reread the events in Orlando East and Mzimhlope, repositioning them, construing them through both a cultural history of widespread witchcraft beliefs and a cultural present of uncertainty, insecurity and change that was widely perceived as „too quick".

As Clifton Crais restated the Africanist historical project in the early 1990s: „The main problematic becomes one of moving away from a history of experience and towards a history of the consciousness of experience".[50] It is then in a consciousness of experience rather than in reiteration of the narratives of experience that we can come to different understandings of the cultural positioning of witchcraft and witchcraft accusations. That witchcraft can exist and flourish is a social fact in Soweto: that witches are not often burned or even assaulted or attacked in Soweto is equally a social fact. The two serious episodes of witchcraft accusation that I recount here then demand explanation as events standing outside the norm. Through situating them within de Certeau's concept of languages of social anxiety we can interpret them as expressions of a time and location-specific social instability: in the largest black township in South Africa, the focal point for many of the major events of the liberation struggle, at a time when the euphoria of the first democratic election had worn off but while expectations and insecurities about the future were equally high, at a time too when gender and generational tensions and anxieties were beginning to manifest themselves more overtly than they had in the past.

---

49 Michel DE CERTEAU: The possession at Loudun translated Michael B Smith, Chicago 2000, p. 1.
50 Clifton C. CRAIS: Representation and the politics of identity in South Africa: an Eastern Cape example, in: The International Journal of African Historical Studies 25, 1 (1992), p. 100.

Jan-Lodewijk Grootaers

„Criminal Enemies of the People": Water Wizards among the Zande, Central African Republic (1950-2000)

Zusammenfassung

Seit der Veröffentlichung von Evans-Pritchards *Witchcraft, Oracles and Magic among the Azande* im Jahre 1937 findet sich das Beispiel der Zande in den meisten ethnologischen Werken zur Hexerei in Afrika. Dies trifft ebenfalls für vergleichende Studien in anderen Disziplinen wie Geschichte, Religionswissenschaften und Philosophie zu. Die Gesellschaft der Zande wird jedoch im wissenschaftlichen Diskurs meist in einer Art Zeitvakuum dargestellt, sodass ihre Glaubensvorstellungen inzwischen für unveränderlich gehalten werden. Der folgende Beitrag beschreibt, basierend auf Feldforschungen bei den Zande in der Zentralafrikanischen Republik und umfassenden Archivstudien, neue Entwicklungen bei den Glaubensvorstellungen und Lebenserfahrungen der Zande. Er betrachtet den Unterschied zwischen (innewohnender) Hexerei und (erworbener) Zauberei, erforscht eine relativ rezente Form schädlicher Zauberei, die als Kannibalismus bezeichnet wird, und erörtert den neuartigen Umgang mit Personen, die der Ausübung dieser Praktiken verdächtigt werden. Die Veränderungen werden aus historischer Perspektive betrachtet, wobei ausdrücklich gegen eine Essentialisierung ethnologischer Erkenntnisse plädiert wird.

Abstract

Ever since the publication of Evans-Pritchard's Witchcraft, Oracles and Magic among the Azande in 1937, the African Zande people have had their place in most anthropological analyses of witchcraft in Africa. This also holds true for comparative research in other disciplines, including history, religious studies and philosophy. Yet over time, Zande society itself seems to have landed outside of history, and Zande beliefs have come to be considered immutable. This contribution, based on fieldwork among the Zande of the Central African Republic and extensive archival research, describes recent developments in Zande beliefs and experiences. It puts the difference between (inherent) witchcraft and (acquired) sorcery in perspective, explores a fairly new form of harmful magic couched in cannibalistic practices, and discusses people's novel ways of coping with suspected evildoers. These transformations are considered from a historical perspective, and a strong argument is made against reifying anthropological knowledge.

My first fieldwork among the Zande of the Central African Republic (CAR) was saturated with allusions to hommes-caïmans or „crocodile-men". I reached Zandeland in eastern Haut-Mbomou Province in June 1991.[1] It was well into the rainy season, which normally starts in March-April, but rains had been sparse. There was heavy lightning above the small town of Zemio, located on the Mbomou River that forms the natural border between the CAR and northern Congo, yet not a drop fell. The farmers were worried, for they had sown their fields with maize and peanuts. When I asked if they thought it was going to rain soon, people answered in the negative: a female prophet of the Zande prophetic church had explained that God was withholding the water in heaven because water wizards were planning to kill somebody in a river. Withholding the rains kept the rivers low and so prevented the murder.

Towards the end of my stay in Zandeland, more than a year later, the prefect of the province came to Zemio – a highly exceptional event – and called a public meeting. A couple of days earlier a young man had drowned in the Mbomou River and several suspected crocodile-men had been apprehended. The prefect warned against the problem of this water wizardry and labelled the offenders „criminal enemies of the people" who threatened the economic future of the entire region. The economic situation in Zandeland is dire indeed and may be summarized as follows: the road to the capital (over 1000 km west) is extremely bad, cash crops have no longer been grown since 1983, very few local merchants subsist to buy the produce, the only existing traffic brings food to a camp of Sudanese refugees 200 km from the border, shortage of money is rampant and people are obliged to eat their surplus production. It was this general feeling of decline, neglect and abandonment that the prefect addressed in his speech, implying that lack of progress, or actual regression, was due to the crocodile-men.

In between these two incidents that marked out my stay in the field, I came to learn a lot about the crocodile-men, also called *kpiri* (or *akpiri*). These perpetrators of a relatively new brand of wizardry were a problem that was on the mind of every Zande I met. Among the CAR Zande at least, witchcraft appeared to have been greatly surpassed by *kpiri* wizardry as the foremost threat to both people's individual well-being and the overall social order. In order to explore this transformation, it is first necessary to go back in time and recapitulate the findings about the beliefs of the Sudanese Zande recorded by Edward Evans-Pritchard in the late 1920s. I suggest that Evans-Pritchard's epistemological construct failed to take account of contemporary changes among the Zande. The remainder of the essay will show what forms these changes – part of an ongoing process of historical imagination – take in today's western Zandeland, how they relate to the lived experiences of modernity, and to what extent the historical analysis of beliefs avoids the reduction of „modernity" to a blanket term.

---

1   The Zande (or Azande) live in three modern states: the Democratic Republic of Congo, Sudan, and the Central African Republic. Fieldwork and writing-up were generously supported by the University of Chicago, the Social Science Research Council (New York) and the Woodrow Wilson National Fellowship Foundation (Princeton). I further thank Birgit Meyer and Kevin Cook for their helpful comments on an earlier version of this essay. My greatest debt is to the Zande people, who accepted me in their midst and welcomed my inquiries.

Evans-Pritchard's triangle

The most striking image Evans-Pritchard's monograph of 1937 conveys, is that of a triangle: „Witchcraft, oracles, and magic are like three sides to a triangle", forming „a system of reciprocally dependent ideas and practices".[2] Witchcraft (*mangu*) was a fairly common internal capacity people possess from birth to harm others; oracles (*soroka*) were consulted to determine the origin of misfortune and, in particular, identify the responsible witch; and magic (*ngua*) was an acquired technique based on medicines and spells to do either good or bad – for instance to combat witchcraft or to cause sickness. The illegitimate use of magic Evans-Pritchard called sorcery, which was much rarer, more feared and more severely punished than witchcraft. Even though he considered these beliefs to be part of mystical thought and therefore empirically untrue, they were not superstitions but explanations, he argued.

In Durkheimian fashion *Witchcraft, Oracles and Magic* also analysed how Zande beliefs were linked to the structure of Zande society. The coherence of apparently irrational ideas was further enhanced by their formal congruence with social rules and relationships. For example, the poison oracle of the members of the ruling Vungara clan was the highest divinatory instance, against which there was no appeal. This warranted royal predominance in judicial matters. Furthermore, witchcraft accusations were restricted to certain domains of the social world, clustering in areas of ambiguous social relationships not buffered by unequal power, wealth or other forms of social distance. Such accusations occurred mainly between neighbouring rivals, but never between husbands and wives, nor between parents and their children; it was equally impossible for a commoner to accuse an aristocrat of witchcraft. In this way domestic and political structures were effectively upheld.

One kind of institution fell completely outside the triangular system, namely the closed associations or so-called „secret societies". Evans-Pritchard discussed them somewhat reluctantly at the end of his book, without really integrating them. In the first part of the twentieth century there seems to have been a profusion of these „societies for the practice of magic" in all three countries where the Zande live (Sudan, Congo and the CAR) – the best-known being the Yanda or Mani association.[3] They were open to all members of society, yet one had to be initiated to participate in their activities. They were hierarchically organized with grades of initiates and several levels of leadership, and their meetings were held in secluded places in the forest. Their main purpose was the divulgence of new magic among their members and the performance of group magical rites to increase the members' good fortune and protect them from any harm, nota-

---

2   Edward EVANS-PRITCHARD: Witchcraft, oracles and magic among the Azande, Oxford 1937, pp. 387 and 512.

3   Just some of the many references: Filiberto GIORGETTI: Brevi note sulla società segreta Africana Yanda o Mani, in: Annali Lateranensi 21 (1957), pp. 9-29. Herman BURSSENS: Yanda-beelden en Mani-sekte bij de Azande (Centraal Afrika), Tervuren 1962. Pierre SALMON: Sectes secrètes zande (République du Zaïre), in: Etudes de géographie tropicale offertes à Pierre Gourou, Paris 1972, pp. 427-440. Douglas JOHNSON: Criminal secrecy: The case of the Zande 'secret societies', in: Past & Present 130 (1991), pp. 170-200.

bly harm coming from the authorities. Other activities included organizing dances, consulting oracles to find witches, and settling cases.

These movements were sternly opposed by Zande princes, Christian missionaries and colonial administrators alike. The royal clan of the Vungara considered them „subversive" and a threat to their authority, insofar as they created an independent jurisdiction and popularized magic that escaped chiefly control. The missionaries emphasized the associations' „immoral" character, mainly because of the close companionship of men and women, and the propagation of what they saw as a false creed. The administrators, for their part, decried the „political danger" that emanated from these societies, owing to their foreign origin and their aversion to all established authority, native and colonial.[4] The 1919 „Unlawful Societies & Witchcraft Ordinance" and similar laws banned the closed associations, some of which went underground. As the historian Douglas Johnson points out, the banning of the societies was also inspired by the ideology of preserving Zande „tribal custom" from exogenous influences.[5] The irony is that there was not, and never had been, a pristine, closed and isolatable Zande culture. Influences from, and exchanges with, neighbouring communities did not threaten some imagined Zande homogeneity; they were, on the contrary, constitutive of the Zande mosaic.

A critical question concerning the closed associations from the past pertains to their origin: are these societies to be understood as responses to external changes or as internal developments of Zande culture? The first students of Zande society agreed that the closed associations did not originate in Zande country, also claiming that their introduction had only been possible due to the conquest of the country by the Europeans.[6] From here it was only a small step to suggest, as Evans-Pritchard originally did, that these societies were a function of European rule itself. They came to be understood as a consequence of the colonial presence and an indication of „wide and deep social change" caused by the Europeans, and were later even described as a „case of native resistance to colonial pacification".[7] Yet the very forcefulness of the colonial riposte to the closed associations has made it difficult to analyse their role independently of the interventions of colonial governments. In a subsequent publication Evans-Pritchard suggested that the associations may have originated in regions affected by, and in response to, the Arab slave trade, i.e. well before the arrival of the first Europeans.[8] The best evidence does indeed indicate that some closed associations existed among the Zande – and the

---

4   Edward EVANS-PRITCHARD: Mani, a Zande secret society, in: Sudan Notes and Records 14 (1931), pp. 105-148. Constant LAGAE: Les Azande ou Niam-Niam. L'organisation Zande, croyances religieuses et magiques, coutumes familiales. Brussels 1926, p. 134; and ANON.: Secret societies of the Southern Sudan, in: Sudan Notes and Records 4 (1921), pp. 204-208, here p. 204.
5   JOHNSON: Secrecy, p. 179f.
6   Cf. LAGAE: Azande, p. 117. EVANS-PRITCHARD: Mani, pp. 106-108.
7   EVANS-PRITCHARD: Witchcraft, p. 511 and William ARENS: Evans-Pritchard and the prophets: Comments on an ethnographic enigma, in: Anthropos 78 (1983), pp. 1-16, here p. 9 respectively.
8   Edward EVANS-PRITCHARD: A final contribution to the study of Zande culture, in: The Azande. History and political institutions, Oxford 1971, pp. 111-120, here p. 112.

neighbouring Mangbetu – as early as the third quarter of the nineteenth century, thus predating European presence in this part of Africa.⁹

The closed societies appear to have had their place in Zande society because they offered their members protection against the „dark underside to Zande political life".¹⁰ The application of Vungara justice through the poison oracle, for instance, was more hazardous than would appear from the idealized scenarios recorded by ethnographers. The Zande state system itself was fraught with internal and external violence, and there was a potential tendency towards royal accumulation and autocracy. It would seem that the misfortune the associations guarded against did not come so much from the colonial regime, as from Zande rule itself. So the new societies were grafted onto existing disenchantment and contradictions within Zande society, even if the latter came to be exacerbated by the colonial presence.

Evans-Pritchard admitted that he was „not entirely satisfied" with his understanding of these associations, which struck him as „foreign and abnormal modes of behaviour".¹¹ The fact that they had been outlawed made it difficult for him to obtain a free and open testimony from his informants. He changed his terminology from „secret societies" to „closed associations" and shifted his interpretation about their origin from post-European to pre-1875. He also noted the disconnectedness of the societies vis-à-vis the self-validating Witchcraft-Oracles-Magic triangle that epitomized his interpretation of Zande beliefs. But above all, the associations threatened the neat division of magic into good and bad. „In the old days", he wrote nostalgically, „there appears to have been two clearly distinguished categories, good medicines and bad medicines. [...] Today] the country is flooded with new medicines and the moral issue has become confused because Zande culture does not prescribe a definite attitude towards them".¹²

I am not convinced that the difference between past and present was as depicted by the author. What Evans-Pritchard knew about magic „in the old days" had become established knowledge, hardly contested or ambivalent any more. His informants, most of them men who had been familiar with court life before 1905, taught him a kind of official history, which was sanctioned by the rulers and in which everything had its place in „clearly distinguished categories". What he himself observed during his stays among the Zande between 1926 and 1930, on the contrary, had not been filtered and aligned; an influx of novelties was taking place under his eyes. Different perspectives were being voiced and different rumours circulated, which made the situation look more „confused". Yet the situation *was* more confused, especially for the Zande themselves. During the early 1920s, for instance, they had undergone various sweeping measures

---

9   Curtis KEIM: Precolonial Mangbetu rule: Political and economic factors in nineteenth-century Mangbetu history (Northeast Zaire) [unpublished doctoral dissertation, Indiana University], Bloomington 1979, p. 90. Enid SCHILDKROUT / Curtis KEIM (ed.): African reflections. Art from northeastern Zaire, Seattle 1990, p. 190. JOHNSON: Secrecy, p. 200.
10 JOHNSON: Secrecy, p. 200.
11 EVANS-PRITCHARD: Mani, p. 146 and EVANS-PRITCHARD: Witchcraft, p. 512 respectively.
12 EVANS-PRITCHARD: Witchcraft, p. 421f.

against sleeping sickness, including the forced resettlement of thousands of „scattered inhabitants" along new roads.[13]

The closed associations were at the centre of Zande ideological and cultural innovation. In Evans-Pritchard's monograph they constitute one of the rare historical loci in an otherwise quite timeless account. I will look at the contemporary association of the *hommes-caïmans* as a phenomenon located in time: rooted in history and at the same time providing a commentary on present-day problems and ambiguities. My intention is to offer an insight into Zande historical consciousness.

How water wizardry operates

The problem of the *kpiri* was a constant topic of discussion during my fieldwork and I dealt extensively with it in the ensuing dissertation.[14] I take it to be symptomatic of the current predicament of the CAR Zande, characterized by failed articulation with the wider world and failed materialization of modernity's promises. People talked a great deal about water wizardry and what follows is a *bricolage* of information gathered from the many stories – rumours, really[15] – that I heard about the crocodile-men. For purposes of comparison and synthesis I also elicited information by direct questioning. Finally, I consulted various archives, especially those of the district court in Obo where suspected crocodile-men were tried. Although not all the stories, testimonies and rumours were consistent with one another – and divergences will be indicated – there is a general consensus about how water wizardry operates.

Hommes-caïmans are humans – men only – who make use of secret and harmful substances to go about their killing business. Zande crocodile-men are not thought to transform themselves into actual crocodiles, nor to be able to tame and control real crocodiles as familiars to commit their crimes; nor do they dress up like crocodiles or use instruments to simulate wounds provoked by actual animals. In all these aspects they differ from crocodile-men elsewhere in Africa.[16] To become a crocodile-man in Zandeland a first kind of *ngua* („evil medicine") is necessary, called *nzati akpiri*. Originally, *nzati* is the name of a magical substance used by hunters who are initiated to be successful in the hunt. It is applied in small incisions on the candidates' wrists by the *ba-nzati*, the initiator or „father of the *nzati*". Because of the incisions, Zande talk about being „vaccinated" with *kpiri* magic. Together with his *wiri-nzati* or „children of the *nzati*", the

---

13 G. K. MAURICE: The history of sleeping sickness in the Sudan, in: Sudan Notes and Records 13 (1930), pp. 211-45, here p. 227.

14 Jan-Lodewijk GROOTAERS: A history and ethnography of modernity among the Zande (Central African Republic) [unpublished doctoral dissertation, University of Chicago], Chicago 1996, passim, especially pp. 225-272.

15 Cf. Pamela STEWART / Andrew STRATHERN: Witchcraft, sorcery, rumors, and gossip, Cambridge 2004.

16 Cf. Carol MACCORMACK: Human leopards and crocodiles. Political meanings of categorical anomalies, in: Paula BROWN / Donald TUZIN (ed.), The ethnography of cannibalism, Washington 1983, pp. 51-60. Kambale MUNZOMBO / Minga SHANGA: Une société secrète au Zaïre: les hommes-crocodiles de la zone d'Ubundu, in: Africa [Rome] 42 (1987), pp. 226-238.

initiator forms a criminal corporation for executing people; *kpiri* always operate in a group.

A second kind of „medicine" is sprinkled into a river while calling a person's name. This will draw the intended victim irresistibly to the water, to bathe, fish, or take a canoe. Yet another *ngua* is used to create an envelope of air around the crocodile-man that moves with him under water, and allows him to see and stay there for hours, even days. It is either ingested or rubbed on the face and hands each time a *kpiri* goes into the water. Still other *ngua* are used by the crocodile-men, including one to make it rain, which delays the search operations when somebody has been reported missing and also erases traces left by the culprits on the river banks, and another to keep witnesses quiet and manipulate judicial authorities so that, if discovered, the accused get away with light sentences.

Once a victim is taken under water, he is usually given a „medicine" to stay alive, possibly the same *ngua* used by the crocodile-men themselves. After a while he is taken ashore in a secluded place and tried: he is told why he has been caught, i.e. in what way he has wronged one of the *kpiri* or their client. The victim is subsequently killed. Parts of his body are sometimes removed – skin, lower jaw, limbs, heart, liver, guts, penis or blood – and prepared to be eaten or sold. The body is then thrown back into the river to be discovered, or attached to a stone or root so that it will not surface. I was told that in previous years maimed corpses were regularly found, but that today the *kpiri* prefer to keep the corpses hidden. It also happens that innocent persons die together with the intended victim. In 1989 a canoe capsized on the Mbomou River near Zemio, carrying an adult man, who had supposedly committed adultery, and five children. All six perished. „Kpirism" was implicated and a dozen or so suspects were apprehended. They were severely beaten at the police station and many men confessed to the crime. Under pressure of the angry population it was decided that all the suspects should be starved to death.

What are the motives behind water killings? Most people believe the crocodile-men to kill out of vengefulness and jealousy – especially as provoked by adultery with their wives. As a Protestant deacon put it to me: „If you don't fool around with somebody else's wife, the *kpiri* will leave you alone". *Kpiri* also kill adulterers (or alleged adulterers) on behalf of their clients. Here a second motive appears: greed. Water murderers agree to execute someone for money. The sums mentioned varied from 5,000 to 100,000 CFA Francs (between 20 and 400 USD at the time), a lot of money in Zande-land. *Kpiri* are also said to make money by selling blood or organs from their victims. I was informed that there was a market for these in Congo (then Zaire), where they were turned into powerful „medicines", and that Muslim traders also purchased them to manufacture *grigri* (Arab amulets) which improve their business. Each corporation of *hommes-caïmans* reportedly has a treasurer who manages the funds.

Finally, crocodile-men are reputed to be driven by a desire for human flesh. One informant thought the liver is used to prepare the *ngua* for staying under water. More widespread is the rumour about the past mayor of Zemio, Koumounoungo. He suffered from diabetes and allegedly used the blood of water killing victims to treat his illness. There is also the testimony of a self-professed *kpiri* who explained, during his trial, why he and his companions had eaten human body parts: „By consuming together the heart and other parts, we unite our fates, strengthen our bond, and become protected against the risk of being disclosed".[17] The sacrificial meal as a ritual of corporate solidarity, in other words. „Zande cannibalism" is an old issue, to be sure, a topic long held in particular fascination by European audiences. I shall return to it.

So far I have been using the term „wizardry" on purpose, in order to avoid the classic Zande dichotomy between „witchcraft", an innate power mostly used in an unconscious manner, and „sorcery", based on external means to harm intentionally. *Kpiri* evil partakes of witchcraft and sorcery, yet also differs from both. It should first be pointed out that witchcraft (*mangu*) is no longer a big problem for the CAR Zande. It is dying out, I was told, because the elderly witches „do no not pass it on to their children". This seems to contradict the famous proposition that *mangu*-substance is automatically inherited by sons from their witch fathers and by daughters from their witch mothers. However, the power of witchcraft could always be passed on in a cool, inactive form. Incidentally, the theory of inheritance of the witchcraft-substance is *really* contradicted by the fact that the substance may nowadays be purchased – abolishing at once the god-given distinction between innate and acquired.[18] Now, the *hommes-caïmans* are initiated in the use of „bad medicines" and therefore practise sorcery. Yet the Zande never refer to them as *mbe-ngua*, „owners of bad medicines" or sorcerers. Indeed, water wizardry shares important traits with possessors of witchcraft, above all the urge to catch people and the uncontrollable desire for human flesh.

Forty years ago Victor Turner warned against an „obsession with the proper pigeonholing of beliefs and practices as either 'witchcraft' or 'sorcery'".[19] Quibbles over terminology are never interesting, but my point is different. The argument has been made time and again that the opposition between witchcraft and sorcery does not hold for most African societies, on the understanding that it was, and continues to be, paradigmatic for the Zande themselves. As is now clear, however, *even* among the Zande the distinction between witches and sorcerers is no longer as clear-cut as used to be thought. This makes it all the more necessary, therefore, to pursue a more historical and symbolic analysis of these beliefs.

Origins of water wizardry

The origin of water wizardry is commonly attributed to non-Zande fishermen, chiefly Yakoma people who live some 400 km west of Zemio along the Oubangui River. From the 1890s on, French explorers, followed by agents of a concessionary company and colonial officials employed countless Yakoma men as peddlers and soldiers to „penetrate" into Zandeland. They were later hired by the colony to operate the ferries that

---

17 Procès verbal d'Interrogatoire. Obo District Court, 4 July 1988. Archives de Tribunal, Obo (CAR).
18 Cf. Pamela SCHMOLL: Black stomachs, beautiful stones: Soul-eating among Hausa in Niger, in: Jean COMAROFF / John COMAROFF (ed.), Modernity and its malcontents. Ritual and power in postcolonial Africa, Chicago 1993, pp. 193-220, for a similar case of commercialization of originally inherited witchcraft -"stones" in Niger.
19 Victor TURNER: Witchcraft and sorcery: Taxonomy vs. dynamics, in: Africa 34 (1964), pp. 314-325, here p. 325.

used to cross the main rivers. Small Yakoma communities settled in the Zande towns, where they now make a living from fishing. They are reputed to employ powerful medicines to attract fish, and to stay under water to place traps or repair nets. It is they, so it is generally claimed, who initiated the first Zande in the art of breathing under water. The criminal use of the fishing magic soon spread throughout Zandeland. Oral sources and archival records agree regarding the appearance of the first cases of „kpirism" in the early 1950s. In a series of typewritten notes on Zandeland, the French trader and planter Edouard Cormon, who lived for some fifty years among the Zande, had an entry on the crocodile-men. In 1953 he called them a „recent phenomenon".[20]

The link between water wizardry and riverside people is further attested by the origin of the term *kpiri*. It is not a Zande word but comes from either the Sango or the Ngbandi language, both of which are closely related to Yakoma and belong to the same Ubangian cluster.[21] Crocodile-men are also known to have operated in Bangassou, a major town on the Oubangui River some 300 km west of Zemio, inhabited by Nzakara, Zande, Banda and Yakoma people. Here the water wizards are known under the Sango names of *bawande* or *talimbi*.[22] Yet however „un-Zande" the term and the phenomenon may be, „kpirism" resonates with a conceptual category well established in Zande culture: fearsome water creatures with an ambiguous disposition. „It is noticeable", the first Zande-speaking administrator in Sudan remarked in 1926, „that they [the Zande monsters] are all said to live in rivers, and none on dry land".[23]

In CAR Zandeland large rivers are the abode of two water monsters or spirits in particular: the older *mama ime* (literally „water-leopard") and the newer *mamiwata* (from the Caribbean or West-African pidgin *mammy water*). Both are described as humans, mermaid-like Europeans in fact, and both used to be called upon for help. One could ask a water-leopard to find a suspected criminal, who would then be caught in the water and tried. If found guilty, the *mama ime* would kill him and suck his blood. If found not guilty, however, the *mama ime* would return him ashore and turn on the accuser. *Mamiwata*, for their part, live in towns under water and can bestow special powers or financial success on those who ask for them. The rules are strict, however, and whatever money one gets through a *mamiwata* must be spent fast, on pain of becoming crazy or dying – a sure sign of „occult economy" and one not limited to the Zande.[24] Crocodile-

---

20 Quelques notes sur la région de l'Est soumises à Monsieur Mabille. Typescript [incomplete]. Kadjema, 23 July 1953. Archives Cormon, Town Hall, Obo (CAR).
21 Raymond BOYD: Etudes Zande [unpublished doctoral dissertation, Université Paris V], Paris 1980 and Erhard VOELTZ: personal communication, 1992 respectively.
22 Unpublished notes of the anthropologist Eric DE DAMPIERRE: Génies des eaux, MSHO-13 („Religion-Magie"). Archives MSHO-Nanterre, Université Paris X (France). Cf. also Anne RETEL-LAURENTIN: Sorcellerie et ordalies chez les Nzakara, Paris 1969, p. 394.
23 P.M. LARKEN: An account of the Zande, in: Sudan Notes and Records 9 (1926), pp. 1-55, here p. 54.
24 Cf. Misty BASTIAN: Mami Wata, Mr. White, and the sirens off Bar Beach: Spirits and dangerous consumption in the Nigerian popular press, in: Heike SCHMIDT / Albert WIRZ (ed.), Afrika und das Andere. Alterität und Innovation, Hamburg 1998, pp. 21-31. Filip DE BOECK: Domesticating diamonds and dollars: Identity, expenditure and sharing in southwestern Zaire (1984-1997), in: Birgit MEYER / Peter GESCHIERE (ed.), Globalization and identity. Dialectics of flow and closure, Oxford 1999, pp. 177-209.

men, though very real, have features of both mythical water creatures. They exercise justice of sorts, like the water-leopard, and have access to superior wealth, like the *mamiwata*. Above all, they are at home in rivers, the non-socialized and dangerous part of the landscape which connects Zandeland with the western part of the country.

The Zande have a particular term for the west, *padi-yo*, shortened to *padio*. It literally means „on the side of/the river/there", i.e. downstream. This refers to the west, because that is the direction in which the Mbomou and Uele Rivers flow, the two main rivers in CAR and Congo Zandeland. In this sense it stands in opposition to *uro-yo*, „[on the side of] the sun/there", i.e. the east. But the term, used as a noun, also denotes the people living west of the Zande, including the Yakoma and, by extension, the people in Bangui (the capital), those in power, the functionaries, the state itself. Even in French the Zande will use the expression *les padio*, which has a negative connotation. These westerners are the antithesis of the Zande: they speak French well, do not cultivate fields or go out hunting, eat at set times and get paid even if they do not work (as was mentioned to me on Independence Day, 13 August). Their bodies too are different, with soft skin resembling that of women and Europeans. Because of their likeness to white people, the *Padio* are also called *avuru musungu*, „subjects of the whites".

It is generally accepted that the *Padio* loathe and fear the Zande, and will do anything to stop their region from being developed. There are many rumours to substantiate this claim. André Kolingba, a Yakoma, was president of the CAR from 1981 till 1993. When a team of German geologists exploitable salt pans in Haut-Mbomou Province, Kolingba allegedly required that the unprocessed salt be transported to his native town for further treatment. That was the reason why the project was dropped, according to those I spoke. It is one of the many examples I heard of perceived attempts by the *Padio* to extract riches from Zandeland, with nothing in return. Nor is the derogatory use of the term *Padio* new. The last French administrator in Zandeland, in office during the country's first year of independence in 1961, viewed Zande „tribalism" as one of the obstacles to economic development. „Do not hesitate to reprimand those who call the non-Zande 'PADIO'", he wrote to his successor.[25] Whereas this Frenchman considered the Zande attitude towards their western neighbours to stand in the way of their economic development, the Zande themselves blamed – and continue to blame – their region's backwardness on the greed of the *Padio*.

„*Padio*", far from being a mere designation for non-Zande people based on geography, turns out to be a term imbued with value and judgement. It has become a figure of speech for the opposition between city and bush, between *haves* and *have-nots*. The CAR Zande scorn the urbanity and effeminacy of their western neighbours, yet at the same time they aspire to their goods. As modernity appears to the Zande in the guise of broken promises of economic growth, their reaction to it is the typical alloy of attraction and repulsion. An analysis of the of *Padio* category reveals how the Zande define certain Others and position themselves. And this brings us back to „kpirism", which is said to have been introduced to the Zande from the west, by westerners. There are many sto-

---

25 Consignes passées par Monsieur Magnin à [son successeur]. Sub-Prefect of Obo, Jean Magnin. Obo, 9 August 1961. Author's personal archives, Fayence (France).

ries about three Yakoma boatmen who are supposed to have started the first *kpiri* corporation in Zandeland. Their leader's name was – fittingly – Pata, which in the national Sango language designates a 5-franc coin and, more generally, means „money". It is worth mentioning, in this context, that Yakoma people were involved in the spread of sleeping sickness in Zandeland during the first decade of the twentieth century.[26]

In other words, these riverside auxiliaries of the whites played a role in infecting the Zande with a disease that weakens the body and leads to death, sleeping sickness, and in assisting the penetration of a power that the Zande could not control but which dispossessed them, colonialism. These are characteristics of „kpirism" too. The modern belief in crocodile-men taps into the *historical* experience of rivers and *Padio* as instrumental in threatening the physical and social integrity of the Zande. At the same time the concept of water wizardry is not a new invention but a transformation of existing ideas about witchcraft, sorcery and sources of evil and wealth. At the *symbolic* level, mythical water creatures like the water-leopard and *mamiwata* constituted an ideological „template" for the *hommes-caïmans* – in the sense of persistent themes in belief which occasionally give rise to new recombinations.[27] What historian Luise White writes about colonial vampires can also be said of the *kpiri*: „a discursive contradiction – firmly embedded in local beliefs and constructions but named in such a way that their outsiderness [is] foregrounded".[28] Before analysing accusations against crocodile-men in general, in order to pursue the issue of their „outsiderness", I will first give a fairly detailed account of one particular instance.

The case of Mbili, the fisherman

Well known to almost every Zande is the story of Mbili, a fisherman of the eastern town of Obo, not far from the Sudanese border. His story, as recorded here, is based in part on statements and reports kept at the Obo District Court.[29] On 13 June 1987, a man named Bassiri left home before dawn to go fishing on the Mbokou River. He did not return home and was reported missing that afternoon. A message was sent from the *gendarmerie* (military police) informing the prefect that someone had disappeared „beneath the water of the Mbokou".[30] Two days later the body was found. The autopsy revealed fractures and first-degree burns all over the body, as well as a rectal trauma; the medical report concluded that Bassiri had died from „torture".[31] Right from the beginning two fishermen, called Mbili and Siberete were suspected. Their canoes had been found on the river bank and a witness had seen them fishing the morning of the disappearance. Mbili's paternal aunt had had a quarrel with the victim three months earlier,

---

26 Rita HEADRICK: The impact of colonialism on health in French Equatorial Africa: 1880-1934 [unpublished doctoral dissertation, University of Chicago], Chicago 1987, pp. 108, 174.
27 Edwin ARDENER: Witchcraft, economics, and the continuity of belief, in: Mary Douglas (ed.), Witchcraft confessions & accusations, London 1970, pp. 141-160, here p. 156.
28 Luise WHITE: Speaking with the vampires. Rumor and history in colonial Africa, Berkeley 2000, p. 29.
29 All the following documents were consulted in the Archives de Tribunal, Obo (CAR).
30 Message porté, police officer to chairman of the court Obo, 13 June 1987.
31 Rapport d'expertise, by Dr. Noel Ngaiwara. Obo, 3 July 1987.

during which she had sworn his death. But above all, the two had previously been accused of involvement in *kpiri* murder; Siberete had even been chased from the village of Kadjema on account of it.

A week after the disappearance Mbili was interrogated a first time. He denied any wrongdoing. He stated that he caught lots of fish with his 67 nets and that his colleagues envied him: „My fellow fishermen are jealous and call me a wizard [*un féticheur*]". So whenever somebody disappeared on the river „I am often suspected and taken to the police".[32] In the course of the police investigation, several witnesses were heard. The deputy-mayor of Obo, Kpourou, stated that he and other town officials had undertaken searches to find the culprits „through various traditional means" – by which he meant a clairvoyant, Madame Mami.[33] The victim's wife testified that her husband had never gone to the river so early in the morning; and although she had tried to keep him home, „he insisted on going and never came back". The victim's older brother told the *gendarmes* about the quarrel between the victim and Mbili's aunt, and was convinced that the latter „financed the *hommes-caïmans* to kill my younger brother out of vengeance". All this was highly suspect and incriminating.

A couple of months later an inhabitant of Obo made a full confession: „I am an *homme-caïman*", Tarakouma admitted. He explained that he had been „vaccinated" and admitted that, together with his companions Mbili, Siberete and two others, „we have taken our booty" in the Mbokou River. The person who had asked for the execution of Bassiri was a man whose wife had been „snatched" from him by the victim, and he had paid 64,000 CFA Francs for the job (about 250 USD at the time). After a short trial Bassiri was killed, and „we removed his heart, his lungs and his liver which we prepared and ate".[34] It was Tarakouma who explained, during his trial in 1988, that body parts are eaten to strengthen the bond between the *kpiri* (see above). Another man also confessed to the water killing of Bassiri and also implicated Mbili. Mbili was again questioned but he maintained his former statement: the two men who confirmed his participation in the torture and death of Bassiri „are lying".[35]

No documents pertaining to Mbili's trial itself were found in the files, but oral testimonies abound. Mbili was sentenced and imprisoned with a number of other suspected *hommes-caïmans* in Obo. The population was not happy with this and called for the crocodile-men to be permanently exiled from Haut-Mbomou or even publicly executed,

---

32 Procès verbal d'Enquête préliminaire, from police officer to chairman of the court. Obo, 22 August 1987.
33 Procès verbal d'Enquête préliminaire, from Commandant de Brigade to Chef d'Escadron de la Gendarmerie à police officer to senior police officer in Bangui. Obo, 18 October 1987.
34 Procès verbal d'Enquête préliminaire, from police officer to senior police officer in Bangui. Obo, 20 October 1987. I am unaware of the circumstances under which this confession was made, but judging by other cases, torture cannot be excluded.
35 Procès verbal d'Enquête préliminaire, from police officer to chairman of the court. Obo, 10 October 1987. (Note that the dates on which the documents containing the statements were written up do not always correspond to the dates on which the statements were taken.)

to set an example.[36] Sometime later, early in 1990, a boy died while swimming in the Mbokou River. Water wizardry was immediately suspected, and footprints were discovered leading from the river bank to the prison. The people of Obo were outraged and demanded that the *kpiri* be starved to death in prison, as had been done in Zemio the year before. The prefect consented, but word reached the prisoners. One night they all escaped, about 15 of them. The alarm was given and the same night the local authorities held an emergency meeting. It was decided that the population be mobilised to look for the escapees and kill them on the spot.

Thus began a manhunt that lasted more than a week. Armed with axes, machetes, spears, sticks and the occasional gun, people roamed the bush and field villages during the day, and searched house after house in town at night. As many as 20 people were killed: escaped prisoners who had been tried for water wizardry, but also suspected crocodile-men, a boy allegedly „infected" by his *kpiri* father and a man reputed to be a sorcerer (*mbe-ngua*). The violence must have been extreme. Once killed, the suspected *kpiri* were burnt. Those who had already been interred by their relatives were exhumed to be burnt. Some men were burnt alive. Among those killed, buried, dug up and burnt – „so that not a single bone of him remained" – was Mbili, the fisherman. Just before his execution he confessed to being a *kpiri* and accused the deputy-mayor, Kpourou, of being their ringleader. Kpourou, whose statement against the crocodile-men is given above, was a rich trader and owned a shop in Obo, the only one that belonged to a non-Muslim. He had already been suspected of involvement in water wizardry before, after a *kpiri* victim was found without teeth a few days before he went to the capital, returning with plenty of goods for his store. People were convinced that his wealth stemmed from selling victims' blood and body parts. Kpourou also perished in the mob lynching.

Accusations against water wizards

Evans-Pritchard's monograph has inspired two main approaches to the study of witchcraft and sorcery: an epistemological one, which investigates the internal logic of beliefs systems and their impact on knowledge and perception, and a sociological one, which focuses on the distribution of accusations, treated as symptoms of social conflict.[37] A closer look at accusations against crocodile-men will indicate loci of tension in Zande society since, in the words of Max Marwick, „Witchcraft [is] a social strain-gauge".[38] However, the sociological approach can easily result in an old-fashioned functionalist framework, reducing society to a homoeostatic system – and anthropology to a science of tautologies. Where accusations against magic evildoers are under control, the model predicts social equilibrium, which in turn is identified by means of institutionalized ac-

---

36 Lettres de plainte („Lettres of complaint") written in 1988 and addressed to the Prefect of Haut-Mbomou Province.
37 Cf. Mary DOUGLAS: Introduction. Thirty years after 'Witchcraft, oracles and magic', in: Mary DOUGLAS (ed.), Witchcraft confessions & accusations, London 1970, pp. xiii-xxxviii. Malcolm CRICK: Explorations in language and meaning. Towards a semantic anthropology, New York 1976, pp. 109-127
38 Max MARWICK: Witchcraft as a social strain-gauge, in: Australian Journal of Science 26 (1964), pp. 263-268.

cusations of witchcraft. Similarly, where accusations get out of control, this is accounted for by reference to a general breakdown of society, which itself is expected to be correlated with a high level of accusations. The rapid examination of *kpiri* accusations that follows will try to go beyond their immediate local social reality and connect them to wider geographical and historical horizons. The purpose is to pursue a dynamic reading of the *kpiri* phenomenon.

Most studies of witchcraft in contemporary Africa reveal the extraordinary flexibility of the ideas and practices involved. With regard to accusations against suspected witches, one finds cases not only where the young incriminate the old but also where the old denounce the young, where the rich accuse the poor but also the other way around, and where villagers inculpate city dwellers but also vice versa. In the case at hand, those who accuse fellow Zande of water wizardry do not seem to have any specific profile. The accusers are members of many identifiable social categories, though the majority are men, farmers of all ages who live in or near towns. People were reluctant to talk about the leaders in the anti-*kpiri* „witch-hunts" but I had the impression that lay Christians closely associated with the missions, both Catholics and Protestants, played an important part in rallying followers against suspects. Contrary to other examples in Africa, however, here this does not seem to be related to Christian demonization of witchcraft, with its concomitant opposition between unambiguously defined good and evil.[39] Expatriate missionaries were shocked by these outbursts of violence and the involvement of their converts. Before examining their reactions in greater detail, I will first say something more about the accused.

In the course of one of my first conversations on the subject, the crocodile-men were described to me as „a secret society for the consumption of humans and the trade in blood and teeth". Today, closed associations seem to have disappeared from the world of the CAR Zande, with the exception of that of the *kpiri*, which is viewed as an association of criminals. Accusations of „kpirism" are not directed against close neighbours, nor is having one's name placed in front of an oracle the way in which most crocodile-men get inculpated. The majority are incriminated by other, self-confessed *kpiri* – the classic phenomenon of group-confessions and mutual accusations by witches. In Mbili's story this happened twice, provoking a chain reaction. A person, once suspected or accused of „kpirism" in a particular drowning accident, continues to be viewed as a water wizard afterwards, unlike witches in the past, although maybe like sorcerers. Suspected *kpiri* are drawn from a fairly limited pool of allegedly identified crocodile-men, who are listed by chiefs and ostracized by the population. It should be remembered that the prefect of Haut-Mbomou Province spoke of „criminal enemies of the people".

When somebody „disappears" in the river, fishermen and canoe owners are among the prime suspects. In order to prevent further water killings, the mayor of Zemio who succeeded the deposed Koumounoungo in the early 1980s (see below) had all canoes destroyed along the Mbomou River within the limits of his district. Fishing was forbid-

---

39 Cf. Birgit MEYER: 'Delivered from the powers of darkness': Confessions about satanic riches in Christian Ghana, in: Africa 65 (1995), pp. 236-255. Mary DOUGLAS: Sorcery accusations unleashed: The Lele revisited, 1987, in: Africa 69 (1999), pp. 177-193.

den unless one was registered at the town hall and in possession of a certificate, and crossing the Mbomou River to the Congolese side was only allowed using the town hall canoe. These regulations are no longer enforced today. Yet there are very few fishermen in the riverside towns of Zemio and Obo. Most of them are Muslims who are said to be stronger than the Zande under water and able to protect themselves from the *kpiri* (the Muslim traders who live in Zande towns are never accused of „kpirism"). In the small villages near the Mbomou River most men are afraid to go fishing. They fear not so much being „caught" under water as being accused in the event that a person drowns or is missing.

In the case reported earlier, Mbili's and Kpourou's economic successes were seen in terms of their using *kpiri* magic and participating in a form of occult economy. It is not only entrepreneurs who get accused of „kpirism" – men without wealth are incriminated too. But, among the accused, one social group in particular stands out: powerful Vungara chiefs. Some people are even convinced that water killing is „a thing of the Vungara". The most notable case of an alleged royal *kpiri* involves Koumounoungo, grandson of King Zamoï himself.[40] He first became mayor of Zemio after independence, in 1960, and then again in 1981, serving in between as a Member of Parliament for Haut-Mbomou Province in Bangui. Koumounoungo is held responsible, by many, for having propagated the new evil in CAR Zandeland. Not a practising crocodile-man himself, he is said to have ordered water wizards to take revenge on his enemies and to obtain blood and organs to treat his diabetes. In his capacity as mayor he allegedly protected suspects and released *kpiri* prisoners. Koumounoungo was arrested in 1983 and transferred to the capital, together with dozens of other suspects. He died in prison in Bangui. His case is not unique among the Vungara.

It is remarkable that members of the royal clan, who in the past were immune from witchcraft accusations, are now so thoroughly implicated in this cannibalistic wizardry. Their political power is no longer what it used to be. Today only a minority of villages and districts in CAR Zandeland is ruled by Vungara chiefs – in contrast to what seems to be the case in Congo and Sudan.[41] There may be historical reasons for this. Zande royals, in the eighteenth and nineteenth centuries, collected large amounts of tribute from their realms, and this was redistributed among their courtiers, retainers and visitors. Yet it happened that a king or prince amassed food and goods without giving anything in return, thus perverting the patron-client relationship. In such cases he was accused of „eating the country".[42] Abuse of power may have occurred in all Zande kingdoms, but there seems to be one instance in which gluttony was more pronounced among the CAR Vungara. This was during the last quarter of the nineteenth century,

---

40 Zamoï Ikpira was the last great king of the CAR Zande. He died in 1912, at about 70 years of age. The town of Zemio is called after him.
41 Cf. Armin PRINZ: Das Ernährungswesen bei den Azande Nordost-Zaires. Ein Beitrag zum Problem des Bevölkerungsrückganges auf der Nil-Kongo Wasserscheide [unpublished doctoral dissertation, Universität Wien], Vienna 1976 for Congo, and Stephen SIEMENS: Azande rituals of birth and death. Ethnography and formal analogy [unpublished doctoral dissertation, UCLA], Los Angeles 1990 for Sudan.
42 DE DAMPIERRE: Les idées-forces, pp. 1-16, here p. 8.

when some of them cooperated with the Arab slave trade. King Zamoï in particular was able to increase his military strength greatly by exchanging slaves for firearms with traders from central Sudan. The use of firearms made raiding ever more efficient and profitable for Zamoï, who once spoke of his slaves as „my wares".[43]

Later, Vungara chiefs were compelled to provide porters and workers for French expeditions and colonial projects. This must have been perceived by those concerned as a form of enslavement, yet another case of extraction perpetrated by the chiefs. Even after the end of Vungara royal rule this pattern continued. In the 1970s the French tobacco company in eastern CAR rewarded chiefs whose village or town produced most tobacco. The above-mentioned grandson of Zamoï is said to have earned a lot of money by obliging the population to expand their tobacco fields or even work in his own. The CAR Vungara have thus fallen into disrepute. People are in no doubt that Vungara chiefs have contributed to the region's moral and economic downfall, and that the country is better off without them in power. In the opening discussion on the closed associations mention was already made of the „dark underside of Zande political life". But whereas in the past this underside could be countered by the independent institution of the societies, nowadays it seems only possible to address it by accusing people of water wizardry and taking the law into one's own hands.

Crocodile-men are not only held responsible for particular misfortunes, such as the drowning of a specific person, but also, and chiefly, for generalized misfortune that strikes Zandeland as a whole. Examples of generalized misfortune related to the *kpiri* include the occasional drought, like the one that hit the district of Zemio upon my arrival; the region's depopulation, imputed to the killings; and its economic backwardness, due to the water wizards' deterrent effect on foreign aid. At the 1992 public meeting mentioned earlier, the prefect of the Zande province declared that the presence of the *hommes-caïmans* scared off international sponsors. This is the reason, he explained, why there is no campaign for economic revival in Haut-Mbomou. Crocodile-men are thus perceived as threatening the livelihood of the entire community and not simply the lives of adulterers. In view of this, people feel it is appropriate, that these agents of misfortune should be dealt with publicly, their identities divulged, and they themselves eliminated in times of crisis. Mob justice appears justified.

Many Zande think that sending condemned *kpiri* to prison in Bangui is not a solution. They are convinced that crocodile-men „live like ministers" in the capital's prison, being well fed, receiving nice clothes, even getting paid. It is imagined, in other words, that once these criminals leave Haut-Mbomou they adopt all the outward signs of *Padio*-ness and success. People perceive this as a perversion of justice: that those who get rich by killing others are so well treated, whereas those who laboriously grow crops are not able to sell their produce. Nor is keeping *kpiri* imprisoned in Zandeland viewed as a solution. The CAR government has no money for provincial prisons. So either the prisoners are kept locked up day and night, in which case they have to be provided for by the local population, or else they are allowed to leave prison during the day to do

---

43 Cf. GROOTAERS: History, pp. 41-54.

menial jobs and acquire their own food. Both regimes have been tried out in the past, but neither is satisfactory. Having *kpiri* walking around freely poses a threat to public safety, whereas having to feed those who feed upon their fellow men is hard to accept.

Processes of normal food exchange and consumption are vital in creating and sustaining social relationships. These processes do sometimes break down, as in the case of famine, witchcraft or cannibalistic practices. The cannibal consumes anti-food and is the embodiment of anti-commensality. The symbolic import of people's reluctance to feed imprisoned *kpiri* became clear to me during the 1992 meeting with the prefect. The questions of who should feed the crocodile-men and whether they should be fed in the first place were debated at very great length. It appeared that sharing one's food – one of the central moral values of community life – with the embodiments of anti-commensality was considered unjustifiable, if not perverse. Starving or burning the crocodile-men appeared to many the only alternative way to purge the community of this evil.

The anti-justice directed against accused crocodile-men finds its counterpart in the latter's own form of justice. These people are not only driven by the desire for money or human flesh, as we have seen, but also have an urge to try wrongdoers. The following statements from two informants sum up clearly how their kind of justice is perceived as fundamentally ambiguous. On the one hand, „*kpiri* do not take people for nothing", since they punish adulterers (it should be remembered that in the nineteenth century male adulterers were frequently punished by mutilation, with the loss of both hands and often also of the ears and genitals).[44] On the other hand, however, „*kpiri* do not pass sentence normally", since innocent people die too. In this they differ from that other avenger, *mama ime*. The mythical water-leopard would never kill a person found guiltless. *Kpiri* justice epitomizes the inversion of true justice: it takes place in the forest, on the sly, instead of in broad daylight in the centre of the village; crocodile-men are most often accuser, prosecutor, judge, and executioner all at once, roles that are always separated in normal procedures; and a *kpiri* defendant stands no chance of being cleared as the verdict is known beforehand.

It is no coincidence that those charged with „kpirism" should undergo the same kind of anti-justice they themselves are accused of imposing upon their victims. And it is no wonder that the few white missionaries who lived in CAR Zandeland during the 1990s took a strong stance against this mob law. Yet relations between Europeans and the *kpiri* phenomenon are intricate, and it is to thesem that we now turn.

European implications

Until very recently expatriate missionaries lived among the Zande. The Protestant evangelical Africa Inland Mission (AIM), a U.S. interdenominational mission, had arrived in CAR Zandeland in 1924, and there had been a succession of Catholic missionaries from various congregations and of various nationalities since 1937.[45] Both groups viewed

---

44 Edward EVANS-PRITCHARD (ed.): Man and woman among the Azande, London 1974, p. 133f.
45 GROOTAERS: History, pp. 190-196.

contemporary retaliatory actions against suspected crocodile-men as a primitive form of settling scores. The missionaries – as agents of modernity – complained bitterly about the widening gap between them and their respective converts. They were exasperated about the Zande's ability „to assimilate everything into their traditions", as one priest put it, acknowledging they had „no longer power over the people". It was the 1989 incident in Zemio, in which *kpiri* suspects were starved to death, that prompted an American AIM missionary to publish an article in the mission's periodical. In it he wrote: „Belief in the *akpiri* creates a cultural barrier that we as missionaries have not yet been able to bridge".[46]

Italian priests firmly opposed reprisals against suspects. They visited the police station and pleaded against the use of torture, threatened to close down the missions if suspects were killed, and even warned governmental officials that *Amnesty International* and other organizations would be notified if these practices continued. The threats were taken seriously by the authorities. A number of years ago two Members of Parliament from Haut-Mbomou Province went to see the priests at the mission in Zemio and asked them no longer to intervene on behalf of suspected crocodile-men. As I was told by a Combonian priest present at the meeting, the message was clear: their business was to pray, not to interfere in matters between Zande. Because *kpiri* wizardry is a „Zande only" thing, the Zande are not surprised that the missionaries do not understand it. The Zande compare „kpirism" to Western science and technology, which are, as they point out, equally mysterious to them.

So far I have not mentioned a striking fact uncovered during my investigation of the *hommes-caïmans*, namely that many men accused of „kpirism" in the past had been employed by European settlers in Zandeland. They include local shopkeepers in the service of white traders and villagers hired to work on the estates of French planters. Notwithstanding the Zande claim that water wizardry is a matter between Zande only, there are quite a few threads that link it to the arrival and presence of the Europeans. I do not argue that the association of crocodile-men is merely a product of colonialism, as was – wrongly – suggested for the closed associations in the early twentieth century. Water wizardry is squarely rooted in the moral landscape of the Zande and I believe it is an attempt to make sense of their contradictory experiences of modernity in a meaningful, if terrifying, manner. Europeans happen to be involved in the history of this modernity.

Connections between Europeans and the *kpiri* phenomenon come into play at different levels: at the ideological level, with the association between water, wealth and white people; at the sociological level, with the Europeans as sources of labour and cash income; and at the historical level, with the introduction by the whites of the Yakoma people, generally considered to be at the origin of this affliction. The first point requires an etymological excursion.

The CAR Zande use the term *putu* to designate Europe or the world of the whites. The word comes from the Kongo language, in which it is an onomatopoeia originally designating water in movement – sea, surf, eddies, rapids, and the like – but also refers

---

46 Les HARRIS: Breaking down strongholds. Bridging cross-cultural barriers with the Word of God and prayer, in: AIM International 75 (1991), pp. 1, 10-11, here p. 11.

to the opulent abode of the ancestors, who create these movements. The first Europeans were thought to have come from this underworld: they surfaced from the sea, were white and rich, and brought unknown luxury goods. The name of their country, Portugal, became *Putulugesi* in many languages of the Lower Congo. Because of its phonetic resemblance to „*putu*", this latter term acquired the new meaning of „Europe" while retaining the connotation of abundant wealth.[47] The term travelled from the Atlantic coast along the Congo and Oubangui Rivers, and reached Zandeland. The watery world is thus associated with opulence and so are the *mamiwata*. Among the Zande, as we have seen, these river creatures look like white people and have access to an inexhaustible supply of affluence. They are both desirable and dangerous. „Kpirism" fits in with these pre-existing perspectives on the ambiguity of rivers and riches.

At the same time this conceptual template is embedded in the history of Zandeland and worked out in social relations. It should be remembered that the first Europeans reached CAR Zandeland by way of the Oubangui River and, as long as they were present, European settlers constituted the main source of wages in the region, playing a role similar to the other wealthy „whites", the aforementioned *mamiwata*. This led to their being suspected of knowingly employing and protecting alleged crocodile-men. In the village of Kadjema nearly all the *kpiri* suspects were employed by Cormon on his coffee and palm tree plantations. It was something the Frenchman was well aware of and greatly worried about. In a long letter about a case of drowning in his village, written to the French administrator of the Zande district in 1958, Cormon made suggestions for securing a fair trial of the accused. The reason he gave for his concern about „kpirism" is worth quoting: „I am personally very concerned that a solution be found that allows everybody to be pacified. There are many bicycle-owners in Kadjémah (this is not a digression). It is supposed, in the more simple circles of the district, that no villager could ever have achieved this if there had not been a traffic in human flesh, with ... my assistance".[48]

In the field I found out that some people still suspected Cormon (who died in 1986) of having been directly involved in water wizardry: firstly, because for decades there was more money in Kadjema than in any other village in CAR Zandeland, and secondly because the Frenchman never admitted the existence of *kpiri* magic and often intervened in favour of accused crocodile-men. Both continued to arouse mistrust. There is a third reason why Cormon may be thought to have been implicated in this wizardry: the fact that he had brought Yakoma boatmen to Kadjema, including the trio talked about earlier – whose leader was called Pata, „money".

The „traffic in human flesh" Cormon mentioned in his letter is a persistent theme in Zande history. It turns out to be a rumour that has not only been spread about the Zande but which they themselves have circulated about others.

---

47 Frans BONTINCK: personal communication, 1995. I gratefully acknowledge Father Bontinck's kind sharing of his encyclopaedic knowledge, built up over the course of half a century's work in Congo. He passed away as I was writing this essay, at the age of 85.

48 Letter from Edouard Cormon to Chef du District Zandé; original dots suspension. Kadjema, 6 April 1958. Archives Cormon, Town Hall, Obo (CAR).

Cannibalism, extraction and ingestion

During the nineteenth century almost every self-respecting explorer crossing the Sudanese Zande region would depict the inhabitants as fierce cannibals in his travel books. In those days the Zande were known under the sobriquet of „Niam-Niam" which, depending on the source, either translated as „meat-meat" or „glutton", or was an onomatopoeia suggesting „the smacking of lips" or „the gnashing of teeth".[49] The anthropologist Evans-Pritchard and the missionary Filiberto (Gero) Giorgetti published detailed analyses to clear „their" Zande from such a bad reputation. Both authors pointed out that the Vungara princes and the „pure" Zande had hardly practised any cannibalism at all, but that it had been limited to the partial consumption of war casualties and chiefly the affair of a few foreign people absorbed into the Zande nation.[50] Even if their view is correct for southern Sudan at the most literal level, cannibalism maintained itself as a discourse and topos in all of Zandeland.

Indeed, suspicions and accusations of anthropophagy also operated in the other direction. Underlying the above ideological, sociological and historical dimensions of European implication in „kpirism" is the ingrained association, among the Zande, of whites with cannibalism. The interest of the nineteenth- century naturalist Wilhelm Junker in human skulls was interpreted in Zandeland as a form of cannibalism. Later, Western doctors in southern Sudan were suspected of performing surgical operations for cannibalistic purposes. In 1949 the (Zande) assistants of the agronomist Pierre de Schlippe, who studied the Zande system of agriculture in Sudan, were suspected of helping Europeans to kidnap and eat children.[51] And in a more recent past, people in CAR Zandeland were convinced that white traders abducted children to turn them into canned meat. Narratives about the cannibalistic appetite of Europeans are not limited to Zandeland, to be sure. What do these stories convey and why are they so powerful and so tenacious?

Several authors have tackled this question. The in-depth survey of man-eating whites in Central and West Africa by Rik Ceyssens traces these stories to sources in the early sixteenth century about the Atlantic slave trade.[52] The capture and disappearance of Africans was explained by their being consumed at sea or in the country of the whites. Similar stories circulated about European cannibals in subsequent centuries, particularly the twentieth, with the widespread tale of African assistants helping whites to abduct Congolese people who were fattened for consumption at Christmas or put into tins for

---

49 See references in GROOTAERS: History, p. 242; cf. also Paola IVANOV: Cannibals, warriors, conquerers, and colonizers: Western perceptions and Azande historiography, in: History in Africa 29 (2002), pp. 89-217, here pp. 92-114.

50 Edward EVANS-PRITCHARD: Zande cannibalism, in: The position of women in primitive societies and other essays in social anthropology, London 1965, pp. 133-64. GERO [Filiberto GIORGETTI]: Cannibalism in Zandeland: Truth and falsehood. The civilisation of the Zande princes, Bologna 1970; cf. also Jan-Lodewijk GROOTAERS: Cannibalism in Central Africa: Culinary pleasure or cultural warfare? [manuscript in progress], n. d.

51 GERO: Cannibalism, p. 176f. EVANS-PRITCHARD: Witchcraft, p. 490. Pierre DE SCHLIPPE: Shifting cultivation in Africa. The Zande system of agriculture, London 1956, here p. 30 respectively.

52 Rik CEYSSENS: Mutumbula. Mythe de l'opprimé, in: Cultures et développement 7 (1975), pp. 483-550, here pp. 508f., 514f.

sale. Ceyssens interprets these colonial stories as an indigenous means of dealing with alienation and acculturation under the new regime, while at the same time linking them to past experiences of the slave trade. This kind of explanation in terms of origin and continuity has been criticized by Luise White, who stresses that vampire stories are locally shaped and situated. Therefore „the white people in each set of narratives have different meanings, different relevances, and different histories".[53] Accusations of European cannibalism cannot be reduced to the unequivocal portrayal of predation on the part of a dominant power, but must be examined case by case. Rosalind Shaw, for her part, has recently argued for a more connective reading of successive cannibalism stories in Sierra Leone.[54] Narratives about man-eating Europeans originated with the slave trade, were transformed and internalized during colonialism, and are again being recast today. But each period carries with it memories of the previous one(s). I would argue that this kind of historical sedimentation also applies to Zande beliefs in cannibalism.

So let us return to the CAR Zande. Earlier I described cannibalism as the consumption of anti-food, but here I wish to highlight how it symbolises one-way extraction of value. In the nineteenth century some Vungara kings participated in the Khartoum-based slave trade, selling people as „wares". Particularly during the early colonial period, the European presence in Zandeland amounted to little more than incessant demands for soldiers, labour, food and products; nothing was given in return, and there was no proper redistribution of wealth. A similar pattern was repeated during the cultivation of cash crops after independence. Tobacco was an important source of income for the Zande in the 1970s, until the French company was partially nationalized. The CAR government – who of course were *Padio* – claimed their share of profits, leaving all road work and bridge maintenance to the tobacco company. In 1983 it pulled out of Zandeland, having been „eaten by the state".[55] It is always the same old story: value is extracted from Zandeland in a way which, in the eyes of the Zande, entails being eaten rather than being fed. The dismembered bodies of *kpiri* victims, whose alienable parts are exported beyond Haut-Mbomou Province, point to and recall present and past dispossession.

I think it is possible to take the exploration of the symbolic significance of cannibalism a little further still. The Zande have always produced large food surpluses. These used to be fed into the social tissue as tribute to the chiefs and offerings to the ancestors, during working beer-parties or at funeral feasts.[56] The latter are on the wane, and the other practices have completely disappeared. Hence the importance of the market getting rid of surpluses. But there are no real outlets in Zandeland and hardly any buyers to export farm produce to the capital. The only possibility, therefore, seems to be eating it oneself, which people greatly resent. Many times I heard the complaint that there is no

---

53 WHITE: Vampires, p. 15.
54 Rosalind SHAW: Memories of the slave trade. Ritual and the historical imagination in Sierra Leone, Chicago 2002, pp. 225-246.
55 „… bouffé par l'état", as people put it. The pioneering study on rapacious „belly politics" in Africa is by Jean-François BAYART: L'Etat en Afrique. La politique du ventre, Paris 1989.
56 GROOTAERS: History, pp. 167-186.

use in growing much at all, not simply because the produce cannot be sold but especially because it ends up being eaten by the farmer. To my question why so few people still grow sorghum (once a staple food), an old farmer gave an answer about raising crops in general: „We've done these things in vain [...]. We just eat them into our belly; there is no money in them". It seems a perverted inversion of economics: among the Zande of Haut-Mbomou, instead of uneaten surpluses being sold, unsold surpluses have to be eaten.

As a rule, crops are not cultivated for self-consumption alone. As Nancy Munn remarks in the (different) context of food transmission and food consumption among the Melanesian Gawa, eating one's own food destroys the food, which loses its capacity to create something new. Such ingestion is „consumption as a nonproductive, self-focused act rather than as an aspect of the exchange process [...]".[57] The current situation in which Zande granaries are filled with products and nobody is there to buy them leads to dispossession. Self-consumption precludes the transformation of food into relations of exchange and reciprocity, and interrupts the life-giving cycle of production and consumption. This too constitutes a form of anthropophagy. *Kpiri* cannibalism appears to address the issue of problematic ingestion – graphically represented by victims of water killings ending up in „the belly". In the case of both extraction and ingestion I interpret organ-stealing rumours in CAR Zandeland metaphorically. However, this may not be accurate for other places in the world, where stories about illicit trade in human body parts are all too palpably materialized in the violence of daily life.[58]

Kpiri rumours and beliefs have not, I would argue, remained the same over time. Historically there seems to have been a shift from crocodile-men being initiated by Yakoma fishermen and employed by Europeans, to their being trained and led by Vungara rulers and elected officials. This changing of the guard roughly coincides with the advent of independence (1960). Even the origin of water wizardry has ceased to be thought of as completely foreign. Many Zande today refer to an indigenous source, the Vungara royal clan, some of whose members are considered to have been crucial in disseminating the new evil. So „kpirism" has been internalized. *Hommes-caïmans*, their teachers, leaders and victims are all Zande. Concomitantly there has been a new turn in the appositeness of anthropophagous imagery. Cannibalism continues to „[root] expansive moral meanings in the naturalizing ground of human bodies" and to „signify unnatural consumption and accumulation".[59] Yet this no longer just happens in the register of predatory extraction but also in that of self-focused ingestion, unproductive auto-consumption and loss of connective articulation. What remains at issue in all these cases is the nexus between morality and modernity in Zande society.

---

57 Nancy MUNN: The fame of Gawa. A symbolic study of value transformation in a Massim (Papua New Guinea) society, Durham 1986, p. 52.
58 Nancy SCHEPER-HUGHES: Theft of life. The globalization of organ stealing rumours, in: Anthropology Today 12 (1996), pp. 3-11, here p. 5; cf. also Lesley SHARP: The commodification of the body and its parts, in: Annual Review of Anthropology 29 (2000), pp. 287-328, here p. 295.
59 Jean COMAROFF / John COMAROFF: Introduction, in: Jean COMAROFF / John COMAROFF (ed.): Modernity and its malcontents. Ritual and power in postcolonial Africa, Chicago 1993, pp. xi-xxxvii, here p. xxvi.

In sum, Zande beliefs in water wizardry come close to what, in classic witchcraft studies, has been called the „standardized nightmare of a group".[60] „Kpirism" provides an idiom of anxiety about the dangers of unregulated consumption and inequitable exchanges. Yet people's sense of conjoined moral and economic decline is also met by an institution that rehabilitates moral sociality. Its responsibility has been assumed chiefly by women.

A female counterpoint

Water wizardry possesses an unmistakable gender aspect. Stories about crocodile-men touch on movements across the landscape, cash crops and money, Vungara authority, and interactions with Europeans. All these are domains that involved mainly men, who were and largely continue to be the intermediaries between domestic production and the outside world. It is no coincidence that the association of crocodile-men is modelled on hunters' guilds, hunting being the male activity *par excellence*. *Kpiri*, as reported earlier, receive the initiatory *nzati* -medicine via small incisions on the wrists and call their leader „father of the *nzati*", like hunters do. Their way of dividing up the victim is also reminiscent of hunters, and like hunters they move back and forth between village and bush, in this case between land and water (even if they remain in an envelope of air when underwater). Yet the *kpiri* society is an inverted hunters' guild: normally game is brought from the wild bush to the village for communal consumption, whereas here human game is lured from the village to the wild rivers for secretive consumption or illicit commerce.

CAR Zandeland is also the cradle of another new institution, a feminine one, already alluded to at the very beginning of my essay: the Zande prophetic church. I have dealt with this example of religious imagination elsewhere[61] but will recapitulate its major characteristics here. This highly organized church used to call itself *Mission ti Africa*, „Mission of Africa" in the national Sango language, and has recently been rechristened MSEP or *Mission du Saint-Esprit par la Prophétie* („Mission of the Holy Spirit by Prophecy"). In this church, which was founded by a woman in the late 1930s, female prophets and female officials play a major role.[62] Twice a week services are held in which songs and prayers (*evanzire*, from „*évangile*" or „gospel") are sung, sermons are given and commentaries made and, especially, problems are solved by prophecy. Men and women submit their problems – ranging from illness and infertility to poor harvests and unsuccessful hunting – to prophets who sleep upon them and receive answers from *Mbori* (God) through their dreams. These solutions are written into the prophets' hands

---

60 Monica WILSON: Witch beliefs and social structure, in: The American Journal of Sociology 56 (1951), pp. 307-313, here p. 313.

61 Jan-Lodewijk GROOTAERS: Zande prophetesses at the articulation of local culture and world religion, in: Danielle DE LAME / Chantal ZABUS (ed.), Changements au féminin en Afrique noire. Anthopologie, Paris 1999, pp. 183-201; also GROOTAERS: History, pp. 273-316.

62 The earliest record of the Zande church I have been able to find so far is in a 1940 log book of the Catholic Mission of Zemio, where it is described as „a religion of sorts which apes the Whites". Cahier de visites / septembre-octobre 1940, B 178. Archives Congrégation du Saint-Esprit, Chevilly (France).

and are communicated publicly in church. The prophets do this by looking into their open palms; they are called *nagidi* (*bagidi* in the case of the few male prophets), which means „(s)he who reads".

The MSEP borrows from the Christian and Muslim religions (including terms like *evanzire* and *ramada*), Western medical science (the image of the syringe, for instance), communication technologies (one type of clairvoyant church official is called *taragaramu*, from „telegram") and the world of literacy. The power to read has been appropriated, mostly by illiterate people, as a divine and divinatory technique for understanding and acting upon the world. This church is, of course, also rooted in Zande culture and its ever-changing traditions. I was told more than once that today's *nagidi* have replaced all former oracles and also assume the task of the now extinct witch-finders and healers, the *binza*. The latter were nearly always men, whereas the new female role of the prophets is consciously emphasized by the church itself. The incorporation of Christian and bureaucratic practices points in the direction of the well-known movements for the suppression of witchcraft, but that is not the main focus of this church. Still, I heard stories about prophets publicly eliminating, in the past, objects used in the Yanda closed association; and more recently, occasional consultations of prophets by official authorities to determine the guilt of a suspected crocodile-man also took place.[63]

Let me end with an admittedly schematic opposition between the *kpiri* and *nagidi*, these two modern transformations of Evans-Pritchard's persuasive yet reifying Witchcraft-Oracles-Magic triangle. Both recapture and recycle older experiences, and cultural patterns run through new world views and globalizing practices. The Zande prophetic church and water wizardry create what have been termed „bifurcated epistemolog[ies]"[64], revealing the constant flux between „tradition" and „modernity". But there are differences. Whereas crocodile-men are accused of destroying the social fabric and vivisecting those that constitute it, the female prophets attend to bodily and social reproduction by restoring health and fertility. Whereas the former are said to engage in selfish urges and occult economy, the latter strive after collective moral reintegration by relying on the power of God's written word and offerings to ancestor spirits (a practice that has all but vanished under missionary influence). Put in a nutshell, the „Mission of the Holy Spirit by Prophecy" and „kpirism" constitute gendered, polar innovations that address expectations and frustrations in response to a long history of modernization. They are at the same time signs and agents of change. And like the closed associations of yesteryear, both of them are linked to existing themes and tensions in Zande society.

Conclusion

Throughout this essay I have treated current wizardry beliefs in CAR Zandeland as dynamic and creative efforts to talk about, make sense of and cope with modernity. My argument is that these beliefs are part of an indigenous ethic whose analysis enables us

---

63 GROOTAERS: History, p. 293 and Margeret BUCKNER: Modern Zande prophetesses, in: David ANDERSON / Douglas JOHNSON (ed.), Revealing prophets. Prophecy in eastern African history, London 1995, pp. 102-21, here p. 108 respectively.
64 STEWART / STRATHERN: Witchcraft, p. 118.

to explore Zande historical consciousness, or historical imagination, and its transformations over time. Stories about cannibalism, for instance, may connect „colonial memories to postcolonial predicaments", while the experiences of colonialism were themselves mediated „by memories of earlier transregional processes".[65] More specifically, the phenomenon of „kpirism" bears upon changing relationships among and between Zande commoners, Vungara royals, Christian converts, European foreigners, Muslim traders, Yakoma fishermen and officials in the capital – many of which entail(ed) new forms of violence and exploitation. „Kpirism" also relates to questions of flow: the flow of people travelling on rivers, the flow of new ideas and practices, of money, commodities and body parts, but also the flow of rumours about the phenomenon itself. In short, then, this analysis fits in with the growing literature on the modernity of witchcraft and the witchcraft of modernity in Africa.[66]

This literature has come under fire in recent years: its authors are accused of blurring cultural differences by imposing sociological abstractions such as „commodification" or „globalization", and of turning modernity into the new omnivorous meta-narrative that organize ethnography; in the process, it is claimed, they cause witchcraft itself to lose its autonomy and become a sign for something else; moreover, disproportionate attention to the occult would prevent them from acknowledging more positive engagements with change and development in Africa.[67] It is important to take these strictures seriously, but some of the criticized authors themselves explicitly repudiate the temptation „to situate our studies at levels of generality that fail to capture lived experience, to grasp the world as produced by ordinary people in everyday activity".[68] My understanding of the beliefs in water wizards and of the violence directed against them is indeed informed by questions of modernity, but this has been borne out by the ethnographic and historical material itself. The analysis of today's occult notions among the Zande has been grounded in diachronic inquiry, and I therefore hope I have managed to avoid turning „contemporaneity into cause, general context into particular explanation".[69]

---

65 SHAW: Memories, p. 226.
66 A few key references: Jean COMAROFF / John COMAROFF (ed.): Modernity and its malcontents. Ritual and power in postcolonial Africa, Chicago 1993. Peter GESCHIERE: The modernity of witchcraft. Politics and the occult in postcolonial Africa, Charlottesville 1997. Henrietta MOORE / Todd SANDERS (ed.): Magical interpretations, material realities. Modernity, witchcraft and the occult in postcolonial Africa, London 2001.
67 Cf. Maia GREEN: Witchcraft suppression practices and movements: Public politics and the logic of purification, in: Comparative Studies of Society and History 39 (1997), pp. 319-345. Blair RUTHERFORD: To find an African witch: Anthropology, modernity, and witch-finding in North-West Zimbabwe, in: Critique of Anthropology 19 (1999), pp. 89-109. Harri ENGLUND / James LEACH: Ethnography and the meta-narratives of modernity, in: Current Anthropology 41 (2000), pp. 225-239, 245-248. Mikael KARLSTRÖM: Modernity and its aspirants. Moral community and developmental eutopianism in Buganda, in: Current Anthropology 45 (2004), pp. 595-610, 616-619.
68 Jean COMAROFF: Consuming passions: Child abuse, fetishism, and 'The New World Order', in: Culture 17 (1997), pp. 7-19, here p. 9.
69 Sally MOORE: Reflections on the Comaroff lecture, in: American Ethnologist 26 (1999), pp. 304-306, here p. 306.

Besides, discourses of witchcraft and sorcery do not simply reflect, or comment on, the world and social relationships, but also create this world and these relationships. They give shape to lived-in realities, including that of modernity: „occult beliefs and practices [are] not only contiguous with, but also constitutive of modernity".[70] It is their illocutionary force that makes these discourses so powerful and so tenacious. Yet beliefs in water wizards' powers, partly intelligible in terms of modernist discontent, do not tell the whole story. In CAR Zandeland they are complemented by beliefs in the prophetic powers of religious leaders. The local „mission" church, only briefly touched upon in these pages, reveals profoundly modernist aspirations on the part of contemporary Zande.

By way of epilogue I wish to mention in short my return to CAR Zandeland in April-May 2004. The country's political situation had somewhat recovered from years of utter instability, and security was now such as to permit travel up-country. After 12 years many things had changed, and during my short stay I became aware only of the most obvious transformations: lorries no longer bring food to the Sudanese refugees, most of whom have settled and cultivate their own fields; Mbororo (Fulani) herders have entered the area with their cattle and generate a new source of income, but relations with them are complex and ambiguous; above all it appears that there has been a lull in the storm of crocodile-men accusations during the past few years. It is quite possible that water wizardry and the violent reactions to which it led have decreased, and more research would be needed to try to account for this. Witchcraft phenomena are known to follow short-term and long-term cycles, an idea first proposed by Edwin Ardener who worked in West Cameroon. The title of his pioneering article is „Witchcraft, economics, and the continuity of belief".[71] Beliefs, occult and other, do indeed have continuity – but they are never constant. Hence the absolute necessity to resist their reification.

---

70 Henrietta MOORE / Todd SANDERS: Magical interpretations and material realities. An introduction, in: Henrietta MOORE / Todd SANDERS (ed.), Magical interpretations, material realities. Modernity, witchcraft and the occult in postcolonial Africa, London 2001, pp. 1-27, here p. 12.
71 ARDENER: Witchcraft.

Veröffentlichungen des Arbeitskreises für historische Hexen- und Kriminalitätsforschung in Norddeutschland

Band 1
Katrin Moeller/Burghart Schmidt (Hg.):
Realität und Mythos.
Hexenverfolgung und Rezeptionsgeschichte
Paperback, 332 Seiten, 12 Abb.,
ISBN 3-934632-04-1, 28,80 €.

Band 2
Ronald Füssel:
Die Hexenverfolgungen im Thüringer Raum
Paperback, 332 Seiten, 8 Abb.,
ISBN 3-934632-03-3, 28,80 €.

Band 3
Katrin Moeller/Burghart Schmidt (Hg.):
Regionale Differenzen – Vergleichbare Strukturen?
Hexenverfolgung im nördlichen Deutschland
1. Aufl. März 2008, ca. 300 Seiten, ca. 10 Abb.,
ISBN 3-934632-08-4, 28,80 €.

Band 4
Burghart Schmidt:
Ludwig Bechstein und die literarische Rezeption
frühneuzeitlicher Hexenverfolgung im 19. Jahrhundert
Hardcover/Fadenheftung, 412 Seiten, 16 Abb.,
ISBN 3-934632-09-2, 39,90 €.

www.dobu-verlag.de